Women and Self-Sacrifice
in the Christian Church

ALSO BY IDA MAGLI AND
TRANSLATED BY JANET SETHRE

Cultural Anthropology: An Introduction
(McFarland, 2001)

Women and Self-Sacrifice in the Christian Church

A Cultural History from the First to the Nineteenth Century

IDA MAGLI

Translated by JANET SETHRE

McFarland & Company, Inc., Publishers
Jefferson, North Carolina

> The present work is a reprint of the softcover edition of Women and Self-Sacrifice in the Christian Church: A Cultural History from the First to the Nineteenth Century, *first published in 2003 by McFarland.*

An earlier version of this work was published in Italian as *Storia laica delle donne religiose* (Milan: Longanesi, 1995).

LIBRARY OF CONGRESS CATALOGUING-IN-PUBLICATION DATA

Magli, Ida
    [Storia laica delle donne religiose. English]
    Women and self-sacrifice in the Christian church : a cultural history from the first to the nineteenth century / Ida Magli ; translated by Janet Sethre.
       p.   cm.
    Includes bibliographical references and index.

    ISBN 978-0-7864-9360-9
    softcover : acid free paper ∞

    1. Women in Christianity — History.   2. Self-sacrifice — History.   I. Title.
BV639.W7M256   2014
270'.082 — dc21   2002155761

BRITISH LIBRARY CATALOGUING DATA ARE AVAILABLE

©2003 Ida Magli. All rights reserved

No part of this book may be reproduced or transmitted in any form or by any means, electronic or mechanical, including photocopying or recording, or by any information storage and retrieval system, without permission in writing from the publisher.

Cover art © 2014 Artville

Manufactured in the United States of America

McFarland & Company, Inc., Publishers
  Box 611, Jefferson, North Carolina 28640
  www.mcfarlandpub.com

Contents

Preface	1

I. CHRISTIANITY: A RELIGION FOR WOMEN

1. The Trauma Inflicted by Jesus: Women Exist	7
2. Women as Christ's "Males"	36
3. A Grand Invention: Let Us Go Outside the World	67
4. The Religious System of Fashion	89

II. THE TRAGIC GAME OF MYSTICISM

5. Mysticism and Culture	105
6. A Custom-Made Lover: God	120
7. In Love Until Death	162
8. If This Is a Woman	184
9. Self-Annihilation in Order to Exist	201

III. RELIGIOUS WOMEN OUT TO CONQUER THE WORLD

10. Acting So As to Exist	225
11. Religious Women Invent the "Welfare State"	237
12. New Martyrs	257
Notes	271
Bibliography	277
Index	285

Preface

In presenting this work, I would first like to make clear to my readers that I have always fought against any form of apartheid, even on dividing narration and the interpretation of historical events into separate compartments. That includes the separateness implied by "women's studies." Indeed, the richest fruit of cultural anthropology, its greatest contribution, is awareness gained of the interdependence of all structures and meanings in each cultural system: their inevitable, intimate interconnection. In speaking of culture, we must speak of a "system," depending on the nature of thought itself, and on the foundations of logic. The system cannot withstand contradiction.

In my previous volume published by McFarland, *Cultural Anthropology*, I attempted to present a fundamental idea of the enormous wealth brought by the discipline of cultural anthropology, that of the American school in particular. In that book, readers may find more complete information concerning the method I have used in all my work aimed at reinterpreting Western history.

Based on the premise of a meaningful, self-containing *form* which each society assumes in a given period and in a given territory, I have always fought, then, against that feminist approach which tries to depict women's history as a separate, cloistered one. From such a viewpoint, this book may at first appear to contradict my own theoretical principles; in a sense, perhaps it does. But in reality, as readers can note, the subject of my narration is women precisely because, until today, the foundation of Christianity has never been elucidated, or even discussed, in relation to what Jesus did. What Jesus did concerned women, above all, because it involved the Judaic roots of blood bonds, the genetic transmission of original sin, and all systems of taboo, avoidance, pollution, and purification whose primary object has been women. In short, Christianity, as it has been understood, interpreted and constructed by Jesus' followers, has almost completely violated the revolutionary action touching on the "Sacred," and therefore on "Power," which Jesus' message implied — a message involving the role and meaning of that fundamental building block of culture which males have, in all cultures, made of the "circulation" of women.

In the history presented here, therefore, women are constantly talked about; but in reality, what we are talking about is "males": about their way of hating-and-loving women; about their way of seeking God by way of female sacrifice; and about women's attempts, nearly always doomed to failure, to free themselves from males by using male institutions. This is a most serious error, since given the very logic of things, no male institution can ever be a female institution. This is one of the most important points I have tried to clarify: Monasticism, for example, is not monasticism when those who experience it are women. A group of women living together is not a group of males living together. The father, the abbot, who represents God (as affirmed by St. Benedict's Rule), is not the mother, the abbess, who obviously does not represent God. And so on, along the tragic itinerary of closure, of gratings, of ecstasy, of visions, of "revelations." Nothing is more false and mystificatory than history "by analogy."

This is a radically new work requiring acquaintance with a vast bibliography; and yet it reaches beyond the perspective I formerly adopted. At the same time, it represents the most fruitful development of numerous previous studies I have made. These have gradually led me to a deeper and deeper understanding of the line of interpretation I have used regarding Christianity, and have confirmed my findings with increasing clarity; I refer above all, here, to my books *Gesù di Nazaret: Tabù e Transgressione; Santa Teresa di Lisieux*; and *La Madonna: Dalla Donna alla Statua*.

I hardly need add that all these books have encountered a vast and polemical interest among the reading public, on the part of practicing Catholics and the ecclesiastic hierarchy, thrown into crisis precisely by the central point of power's theological construction: the need for a sacrificial victim; but also on the part of feminists, believers and non-believers alike, erroneously convinced that the importance attributed to women mystics and the Madonna cult could somehow favor women's power. I have fought against this erroneous idea for many, many years, with hundreds of articles in Italy's major daily journals and weekly magazines (as well as French ones, German, Spanish, and Swedish), in debates and talks on radio and television, but I have failed to convince either secular or religious women that maternal power, such as that hypothesized in the "matriarchy," *is not* power.

However, two main factors give me reason to hope that the situation in the United States is different: the lesser political and social power of the Catholic Church (which in Europe, instead, is still considerable); and the need for everyone, women especially, to look the strength of Islam in the face. This strength is based on an unquestionably "male" God and on the certainty of a need for sacrificial victims. Such, in fact, are today's kamikazes, who—significantly—call themselves "martyrs."

The West, then, needs to start out once again from Jesus, constructing a Christianity which, as Jesus wished, is truly detached from the Old Testament; and in which the social organization of power is therefore detached from the "sacred." At this moment America is the only nation capable of confronting this problem, both on a practical level—as it is now doing—and on a theoretical one, where the contribution of women may be crucial, since they may understand and lead others to understand the dialectics of sacred sacrificiality as something necessarily separate from the battle for freedom and for the safety of their homeland.

At this point I shall stop, so that my readers can judge. However, I wish to point out one more thing, which gives me great joy: the fact that I have begun to trace the first lines of a history that no one has yet narrated. It should tell of the immense, incalculable contribution which religious women have given to society, in caring for the poor, the ill, and children; the contribution which they have given, above all, to women, who in all societies have been the ones to bear most of the burden. Most of this story still remains unwritten, because women have never told about their own work, objectifying it. To see with such eyes the *Dizionario degli Istituti di Perfezione*, which lists all the Catholic orders existing in the world, dramatically reveals the appalling emptiness of any bibliography regarding female religious institutes. It makes us perceive the enormity of visionary delirium to which the literature has been subject. Almost nothing has been said about the hands that have touched, washed, medicated, caressed, and comforted innumerable derelict bodies, helping them to enter life and accompanying them in death.

To all the religious women who have died in the same poverty of their poor—of pestilence, hunger, cold, filth, wounds, fear—this book is dedicated.

Rome, 2003
— *Ida Magli*

I. Christianity: A Religion for Women

Whoever has lost her liberty loses everything.
— Arcangela Tarabotti

1

The Trauma Inflicted by Jesus: Women Exist

A Poet Contemplates the Work of Women: Jesus' Ethnological View

In order to truly understand the revolution wrought by Jesus, one must contemplate his actions far more than his words. The reason for this is quite simple: like all men, Jesus had to express his ideas in the language spoken around him — the language he had learned as a child, and in which he had learned to think.

As innovative as language might be, it cannot be invented. Anyone who speaks learnt his language little by little, when he was still unable to analyze it, from those who spoke around him. The human brain is such a *tabula rasa* as regards language that an individual born deaf is also mute: he does not speak because he hears no one speak. In other words, human language is a "potentiality" which needs the human environment in order to be activated. In this respect, Claude Lévi-Strauss is mistaken when he states that it is the sexual instinct that gives birth to the social life, sex being "the only instinct which needs another person in order to be activated."[1] For in the human species, language, like sex, is incapable of being activated without another person's presence (apart from the possibility of coming to know sex through masturbation and bestiality). If we take a newborn baby — say, the son of Japanese — and immediately transfer him to an Italian-speaking family, the growing child will speak Italian. He will understand neither Japanese nor any other language except Italian. But language is the fruit of culture: It reflects all that culture's meanings, customs and values, implicitly much more than explicitly; so that in speaking, the individual is not even aware of the social rules he is obeying, nor how much of his cultural history he is referring to. At school they must explain the rules of grammar to him since, when he begins to speak, the child does so simply because he has heard others speak; he is unaware of the "whys." However, the concept of a grammatical "subject" is actually present within him; and it is reinforced simply by using the term "I." We cannot stop here to examine the enormous problems entailed in analyzing a language; one reason being that many disciplines are involved in such analysis—from epigenetic biology to anthropology. Our brief mention here only serves to illustrate why the speech and parables are the most difficult part of the Gospels to interpret, especially when they are separated from acts.

In the radical revolution achieved by Jesus in the context of Judaic society and culture, his speech—including the parables—represents the most uncertain element as to authenticity, and the least innovative part. For in expressing his thought with words, Jesus was conditioned both by the need to speak in such a way as to be understood by his listeners, and—above all—by the impossibility, for him as for anyone else, to "create" a language *ex novo*. It is not, nor can it ever be, the single individual who creates a language, because language is always the fruit of long-standing group communication and action. Moreover, it is not through the immediacy of conversation (Jesus is never said to have *written* anything) that one can elaborate and explain new concepts and new theories of thought. Not even a genius—and Jesus was *that*—can do so. Indeed, he realized that fact, from the moment he refused to comment on the Scriptures in the synagogue, and he remained silent for 20 years. When he acted, he did so with a highly determined strategy: *to act before speaking*. First of all, he performed gestures and actions so totally in contrast with the values and laws of the group, that he *scandalized, traumatized* (Jesus himself recognized this as an "indispensable violence") those who stood around him and *watched* him: that is, the disciples, and the crowds as well. If words came (and they did not always come), they came *afterwards*; there were attempts to explain the gesture that had been performed beforehand in words. These words were "weaker" than the gesture, since words could not evade the conditioning of the codified language. If the liberating power of Jesus' thought has reached us today—in spite of the two thousand years that have been spent imprisoning it, distorting it, limiting it, and destroying it from the very beginning (starting with Paul and the Gospel writers)—that is because speech can be filled in, interpreted, and transferred to other forms and other languages, whereas gestures cannot.

Least of all, the gestures that traumatized those who witnessed them; and Jesus' gestures traumatized people particularly since they appeared suddenly, out of the blue, with no prior explanation. What is indelible in Jesus, what we can understand even today as if nothing had ever been said about them, are his gestures.

In ancient societies the male was *masculine*. The only active subjects, whatever the action involved, were males; therefore language never presented any ambiguity, because it never occurred to anyone that women might be included in male actions. Women simply obeyed. In the famous parable of the Prodigal Son, for example, the fact that no mother or sisters are mentioned does not mean that they did not exist. They are simply not mentioned, because it was *as if* they did not exist. The actors in the story are men exclusively, because they were the only free, active figures in society; that was clear to everyone. In this respect, we can observe how culture conditioned Jesus, leading him to choose an exemplum valid only for males. In fact, in the Judaic society of the time, a woman could never leave home alone, nor receive any part of an inheritance. And since Jesus was wont to give great attention to women, one might even suppose that this parable is not attributable to him.

Indeed, it is through Jesus himself, and through his actions, that things change radically for women: Women appear as subjects, as first-person interlocutors, in the relationships Jesus initiates with them. However, in the Gospels—even though they do report episodes that were upsetting for the disciples—no theoretical explanations are given for such behavior: Jesus simply acts. The examples are numerous. All are radically and meaningfully fundamental.

One need only recall the Samaritan woman, Martha and Mary, Mary Magdalen, the woman from Canaan, the adulteress, the woman with a hemorrhage; and, in contrast with these, the impatience with which Jesus speaks to his mother, precisely because Mary would not let herself be "liberated" from the role assigned to the Jewish woman and mother. What counts, then, are Jesus' actions, more than his words.

Jesus never explained anything (or perhaps the Gospels did not transmit such explanations because the disciples were afraid that the theoretical implications of Jesus' behavior toward women would be intolerable to Jewish society). And Jesus never pointed out how absolutely revolutionary his way of treating women was: women as subjects, whether in interpersonal relations, society, or theoretical knowledge. Nor does Jesus even explain this to the very women with whom he speaks: he knows that acting is more powerful than any theory. His "give me something to drink!" for example, addressed to the Samaritan woman, constitutes an immediate breakage with the concept of Samaritan women's *impurity*; a Galilean would never have spoken to a Samaritan woman, much less touched any object (a water jug, in this case) that had been touched by one. But at the same time, the episode reveals the "ethnological" vision Jesus has of the world in which he lives, because he chooses to propose one of his most difficult theoretical thoughts to a woman, in terms that a woman could best understand: "water."

Who, more than women, has always been involved in using water? Throughout the world, in all societies, it is they who are the water bearers. It is their task to clean house, to cook, to wash the bodies of others: children, males, the elderly, the sick, guests, pilgrims, as well as all their garments and eating utensils. So no one better than women can appreciate the fundamental value of water.

Jesus acts in an I-you relationship with the Samaritan woman. No witnesses are present. And he does not explain why he has revealed one of the most important themes of his thought to such an inferior, ignorant being as a woman, and a totally impure one at that, being a Samaritan. We can say that Jesus is an "ethnologist on home ground" (and in this respect, a thoroughly modern man), because ethnologists and anthropologists, though studying different, faraway peoples, have always had an eye to daily life, and therefore, to women's life. Jesus goes much further than his, however: he observes the world around him, then singles out the work of women in order to propose his "revolution." Nothing could be more surprising. Indeed, not even in the modern world has a revolutionary ever taken the example of the "banality" or the lack of the "epic" in the life and work of women, in order to incite a revolution. Nor would he ever do so.

Jesus' thoughts, feelings, and inner reflections, and the resulting conclusions which influence his external actions, seem to be uniquely nurtured by this particular attention to everyday events—and not those events that journalists and politicians still today consider as such: wars, political strategies, and anything that has to do with power; but what, on the contrary, does not even exist in male eyes. Indeed, more than attention, he possesses a "vision"—that of a poet or a painter; he contemplates an unchanging landscape with new, modern eyes: those of a Leopardi or a Pascoli. The extraordinary force of his examples, criticism, comments, and parables springs forth above all from his capacity to analyze, to use and to consider daily things that are visible to everyone, and are so *obvious* that no one is aware of them. Herein, above all, lies the force of his intelligence: in reflecting upon the obvious. And the force of his revolution: in denying the necessity of tradition, of the customary, of the obvious. By using such a non-masculine method as anthropology (with good reason anthropology is somewhat ridiculed as being a "science for women" today), Jesus describes and comments on the world surrounding him —fields, birds, flowers, sand, wind, and stones—in their continual interaction with the troubled life of humanity. He describes this world sometimes with critical violence, sometimes with the sweet sadness of one who has experienced the heartrending, unrequited desire for joy, for beauty; and for the will to exist that is inexorably threatened by an awareness of the "end." As expressed in Leopardi's poem, "Sabato del villaggio," Jesus has infinite compassion for the condition of humanity and nature, which, being fragile and transitory is menaced by the immediacy of death even while wearing the lovely robes of a field lily. The very spontaneity with which certain images come to his mind reveals that he must often have stopped to contemplate such things, and that perhaps this was the strongest motive leading him, first, to renounce any action aimed at changing the reality of life around him, and then to leap suddenly into the fray.

The impetus of his rebellion appears, above all, in his refusal of an injustice which was intolerable in that it was obvious, "natural," or rather, because it was *considered* just and natural: the human limitation of the freedom that Jesus has us behold in the birds of the air, the violence exerted by everyday norms on people who are not even aware of the misery forced on them. If Jesus is a dreamer, it is in his romantic rebellion against a reality rendered vulgar and coercive by the falsity of the powerful; he is a dreamer because he is totally extraneous to the violence of his own culture. In fact, it is his acute sensitivity in grasping the essence of the inner and social aspect of daily, infinitely repeated gestures that makes Jesus appear so different and distant from the majority of men. And finally, in spite of all the picking and choosing done by the Gospel writers in narrating his life, the Gospels remain an absolutely "new" document; somehow similar to and close to the sensitivity of the so-called new history of the French school of the *Annales*. This was certainly not the purpose of the Gospel writers. But apart from the inevitable hagiographic commonplaces used by anyone wishing to narrate the life of a prophet and an exceptional man, we find speeches and acts that the Gospel writers were incapable of inventing, and that quite clearly belonged to a leader and someone who had nothing to do with a Jew or any other man of antiquity.

Moreover, the very abundance of these details in relation to the essentiality of the Gospel accounts allows us to realize that the writers of the Gospels could in no way recount the life of Jesus without using such "narrative" material, unwilling as they may have been to do so, because it represented Jesus' usual manner of speaking and acting. After all, we need only read Paul, with the brutish masculinity of his arrogance, to understand that the world revolving around Jesus and his first disciples was totally different from him: it was a world brimming with the usual male desire for power and all its violence.

Women were assigned nearly all the tasks indispensable for daily life: food preparation, the care of clothing, cleaning, the care of the "body." Thus no one ever told their story prior to the birth of anthropology. And since this work is indispensable and obvious, it lacks meanings that can be theorized and therefore is not of interest in the eyes of men.

Except for the eyes of Jesus.

Certain images come to his lips so spontaneously that we can only surmise that he had long observed everything that went on around him; above all, what went on at home. Consider:

> The kingdom of Heaven is like the yeast a woman took and mixed in with three measures of flour till it was leavened all through ... be on your guard against the yeast of the Pharisees and Sadducees ... of two women grinding at the mill, one is taken, one left.... Think of the flowers growing in the fields; they never have to work or spin; yet I assure you that not even Solomon in all his royal robes was clothed like one of these. Now if that is how God clothes the wild flowers growing in the field which are there today and thrown into the furnace tomorrow, will he not much more look after you, you who have so little faith?... No one puts a piece of unshrunken cloth onto an old cloak, because the patch pulls away from the cloak and the tear gets worse.... Do not store up treasures for yourselves on earth, where moth and woodworm destroy them....[2]

All these examples are taken from the work which, in the Jewish society of the time, only women can and must do. The man-male does not do this work, not because he does not want to (though it is true he does not want to), but because he *must not do it*. Unless we understand this absolute, obligatory division of labor between males and females, we will not be able to understand the importance and exceptional nature of Jesus' speech. Was he perhaps speaking only to women? This must be excluded, because his disciples were males, and because women counted for nothing in the ancient world, particularly in the Judaic one. Jesus certainly could not have thought (not even from a realistic point of view) that he could actuate a radical social revolution with the contribution of women. And finally, because from the very beginning, commentators, theologians, church fathers and saints have always interpreted these parables as being addressed to all Christians, but *above all* to men: preachers, priests, bishops, missionaries.

It is important to analyze a few details of these texts. A Jewish woman prepares bread every day because the Law forbids her to prepare a quantity superior to the daily need (an oppressive norm, given its lack of economic functionality)—except on Friday, when she also has to provide for the Sabbath when all work activity is forbidden. The task is performed in a courtyard encircled by windowless huts; this is the place where the women carry out most of their work and life in common. The preparation is toilsome. The grain, which is kept at home, is poured into a small bucket in the correct dosage, and taken into the courtyard, where the gristmill sits. This is formed by two massive stones, one on top of the other, which rotate around a pivot. The women often work in couples in making it turn, to lighten their fatigue. One carefully throws the grain into the pivot hole, while the other sets the mill turning; they take turns at these tasks. Then the dough is prepared by mixing the flour with water drawn by women from the well; and the yeast is added, a lump of dough from the day before. If someone has forgotten to save a lump, she asks her neighbor to lend it her. The dough is then shaped into loaves and put into a clay oven, generally used by several families. Each person must thus wait her turn; each must bring her own cooking fuel. Even the gathering of dry roots, thorns, briers, and thistles needed for the fire is the women's task. Forced to walk long distances to find a sufficient quantity, they tear briers and thorns out of the ground with their bare hands and form a large bundle, pressing it down so that they can carry it on their heads from the fields to the courtyard.

Such toilsome, yet habitual work has never been considered "work" by anyone ever, not even by Marx.

But Jesus observed it with such an attentive eye that he drew many of his teachings from it. Some reflections strike us more than others. The woman who "hides" the yeast in the dough, for example: This involves more than a glance; it involves attention to the meaning of gestures, which not even the most scrupulous anthropologist has ever held to be necessary. What about the woman who forgets to set aside yeast for the next day, and has to ask her neighbor for some? And the two women who turn the gristmill? What man has ever observed the domestic work of women with such close attention? And the grass that grows in the field today, and tomorrow is cast into the oven? Women, women, women…. It seems Jesus has done nothing else but observe them, and in doing so, he has drawn his respect and trust in their capacity to understand him even in the most challenging depths of his thought. Furthermore, the detail of spinning and weaving is even more significant, because Jesus could only have observed his mother doing it. The reason is very simple. If, as it appears, there was no other woman at home, Jesus watched his mother spin and weave, sew and patch, and pull out moth-eaten clothing from the little chest that contained their most "precious" things. Unlike making bread, women had to perform all these other tasks indoors. For they needed to see what they were doing clearly, and only at home could they take off the veils that covered their entire faces and shoulders and, light as it might be, blocked their vision. Moreover, as they raised their arms to spin and weave, their sleeves slipped to uncover their arms, something that was forbidden for any respectable woman.

So, then, Mary obeyed the law obliging women to keep their hands perennially occupied; a law based on a supposition that lasted until a century ago, according to which women must not "think," since their silly little heads would only be full of futile, sinful thoughts. It is well-known that women have always observed this obligation, one inculcated by their fathers, husbands, confessors and spiritual directors; so that even noble, rich bourgeois women never stopped embroidering at their little looms, even when they received with illustrious political and cultural personages and conversed with them in their salons. Even today many women often knit as they watch television, which goes to show how heavily laws and customs of remote origin still persist in daily life. After all, the justification for this is immediately ready: this is an "automatic" task, which does not keep one from following what happens on the TV screen. But everyone well knows that this is not true; as soon as the images require more emotional concentration, the women stop wielding their knitting needles. The ancient legislator of Ecclesiasticus has, at any rate, reached his goal: even today, a vague sense of guilt dogs women's heels when they "think."

It is clear that like all Jewish women who work when there is no immediate need to, Mary arranged blankets and clothing in the linen chest, from which they frequently emerged with moth-holes. Without saying so explicitly, Jesus denies that women must do unnecessary work; and it is above all in connection with women's work that his talk of "not putting up treasures on earth" becomes revolutionary, because in freeing them from the precepts of Ecclesiasticus, he puts at women's disposal the limitless space of "thought."

Who Decided to Baptize Women?

Immediately after the death of Jesus, the apostles and disciples betrayed the fundamental parts of his works. But what do we understand when we say "betrayed"? In part, they did not in the least understand what Jesus had proposed doing; and in part, even while understanding, they attempted to transfer Jesus' message to an organized social reality, virtually conceiving a new type of religion, with well-defined structures such as the church, the ecclesiastical hierarchy, initiation rites, the sacraments,

The Trauma Inflicted by Jesus: Women Exist 15

power. As it turned out, they immediately rebuilt all the foundations of the sacred. But at the same time they betrayed the radical liberation proposed by Jesus, which was liberation from the sacred itself; they made a cultural "leap" which can be defined as a work of genius, not only in relation to Judaic society, but to all other societies and religions existing in the ancient world. Their keeping faithful to the revolution proposed by Jesus in those areas where they were able to do so was the fruit of what they had been able to grasp, but this in turn depended on how traumatized they were.

The trauma that left the deepest scar was the one regarding women. In fact, the only society in which the initiation rite is the same for men and women is the Christian one. Christian baptism is perhaps the first "communist" social structure, because wherever women are placed on a level of social parity, you can be sure that everyone else is as well. Probably one of the decisive reasons for the Judeo-Christian (Jesus' disciples were Jews) renunciation of circumcision was that it could not be performed on women. When we consider how powerful the circumcision rite is today in a modern society where both Jews and Muslims continue to be circumcised, we are able to realize that the decision to renounce circumcision was virtually unthinkable. The only equally unthinkable thing was the need to recognize women as equals.

When attempting to sketch out a history of women, we never stop marveling at the fact that we find nothing which interested historians; nothing stimulated any doubts, any questions on their part; nothing presented itself to their eyes in the cloak of newness, urging them to seek specific causes and motivations for given forms of behavior. Baptism constitutes one of the countless examples of this void. A rite of initiation that is offered to women as well as men is an absolutely original, revolutionary fact in the social institutions of any era and any ethnic group.

But if we seek a debate on this subject, we come up against an absolute void both in the *Acts* of the primitive church and in the reflections of the church fathers; that is, those who in the early centuries argued about practically everything, any theory or theoretician who brought up even the most subtle practical or theological problem in Christian life. In turn, the historians who have handed down these arguments—even the most extravagant, futile ones—limited themselves to observing phenomena which appeared in the immediate foreground, for such phenomena were discussed without their making the slightest intellectual venture of a personal nature or queries outside the scope of the already existing ones.

Who, then, decided to baptize women? No one tells us this. The baptism of women thus appears to be so *obvious* that there is no need to emphasize its absolute newness. But ethnologists and anthropologists well know that initiation is an exclusively masculine institution. There are rites that prepare young women for marriage, but they are referred to as "initiation" rites only because of the mental and linguistic inertia of scholars. As the French ethnologist Jean Poirier points out, "woman is par excellence not initiated nor can she be initiated."[3] After all, this is a logical, inevitable fact: the function of initiation is to introduce new members into a group of male adults who hold leadership. But the only reason they hold leadership is because they know the founding myths, history, and secrets of the group itself; and they have testified that they are worthy by keeping silent about these revelations through their courage in overcoming the terrifying, bloody ordeals of initiation. On the other hand, women are weak and vile by definition, so that the circle closes with facile logic: only men are courageous and can overcome the trials of initiation; the knowledge of secrets presupposes the courage of initiatory trials, and so only men can know them.

In Judaism, initiation consists of circumcision, to which all males are submitted the eighth day after birth. But Jewish circumcision has a different, much more powerful finality than initiation as it is conceived by other ethnic groups, because the Jewish male stipulates a pact of alliance with God: a "nuptial" pact in which, as is only right, God is offered a "sexual" gift: the prepuce.[4]

Initiation through baptism thus marks a radical rupture with Judaism. First of all, because once marriage with God had been fulfilled through the procreation of the Son of God, circumcision, the sign of sacrifice and the sexual submission of virile potency to God, is no longer necessary. The choice of a purification rite by water was the most obvious thing that could emerge from Judaic culture, in which an Orthodox male performs more than a hundred acts of purification a day. But it is also a different rite of initiation — not only from the Jewish one, but also from those of other societies we know — in that it is not inscribed on the body. This choice constitutes an enormous cultural leap. The conceptual passage from the concrete to the symbolic, of which we find numerous examples in Christianity, is most clearly and meaningfully demonstrated precisely in the passage from the initiatory rite of circumcision to baptism.

Though we have received no word of the discussions that must, in any case, have transpired, regarding whether or not to baptize women, we have nonetheless received word of the conflict between Peter and Paul over whether or not to preserve circumcision alongside baptism. Peter was strongly bound to the Jewish identity, which in circumcision found not only the sign of the covenant with God, but also the ethnic seal of his group, an ethnic seal that makes every Jewish male even today, be he a believer or not, view circumcision as a sign showing that he belongs to his people, one distinguishing him from other peoples. Paul, on the contrary, imbued with the Greco-Roman mentality and determined to carry the Gospel outside Palestine, insisted on the need to eliminate circumcision, and was well aware that it would be an insuperable obstacle in the conversion of the Roman world. In fact, the Romans were horrified at this mutilation of the male genital organ, so that Jews were ridiculed with the nickname *curti*. In any case, there are numerous records of the dispute, including the mosaics in the Roman basilicas of Santa Prassede and Santa Sabina, which are among the most ancient in Rome, and which document for this reason the extraordinary importance of women in early Christianity. These mosaics represent Peter together with the Church of the Circumcised — this Church *obviously* in the figure of a Woman; and Paul together with the Church of the Gentiles — this, too, in the figure of a Woman. Conversely, there is absolutely nothing about the decision to baptize women.

This silence cannot be explained unless we look back to the deep, ineradicable trauma wrought by Jesus' behavior with women, and at the same time, to the disciples' desire not to attract people's attention to it. They feared that it would find excessively strong opposition in a world like the ancient one, both Judaic and Greco-Roman, where women were barred from social life and considered inferior to everything that gave men their "male" character. But it is precisely from this perspective that we can realize how Jesus' companions, who saw how easily and trustingly he communicated with women, were neither willing nor able to betray his scandalous, new way of behaving. And so, in profound silence, they chose as a seal of their membership in the Christian community that "water of true life" whose meaning and mystery Jesus had first decided to reveal to the most "impure" of women.

In reality, with Paul's elaboration of the coming of Jesus as the Savior, the concept of initiation and the social category entailed by it totally change function and meaning. More than an initiation, baptism is a "conformation" to the life beyond, to eternal life, to Paradise. It is something entirely different, then, from the rites that make new members similar and suitable to the social life of the group, to the knowledge and power of the group in the reality of life "down here." The total rupture that occurred between Christianity and the institutional establishments of different societies of the time is rooted in this premise: With the advent of the Savior, human exile on earth which was caused by original sin has ended; baptism annuls it through the death and resurrection of the Son of God, and lets humanity enter the eternal life of the hereafter which is the only true one. Baptism, then, at least in the early centuries, is a rite that concludes earthly life and exile. As so conceived, on the basis of Paul's elaboration of the redeeming death of Jesus, Christianity thus has no longer anything to do with Judaism, in which circumcision ratifies a pact of alliance with God for life on earth, even though, as we have seen, circumcision in turn constitutes an initiation rite which is entirely unique in relation to the "initiation" phenomena present in all other social groups.

The betrayal of Jesus' thought was logically perpetrated by his disciples, who were Jewish, and by Paul, with his abnormal sacrificial personality, who were seeking the theological conclusion inherent in Judaism. The spurning of such logic as proposed by Jesus was a spurning which, in modern terms, we might define as "secular." This intolerance was for the entire sacred structure inherent in Judaism, an intolerance that opened up a life free from the sacred, for the sake of reality "down here." The disciples were unable to face the consequences—to live without rituals, without a synagogue, without priests, without original sin. And so they concluded that this meant that "time" had ended; therefore, exile had ended, and nothing remained but to prepare for the end of the world.

But if the whole system of the sacred ended, then the inferiority and impurity of women ended as well, for they represented a consequence of original sin and a condemnation to earthly life; and so women, too, now returned to the primary condition: that of life prior to the existence of death. As a sign and symbol of this return to original "purity," as a cancellation of original sin, baptism had to pertain to women as well. Indeed, to women first and foremost, for they had been more heavily condemned than men, for having led Adam to sin, for having brought about the condemnation to death for all humankind. Only in this context can we explain the events immediately following the death of Jesus, with the massive, free, joyful presence of women in Christian groups. Even the purification bath, by which the baptismal rite was originally performed, was both obvious and liberating for women, since they had always been obliged to perform it in a special pool on the roof of the synagogue, after each menstrual period, childbirth, and puerperium, as a sign of their obsessive "impurity." Water, the most precious possession in a land where water was scarce, which women had to procure, but which they could not use during their periods of impurity, because it was logical to think that if it functioned for purification, it could not be utilized during a state of impurity (not to wash oneself during menstruation, and during the terrible hemorrhage following childbirth, was one of the heaviest "penances" women were condemned to by the obsessive system of taboos in Judaic culture), now became the joyful celebration of their return to innocence: the sign of that white baptismal gown robing both male and female in the eyes of God.

But there was something else that was an innovative and traumatizing trait in Jesus' behavior that implicitly ended the inferiority of women. During his public life, Jesus had called upon single persons, not groups. If, at a given point, a group ended up following him, it had formed freely; but Jesus never gave official sanction to a group as such; he never theorized the existence of a group, much less an organization with him as its head. Whatever could have been more radically different, even in the general context of ancient society, than the "group" by definition — that of men? On the contrary, it is the single person in the Gospels who counts, even women, though they were "objects," property belonging to fathers, husbands, sons (we often only know their names).

The "name" or the "person": something that was not recognized as a right of women in ancient society, particularly in Jewish society, to be a "person," self-sufficient, autonomous, *compos sui*, as indicated by Roman law. Suddenly Jesus tells the women he encounters: go, act, speak, change your life, choose, you have acted rightly, I accept your love, your gifts, your caresses, your hair ... as if each one of these women were really *compos sui*, capable of deciding, thinking, acting, speaking, loving. Here, again, we must conclude that Jesus' message proposed the freedom of the single person, and not of a group as such; and in the eyes of his listeners, whether they were disciples or not, the fact that he offered freedom to women was the most undeniable, traumatizing, powerful proof of that message.

We thus see here a radical, nearly unthinkable change that explains the contradictions already present in St. Paul. He greets and thanks large numbers of women in his letters, calling them by name, and yet he forbids them from speaking, and preaching in church; he commands them to obey their husbands, and cover (that is, "bow") their heads before God and man. In any case, Paul's position bears witness to the enormous discrepancy created in the condition of women right from the beginning. When had women ever been capable of even "thinking" about disobeying the authority of fathers and husbands, their masters over life and death, be they in the Oriental or the Greco-Roman world of the West? Whenever had they been able to address an assembly (or even participate in one)? When had they ever been allowed to listen to the explanation of the Scriptures, if they were prohibited from entering the synagogue, since they had to keep to their domestic chores, and be content with what their fathers or husbands might bother to recount on returning home? The fact that Paul expressly imposes silence on women in his writings to the different communities is a clear sign that such behavior, inasmuch as it was subversive to an orderly masculine life, not only occurred, but had also become customary.

As time went by, the contradictions became more and more conspicuous. The Church strove in every way to drag women's behavior back into the fold of subjection and inferiority. One of many examples can be found in the problem of female impurity linked to the processes of sexual physiology. This problem had always been obsessive in the Judaic environment but, with the spread of Christianity, it extended as far as the West where it was present, however, not in the strongly tabooed form set forward by Jewish culture. And yet doubts continually reappeared in the writings of various Christian authors throughout the centuries with respect to this problem, and they perhaps reveal better than in any other context how strongly the advent of baptism and cultural parity of women had influenced male thought. For example, toward the end of the second century, Dionysius of Alexandria, when questioned by Basilides about menstrual impurity, answers that "in his opinion [therefore there was no common norm], pious, faithful women in that state should not approach the altar to receive the body and blood of the Lord."[5]

Entry into church and communion are still forbidden during the menstrual period in the eighth number of the *Spiritual Canons* attributed to the 1st Ecumenical Council of Nicea in 325. Gregory the Great, in turn, replies in kind to the Bishop of Canterbury, Augustine, advising women to abstain from communion, mostly out of respect and devotion.[6] One could continue with St. Thomas who, even while acknowledging in the *Summa Theologica*[7] that all bodily impurities which, according to the law of Moses, impeded entry into the temple, such as the impurity of women who had recently given birth or those who were menstruating or hemorrhaging, do not impede eucharistic communion according to the new law, yet leaves the various confessors and spiritual directors free to advise their penitents according to each single case. At any rate, the taboo of menstruation remains, thus signaling how difficult it was for men of the Church to fully accept the equality of women in the light of the purity conquered by baptism. The problem of the "opening" of the female body, so blatantly verified during the rhythms of sexual physiology, obsesses male mentality profoundly. It is no coincidence that many saints think of the Madonna as being absolutely "closed": an ivory tower, a sealed fountain, devoid of menstruation; for this was the only system — besides that of virginity — guaranteeing her from any "passage." It is in the Madonna that all the aspirations of men are found enclosed, and it is in her alone that their fear of the "opening" can be assuaged, for as the hymns of the ancient church of Tarragona intone: "God did not violate the gateway to her virginity, either by entering her or by going out of her."[8]

Going Against the Tide: How Lovely to Be Old Widows, Old Maids!

In spite of the numerous studies dedicated to them, the early centuries of Christian organization still remain quite obscure. The conviction that Jesus was really the Messiah, and that Judaic culture had consequently ended, also implied that the life of men on earth had ended, and that nothing more was necessary for "life down here" except to spread the good news of salvation to the whole world. But the end of Judaism meant the end of the fundamental traits marking it: in particular, the time concept. Judaic culture was (and is) characterized by expectation: A change will occur in the relationship between God and the Jews, their exile will come to an end. But because the expectation is a basic feature of the Jewish cultural pattern, and the direction of time is not cyclical (i.e., does not continually turn back upon itself), as it was in all ancient societies until the advent of Christianity, the end of the expectation cannot occur, because that would mean the end of Judaism. However, that is precisely what the proclamation of the death and resurrection of the Son of God inevitably signaled: the end of *time*, the end of earthly life.

Jesus' disciples were Jews: Everything they had believed pertained to Jewish thought and yet, without their being aware of the fact, it was totally new. The end of Judaism opened up canyons of "possibilities," making them totally *free*, incredibly free, creators of a new world no longer restricted to Palestine and the Jews. The cultural *rupture* was total on every front: rupture not only with the Judaic sacred structures, but also with the universal structures of the sacred, because these are an arrangement made to guarantee life "down here," and no longer serve in the life "hereafter." Jesus urged his followers to bring the news of redemption to all peoples; but this in itself contrasted with the Jewish mental world which was concentrated and withdrawn into itself, the world of the chosen people. One is born a Jew (born of a Jewish mother); one does not become one. Circumcision, in fact, is not a customary rite of initiation in religious phenomenology; a person who is circumcised ratifies his pact with God by affirming his Jewish identity. The urging to "go among all peoples," though, was an affirmation that all men are equal, and that no people is "chosen." In this way Jesus virtually uprooted the fundamental structures, not only of Judaism, but of the sacred.

The hypothesis has often been made that the initial organization of Christianity aimed only at the sanctification of individual converts, while awaiting the final coming of Christ, and that those institutions which gradually formed, with their church- communities, functioned in the context of this final sanctification. In fact, in the *Acts of the Apostles* and in the *Apostolic Letters*, we find the names of several women who dedicated themselves to continual service to God and the Christian community, renouncing marriage, or else preserving their widowhood. They spurned the only roles assigned to women, that of being "circulated" among males and that of procreation; this choice inherently implied the end of the world. Even while living with their families or else, as in the case of rich widows, in their own homes, these women were responsible for carrying out a variety of tasks in their church. St. Paul speaks of a deaconess, in his *Letter to the Romans* (16:1), a text held to be authentic, and written around 58 AD: "I commend to you our sister Phoebe, a deaconess of the church at Cenchreae. Give her, in the Lord, a welcome worthy of God's holy people, and help her with whatever she needs from you. She herself has come to the help of many people, including myself." It is hard to tell exactly what her role was or whether at this date the deaconate can be considered an "order" in the restricted sense that it would assume for males later on. In the centuries that followed there doubtlessly existed an "ordination" of elderly women, who played an official role in the Christian community: in the liturgy, in assisting women in the baptism rite (which was performed by immersion, and so entailed the need to disrobe); and above all, in a certain "charitable" duty which is also called "ministry"; we do not know how that began, or what functions it entailed. These women were chosen among widows or among elderly "virgins," meaning unmarried women, since at the time it was unthinkable that an unmarried woman might not be a virgin.

The *Didache* and the *Apostolic Constitutions* describe their tasks and state that they must be 60 years old (women of that age were rare, given the short life span of women at the time). At the end of the fourth century, instead, they were admitted at the age of 40, by decision of the Council at Laodicea (perhaps to make up for the small number of eligible women). The inclusion of elderly women in some function of a social nature is a phenomenon found in nearly all cultures, and bears witness to the fact that it is the female sexual physiology which gave rise to the institution of "avoidance," for only elderly women are devoid of menstruation, and are safe from the dangers inherent in the use of sexuality. We can therefore affirm — and we shall see how important it is in the history of Christianity — that this is a "constant" in male thought. Either through virginity or with the end of the menstrual cycle, the woman's body must be "closed" to the risk of the unknown, to the perilous mystery of the transcendent, ultramundane world which her "opening" causes.

Scholastic theologians are careful to explain that the ordination of women had nothing in common with the sacrament of the holy order as such, in its canonical definition. Such emphasis is superfluous, for the exclusion of women from any true hierarchy of power is so *obvious* that the theologians' statement cannot in the least be doubted. The almost incredible cultural "leap" made by making women equal to men in Christian society through baptism finds its justification not only in Jesus' actions, but also in the fact that people believed baptism was a way of preparing themselves for the soon-to-come world of the hereafter. On the contrary, it was impossible to make that other "leap" — a far more dangerous one, since it pertained to earthly reality — which would have been the investiture of women in the function of "mediators" with the divinity, the maximum power that can be exercised in any society. In other words, baptism confers no power over others; the orders, instead, establish hierarchies of power. In fact, baptism is the only sacrament that can be imparted by anyone in case of need, and does not require a priest.

Among the most illustrious deaconesses we can recall Olympia, the friend of St. John Chrysostom, and perhaps Macrina, the sister of Basil, whose biography was written by his famous brother, Gregory of Nyssa. We find records of deaconesses in Byzantium up to the 13th century. Their role was even more important in Syria. Among the eastern Syrians, some canonists, such as John of Tella in the sixth century and James of Edessa (d. 708), tended to limit their powers, but did acknowledge their right, particularly in female communities (and so not in public), to read the scriptures, recite the deacon's prayers, and even distribute the Eucharist. And in eastern Syria, deaconesses could read the liturgical texts even in church, and offer the consecrated bread and the chalice right up until the Middle Ages.

In the West, on the contrary, we note a kind of repugnance toward the title of "deaconess" as early as the Councils of Nimes (394–6), Orange (441), Epaona (517) and Orléans (535); and the repetition of these warnings perhaps testifies not so much to the difficulty in uprooting a venerable custom as to the resistance raised against an Eastern custom that some were attempting to introduce. The same thing occurred with the institution of "canonesses," a designation which seems to have been unknown in the West until the eighth century, when it was used synonymously with the term "nun."

Scholars give no particular explanation for the greater rigidity of the

Western Church in contrast to the Eastern one, as regards the attribution of institutional responsibilities to women. In any case, it is arguable that this difference depends on the greater awareness of the importance of "law," and thus, of the institutionalization of customs in a society dominated by the influence of Roman juridical thought. Furthermore, the introduction of elderly women into social life appears easier in a "traditional" society such as the Eastern one, in which (as also occurs in various societies of an ethnological level) menstruating women were avoided in a conscious, explicit manner. In the West people kept silent about this custom, an embarrassing one, and perhaps regarded as a bit uncouth.

Moreover, as we shall see, it was perhaps a greater awareness of the institutional meaning that the social organization assumes that later caused women in the West itself to abandon the cloistered, contemplative life, in order to embrace one of educational and social assistance, an explicit choice, and much more common than in the East. In any case, monasteries for women soon sprang up and developed, in the West, little by little absorbing nearly all previous forms of consecration of women.[9]

Umpteenth Exchange Between Death and Sexuality

Jesus had proposed an entirely new vision of the world *down here*, whereas the disciples, guided by St. Paul, held that their work would serve as the final phase — one of unspecified length — for preparing humanity's return to the world *hereafter*. The elaboration of the sacred structures such as the symbolic sacrifice, the sacraments and the ecclesiastical hierarchy developed little by little, together with a corpus of theological thought. With the gradual passage of time, the conviction that Christianity constituted a preparation for the kingdom of God and the end of the world became more and more remote, while the institutional organization sank its roots into the social life of this earth.

Some of the earliest organizational forms testify to the "final contingence" for which Christians believed they had to make themselves ready. The foremost of such forms was the consecration of female virginity. What more than the cessation of the matrimonial exchange of women could actualize the end of society, the very end of the world? The consecration of virgins was chosen and propagandized by the most important men, those of the Church, with a force that in itself would be incomprehensible if it had not been the clearest sign of the very transcendence of the Christian community. But aside from the concrete logical motivation — the belief that the world was about to end — the male renunciation of the use of sex, projected onto the enthusiasm for consecrated female virginity, hid the real cause that, from the very birth of Christianity, made sexuality its fundamental problem: Men have really become the "brides of God" and therefore, more or less consciously, the end of the world has actually arrived. Or rather, the end of "earthly" organization has arrived, and it is men who must impose the new one, the one without sex.

It would suffice to recall the invention of "continence" (pauses in sexual relations between spouses) to understand the limits that the problem of sexuality had reached in the eyes of Christians. Married people who had received baptism were "allowed" to maintain the bond that had united them previously, but they were urged and encouraged to renounce the use of sex in order to establish a new kind of relationship, a "spiritual" one. This is an aspect of the Christian social setup that is never discussed in its concrete implications; in any case, the fact that baptism could entail the renunciation of sex even within the marriage bond, which in antiquity was aimed at producing the largest possible number of children, is an almost more significant fact than chastity outside of marriage. All the more so for women, who were subject to the will of males during their entire married lives, just as they were in the realm of sexuality. They now suddenly became "companions" in marriage, on a level of parity, once the marriage bond was based on a spiritual and not a sexual plane. And yet, as much as one might be tempted to explain the obsessive renunciation of sex during the early centuries with the choice of ascetic practices and penitence for one's sins, the fact that marriage could subsist without sex is so absurd on a natural, social, and cultural plane that it could only mean one thing: Christianity had made sexuality useless.

Naturally, to look this conclusion squarely in the face in all its logical rigor was impossible even for the most fervent Christians, so that the idea of a ladder of merit slowly developed: the idea of a hierarchy in spiritual life. Proceeding from the highest to the lowest plane, from the maximum to the minimum, "perfection" is found in martyrdom, in virginity, and in marital continence. In a passage of his *Commentary* on the *Letter to the Romans*, written around 243–244 (quite early, then), Origen expressly declares that this three-part division was the most widely-observed one in the Christian communities of his time: The sacrifice most pleasing to God is that of martyrs; second comes that of virgins, and third, that of persons practicing sexual continence. Therefore, Christianity *is sacrifice*, and immediately after the sacrifice of life comes that of sex. In the Latin sermon of Pseudo-Cyprianus entitled *De centesima, sexagesima, tricesima*, we read a series of exhortations to put into practice the Christian values of martyrdom, virginity and continence. The structure of this sermon, of African origin, dating back to a period between the late second and the mid-third century, corresponds exactly to what Origen affirms regarding the Christian East. Therefore, if the fundamental demand for the renunciation of sex is the same in the East and West, then the supposition often made by historians, that the Greco-Roman school of philosophy of the skeptics and gnostics influenced this demand, can hardly be considered valid. Moreover, the renunciation of sex is nearly unthinkable in the customs of Eastern cultures, unless it is linked to some absolute, indispensable need.

According to that same anonymous African sermon, each of the three stages of spiritual life corresponds to a prize: Martyrdom obviously merits the most, 100 points; virginity, 60; and marital continence, 30. The percentages adopted to express the existence of a hierarchy of awards, corresponding to the hierarchy of values achieved by the Christian, are derived from the Gospel parable of the "sower," according to which good seed bears fruit in the one receiving it 100, 60 or 30-fold (*Matthew* 13:8–23); but in the end, the good seed ended up being identified wholly with the exclusion of sexuality.

From the mid-third century onward, in fact, the distance from the scheme of the African sermon increasingly widened. The first interpretation to be thrown into crisis was that hinging on the number 30, which the most ancient tradition had awarded for marital continence. Again in his *Commentary* on the *Letter to the Romans*, Origen maintains that even married people can offer their "bodies" as holy and immaculate hosts, or victims pleasing to God, if they behave rightly and abstain from sex only sporadically, dedicating themselves to prayer. A few years later, in 249, in commenting on a passage from the *Book of Joshua*, Origen formulates a new scheme: After martyrs and virgins, in the place assigned to the sexually continent, we find widows for the first time. It is interesting to note that Origen himself emphasized the value of the renunciation of sex by widows. On the one hand, more women were taken off the marriage market; on the other, a sexual value was attributed to women, even when they were no longer virgins. During the third century, both because the danger of persecution lessened and, perhaps, because faith in the imminent end of the world was attenuated, people began to believe that the highest degree of evangelic perfection did not necessarily demand the actual death of the martyred victim; and asceticism, in its rigorous renunciation, little by little assumed the aspect of a death similar to death by martyrdom. At the beginning of the century, Clement of Alexandria had not hesitated to speak of a "gnostic martyrdom": that is, that type of martyrdom faced by every pure soul in the effort to know God, and in obedience to the Commandments; a martyrdom which, in a way, even surpasses blood martyrdom in that it requires a perseverance in time which is more difficult than the heroic but immediate act of death.[10] In this as in many other third-century texts, we can witness a progressive development of the doctrine of asceticism as spiritual martyrdom: a doctrine which, starting with the consideration of a parity of value between a cruel form of martyrdom and the exercise of ascetic virtues, would shortly end up by simply substituting martyrdom with virginity, at the apex of the hierarchy of values in Christian life.

It is superfluous to repeat here that any theological theory, like any "rule" of perfection, functions exclusively in relation to male experience. As with monasticism later on, consecrated virginity represents liberation from the martyrdom of married life for women; needless to say then, women would never have considered the renunciation of sexuality as the supreme martyrdom. It is no coincidence that one of the theoreticians of the three grades of perfection is Origen: that is, a male so totally convinced that the sexual impulse could not be tamed by the will, that he went so far as to castrate himself with his own hands.

Apparently, it was Athanasius who first attributed 100 points as a prize for virginity, reserving the minimum, 30, to married persons, in his *Letter to Virgins*. In Athanasius's scheme (which never mentions the number 60), we find for the first time a consideration of the common matrimonial condition, recognized as deserving of legitimacy from the Christian point of view. This acknowledgment had somehow become necessary in order to combat the persistent supporters of sexual abstinence as a "sign" of the Christian — they were still numerous in the fourth century: For the first time, martyrdom now disappeared from the list of Christian virtues, substituted by virginity. Ambrose of Milan, whose first tract, *On Virgins* ("virgins" being used in the feminine case), was written in 377, was surely influenced by Athanasius's *Letter to Virgins*; among Western authors, he appears as the first to be familiar with the attribution of 100 points to virginity. However, Ambrose does not limit himself to fixing the superiority of the virginal state with respect to matrimony, but inserts widowhood between virginity and marriage as an intermediate state, perhaps taking into account Origen's view. At any rate, we now find sexuality referred to women alone: a critical sign of the passage from a Christianity that is experienced and meditated upon as the final state of the world, as physical death by martyrdom, and individual or group death by the renunciation of sex and procreation, to an early adjustment of Christians to life on earth. It is no longer possible to know how long the "expectation" of the end will last, so it becomes necessary to establish what distinguishes the Christian from the non-Christian in the persistent conviction, however, that Christianity coincides with the "perfection" of humanity.

Indeed, it is at this point that Ambrose writes his tract *On Widows*, for it has become imperative to define the social condition of women, which has almost universally been determined by their sexual relation to men. Widowhood, in fact, is a "state" assigned by society exclusively to the woman, indicating a woman mutilated of the male element—*vir*. She must remain chaste; any sexual relation with a widow is included in the category of *stuprum*.[11]

The scheme based on the distinction "virgins-widows-married persons" is later taken up by Jerome. In order to defend himself against the accusation of having exaggerated in deprecating matrimony in his polemic against Juvinianus, he once more repeated that martyrdom must not be excluded from the list of Christian virtues: Otherwise, it becomes impossible to insert matrimony at the bottom line (!)—while matrimony does deserve a place among the states of the Christian condition.[12]

This entire debate leads to one clear conclusion: The Christian is defined as such in relation to sexuality.

Finally Free: Long Live Virginity!

From the beginning, one of the fundamental traits of Christian organization has been the "consecration of virgins." Regarding the conviction on the part of Jesus' disciples that his coming coincided with the end of the earthly world, no proof is greater than this: the stoppage of the matrimonial exchange of women. At least on a conscious level, only this conviction can explain the force with which the consecration of virgins was desired and propagandized by the most important men of the Church, until it became the absolute symbol of the holiness and transcendence of the Church itself. But the manner in which this symbolism formed on the psychological level is one of the most difficult puzzles to resolve, unless one refers to the sexual roles present, from Judaism onwards, in the relationship between men—males—and God. In the Gospels, in fact, Jesus does not require virginity of the apostles, nor of the other disciples, even if we were to admit that he actually stated that there are those who "make themselves eunuchs for the kingdom of heaven." It was on this affirmation that the Church founded the primacy of virginity.

In reality, it is extremely improbable that Jesus exploited the condition of eunuchs in order to inculcate the virtue of virginity. The reason is clear. In ancient (as well as medieval) Eastern societies, especially in Egypt—and therefore, in the world that the Jews knew—eunuchs constituted a well-defined social class: a codified institution carrying out an administrative function of responsibility and trust, at the service of men of power and the court. Although not many studies have been made regarding this institution (given the usual male fear tabooing the negative functioning of the penis), still, there is no doubt about the social place occupied by eunuchs: a very important one from the point of view of administrative and political strategies in the Eastern kingdoms. And the best-known fact — that they were also in charge of guarding the harem — has always served to hide the public social importance of the true statue of eunuchs. The operation that they underwent as boys was total. Unlike what is usually thought, in antiquity castration was not performed by the mere crushing or cutting off of the testicles; it also consisted of the partial amputation of the penis, because the male sex organ was seen as a total entity: testicles and penis together.

Eunuchs therefore did nothing "virtuous" in the Christian sense of a renunciation of sexuality. They were instead submitted to this mutilation only with the intent of introducing them into the social class destined to them. In ethnological terms, we might thus define it a mutilation by "initiation." The taboo regarding anything that has to do with the potency of the penis and the male fear of losing it has seen to it that the bibliography relative to this subject is practically nonexistent in the Bible.

Nor can we suppose that Jesus' disciples held the eunuch to be a symbolic example to be followed. Jesus' entire message is centered on "what comes out of the heart of man," since only this can contaminate him. True, this concept is totally contrary to the Judaic religion and culture, with its concrete purification rites, concrete sacrifice of animals, and concrete division between pure and impure foods. But Jesus' words were too clear to be misunderstood. For the Jews, the "heart" was the central mover of the person as a whole: thought, will, feeling; and in the view of Jesus, these are the only agents responsible for human actions. Nothing to do with eunuchs, then, who, lacking the organs necessary for sexual activity, are without libido, incapable of desire, and therefore also incapable of "virtue" in this area.

The Institution of the Canonesses and the End of Freedom

The consecrated virgins included women designated by the particular name of "canonesses": a group apparently linked to the male group of "canons." However, we must immediately make a distinction here that will be necessary during our entire journey down through the history of Christian women. Calling a woman "canoness" is an example of the banal custom, in force for centuries, of transforming to the feminine form those terms that refer to male institutions. Under the veil of an apparent analogy, the custom hides the fundamental differences between the social statute and the concrete forms of the lives of women, in comparison with those of men. True, it was the parity of women established by Jesus which encouraged linguistic usage in which the masculine form included the feminine one; in ancient society this would have been illogical. The masculine was "masculine," since the subject of an action was exclusively male. It was with the revolution wrought by Jesus, as we have seen earlier, that women became the subjects of actions as well; but the dogmatic cultural and psychological attitudes of men have led them to continue using the masculine form even for women's actions. The use of names in the feminine form, derived through a kind of inertia from the masculine, has given rise to the nearly absolute falsity with which the condition of women has been narrated and perceived by historians, as well as the nearly insurmountable difficulties we meet today in trying to highlight the *real* historical phenomena marking the lives of women.

But let us get back to our canonesses. Both specialized monographs and encyclopedias define them as "virgins consecrated to God," whereas canons were so called either because of membership in a particular "collegium" on the basis of which they were assigned service in the corresponding church, or because of their promise to observe a given rule, which was also called a "canon." Canonesses, then, appeared alongside canons, but the analogy with the male institution was more apparent than real, and the name was given them for convenience's sake. The designation "virgins," which actually distinguishes the female institution, does not emerge as an indication of the canons' statute. Although the origin and history of canonesses cannot be precisely determined, we do know that their presence was particularly felt in the East, since they are repeatedly mentioned in the writings of the church fathers. St. Basil speaks of the punishments awaiting canonesses who break the rules (thus revealing an early decadence of this institution), and sends a letter to the "canoness" Theodora. St. John Chrysostom, instead, entitles a pastoral booklet: *Canonesses must not live with men*;[13] the title suffices to indicate fears regarding possible sexual abuses. In addition, it leads us to conclude that these canonesses did not live together in a special building. On this point scholars disagree, or are uncertain, but this is relatively unimportant. Since women's lives were so totally confined to the home, and to a part that was separate from that of men, their virginity was never at risk; however, with monasticism community life assumed a particular meaning for women as well. One may suppose that these women were attracted to an intense religious life, precisely because of that "virginity" which marked female Christianity from the very beginning, and that they were members of a college, and assigned service in a particular church. The scholars' mention of "assignment of a particular service" is, however, the consequence of that imprecise language of convenience stemming from the masculine form, which we have already mentioned; one must not be led to believe that the liturgical and pastoral roles of canonesses were anywhere near those of canons.

It must also be stressed that the development of female consecration in the West took shape differently from that in the East, where the institution of deaconesses and canonesses survived for a longer period, and the participation of women in certain church activities was more deeply-rooted and functional. The Western church obviously recognized the services of baptismal assistance and charity toward the needy that were carried out by women, but we do not exactly know to what degree it agreed to confer on them what is known as "ordination." Jesus' stress on the need to help the poor and weak doubtlessly influenced the immediate introduction of women into Christian social life, since it is women in all societies who perform the task of assistance in physical needs; but only a faded memory has remained of the institutional meaning that this assistance implied in the early centuries, probably because it was women who provided it.

We cannot stop here to consider the long, complex historical itinerary of the institution of canonesses; at this point, what most interests us is to demonstrate how the "consecration of virgins" in all its forms soon became a fundamental structure of society. It created a true and proper "class" that had nothing to do with a religious "vocation" for those women who could not be given away in marriage for economic or social reasons. Naturally, this practice gave rise to many deviations from disciplinary restrictions. In the Carolingian era, the great majority of canonesses, called "secular" because they did not follow a monastic rule, were from noble families. Without taking vows, they lived in convents sustained by the "benefits" assigned them, and could administer their own personal incomes. Their only liturgical obligation was to participate in the "choir" on the days prescribed by the rule, and, of course, they had to remain virgins. In this case more than any other, it clearly emerges that the primary aim of the institution was to officially remove designated women from the matrimonial market.

Indeed, until 1900, it was virtually impossible for males to think of women as autonomous subjects, apart from their matrimonial and maternal roles. Whenever it was impossible to utilize them for earthly matrimony, they were given away in marriage to God. This was the only way to preserve them, even conceptually, in the role of brides: They were made into spiritual "mothers" and made "fecund" with prayer, thus annulling any doubt that might emerge as to the organization of society. As we shall see, herein lies the main reason why the Church fervidly opposed the "active life" of religious women; for the active life was the first sign of the possibility for women to "work" within society, aside from maternal and domestic tasks, and an indispensable step toward their psychological, social, and economic autonomy from male and family authority.

The "regular" canonesses were distinguished from secular ones, in that they took vows and followed the rule of St. Augustine (which was also the rule of the canons). Every canoness wore a tunic that varied in form and color according to local custom. Over it she wore a rochet or knee-length vestment that, as in the case of men, marked her status as canoness. The number of convents for regular canonesses was enormous and spread throughout Europe. But as time went by, the distinction between "canonical" and "religious" women belonging to the monastic orders became less and less clear, at least in the eyes of the public, both because they were not confined to a convent and moved about in society dressed in the sumptuous robes of the nobles, and because, as had occurred in the case of men, membership in the religious order was associated with membership in a higher class, and had little to do with religious choice. However, if this was the social reality, in no way did the Church intend to acknowledge it, at least regarding women. In fact, it is more exact to say that, for the Church, and therefore for the whole of society, it was obvious that the institution should be respected, above and beyond any religious sentiment or aspiration on the part of the individual. After all, that was the way things worked in earthly marriages that were imposed by fathers as well. Women were obliged to love and obey their husbands, who were assigned them by their fathers, and to behave according to the duties imposed by society, both in feeling and in action, for it was unthinkable that they might be "subjects" with wills and desires different from those prescribed.

This situation gave rise to invocations of the religious obligations imposed by the social structure of the canonical institution. Such calls to duty were often harsh. For example, Canon 26 of the Second Lateran Council (1139) expresses its scorn for any kind of female liberty, decreeing that "a stop be put to the hateful, evil custom of certain women who wish to be called nuns by the people, even though they do not live according to the rule of Benedict or Basil or Augustine [...] We prohibit and forbid them, under pain of anathema, to continue this hateful, dishonest impiety."[14] Naturally, the fact that such women passed themselves off as nuns depended on the impossibility for unmarried women to move about with any freedom in society, unless they were covered by membership in a religious institution. Shortly thereafter, the Council of Reims (1148) feigned to know nothing of the decisions made by fathers for their daughters; or rather, it decided not to leave room for any freedom for those condemned to the claustral prison, stating:

> Preoccupied with maintaining greater decorum in the house of God, we have established that the nuns and women calling themselves canonesses who live outside a "rule" must repent and correct themselves, and observe the Rules of Benedict and Augustine; they must abandon their luxurious, improper clothing; they must continually reside in the convent; they must be content with the choir, the refectory and dormitory; and, leaving their incomes, they must satisfy their needs with things of the convent.[15]

So the turn of the screw regarding women's institutions was continuous, even though everyone knew that they were imposed prisons that for many centuries now had nothing to do with any voluntary choice of consecration to God.

During the last two centuries of the Middle Ages, the institution of secular canonesses became the equivalent of that of "noble" women, and was particularly widespread in the German empire. Scholars have failed to study it in depth[16] not only because of the afore-mentioned general lack of interest in the history of women, but above all because it is a social phenomenon vested as a religious one, and therefore evades the scrutiny of both church historians and historians in general. Until scholars realize that until 1900 the history of women coincided with the history of ecclesiastical thought and organization of society, it will be impossible to understand it. After all, it is impossible even today for the men who guide the Catholic Church to think of women except in their matrimonial and maternal roles; suffice it to read the Vatican document prepared for the Fourth World Conference on the Rights of Women in 1995. A few concessions may be made at an economic level, such as proposed increases in family allowances and compensation for domestic work, so that women will not have to leave the house and can continue to be instruments of procreation. Lest there be any doubt regarding the fact that ecclesiastics are completely incapable of considering women as "subjects" in society, the document concludes that "the world of politics, in its structures and functions, remains a male world essentially."

In any case, as admission to convents became restricted to the nobility, the canonical rule of living became increasingly widespread, precisely because it was less harsh and penitential than the monastic one. The chapters of noble women were located almost exclusively in the Germanic empire: In Lotharingia in the North (Andenne, Nivelles, famous for some of its mystical women; Mons, Moustier, etc.); in the South: Remiremont, Epinal, Bouxières, Poussay; in Alsatia (Andalu, Erstein, Sainte-Odile); and then in Burgundy; in Saxony (with its famous Gandersheim, Quendlinburg, Nordhausen, Gernrode, etc.); in Franconia (Essen, Cologne, Kaufungen, Herford); in Bavaria, in Lorraine and in nearly all the imperial territory. Unfortunately, though the geographic extension itself indicates the social importance of this institution, we lack statistical studies showing how it influenced the life of the nobles, and we do not know how many women were condemned to become the brides of God. Although convents everywhere performed the social function of removing excess noble daughters from the matrimonial market, in France and Italy this function did not become so explicit as in the Germanic empire.

There, in fact, the Church made no attempt to conceal its ruling role in the politics, as clearly appears during the Ottonian era when bishops were "princes," and many abbots and abbesses of court monasteries were attributed royal ranking as well. The ecclesiastic aristocracy thus performed an important political role. Moreover, the interchange of powerful laymen with powerful ecclesiastics reciprocally increased their power until, after the secularization of the Carolingian period and the "manumission" of the officially-recognized lords, the richest abbeys passed under the direct control of the princes. Some monasteries then became institutions reserved exclusively to the nobles, with increasingly rigid disciplinary conditions; and the papacy was unable to maintain its supremacy and authority over them. The chapters of noble ladies offered girls of the aristocracy the prebends and education held to be indispensable for their place in society; while all the abbeys, which in practice had always reserved places for the nobles, ended up adopting exclusive, explicit rules to assure this aristocratic prerogative. In 1207, for example, at Andenne, it was decided that each new recruit had to be the daughter of a knight, though it was probably not until the 14th century that this rule was fixed by decree: at Remiremont in 1395, Nivelles in 1462, and Moustier in 1496.

As time went by, the noble class became more and more self-confined, with the aim of maintaining its prestige and privileges that were now at risk given the excessive expansion of knighthood. Direction of the canonical abbey was entrusted to an abbess, elected by the chapter on the basis of her membership in one of the illustrious families; sometimes the abbesses of a given convent belonged to the same family, their offices becoming virtually hereditary. Many abbesses were princesses of the Germanic empire for example at Gandersheim, Herford, Essen, and Remiremont, so that it is absurd for historians to keep pretending that this institution was separated from society as a whole, and that religious institutions cannot be placed in a global framework. The canonesses were accepted into a convent at a very tender age; they attended the convent school, where they received an education in conformity with the demands of the noble class, and prepared for marriage, or else to succeed their relatives in the most important offices of the convent itself. At this point, we must try to understand to what degree the placement of women (though apparently "passive") within the immense area of religious organization, allowed the Church to dominate society, both concretely and theoretically, given the high number of consecrated women, and their formal acceptance of the values asserted by the Church itself. It was an acceptance propagandized by their very presence.

2
Women as Christ's "Males"

The Scandal: A Woman's Word Is Worthy

It seems that the concept of "martyrdom"—accepting or even seeking out death in order to testify, to publicly affirm, under the dominion of juridical law, an *idea as the absolute truth*—is particular to Christianity. A new fact. Studies on the topic, though abundant, give no true explanation. It would almost seem that martyrdom is *obvious*; a *value* that is self-evident, given that it leads to the loss of life. Under the entry "martyr," in the *Nuovo dizionario di spiritualità* of 1985,[17] there is still no clear explanation for the act of "witnessing" (the Greek term *martus* means "witness") as it appears in the earliest centuries of Christianity. Indeed, in the New Testament the term *martus* does not have the exclusive technical meaning—implying acceptance of death—which it assumed from the second to third centuries onward.

The particular meaning given to Christian martyrdom seems to rise, in particular, from the thought of St. Paul, who sees in Christ the only true "victim," the only one capable of annulling the sins of the world, who accepts the sacrifice willed by God without rebelling. Every Christian is *alter Christus*, and with his renunciation of life, bears witness to the truth of his faith, identifying himself in the role of "Christ the victim." Indeed, in the delirium leading him to equate himself to Christ, Paul states that with his own sacrifice he completes what was lacking in the sacrifice of Christ. Paul then adds an ulterior meaning to that of "witness"; the concept of "martyr" no longer coincides perfectly with that of "sacrificial victim," but is instead superimposed on it. The martyr marks a deep cultural rupture with the thought and behavior both of the Judaic world and the Greco-Roman one. If we read some of the acts of trials that the Roman authorities were called upon to hold against Christians, we clearly note their *surprise* over the matter of contention, and their reluctance to pronounce death sentences against individuals who had not committed any crime, and of whom very little was asked in order to be saved. The Romans' traditional tolerance toward all religious cults and ideas clashed with the intolerance of the Christians who, in their refusal to recognize any degree of "transcendence" in the person of the emperor, committed the *crimen maiestatis*.

At any rate, two aspects, neglected by scholars, can shed a great deal of light on the absolute newness of Christian behavior in the context of ancient society. One is the valence of the "potency of the word," which passes from its well-known use in affirming truth in court, to that of affirming the "truth" of religious faith, thus becoming analogous to the potency of death in "sacrifice." Tied to this new potent aspect of the word is another aspect—a surprising one indeed, which no author has stressed, as if it were too obvious to mention: "witnessing" on the part of women. This is an absolute novelty, having no equivalent in any other society or era; by itself it furnishes the strongest proof of the traumatic, irrepressible "leap" which the behavior of Jesus of Nazareth forced on the ancient psychological and cultural pattern.

We must start by considering the "potency of the word," for that is the point where the diverging newness of Jesus begins. The concept of "message," the word of salvation which must be carried to all peoples, does not correspond to the "magic" force of the potency of the word, present in all cultural systems, but is "historicized": transformed into an instrument of becoming, of transformation, of the future, and not a "repetition" founded in the past. This message concept would have been an impossible one in the Judaic context, since an individual is born a Jew: He does not become one.

"Affiliation" is fundamentally important in Judaic culture precisely because one's history, one's identity, is not acquired, but inherited. Only one who is "the son of" receives his identity.

This category of Judaic thought is so consequential that in order to give absolute force to his figure and message, the disciples of Jesus could only affirm that he was "the son"—the son of God. And yet the contradictory newness of Christianity is precisely this: One *becomes* a Christian through the force of the word. Preaching and baptism are linked by the potency of the word. Even though, according to Jesus' thought, neither baptism nor any other gesture is necessary, since it is inner conversion that counts: the transformation of one's thought and will. In any case, baptism, which the disciples invented because they were incapable of getting along without some rite, does mark the cultural "leap" inculcated by Jesus. With baptism, *one becomes*, annulling the value of what one *is*.

That is why all of a sudden, all people are equal: free or slave, rich or poor, young or old, barbarian or civilian. Even the "difference" par excellence — that of gender — is cancelled. Indeed, we might suppose that, precisely because the sexual difference falls into decline, all other differences would be prevented from doing so. But once this totally new logical category of "being" has snapped into action and one *becomes* a Christian, the fundamental structure underlying ancient society is virtually annulled. Society is liberated from any conceptual bond associated with "descent": a noble because he is the son of nobles, a slave because he is the son of slaves, etc. In the history of Christianity, the contradiction between everyone's being equal and their not being so has undergone every imaginable contrast and return to the past; but the seed sown in the beginning by Jesus of Nazareth has never disappeared. Therefore, the concept of "bearing witness," which originally meant to confirm the truth of a fact that has already occurred, assumes a much stronger valence. Now, in declaring a reality one makes it be or keeps it viable by strengthening it.

However, along with the decline in the continuity of inheritance or descent, we also note a decline in the analogous way of conceiving time (which characterized all ancient societies): that of long duration, of the concatenation of events, parallel to that of equality through affiliation. The conception of time is one of the fundamental principles of a culture and, at the very moment in which Jesus of Nazareth affirmed that salvation had come, he changed the direction of Judaic time, which was informed by the concept of expectation. *Expectation* is simultaneously a projection toward the future and continuity with the past: It is because one expects that time is projected forward, yet also remains "immobile." The coming of the Savior "closes" Judaic time.[18] But Jesus' disciples, for whom it is unthinkable that life can subsist outside Judaism, are convinced that the moment has also come for the world to end, and that the only future is that of the afterlife.

Herein is the origin of all the ambiguities and contradictions of the history of Christian Europe. Included are those regarding human equality, even today. In reality, one's way of conceiving time determines one's way of conceiving the life of man, because time and human life are one and the same. Equality through affiliation is thinkable only within a time that *does not become*, that flows along oblivious to the individual, that *continues* beyond the life duration of each single person. Continuity by blood is the continuity of time. This is one of the main reasons why, in many societies, women are denied survival in the afterlife, and why the female sex is the fragile sex: a fleeting reality, prey to contingency and negativity, evil in itself, because it is the absence of good. As affirmed by the Nambikwara Indians, so beloved by Lévi-Strauss: "After death, the souls of women and children are dispersed in the wind and rain."[19] Clearly, if the continuity of generations occurs through paternal descent, it is in males alone that the continuity of time is manifested and achieved.

Therefore, it is only the male that counts, beyond his biological life, and only the male son guarantees the continuity of both *time* and *being*. Ancient Greece provides an illuminating example of this cultural "pattern" or "complex." In Greek tragedy, in Aeschylus, Sophocles, and Euripides, justice is revealed only with the *passage of time*: that is, events are concatenated (for example, from Clytemnestra to Orestes) in such a way that the single individual is never either entirely guilty or entirely innocent. In other words, the concept of an individual, of a *subject unto oneself*, cannot coexist with that of time as duration—whether this duration is expressed in a time cyclically turning back upon itself or instead in expectation—though the expectation inasmuch as it already indicates a certain type of movement toward the future, has made possible the fundamental passage to the concept of "becoming." It is therefore the cultural problem of time and the individual, family (or group) and subject, that comes to the fore. Clearly, the concept of "subject" implies a danger for the continuity of the group. And this is one of the fundamental reasons why Christianity, even while giving forceful substance to the history of Europe in its journey toward individual liberty, at the same time led the Church to place itself within this very history as the principal source of *conservation*: defense of the family as the primary social factor; of liturgical time and the cult of the dead as continuity, cyclicity, tradition, and past; of the necessary subordination of women and the negativity of the value of the individual. (Thus not allowing it to be understood that the Enlightenment was in reality a child of Jesus.) Such positions are in patent contradiction with the equality of all men that the Church defends. But in reality the only equality that the Church can sustain is that of "continuity," conceptually carried over from the continuity of paternal generation to the continuity of divine generation.

Herein lies the greatest misunderstanding among the followers of Jesus. After Jesus denied the importance of "blood" and family bonds, they transferred this importance to the greater "family," that of humanity: all men and women are children of God and consequently all are brothers and sisters. The early Christians, in fact, called one another "brother" and "sister," as attested in the *Letter to the Romans* which we previously cited; Paul calls the deaconess Phoebe "sister." But when Jesus denied his bond with his mother and "brothers" (*Mark* 3:31 ff.), indicating the unrelated people surrounding him as "brothers," he did so in order to break the concept of family and blood ties which was extremely strong among the Jews, not to create a category analogous with that of family. If we eliminate the blood bond, in fact, it makes no sense to speak of "brothers." In Jesus' thought we thus find a total negation, represented by the strongest kind of logical contradiction. To say before one's own brothers that others, strangers, are brothers, means to say "no brothers exist": no one is a brother. But the Jewish mentality of the disciples was unable to overcome the force of the family bond and so—though this, too, was extremely difficult—it merely carried it over to group bonds, leaving the point of reference intact. God has become the Father of the great human family, giving rise to the *contradiction*, both theoretical and concrete that pervades the entire history of Christianity: that of the inequality between male and female: inequality centered on the figure of God the Father — unavoidably male — and the "continuity" of the value of the father with the value of male sons. Even today the Church defends this difference, denying the value of the individual as a "subject," which would necessarily force it to acknowledge the identical value of women.

At any rate, the impossibility of imagining a relationship of friendship and equality among men outside of family bonds and the analogy with family bonds is highlighted by the French Revolution — the revolution par excellence against the importance of blood: the blood of the nobility. The revolutionaries called one another "brothers," just as Christians have done; and in order to achieve the concept of equality among individuals, they were forced to eliminate affiliation with God in the only way they could imagine: by eliminating the existence of God. For this is the prison: If He exists, God can only be a Father. Therefore, we are still far from any *real* equality, outside any family bond. In order to reach such equality, today we have been obliged to throw the "family" into crisis: with divorce, with the refusal of the father's authority; and finally, it was necessary for feminism to arise and with it the rebellion of women against their inferiority and submission. But not even feminism has been able to think in terms of "equality": Indeed, it struggles in favor of the "difference" of women.

The fact that this difference is conceived as superiority, is not only a logical snare that does not hold up in concrete reality; it changes nothing of the true problem: that of "affiliation." Even were it theologically possible to include "maternal" aspects in the image of God, as the feminists would like to do (a senseless, useless thing, obviously, since it is the structure of earthly society which has been projected onto God, and this society is still founded on male power), women's only hope is to struggle for a type of equality *outside* any analogy with family relationships: The only true equality possible is equality among *individuals*, among *subjects*. And each individual, as such, is different from the next.

Taking up the question of martyrdom, then, its two totally new aspects are the potency of the word when attested by death, and the extension of "witnessing" to women, made possible by the fact that witnessing has been liberated from the potency of male sexuality. Indeed, the Jews formerly bore witness, or swore, while placing their hand upon their genital organs, explicitly demonstrating that the "truth" of their word was attested by, and in function of, "potency" par excellence: that of the penis. Women's word, instead, counted for naught, since it was devoid of the guarantee of sexual potency. In fact, nearly everywhere, women were prevented from testifying, swearing oaths, or establishing contracts; all these transactions had to be guaranteed by the male word-sexuality. Even now, moreover, one *raises* the *right* hand (right also means correct and upright, that which is perpendicular, while to fail is to fall down)[20] in order to swear an oath in court, an unconscious but palpable analogical demonstration of erective potency. (Funny that even women must do so!)

The equality of women in martyrdom depends on the fact that the word is confirmed by death; a death which, as Perpetua and Felicita sing on the way to their execution, makes them "equal to males," because it eliminates the need for sexual potency. However, though arriving by a different path, do we not find that "feminization" of males that we encountered earlier as one of the characteristic problems of Christianity? One who bears witness through his death demonstrates the "truth" of what he says, the reality of his word. The martyr links truth and word through *blood*: a blood which is not the Jewish blood of generation or affiliation, but blood that is shed: his *own* blood, which has value in itself inasmuch as it is individual and unique, just as death is individual and unique. In shedding blood, the martyr bears witness to the reality of the blood shed by Jesus, the Son of God, so that martyrdom substitutes baptism. In fact, it is the strongest baptism, because it assures salvation whatever the martyr's faults and virtues in life. Word and blood become interchangeable; they coincide, absolutizing the potency of the sworn word. All the differences of gender, age, or social status, which have always attributed a value to the word in any society and in all eras, are annulled in martyrdom because the potency of death substitutes sexual potency.

Thus an irreducible contradiction arises, which has pervaded Christianity from its beginnings until today: Sexuality and death are no longer interchangeable, as they had always been in all societies, on the basis of the potency of *vis* (that of the penis).[21] In Christianity, death takes precedence and, like St. Paul, cries victory at the very moment it "loses." Christianity is the religion of death. As such, it is the enemy of sexuality, and creates the conflict that still tears it apart. Studies of martyrdom give no explanation for this fundamental cultural transformation. Indeed, they do not seem to take it into account, and are limited to exalting the "heroic" aspect. But this new heroic quality is quite strange in a world where the hero has always been defined as the male who fights to the death and kills his enemies, who even kills himself in order not to fall into the hands of the victor. Christians, instead, are "heroes" who do not fight; they surrender to their executioner like meek and defenseless "lambs." Therefore, the judges and common people present at their trials and executions found themselves facing the most absurd thing they had ever thought or seen: Men, who were obliged to fight to the last drop of blood against other men and ferocious animals not only in war but also in games, whether or not they were gladiators, responded meekly and serenely to those accusing them of crimes they had never committed. They were happy to flaunt the force of their meekness; they went off to meet their executioners, gladiators, or ferocious beasts, without raising a finger in self-defense. Nor, during their trials, did they make the slightest gesture to save themselves; so that it was the judges themselves who urged them to make just one tiny compromise, that of obeying the state's authority by recognizing *maiestas*, the sacredness of the "potency-power" of the Emperors. Such acknowledgment was a mere momentary formality, since in the immense, hard-to-control territory administered by the Romans, each person could behave as he wished, as long as he did not disturb the peace with excessive noise.

Why, then, did the Christians stubbornly raise hymns to the glory of God in court, when they could have saved themselves from torture and death with a mere nod of consent before the judge? Such a gesture would not have kept them from being Christians. The motivations that the Church has always put forward to strengthen itself—exalting the faith and courage of its martyrs, and identifying in their sacrifice the foundation stone underlying the expansion of Christianity—are not sufficient. Such expansion, at any rate, remains surprising in a society like the Greco-Roman one, self-satisfied because it was based on the military valor of its men, its architectural works, its philosophical, historical, and juridical achievements, the well-being of daily life. In practice then, it represented the opposite of what Christianity offered: "renunciation" as a fundamental value, renunciation of all benefits or possessions in favor of a "sentiment," an incomprehensible one at that, requiring humiliation and "service."

Furthermore, the Romans' religious experience was devoid of any emotional relation—least of all, love—with the divinity: Homage to the gods was a mere ritual formality, whose intent was almost solely to assure good fortune for oneself—the happy achievement of one's daily destiny. The first centuries after Christ, with Christianity's rapid conquest of the Empire's key cities, have not yet found a satisfying historical explanation, and the presence of martyrs certainly cannot provide one. The debate over the real number of Christians who were killed, and the virulence of persecution, has not yet ended: Figures range from ten thousand to a hundred thousand or two hundred thousand. However, that is not what counts. What counts is the birth of a totally new cultural value, which crucially informs the history of Christian institutions, and the fascination that it exercised over peoples distant from its spirit: the new vision of *sacrifice*.

There was nothing in Jesus' message that endorsed sacrifice as a search for death — one's own or others'; indeed, he denied the value of sacrifice as an "instrument" of mediation with the divinity, driving from the temple all those who were involved in its processes; he denied the very need for a temple. Paul, on the contrary, overturned the annunciation of liberation. He attested the need to imitate Christ by being sacrificed like him; with his blood, he confirmed his own truth. The sacrificial "game," present in all religions, is supremely concretized in Christianity, becoming the absolute symbol of the Christian meaning of existence. Man is the victim of this sacrifice, while in various other eras and societies, including the Judaic one, human sacrifice had long ago been substituted by other less burdensome sacrifices: animals first of all, but also the first fruits of the harvest, and other objects. Christians, who live out nearly all their cultural themes on a symbolic level, have never been aware of how terrible their sacrificial origin is; they were horrified at witnessing human sacrifice among the Mayas and Aztecs. It was through human sacrifice, though, that Christianity was constituted as a sacrificial religion. The "repetition" of the sacrifice of Christ, presented as the symbolic-concrete repetition of the Eucharist, has meaning and power only if it is sustained by the existence of true victims. In fact, martyrs have never lacked in the two thousand years of Christian history; it was even debated on a theological level whether or not it was licit to seek martyrdom by accusing oneself to the Romans. The Christians were dissuaded by the ecclesiastic authorities themselves from performing gestures that could cause them to be persecuted on numerous later occasions, during missionary activities in hostile countries, and even during the French Revolution. But what counts most here is the fact that the spirit of Christianity boils down to an essentially *sacrificial* spirit, actuated in the search for suffering, penitence, "death to oneself"; in making oneself a victim with one's own hands through asceticism, humility, and renunciation, acts which the Church incessantly advocates as the only ones guaranteeing salvation. With monasticism, these paths became institutions for Christian "perfection."

In Christianity, each individual is a victim; thus the sense of guilt passes from being collective to being individual, and can no longer find an "outlet." The "sacrifice" present in all religions for this specific purpose loses its true valence and makes way for the celebration of death.

Door-to-Door Christianity

Therefore, martyrdom is the Christian choice par excellence, and the early martyrs light the way to salvation and resurrection. It is the martyrs who establish the category of "holiness." The saints arise with them, for not only through martyrdom will they receive the baptism by blood that will carry them directly to paradise, placing them at the head of the parade accompanying Jesus in heaven. They also constitute the identity of the saints who will come afterward, those new martyrs who, through their religious and monastic vows, will be transplanted directly on Earth in the sacred space of the monastery, as in the Heavenly Jerusalem, where there they will serve God and help their brothers who have remained in the arena of life. Devotion to the martyrs and their burial sites, the search for their bodies and blood as "potent objects" and relics capable of any miracle have little by little come to characterize the cult of other saints: those who in one way or another have complied with the pattern of self-sacrifice, incontrovertible proof of their holiness. The process of "beatification," in fact, came to declare the *heroic* nature of their virtues, virtues which are essentially sacrificial, involving deprivation and the death of oneself: chastity, poverty, humility, and obedience. In Greece, an ancient custom existed in which homage was made to the tombs of "heroes" and to their "relics"; it may have influenced the Christian devotion to the tombs and relics of Christian martyrs.[22] However, aside from the fact that no proof exists of this, and no historian of Christianity affirms it, we must still find an explanation for the fundamental fact that the Christian martyr is a very peculiar kind of "hero" and totally different from the Greek one. The Christian is exalted as one who does not kill, who does not defend himself, who does not win, but "loses"; and neither in Greek nor Roman epics was sacrificial passivity ever seen as a quality of heroism. Indeed, the Christians' behavior seems so inexplicable, both in the eyes of society and in the eyes of court judges, that they are considered "strange," "mad"; many Roman procurators felt ill at ease in condemning them. In addition, we must not forget that in any society, "diversity" or "strangeness" takes shape as a "danger" (it is nearly always the perception of an incomprehensible diversity that triggers fear and refusal). Without a doubt, Christianity, with all its apparently senseless forms of behavior performed in function of an afterlife, appeared as a subversive risk: a radical revolution for the entire ancient world.

Therefore, it is all the more difficult to explain the force with which Christianity succeeded in prevailing in the immense Roman dominion. This remains totally unexplainable, unless we take into account (as historians to date have failed to do) a socio-psycho-cultural aspect of enormous vastness: the rapid, capillary penetration of Christianity in the Empire, from Northeast Africa to Greece and Italy by way of the connective tissue formed by women, and their "martyrdom." In all the history that we know, the spread of Christianity represents virtually the only case in which women participated en masse in a cultural revolution on an equal footing with males (though with an immensely higher expenditure of energy), acting personally in all its aspects: theoretical, political, economic, and institutional. In fact, women have nearly always waited at home to hear the results of men's choices and deeds; the most they did was to care for the wounded or feed fugitives and prisoners. If any woman participated in the forefront (whether in battle or in the formulation of aims and goals), it was an exception and to be recorded as such in history. Not even in the greatest revolutions of the modern era—the French, American, or Russian—have women been active subjects of theoretical elaboration or concrete militancy in such numbers as to influence those movements' success.

On the contrary, regarding Christianity, not only did women spread the message by living it and making it live in daily life, in a kind of "door-to-door" exchange, but they also faced torture and death in such a way as to arouse the admiration of judges and executioners, leading them to believe in the "truth" of a massage capable of giving rise to heroism in those who in any era or any society had never been called to "heroism": women, the weak sex.

The martyrdom of women in itself is enough to proclaim that a new culture has been created; that ancient society has been overcome and conquered; that Western culture is about to take its first steps—slow, uncertain, contradictory, blood-soaked though they may be—toward the liberation and equality of women. Not so much because women demonstrate a heroism similar to that of males, but because society *calls* upon them to demonstrate it, acknowledging their right to do so.

We have mentioned the meaning of the hero in Greek culture; but in Greece—or rather, in the various Greek realities prior to the spread of Christianity—what was the condition of women? Society was male, a group of men who exercised absolute leadership, from which all "minors" were excluded, including women, children, slaves, and foreigners. The wives of "heroes" who went off for years to fight fierce battles were rich, but they remained at home with the slaves and children. Though they might be queens, their only dominion was the home, where they shared the marriage bed with slave women and female prisoners of war. They were given away in marriage as in all other societies as an "exchange" between families, decided on by the fathers. The male—father, husband, son—had all rights over the woman, who was confined at home to spin and weave, including the right to kill her. Says Telemachus: "Speaking becomes men, and me above all, for I am the master of the house." Although women sometimes spoke in Homer, this never occurred in the reality of the *polis*: Women remained closed in their rooms, married the men assigned them by their fathers, and could not speak in public. In any case, Greek women were excluded from political power.

When the men went off to occupy lands for settlement, they sometimes took along their women and sometimes not, but wherever they were, the women occupied themselves only with domestic life; and if the male supporting them died, they would depend on another male guardian (if not a father or husband, then a son or brother). Perpetually *minor*, they were obliged to perform chores similar to those of slaves. In Athens, the woman was not a "citizen"; she could not participate in assemblies or court hearings, even passively. Punishment for adultery was extremely harsh: exile, which in ancient society was the equivalent of death, and when it was not actual expulsion from one's homeland, it was psychological and social. In any case exile at best almost certainly meant becoming a prostitute in order to survive (as occurs for so many immigrants today). Moreover, the loss of virginity before marriage was punished with the severest measure: death by drowning.

In the Roman world, women had it a bit better in some ways than in Greece, at least economically. Women could inherit and administer their possessions when they remained widows, and no longer depended on male guardians.

But in many respects, when Christianity began to spread, the situation was similar to the traditional Greek one. Marriage was decided on by the father, according to family strategies: The daughter was promised at the age of 12, the son at 14, with any eye to increasing the father's power, prestige, and wealth. The precocity of marriage—and so of sexual relations—seriously harmed the health of the bride, still in early puberty, both because of the difficulty of childbirth and the impoverishment of the body at a stage when it was still growing. The Roman woman was not considered responsible, *compos sui*, and depended on the *pater familias* who could even decide on her death (and who, in such an event, was obliged to consult the other males of the family; for the Roman state always avoided intervening in family power). The famous formula, *Ubi Tu Gaius, Ego Gaia*, exalted by historians as a sublime conception of nuptial union, actually attests the wife's identification with the husband; her total belonging to him, body and soul; the annulment of any personal identity for the woman. In public life, furthermore, the Roman woman had no rights and could hold no office, except in a narrow religious ambit, as a Vestal; and if she was honored, she was so only as the wife of some male power, and bore his title in a feminine version—Empress, Flamina—without receiving any formal power except the implicit influence that the women of the powerful have always had.

Regarding the Judaic world, in speaking of Jesus' behavior and choices, we have seen that women enjoyed no liberty; they were allowed to speak only in private, and even then by authorization of the male—father, husband, or son. The domestic environment was their only life reality. It was even physically separated from the males' space, the only part of the home open to the outside world.

Virginity, the Eternal Male Obsession

The history of women, first through martyrdom, and then through a "holiness" that is also a form of martyrdom, continually retraces the model of the virgin—a heroine in being virgin—both concretely and in the collective fantasy. This fantasy enlarges, interpolates and completes the image with miraculous, legendary phenomena, constructing its fixed topics, its *topoi*, with inexhaustible energy. Invention aims to create phenomena marking the predestination of an important person from birth, which in itself places women on a par with men, since in ancient society, both in the Greco-Roman and Egyptian, this type of *topos* was limited to male personages. Dreams or visions (generally not differentiated because they appear as transcendent messages in either case) predicting the exceptional nature of the child to the mother, either during pregnancy or immediately after birth, are frequent in the biographies of saints, both for women and men. But one *topos* is specific to the little girl: She consecrates her virginity to God in the earliest years of childhood. Furthermore, she is often forced by her father to marry, against her indefectible will. At this point, the path opens up to other *topoi*: On her wedding night she persuades her husband to respect her virginity, so that both remain chaste, offering themselves to God; or else she accepts the duty of wife and mother, attesting the heroic nature of her virtue of *obedience* to father and husband. Or again, in the most legendary version, she succeeds in fleeing this destiny, taking refuge from the danger of losing her virginity in a manner that is both miraculous and heroic, in a "repetition" of the initial gesture of female martyrdom. Women who tear out their eyes with their own hands, or who cut off their noses and lips in order to make themselves so horrendous as to annul the libidinous desire of the male pursuing them; women disguising themselves as males, in order to live out the rest of their life in a male monastery, silently letting themselves be blamed, in the place of a brother monk, for having made a girl pregnant.

The *Acta Sanctorum* reports the story of Ebba the Young, an abbess in the convent of Coldingham. In 870, with the invasion of Scotland by the Danes, and fearing a collective rape, she cuts off her nose and lips with a razor. Her nuns do the same. Horrified, the Danes renounce their intention and set fire to the convent, where everyone dies. (In book XV of his *Annales*, Caesar Baronius mentions them among the martyrs.)

How far are these tales from reality? Or rather, how far are they from credibility, for those who hear them? Nowadays, it is hard for us to realize how deeply Christianity infiltrated not only social structures, but the global cultural fabric, in which *events* assume "meaning" only because they stand out in an *obvious* background, which need not be explained because it forms the shared terrain, the linguistic or semantic code, now incorporated into the collective imagination.

It is impossible to present here a complete picture of the various episodes of female martyrdom which the Church deems to be worthy of mention in the *Acta Sanctorum*. We shall only mention the most significant personages: significant in the historic reality attested by their lives, or else in the fascination that they have exercised over the imagination of Christians, arousing extremely strong "devotion" throughout the centuries, a devotion which cannot be explained on the basis of *facts*. These are figures of women, sometimes wholly nonexistent but which, with their recurring *topoi*, allude to the psychological and cultural needs that believers have projected onto them. Let us make one point before proceeding: Although there are no specific statistics dividing the number of martyrs according to gender, the number of women is striking. It is striking especially because women have always been excluded from wars, from any and all wars, whether ideological, political, or territorial. Here, however, not only is their number nearly equal to that of men, but it was probably they, with their courage and the force of their testimony, with their capacity as women, who led people to believe in prodigious, fantastic, irrational events and tales, who urged believers and non-believers alike to join together around the martyrs and gather strength from them, thus making them one of the fundamental tools in propagandizing the new religion.

It is probable (as usual, we lack documentation, since the events are narrated by male historians) that women gave rise to customs associated with the new concept of virtue: Christian "charity." It was surely women who visited imprisoned believers in order to comfort them, risking their lives in doing so; they bore not only food and clothing, but above all, the community's support and prayer. It was almost surely women who collected the blood of the victims and, whenever possible, the body itself, burying it in tombs acquired with their own money. Those burial sites immediately became places of worship, preserving the name and memory of those who had borne witness to the faith with their life. One might even suppose that through the tender, romantic gestures of women — who have always remembered to keep some object belonging to the beloved — a baby's lock of hair or the first flower from one's lover — the passion for "relics" arose. This became an imposing phenomenon of Christian worship. Among the many pieces of evidence supporting such a hypothesis is the fact that we find St. Crescentia listed among the martyrs of Rome. She was almost certainly a pious matron of the third or fourth century who became such a benefactress of the Church that she was considered a martyr for having given a *Domus Ecclesiae*— a house belonging to her — to the Christian community as a place of worship. It later became customary to preserve the name of the owner (*titulus*) on all donations of this kind.

Buildings erected in memory of a martyr are pieces of historical evidence poignantly testifying to the persecutions against Christians. From our perspective — according to which it was women in particular who guided and developed Christianity in the early centuries — it is significant that the most ancient, important churches of Rome are "entitled" with feminine names: Praxedes, Sabina, Cecilia, Agnes....

A fundamental point to consider is that the great majority of women martyrs are remembered by the Church as "virgins." In the social environment (apart from the religious value attributed to virginity by Christianity), all women, from antiquity until today, have been obliged to remain virgin before marriage; indeed, in the Roman world the term *virgo* indicates a girl in puberty, ready for marriage and so suitable to receive the *vir*, and those who dare to disobey are condemned to die.

But in Christianity, as we have seen, virginity became the supreme virtue of women, and in the biographies of women martyrs, it is taken for granted — though considered a heroic choice — that the virgin prefers to die rather than to save herself by giving in to the libidinous desires of her persecutor. At any rate, this narrative commonplace of female martyrdom is hard to believe: not only for concrete historical reasons, but above all because it corresponds all too perfectly to a psychological, social, and cultural perspective which is visibly masculine. It may be superfluous to mention that, in all eras and in all the societies we know of, women prisoners have been raped by their jailers, whether these were victors in battle or simple civilians assigned to the task. Refusal has never prevented a man from raping a woman at his mercy. (Even today, sexual violence toward women prisoners is constantly denounced by Amnesty International.) On the contrary, in the *Acts* of women martyrs, death is exalted as the supreme form of female heroism when it is chosen to avoid the loss of virginity. Moreover, even today the Church preserves this value; it has beatified Maria Goretti as a "martyr." However, even though it is well known that males as well, if made prisoner for any reason, are submitted to sexual violence by sodomy, no one has ever claimed that they could be defined as heroes or martyrs for that reason.

In the case of male martyrs, the judges and public present at trials found themselves facing an entirely new spectacle, that of peaceful, unresisting "heroes." But the absolute, traumatically new thing was to see women as "heroes." And it was certainly not male martyrs who inspired an appreciation for Christianity in a world that had made virile courage, military virtue, the supreme value. Other martyrs, women, are the real "heroes," because society does not *expect* "courage" from them; that is, "public" courage, for that is the exclusive prerogative of males. It is women who astonish those who actually hear them *speak* for the first time in the male sense of the term; they hear them express thoughts, concepts, theories, in short, all those fruits of reason from which "nature" had supposedly excluded them. And above all, they now hear women affirm a "truth": a truth which everyone *must believe*, even men invested with the highest authority in a courtroom, along with those other men—fathers, brothers, husbands, sons—to whom women have always been subject. For it is they, women, who proclaim that truth aloud in public, and who bear witness to it with their death.

Historians have often mentioned the "scandal" of Christianity. But this is the true scandal: the revolution in the woman's role; the shifting of women to the foreground; the force of their self-presentation as subjects, as guides, as leaders in action; the potency of their word; the proud, indomitable certainty of their blood's value. No longer "maternal" blood, now; not serving to give life down here on earth—once the only task ever assigned women anywhere, a task that has never been recognized as "heroic" because it belongs to nature: to the laws of nature whose mere instruments women are and must be. Suddenly, and apparently without anyone giving a go-ahead, women's blood, too, serves for the hereafter, for culture which dominates nature, subjugating it and transforming it into transcendence. If, as Lévi-Strauss claims, this is what men have always feared and continue to fear — that women will free themselves from the yoke of the natural order; that they will put the cyclical laws of day and night, raw and cooked, life and death, at risk — here now, through a martyrdom that is desired, sought out, pursued with all their might, women deny nature; they contradict it and overcome it. Nature allows and obliges them to sacrifice themselves *only* in order to give life, to assure the biological continuance of a life that is not life, since it requires the death of the individual in order to guarantee the life of the group down here. The women martyrs, on the contrary, suddenly assume the *heroic* role of giving true life, that which overcomes nature and transcends it, defeating death once and for all.

With Christianity, then, as female martyrs go off singing to the site of their execution, women *become males*. The tragedy inherent in this conquest by women is in having assured — by unwavering deeds of courage down through the two thousand years of Christian Europe — victory for the religion of sacrifice, victory for the primacy of victims. They have done so by offering themselves up as victims but at the same time by *serving* the needs of a power demanding more and more victims in order to reinforce itself as power. Now that women no longer die in childbirth, John Paul II has become aware of the danger of which Lévi-Strauss speaks: that women might free themselves from that other law of nature, procreation, and so he has begun to sanctify those who *voluntarily* die in giving birth, transforming the subjection of women to the continuance of biological life into *martyrdom*. Thus, they are cheated once again. Moreover, from the very beginning men have tried to eliminate the "male" value from the martyrdom of women by claiming that they died in order to defend their virginity, since the only value that men, Christians and non-Christians alike, have assigned to women is the orderly use of sexuality. The battle that excludes women from culture and from power and which actually implies control and dominion over the hereafter continues. But the misunderstanding by which, during the flow and change of Christianity, both women and men have collaborated in "producing victims" is about to end. Or rather, it *can* end. On the razor's edge between being for the sake of nature "down here" and being for the sake of the transcendent "hereafter," women have always had to kowtow to power: the only power existing which is that of men and which has always made them function in terms of sexuality, mothers for the Earth or virgins for Heaven, but "victims" one way or the other.

Today, women are called upon to take a further step toward liberation: to unveil the principle of male sexuality in which Christianity is rooted; to destroy the need for "sacrificial femininity" which is ineluctably linked to it, and to deny the need for a "victim," which only the capillary contribution of women has allowed to dominate the history of Christian Europe, and remain intact until our time. This is a matter that has to do first and foremost with the liberation of men, their sexuality, and the cultural construction they have built on it, which has reached the greatest historic expression possible through Christianity.

The greatest expression, because with the vocation of sacrifice for everyone — women and men alike — Christianity proclaimed the feminization of males, that they had become the brides of God. Nietzsche was aware of this feminization; indeed, he found Christianity repugnant because its "femininity" was incompatible with the force of willpower and the supremacy of man in the face of any power. But Nietzsche did not understand at all where the bases of this femininity lay; and above all, he gave no explanation for the triumph of Christianity which, indeed, remains incomprehensible precisely because it seems to go "against nature" in calling upon males to become females and victims.

Women, instead, immediately responded to and embraced suffering, for they had always been victims and assigned to sacrifice in every era and society. Now, with Christianity, they passed from a victim hood that was imposed as if it were "natural" to a freely chosen, conscious one proposed as a "value" and therefore, "cultural." A value equal to the one inculcated in males, it freed them from living "in the service of" fathers, husbands, brothers and sons, as did children and slaves. For the first time, freedom was presented to women as such: to live — and die — for themselves, albeit "in the service of God."

As we shall see, the sacrificial choice would almost immediately impose the renunciation of sexuality (naturally, it was Paul himself who proclaimed this, having theorized the need for Christians to become victims). But this very renunciation (in total contrast to the males' situation) brought liberation. Freedom from the brutality of male sexuality; freedom from motherhood, a terrible yoke, given the ever-present threat of death in every childbirth; freedom from the fatigue and suffering of raising children who were exposed to the continuous aggression of disease and death; liberation from the obligation of chastity under pain of death according to male laws. With the consecration of virgins, this obligation now became a cultural virtue, a transcendent, freely chosen one.

During the historical development of Christianity, "suffering" would remain the main theme, even when the phase of martyrdom had been surpassed. Women would always be in the fore, in driving the sacrificial spirit to its extreme consequences, whether for themselves or on behalf of others, with all the pathology, injustice and actual perversion that this entailed.[23] This dramatic condition has always accompanied women in Christianity and under Christianity: after "liberating" themselves by absolutizing their condition as victims, they have spurred on other victims entrusted to their care—children, the poor, the ill, slaves, the ignorant—to accept and embrace their own condition as victims. Unconsciously, women have thus favored the construction of a stronger and stronger power in the ecclesiastic hierarchy, for nothing favors the powerful so much as its vassals' attitude of subordination and sacrifice. Women, therefore—for good or evil—have been the support of Christianity: They have allowed the men of the Church—the popes, bishops, abbots, theologians, and saints—to concern themselves with its power, increasing and extending it further and further. In the meantime, in silent obedience, in the charity of *sequela Christi*, women have spread the message by which that power found self-justification, testifying to it with their presence, their actions permeating the capillaries and connective tissue of society. It is difficult to make any statistical study as to the number of women—martyrs, consecrated virgins, nuns, missionaries, religious nurses and teachers—who have "worked" to spread Christianity simply by their presence, which has now become quite visible and contrasts with the invisibility of the housework of all other women. As for martyrs, who actually represent the fulcrum of women's lives as Christians, we can form only a vague idea of their number, by culling the female names from trial records. This is the consequence of two precise factors which we have already mentioned: history has been narrated by men, who have handed down only what seemed important to them; until our time, women have never been aware of the importance of their own lives and so have never felt any need to recount them. If we then consider that they were obliged as "religious" to comply with the rules of "humility," which led them into hiding and silence, then we can well understand why nothing has come down to us of their story. As we shall see, it was almost exclusively the mystics who "spoke," spurred on by their confessors and spiritual guides, but with the logical premise that it was not *they* who were speaking, but God.

Therefore, the only thing that remains of the story of religious women is a few *false* words, those of the mystics, together with immense, boundless pools of silence.

Simple Little Women and Housewives Have Their Heads Cut Off

Many questions regarding the martyrdom of women, therefore, have never been raised until now, and it is hard to find answers. For instance, why did the Romans bring women to trial and condemn them to torture and death, as they did with men, when women's word carried no weight at all? After all, no one had ever heeded the beliefs of women who certainly posed no threat to law and order. But more important, how can we explain the presence of so many women from the very beginning in the trials against Christians, even in the remotest corners of the Empire where women were even denied those limited possibilities of social life that certain noble, rich matrons of the capital enjoyed? The martyrdom of the Scillitans, which marked the beginning of church history and Christian persecution in Africa, is exemplary in this respect. We are in the year 180, during the empire of Commodus, in a village of proconsular Africa called Scillium, which lent its name to the "Scillitan martyrs." The trial is recounted in the *Acta*, the most ancient document of Latin Christian literature. But here we find that the masculine form of the name by which the "Scillitan martyrs" are remembered in history once more obscures a surprising reality: They are seven men and five women. It is only through Roman juridical formality, however, that we discover that five out of the 11 condemned are women; otherwise we should never have known it. (It has never been customary for historians to count or stress the number of women in relation to men). It is the women's names, called out by the herald in proclaiming the death sentence, that informs us of this surprising presence: Gennara, Generosa, Vestia, Donata, Seconda.

What could five humble little women in an African town have done to endanger the powerful men of Rome? They surely held no public office, and their words — supposing they *had* spoken in public — were considered idle, superstitious chatter, as women's words always had been. And yet the trial was identical for all the accused, as the determination and courage of the accused were identical. The magistrate (like nearly all Roman judges in such trials) does everything possible to avoid condemning them, urging them to change their minds and swear loyalty to the Emperor; on their denial, he even offers a 30-day delay so that they can think over their decision. But everyone, men and women alike, rejects the proposal: "their cause is too just for reflection." The sentence of death by beheading is the same for each person, and is to be carried out at once. And everyone responds: "Praise God." Is everyone equal, then? How can that be, in a world where the *difference* between men and women is radical and immeasurable? How much more courage was suddenly demanded from women! For they had never before had to face the violence of giving or receiving death — something that men, on the contrary, were obliged to do on many an occasion, for it was an inevitable part of their lives.

And yet, aside from the general neglect shown in remembering women martyrs, one clear piece of evidence points to the difficulty found among Christians of the time — and later, of historians and commentators — in understanding their martyrdom. This evidence is the male recourse to the only "just" motivation in the eyes of the world, the "defense of virginity." One example among many of the "woman-virgin-martyr" associational chain is the story of Cecilia. Her story is more complex than similar ones, but perhaps more meaningful. As in the case of similar tales, we cannot count on the historical accuracy of her *Passion*; but what matters here is that Cecilia is one of the most beloved figures of early Christianity, perhaps because it was around her figure that little by little, the essential *places* of a profound emotional imagination arose.

Cecilia: Why a Martyr?

On her wedding night, Cecilia, a young Christian girl from a noble Roman family, reveals to her pagan husband Valerianus that the Angel of God protects her virginity, which not even her husband must try to violate. She is so convincing in her defense that Valerianus agrees to live in chastity, and to be baptized. (As time went by, the refusal of one's body on the wedding night became such a fascinating theme that it turned up again and again, not only in many other hagiographic accounts, but in various types of literature, right up to the modern era.) In the *Passion*, events become more and more confused: Valerianus, together with other neophytes, is discovered, condemned, and killed. Cecilia, then, carrying out the task that has always been assigned to women, takes care to bury them; but in turn, she is condemned to die, first in her house which is set afire, from which she nonetheless escapes unharmed, and then by decapitation.

It is hard to kill a virgin; indeed, it is forbidden among many peoples. The Roman Vestals were left to die, locked up with little food and water, so that no one could raise a hand against them; even drowning, foreseen as punishment in Greece, was meant to be an indirect way of killing. The executioner strikes Cecilia three times, but she survives for three days, her head nearly detached. She leaves all her possessions to the Church, and asks Pope Urban to consecrate her house as a church, *ecclesiae nomine*. Scholars have made differing hypotheses about the date of her martyrdom, ranging from the beginning of the empire of Commodus (June 177) to the death of Marcus Aurelius (March 180). However, the papacy of Urban I, to which the author of the *Passion* refers, lasted from 222 to 230. At any rate, Cecilia's story does not end here. The events accompanying the fate of her body are highly complicated. When considering these events, we confront the central theme of Christian piety—the cult of relics—something the Church avoids discussing even today. In fact, modern man's sensitivity has distanced itself from such forms of piety, perceiving them as embarrassing in their implication of "magic," or else because they seem to hint at a macabre, fetishistic kind of psychopathology. The itinerary of Cecilia's body is indicative of the entire psycho-cultural-religious-magic-artistic framework that envelops and develops meanings, emotions, and expectations; the expectation of a liberating power surrounding "holy bodies," and the history of their lives after death, elaborated by a "total" religion—or at least, one permitting totality, Christianity. It is on the basis of these interconnected meanings that the still-vibrant figure of Cecilia has reached us today.

First and foremost, she was a lovely young girl on the threshold of female maturity. In fact, the *virgo* is the girl who saves herself from becoming a flower that is "picked" or "enjoyed," by preserving her virginity just as she is about to lose it, on her wedding night. It is this fragile woman who conquers the man, dominating him through what the male himself has assigned to her as a more potent element than the male himself: virginity. Men want to gain mastery over this virginity, but at the same time, they fear it, attributing to it an absolute value: a value so absolute that it is *on a par with death*, stronger than death, beyond the transcendence of death. Moreover, the more they fear it, the greater its value. It was for good reason that the Romans, who had elaborated a legal system with greater rational coherence than any other society had done, had established that a person condemned to die was to be pardoned if he met a Vestal on his path, and that a virgin could not be killed by the hand of man, but only "entrusted" to death. All the tales describing the extraordinary lives of women saints and martyrs stress this impossibility of inflicting death on them, either by the hand of man, wild beasts, or natural elements. Though not a virgin, Perpetua seems to become one again, since in the *Passion* her husband is never named. She is forced to direct the executor's sword with her own hand, since he is unable to strike the mortal blow to her neck, but that only happens after the wild, ferocious beast sent to attack her in the arena—where she stands at length, immobile, her face shining with ecstatic sweetness—fails to do anything more than throw her to the ground and tear her clothing.

In reality, killing is equivalent to the ending of virginity, to the taking of virginity; that is why it is just as difficult — nearly impossible. For this reason, the pathway traveled by the male imagination in constructing female martyrdom upon the defense of virginity, rather than on the witnessing of faith, was almost "natural." Woman and death are the same thing; virginity and death are the same thing. Only if the woman "wins" in virginity, can man be guaranteed his victory over death: that is, life in the hereafter; life without death. The docile gesture of Cecilia, who gathers up her long hair to expose her slender neck to the executioner's sword, has never lost its fascination for the artist. For it is the equivalent of the gesture of one gaining mastery over virginity *without destroying it*: that is to say, the gesture men dream of, and impossible to achieve on earth.

We have already seen Cecilia's devotion in action: Like so many other Christian women, she takes it upon herself to bury the dead — the "husband/non-husband" whom she herself has led to death. (The poet's fantasy eternally crystallized such devotion in Antigone, whom two thousand years of critical studies have failed to explain — precisely because the indissoluble nature of the association "woman-death-life beyond death" defies explanation.) Cecilia prepares a sarcophagus at the "fourth mile along the Appian Way," and has a phoenix sculpted on it — a symbol of the resurrection. She thus exposes herself, a new Antigone, to the risk of death; a death that will take three days to gain perfection in its work of killing her, even though her head is nearly detached from her body. Of course, this body will become the object of extraordinary devotion, and its transference from one place to the other, whether true or presumed, nourished the miraculous, emotional legend of her figure through the centuries. Evidence of the uncertain memory and wanderings of Cecilia, as a martyr and prototype of the virgin-martyr, begins in Rome with the "entitlement" S. *Caeciliae*, appearing in the fragment of a stone inscribed by a *clericus Saecularis*, dated between 379 and 464 (as reported by the *Acta Sanctorum*). During the exploration ordered by Cardinal Rampolla at the end of the 19th century, an inscription by the presbyter of the entitled church, Giovanni, appeared, dated between the fifth and sixth century.

The *titulus Caeciliae* is later attested to by the signature of two presbyters at the Synod of 499, and of one during the Synod of 595; it again appears as the *titulus beatae Caeciliae* under Leo III, in 806. In devotion to martyrs and saints, even the oil gathered at the base of lamps lit above their sepulchres almost immediately became a "relic" (flames and oil in themselves are "potent" objects), and among the collections of oil gathered at the time of Gregory the Great (590–604), we find the name of Cecilia. We know that the church of Santa Cecilia already existed in November 545 because it is mentioned in the biography of Vigilius in the *Liber Pontificalis*, though we do not know when or by whom it was erected. In the *Liber Pontificalis*, again, the biography of Pascal I narrates that this pope sought out the body of Cecilia in the cemetery of Pretestatus, guided by a dream in which Cecilia appeared to him, urging him to place the relics of her body in the church dedicated to her, which he was in the process of reconstructing. Having found the body, Pascal dressed it in golden robes, and in 821, he had it carried to the basilica consecrated to Cecilia in Trastevere, closing it up in a cypress coffin that in turn was enclosed within a marble sarcophagus. However, the Pope set the martyr's head aside in a little silver box (the breaking up of holy bodies with the aim of multiplying relics has always been a Christian custom, as widespread as it is disconcerting); the box was then moved by Pope Leo IV to the church of the Quattro Coronati. The adventures of Cecilia's relics, however, do not end here. In 1559, Cardinal Sfondrati, titular of Santa Cecilia, executed the "recognizance" of the body (this, too, was a constant practice, meant to originate or confirm official devotion to a saint by guaranteeing the authenticity of the body). In memory of the event, he commissioned a statue that would reproduce the exact position of the saint "lying intact in her sepulchre" from the young sculptor, Maderno. At any rate, the artistic iconography inspired by Cecilia is extremely vast; suffice it to remember that the saint is represented in the procession of the virgins and martyrs in the Ravenna mosaics.

We have stopped to describe the adventure of Cecilia's corpse, and the obsessive perseverance with which this corpse has been pursued, preserved, and celebrated, because all the meanings and behaviors that emerge here, right from the beginning, have linked the saint (of which the martyr is the most powerful prototype) to the world of the living. Such an intimate link is proper to no other religion except Christianity—Catholic Christianity, in particular.

The concept of "relic" pertains to many sacred contexts. In the Greek religion, for example, body parts and objects belonging to "heroes" were celebrated, even when those heroes were mainly mythical figures. The Roman cult of the Penates also included the cult of relics. In this cult, however, we do not find the fundamental cultural "leap": that of the "potency" of the body, which instead deeply characterizes the relic of the Christian saint. Not even in Judaism—despite its strong sense of "contagion," of pure and impure things—do we find the concept of "relic" as the holy body of a figure qualified by exceptional virtues, and so charged with miraculous powers. The dispute over relics, on the contrary, which raged during the Protestant Reformation, depended mainly on the need to defend absolute monotheism, put at risk by the identification of saints almost as "divinities"—albeit second-class ones.

At any rate, the sense of the saint's *physical* importance has never stopped growing. This sense implied the potency springing from a sacred space (the place of martyrdom, the tomb), attracting pilgrims as a mirage of earthly health and heavenly salvation. The body parts which most meaningfully identify a person — head, arm, and heart — work extraordinary miracles; and gradually the clothing and any other object that has come into contact with the body gain specific importance, following a tacit but ever more explicit tendency, aimed at filling up the distance between the holy man and God. The apparent contradiction in Catholicism between the renunciation of the joys of the body (chastity, fasting, and penitential ascetic practices) and its exaltation is firmly guided by the expectancy of the body's resurrection, which only a "total" religion like the Catholic one has been capable of promising man. In this respect, it is especially illuminating to observe the identification of a Christian body closed up in prison and about to be martyred with an "altar" upon which the consecrated communion host was concrete! In the still-living body of the martyr, the opposing categories of sacred and profane are thus overcome, through the absolute trust that every Christian — as St. Paul says — is *alter Christus*, completing by way of his own sacrifice what is lacking in the sacrifice of Christ. It was precisely this stated identification with Christ-male, which even women achieved through baptism, that made women martyrs and saints on a par with men.

However, enormous though the cultural leap made by Christianity was, the men of the Church have failed to elude the sexist logic which, in all societies, underlies the place reserved for women. They have therefore reduced the value of martyrdom, which made women equal to men, to the defense of virginity, virginity being valued as the supreme womanly value. In the collective fantasy (thus, in that of women as well, since women are part of the global culture), virginity has become equal to a testimony of faith, and superior to martyrdom by death. That is why in our times, a girl like Maria Goretti could be canonized as a "martyr," having been stabbed to death after resisting a rape attempt. Very recently, two other girls have been canonized for the same reason; Pope John Paul II clearly believes that the only value of women lies in their use of sexuality.[24] After all, nothing expresses this fact more explicitly than liturgy. In the Roman missal, the ritual foresees a feast for virgins and martyrs, non-martyred virgins, and widows. Thus, the qualification always accompanying women saints defines and places them in relation to their use of sexuality. After Christianity was recognized as the religion of the Empire and the danger of martyrdom thus became an increasingly rarer prospect, the renunciation of sex, virginity, was assigned to the positive image of the nun as a supreme

60   I. Christianity: A Religion for Women

value. The nun became the bride of God, "dead" to the world in a symbolic-concrete martyrdom, a "recluse" in a cell-tomb, "buried alive" in solemn cloistered life; her "vow" was as definitive as death. (Only the Pope could release her from that vow, for serious reasons.)

If we take a look at the more or less historical accounts accompanying the names of the martyrs, what strikes us most, besides the fundamental theme of the defense of virginity, are certain recurring traits characterizing women's martyrdom. We can cite here only the most meaningful ones; they assume importance precisely because they are linked to femaleness; or rather, to male imagery aroused by femaleness.

The Beauty and the Beast

We can mention here only a few of the topics accompanying the biographies of martyrs; they may serve as points of reference. We shall try to group them according to similar characteristics, reflecting the transcendent, prodigious meanings assigned to female martyrdom, and the fantasies that have grown throughout the centuries around the tales of the *Passion* (written, obviously, by men of the Church who were the only ones then able and entitled to write them).

We have already mentioned the virgin Cecilia. She is represented sixth in line in the famous procession of the virgin-martyrs in the mosaic at Sant'Apollinare in Ravenna; it dates back to the sixth century and depicts 22 women and 25 men, proof of the extraordinary number of women martyrs. Cecilia is joined by many other women whose martyrdom is marked by countless, cruel acts of torture, which they miraculously succeed in surviving, until the executioner is forced to behead them in order to kill them. Thus, for example, Philomena, martyr of Rome (archeological evidence of her existence is in the cemetery of Priscilla), presents the chief themes of the female *Passion*. At 12 years of age — that is, marriageable age — she takes a vow of virginity. Then, there is a fantastic tale of her encounter with the Emperor Diocletian, who falls in love with her but fails to bend her to his will. The man of power, defeated by the virtue of a poor young girl, is a fairytale prince: the other face of the fairy-tale prince — a permanent fixture in literature even today. We then have a sequence of acts of torture that fail to kill her, an analogy of the potent man, demonstrating that it was not the male's lack of potency that was defeated: whipping, drowning (the anchor tied to her miraculously breaks), pierced by arrows (the arrows bend backwards), and finally, decapitation.

Regarding the near impossibility of killing a virgin, we can recall, among many, Theodosia of Caesarea. We are in Palestine, in the year 307, during the persecution of Maximian; we cannot help but note that the biographers' fantasy has been unleashed over this martyrdom with uncontainable fury. At the beginning, we see the usual heroic gesture of a woman bringing help and comfort to Christians awaiting judgment, and so running the risk of being arrested; then, the refusal to sacrifice to the gods, despite ferocious torture: iron rods stuck into her loins, breasts, bones, and finally, condemnation to death by drowning. What had been narrated by Eusebius of Caesarea up to this point was added to by the other terrible and miraculous forms of torture recounted in the Latin *Passion*: Theodosia emerged unharmed from the sea into which she had been cast; she was then exposed to ferocious beasts in the amphitheater but, as she continued to display a sweet, luminous face, the beasts were calmed. The calming of beasts is one of the *topoi* characterizing women's *passion* in particular, because the soft, fragile physical nature of women demonstrates their potency in contrast to the violence and force of the beasts. This seems to be a first step toward the fantastic construction of another theme whose symbolism has been handed down to us: *The Beauty and the Beast*, with its innumerable manipulations and adjustments from fairy tale to Tarzan and the King Kong film. At any rate, once more, we find proof here of how *virginity* is the central element of female potency; it is the sole invincible weapon against any other "natural" potency: that of the beast and that of man when they are not domesticated by "super-nature," by the "beyond nature" which only the female virgin reveals, points out and promises. After she emerged alive from this last attempt as well, Theodosia was finally beheaded.

The story of Christina is quite similar to that of other virgins and martyrs, given the incredible tortures she suffered. With one difference, however, that of her relationship to her father, in which Freud — had he known the story — might well have found confirmation for his theories. Christina, who is too beautiful and requested in marriage by many, is shut up in a tower by her father. This theme, as well, has inspired a number of fairytales. Officially, however, the father turns her over to the judges because his daughter has converted to Christianity, and refuses to make sacrifices to the gods. She is tortured in the most atrocious manner, but does not die. Christina is then taken back to her cell where three angels heal her wounds. So her torturers try to drown her, the classical way to kill virgins. But after being thrown into the sea with a stone tied to her neck, she is saved once more by an angel. The torture continues: whipping, the red-hot grate, the fiery furnace, poisonous snakes, the tearing off of her breasts, but Christina still does not die. It is not until two spears pierce her heart that she does.

62   I. Christianity: A Religion for Women

What can we say of the fact that a number of great artists have been inspired by her resistance to all forms of death, representing her in a kind of iconographic furor? She is 20th in the procession of virgins at Sant'Apollinare, where she bears no particular sign except the crown of martyrdom. Gradually, however, sadistic fantasies take over, and Christina is presented together with the millstone of drowning, the wheel, the snake den, the flaming grate, and the fiery furnace. In 1515, Luca Signorelli painted scenes of her passion as her torturers whip her, pour out boiling oil, turn the wheel among the flames, throw her into a lake, and finally, while archers shoot arrows at her heart.

Another account presenting nearly every imaginable form of martyrdom is the legend of Euphemia of Chalcedon. Her *Passion* includes: torture by the wheel to tear her to pieces, flames to consume her, a well to drown her, sticks and saws to cut her up, ferocious beasts to rip her flesh. Finally, Euphemia decides to die from the bite of a beast as heavenly voices and the quaking earth terrify the onlookers.

In our brief list, we cannot help but mention the names of Agnes, Agatha, and Lucy: all very famous because of the cults they have ceaselessly inspired.

We know that Agnes's martyrdom dates back to the end of the second or the beginning of the third century; she has been venerated in Rome since the first half of the fourth century, together with the martyrs buried on the Via Nomentana. St. Ambrose speaks of her in his *De Virginibus* (II, 5–9), written in 377, comparing her to the Greek heroine, Leona. Comparisons of martyrs to certain famous women of Greek and Roman antiquity were often made down through the centuries, which only shows men's incapacity for understanding or even acknowledging women's martyrdom: an absolute novelty, which totally changed their situation as "subjects" of society. Even the most frequent comparison, that with Lucretia, the Roman woman whose courage appears today as a symbol of supreme virtue and heroism, demonstrates that men (and therefore society as a whole, since it has always been males who interpreted the meaning of events) have failed to "see" women outside of their sexual function; their courage in facing death could only be a price paid in exchange for the only female "value": that of not being sexually possessed.

Lucretia killed herself after being raped, because she felt dishonored before her husband and children. Innumerable words of praise have been heaped upon her, from the male point of view.[25]

In referring to the attribute of "chaste" given to the name of Agnes, Ambrose states that this is praise in itself, since, at only 12 years of age, she underwent the double martyrdom of modesty and faith. As we have noted more than once, no one tells us why women like Agnes, not yet marriageable nor old enough to act as witnesses, were taken to trial personally, whereas by law they depended on the father's authority; nor is it explained why they were condemned to die, though what they believed or did had no importance socially. And yet, we must believe Ambrose when he declares that Agnes was a minor, and that she was condemned to public exposure: *flexu in plateae sistere virginem*, says Ambrose who, like all hagiographers observant of the taboo of obscenity in relation to virgins, fails to specify that women were condemned to appear naked in the square, and placed in a sort of prostitute's cell (*cella meretricia*), before being taken to be burnt at the stake or beheaded. Of course this—making them lose their virginity—was the simplest way to get around the problem of killing a virgin. But regarding Agnes, the psychological tension toward a virginity which "is about to be lost" reaches its height precisely because "it stops short" at the exposition of nakedness; around which erotic and transcendent fantasies have collected which only female nudity can arouse. The *Acta* recounts that a man loses his eyesight for "having looked lustfully at the nude body of a young girl," and Agnes miraculously restores it. Further legends, instead, tell us that her long hair covered her, protecting her nudity: It is a theme that appears elsewhere as well, partly indicating (as in the case of Mary Magdalen and Mary of Egypt) a supreme degree of deprivation, penitence and refusal of the world, by the renunciation of clothing (see Part I, Ch. 4 of this book), and at the same time it reflects obscene-erotic male fantasies about women's hair. The form of her martyrdom being uncertain, the iconography represents Agnes as very young, holding a lamb in her arms—the symbol of her purity—and enveloped by flames, or else at the moment the sword is about to decapitate her. In any case, she constitutes the prototype and emblem of martyrs exalted for their virginity.

We cannot stop here to recount the influence exercised by the figure of Agnes as an image of reference and identification for female virginity. It constitutes the only true reason why both men and women have kept her alive and active in their historic memories; the martyrdom of women for the sake of "faith" has merged with, indeed has been "covered by," martyrdom for sexual untouchability. Imprisoned in their sexual function, whether negative or positive, women did not disturb the logical adjustments that men of the Church, and public opinion in general, were forced to make in the face of the "maleness/femaleness" revolution, ineluctably included in Christianity.

Not even as martyrs did they disturb the system.

And yet, a global history has yet to be written—one not only "from the man's viewpoint" or (with a banal descent into the obvious) "from the woman's viewpoint": a history that will enable us to understand something of the intricate, dense, unexplored problem of male sexuality. Unfortunately, like nearly all "secular" historians up until now, Freud never thought of reading the *Acta Sanctorum*, let alone regarding it as one of the richest, most significant sources for an understanding of the deep motivations of Western history. Yet certainly, the way in which males have watched, recounted, preserved, and interpreted *themselves* through the martyrdom of Christian women, reveals the fact that for them women are the objects of sexual prey, and at the same time, of inexhaustible hate, because they are necessary sexually and cannot be eliminated. Moreover, men must remain in the absurd, unsolvable position of desire and hate. They must never let up. Hate must be made manifest in all its violence and so insatiable as to desire and hope that the object will not be destroyed by it. This explains why the continual acts of torture, such as the cutting off of breasts and the prostitute's cell, are vulgarly sexual in their denial of any sexual attraction; it is torture of an almost unimaginable ferocity toward the weakness of the female body. Torture which, however, fails to destroy the victim, for her indestructibility assures man both that the woman's body will belong to everyone or to no one, *and* that it will always be a victim, a shield against what man does not want to know: that he is identical to the God he himself has created; a God which, as God, *has no need* to possess women sexually. God's kind of "possession" is male — a destructive possession, that of death; and death is that power which no woman possesses, which no woman can or must possess. The only holder of the power over death, analogous to that of God, is the male, and therefore the only object of possession belonging to God is the male. Male sexuality, the "penis," is a destructive instrument that associates sexual possession with killing: therefore any sexual object of possession is a "victim." The only true "victims" or objects of God's possession are men; and no matter how many women males have offered Him and offer Him, the fact remains that men are the only victims pleasing to God. Therefore, when women martyrs thank God while going off to their execution for having made them become "similar to men," they unconsciously perceive the deep meanings of the cultural system, they "reveal" those meanings, but they are, just the same, "manipulated" by them. They will never directly be victims of God, since God — the god created by men — has no use at all for the sexual possession of women.

Female virginity thus manifests its true face, in the multifaceted game of "mirrors" which males have constructed on and around themselves: Women are and must remain "virgins," because culturally, neither God nor men need their sexuality.

That is why they cannot expunge them despite the most ferocious torture, for they do not *want* to expunge them.

Therefore, only rape — individual, or, even better, collective — responds to the deep needs of males: hate toward women, destructive violence toward them, use of the penis as a weapon which, at the very moment it possesses them, kills them. This should be a starting point for reflecting on the true essence of prostitution: male needs. But we are tacitly forbidden to speak about this, too. Any study or research on prostitution, today as in the past, only considers the figure of the prostitute — without noticing the absurdity of such a position. It is even frightening, inasmuch as it reveals an unconscious taboo afflicting men, to see male and female interviewers, journalists, sociologists, and priests, ask a woman standing under a street lamp: "Why?" when no one asks the same question of a client passing in his car. More than a century has gone by since Cesare Lombroso declared his certainties concerning the genetic perversions of the woman prostitute, but as for male "needs"— the only clear cause of prostitution, present everywhere and in all known eras— we are forbidden to ask.

Many other cultural "themes" could be highlighted and analyzed on the basis of the precise meanings attributed by males to female martyrdom: Lucy, who tears out her eyes so as not to be raped, becomes the prototype of all those women who later, even though they may not be martyrs, tear out their eyes (and miraculously reacquire them), or else cut off their noses and lips in order appear monstrously repellent in the face of their persecutors' lust. Finally, the theme of mothers who, like Sinforosa or Felicitas, witness the martyrdom of their *seven* sons, encouraging them to accept death, in perfect correspondence to the destructive violence of male torturers who expand their hate to the full limit: that of making their victims resemble them.

And who continue to do so today.

In the future, other scholars can take up studies centering on such themes. At this point, it remains for us to marvel at the fact that men, even while hiding behind the fragile pretense that it was "pagans" who performed similar atrocities, have not realized, while exalting only these aspects of female martyrdom, that they were identifying themselves not so much with the persecutors of faith as with torturers. Indeed, they themselves were "projected," psychologically, and, above all, physically, into the beings of torturers. This identification palpably emerges in the pleasure with which artists— even the greatest ones— have painted scenes of female martyrdom, almost always neglecting any causal element linked to theory, ideology or faith, showing the spectator merely the physical nature of a tortured, dismembered female on the point of being eliminated, destroyed.

These victims are so "happy" to be victims. They bow so serenely to the violence of the most ferocious torture, carrying around cut-off breasts, torn-out eyes, and detached heads, while wheels crush them, flames devour them, beasts tear at them with sharp teeth, arrows pierce them, and swords decapitate them, so that it is impossible to nourish any doubt: The person who portrays them, stopping to work with brush or scalpel as he traces the details of such gestures, identifies himself with the torture at the very moment he is convinced — while imagining the ecstasy and enjoyment of the victims— that nothing could be more "just" or more "beautiful."

Art history is still waiting for someone who will really "look" at these works.

3

A Grand Invention: Let Us Go Outside the World

A Room of One's Own

In order to understand the nuptial adventure in relation to God inherent in Judeo-Christian culture, we must consider the importance of symbolism in mental activity, in the very formation of concepts giving substance to the "superior consciousness."[26]

Of course, symbolism has been studied in innumerable works pertaining to philosophy, anthropology, art, and psychology. However, scholars have never openly acknowledged what symbolism simultaneously reveals and hides until now: the concreteness that always informs symbolic activity, its perennial readiness to spring into *action*.

Until it wears itself out and is lost, any symbol within the culture in which it was formed and subsists is based on the possibility of real, concrete action. Only the "obviousness" of our living habits prevents us from seeing this possibility. The potentiality of concrete action comes to the fore as soon as power—be it religious, political, or cultural—perceives a need for it. The power of symbols and the symbols of power, in fact, are interchangeable.

In all known societies and cultures it is the "sacred" which absorbs most symbolic activity. Any "magic" behavior, for example, is founded on the belief that certain words or gestures can cause a desired event to happen. The potency of the word, pronounced by given figures—priest, sorcerer, shaman—creates a reality. The clearest example in Catholicism is the sacraments. I say: "This is the body and blood of Christ," and the bread and wine become what the priest says they are; I say: "I baptize you" and original sin is washed away. In Judaism, the logical outcome of this concrete force of symbolism is the covenant between males and God, which is a nuptial pact. In Christianity, instead—because males are really the brides of God now, since the nuptial pact has been completed—we see a symbolic-concrete transferal of femininity onto the Church. In theory, the Church should represent the collectivity, the Christian people. But in reality, as in any "representation," it achieves concrete reality in those who hold power; so much so that it gives rise to the Pope, whose figure assumes all the meanings of maleness-femaleness present in Christianity, becoming their undeniable testimony. A man/male, he is both "male/bridegroom," as God on earth and man of the Church; and "female/Church," as bride of God. Clearly, there is no longer any place for women, in this theorization of the man/male relationship with God; therefore, men gave women over to God by means of the promptly formed institution of "consecrated virgins," and later, by means of monasticism. In reality, female monasticism has always been "added" to the consecration of virgins, but what really counts for women is "virginity," and not the observance of a particular rule. We find proof of this in the fact that cloistered life was invented and imposed only on women. A "taboo" of women emerges here, which was already present *in nuce* in Judaism, once they have been offered up to God; they are separated from the human community, consigned to death and transcendence; possessed bodily by God, their bodies must therefore become invisible to the living. This situation gives rise to a highly complex psychological structure, eventually leading to the absolutizing of such meanings on the part of the "mystics." Driven by the eagerness to be "true," real, they find themselves with their visions and ecstasies in a world of total unreality.

On entering the convent, women free themselves—and this is the fundamental fact—from dependence on male authorities, fathers, husbands, sons; they free themselves both from juridical dependence and the daily dependence of domestic life. Female monastic orders are subject to the authority of the corresponding male branch, or of the bishops. However, it is a distant authority, and does not intervene in the normal organization of work, in the dynamics of interpersonal relationships among nuns, or between nuns and the abbess. It is hard to fully realize what a male figure means in daily life, in the restricted space of a dwelling, with the weight of his predominance, above all, physical predominance with the authoritarian power of a voice that is so different, potent, and deep in comparison to a woman's voice. The oppression which male physicality creates is hard to assess partly because it is not spoken of, as if physical force intervened only when the male, husband or father, raises a hand to strike. But many of the quarrels and conflicts, expressed and otherwise, which break out in daily family coexistence, are due to this disparity of concrete corporeal "weight." By itself, it establishes who the boss is and who holds the power. When she reaches the convent, then, the woman first of all experiences the ecstasy of "possessing a territory"; this possession derives above all from feeling free of the encumbering male physicality, a physicality whose aggressive, intimidating weight is forgotten by men, since they are used to possessing it and to taking advantage of it, but which makes each gesture they make and each word they pronounce seem out of proportion to women, noisy, violent, dangerous. Only when we think of the meticulous measurement of weight in boxers prior to a match, can we perhaps realize the effort women make to convince themselves that they are on a par.

Therefore, women's life in common, though causing psychological problems and conflicts of various kinds, does provide a fundamental liberty: a physical one, free from the domineering presence of males. Furthermore, women know how to tidy and enjoy their abode, how to keep order and keep things clean in the intimacy of physical needs; they know how to compensate for the destruction unconsciously wrought by males every day.

It was men who invented monasticism, and therefore separation from the female sex. Women only copied it; at any rate, the subjective and objective differences between female and male monastic life are total. The first and fundamental freedom which the convent assures women, besides freedom from physical fear, is freedom from the fear of "maleness"; of what is hidden in maleness, of the "danger" which women fear all the more in that they have been condemned by men themselves to know nothing about it, except that it *is* something to fear. A gathering of women allows an immediate lowering of the defensive, fearsome tension that, even when not expressed, nonetheless accompanies them constantly through life. This lessening of tension in the atmosphere immediately allows the possibility of introspection, of reflecting on one's own thoughts and feelings, of finally closing one's eyes and ears to the surroundings. But the walls of the convent protect with even greater solidity in that they establish a space or territory outside of the world and the flux of worldly time where women can finally experience the cultural structures that men have created, but always prevented women from using, since they have assigned them to "nature": to the maintenance of biological life and the monotonous domesticity of everyday routines.

In separating himself from the female sex, the male actually abandons himself to himself. In appearance he does so out of the need to find protection from the temptations and sins that the nearness of women might provoke in one who has made a vow of chastity. But living with other men in a special building with the preordained purpose of eating, sleeping, praying, and working for one's entire life together with other men is quite different from distancing oneself from the world, from doing penance, from trying to practice ascetic exercises, as occurred in the life of hermits. In monasticism we find a psychological and social "leap" implying a sexual, emotional, and intellectual choice, not to renounce or distance oneself from the world, but to construct a world. It is true that hermits often placed themselves quite near one another in a given territory, but this was for contingent, practical reasons, in order to assure themselves of help in case of need, and it did not touch on the choice of solitude. Benedictine monasticism requires and provides for just the opposite type of situation: It is a community of men only, who promise to live together all the hours of their lives, their whole life long. Furthermore, this community constitutes a "family" of men only, defined as such, in which the abbot is the father. It is not interchangeable with other communities of the same order, since the monk makes a vow of "stability": He will remain in the same group until death, in the same monastery that he entered as a novice. Finally, there will be children as well, as foreseen by the Rule of St. Benedict. Not only will they provide visible truth that this is a family, they will also assure the continuity of the group, beyond any need of procreation.

With monasticism, therefore, men create a type of society and culture which changes the face of any and all preceding cultures and societies, organizing a system of living that deliberately, consciously exists without the presence of women: not for the ascesis or salvation of one or more individuals, but in order to construct a different world. The fact that this is a sexual choice is clear: Only sexuality makes possible the acceptance of a physical community among adults. As soon as children grow up, in fact, they wish to—indeed they must—leave their parents' home; similarly, no guest, friend though he may be, can stop long in a house offering him hospitality. The programmed, absolute physical togetherness imposed by the monastic rule excludes only the concrete sexual relation, so that the monk will never be alone, even at night (a curtain separates him from the rest of the community, in a single dormitory). Such acceptance would be unthinkable without the sexual acceptance of the other, of others. It reflects an implicit homosexuality, surely "mental," when not sensual as well. Moreover, the expansion, the socially constructive capacity that monasticism has manifested and achieved during nearly a millennium, covering the European territory with innumerable monasteries, assuming leadership in all fields, from the theological to the moral, from the artistic to the political, from the social to the economic, gives undeniable proof of its "worldly" vitality and its intellectual and emotional force, which has nothing to do with the "renunciation" inherent in ascesis. For many centuries, Europe was organized around abbeys; the presence of monks constituted the supporting structure of the Church, its true power; with the monks, it emerged as the dominant social structure.

Clearly, none of these characteristics is found in female monasticism, which copied only outwardly the life of male monks, remaining incapable of creating any power structure outside the monastery. In fact, nuns have never assumed leadership in society in any area of power. Therefore they have not created any model for society, but instead have passively accepted one. At least in most cases, living among women was thus not an expression of homosexuality, but a flight from sexuality, and above all, a flight from the power of males. It was a search for autonomy and self-achievement for their own sakes: an autonomy and self-achievement that they could reach only by freeing themselves from the authority and physical presence of men.

In monastic living then, the woman discovers the contradiction that has always been imposed on her life: the same contradiction that has always rendered history incapable of noticing women's presence.

This is the contradiction: Precisely because she keeps life alive by caring for the physical needs of everyone—children, adults, old people, the ill—she does not theorize life. Precisely because it is she who keeps the fire lit and draws water from the well; precisely because it is she who prepares the food and washes the dishes and garments for everyone; precisely because, without her work, no one could survive from one day to the next, it is she who founds history: that is, man's reflection regarding himself and the world surrounding him, which makes man be man. In short, a woman who knows very well how long it takes to cook soup and how long it takes to put a child to sleep, does not "know" what time is: that time which males, even when doing nothing, have learned to know in depth. It is in the convent, then, that the woman discovers to her great surprise, along with Augustine, that time "does not exist." For the only true time, the time that is not consumed, since it is man who creates it, invents it, and wants to live it out, is liturgical time, monastic time. That is why the "little" Thérèse, on hearing through the cloister wall one freezing winter night the faraway music of the world, and setting her eyes on the grey stones of her poor Carmel, feels a great joy flood her heart: for those stones are "perennial"; they are "outside the figure of the world that passes."[27]

For women, then, the monastic experience presents a radical difference: the passage from "nature" to "culture"; indeed, to a "superculture," since the great founders of the monastic life, from Pacomius to Benedict, from Colombanus to Bernard, sought in it a liberation from "culture" in order to experience the immensity of sin and separation from God in the harshness of a grinding, penitent life. For women, instead, there is a double "passage": For example, whereas the monk excludes meat from the monastic diet, since hunting pertains to that culture which the male repudiates in order to punish himself for the aggressiveness, violence and pride that Christianity condemns, for the woman, the refusal of meat becomes primarily the discovery of the "cultural" valence, and not only the natural, nourishing one of meat; then, she makes the happy passage to the "superculture" of renunciation, since the woman has nothing cultural to repent of in eating meat.

Analogous pairs of differences can be noted in nearly all monastic practices. In his Rule, St. Benedict says a surprising thing: Even though he had wanted to do so, he had not been able to remove wine from the diet because the monks would never have agreed to give it up (*Regula,* chapter XL). Naturally, in antiquity and the Middle Ages much more than today, wine was imbued with "virile" values; besides being considered an indispensable element in the nourishment of rich and poor alike, it was considered capable of giving a force and vitality which were partly analogous to sexual potency. For that very reason, women were excluded from partaking of this kind of nourishment both in Rome and Palestine. Even in modern times we find traces remaining of this prohibition: Women could not enter taverns, they could not serve alcoholic drinks in bars, they had to leave the dining room when males drank liquor, and so on. In this perspective it is surprising that in the literature of the early centuries, we find no discussion regarding women's drinking of wine during the Eucharist; at any rate, we may suppose that in this case too, as in baptism, the parity of women was silently held to be obvious. From this detail alone, one can understand that the monastic rules were conceived exclusively for men, and that the small quantity of wine allowed, while penitential for males, was culturally significant and gratifying for women.

Examples of this kind could be extended to all the regulations of the monastic system, however, only the fundamental structures and their relation to the female experience are mentioned here.

The Angel of the Hearth Puts Out the Fire

The fact that even up to modern times, historians have always spoken of female monasticism as if it were a version of male monasticism, is macroscopic proof of the scholars' blindness in the face of the history of women. The refusal of culture, the abandonment and contempt for the world inherent in the monk's choice—culture and the world being perceived and theorized as passing values, pleasures which hamper the relationship with the divinity at the very moment they satisfy the "flesh" —cannot in the least be shared by women, and by themselves are no motivation for the monastic choice. The theme of "dualism," present in philosophical speculation during late antiquity, finds no equivalent, or psychological or cultural verification in the experience of women. First of all, women did not participate in the intellectual life of the time, and therefore were excluded from any philosophical knowledge of the problem of dualism. But above all, this problem never arose for them in realistic terms, since the world did not offer itself to a woman as pleasure, temptation, or satisfaction of the flesh. Lacking juridical independence and economic power, and belonging to the social structure only through a marriage imposed on her by the father or other male relatives with no possibility of choice, her destiny was to die at a very young age in childbirth, or else be subject to a great number of pregnancies, and many years of nursing and childcare. Totally illiterate in most cases, devoid of any intellectual nourishment, the women of antiquity and the Middle Ages knew relations with men only through "sexual brutality and absolute authority," as Marc Bloch states.[28] In looking at herself, the woman was urged to see only her "inferiority," proclaimed by the greatest Greek and Latin sages, or her essence as *caput malorum*, which men of the Church agree to attribute to her. What worldly pleasures, then, did she sacrifice in becoming a nun? The two paths leading to early monastic ascesis, sex and food, presented themselves to the woman in their existential meanings of liberty, which were quite different from (when not contrary to) those of the male. The renunciation of sex takes shape as liberation, and not as sacrifice.

A partly analogous observation can be made about food. Without a doubt, sex and food are linked, and it was not at all necessary to await modern studies in psychology and psychoanalysis to realize the fact. Indeed, monks themselves have emphasized this bond on more than one occasion, stating that gluttony and the sins of gluttony inevitably lead to sins of the flesh. Chastity can be protected above all by the emaciation of the body: "Gluttony is the first among the vices which the monk must avoid. It is not only the quality of foods, but the quantity as well which endangers chastity. There is a close relation between impurity and the belly full of foods, especially vile ones."[29] Moreover, Lévi-Strauss clearly demonstrated the "cultural" meaning which food and its various modes of preparation assume for man.[30] Yet the most palpable proof of monasticism's radical refusal of culture is the abstinence from eating cooked food on the part of hermits and monks (institutionalized in nearly all the monastic rules, at least during the liturgical periods of penance). St. James of Nisiba nourished himself on berries and grasses growing in the fields without ever cooking a thing; St. Jerome, who has always been looked up to as the supreme ascetic, lived for many years in the solitude of Chalcis where "eating any cooked food was considered an intemperance" (*Epistula XXII ad Eustochium, 7*). The ascetics tried for years, or even all the rest of their lives, to eat only what they found in nature, excluding any manipulation, and they felt a real horror for meat: a horror which has persisted in the monastic rules down through the centuries and through the various "reforms" up to the Abbot of Rancé, the founder of the Trappist community in 1664, who totally excluded meat from the diet of monks (except in serious cases of illness). The exclusion of meat can be explained by the refusal of that basic element of culture which is *fire*, and immediately following it, hunting.

However, in the case of women, abstinence from food and from the use of fire assumes a radical meaning, totally different from those perceived by the male. In all known societies, women have been assigned the primary task of keeping the fire lit, and using it to prepare food. Of course, the examples are countless (suffice it to recall the religious task of the vestal virgins in Roman society). Furthermore, for a woman, sex and food are closely connected because they imply not only her personal satisfaction, but her role in maintaining the group. The woman feeds the newborn baby, but the breast is also an erogenous zone, simultaneously linked to sex and nutrition. Given the growing psychological and cultural awareness that biological functions assume for women, especially in the West, this fact causes many of the disturbances that accompany puberty, and often, nursing as well.

Psychiatry today tends to take such factors more and more into account when confronting the problem of mental anorexia. Refusing food, failing to eat, or eating only particular foods cooked in particular ways, is nearly always a disturbance afflicting the female sex, often associated with the anxiety felt when the breasts and menstruation first appear.

We find an "opposition" between menstruation and the handling of food in all those cultures where, during menstruation, the woman is tabooed, forced to fast and to take purifying baths; she is sent away from the house for it is feared that, in cooking, she might poison her husband.[31] The negative meanings attributed to the menstrual cycle in all eras and all societies are well-known by now; but unfortunately the orientation of psychiatric treatment does not sufficiently consider the conditioning which society and culture exercise over women's psychological experience. Anorexia (and this is just one example among many) is closely tied to the sphere of sex, but it could never have become a female mental "disturbance" endemic to modern European history, if this tie had not been codified by the environment, by socialization, and by cultural values. "Woman-and-food," and "woman-and-cooking" appear as binomial pairs within which women have been forced to express themselves, even in a pathological sense. In psychiatric analysis explicit reference is made to the refusal of food as emaciation of the body: "The real ethico-ascetic aim of anorexic women is to crush the strong body in order to magnify the weak spirit."[32]

The earliest medical information concerning "ethereal maidens" is found in texts of the 16th and 17th centuries; it becomes increasingly frequent in history until the explosion of our times. Were there no anorexic women in the Middle Ages? This question is poorly framed (even though research is underway in this area), for the ascetically-motivated refusal of food, foreseen by the group and "sanctified" in religious life, prevents it from being considered pathological.[33] At any rate, it remains to be explained why, among the ascetics declared as "saints" by the Church, only female cases appear significant as far as anorexia is concerned.

In reality, everywhere and in all eras, the woman is socially assigned the role of preparing food. This task has been given to her as if it were "natural," so that it is not even considered a job. She cannot avoid it because she herself considers it an obvious part of her nature. For women, then, the refusal to handle food, assumed as a virtue — indeed, a virtue theorized and adopted by men themselves — becomes not a penance, but a positive, radical rebellion against their social function. It is not a "technique" for reaching particular states of mystic purification and sanctity, but a negation of the values proposed by the cultural pattern in which they are immersed. Soon after their entry into the convent, there is often a suspension of menstruation, largely due to the change in diet, environment, and the daily routine, which nonetheless takes shape psychologically and concretely as a victory over their contaminated and contaminating physicality; and consequently, as a liberation from that biological-cultural clock that inexorably marks off their time and binds them to "nature."

Another fundamental aspect for women leading the monastic life is the value given to *silence*, present in all convent rules. Silence is imposed with greater or lesser stringency, according to the rules of different communities, but in any case, it implies the negation of external culture, and the potent re-founding of the "word." Here again, we find ourselves facing a fundamental difference with respect to monks, since women have never been entitled to the use of an efficacious word: a "true," culturalized one. (Only today, in Western culture, are they beginning to be so.) As Lévi-Strauss writes, "May the woman be mute, or stopped up from above,"[34] because of the opposition between the female sexual opening (the "below") and the use of the word, which is found in all cultures. Restrictions on the possibility of speaking are imposed on women, and are a constant in all societies: the prohibition against speaking in public, or in the presence of males, unless addressed beforehand by a male; the obligation to speak a "female" tongue: that is, the prohibition against speaking the same language as men, and the obligation to use a language "of respect." The prohibition against taking oath and testifying that was present in Europe until the modern era corresponds, instead, to the obvious lack of that sexual "potency" in women that can guarantee the potency of the word. The lack of the potency of word also gives rise to the impossibility of preaching and becoming priests; it even touched on the exercise of the political vote, denied to women up to the time of modern democracies.

In the convent, then, where primary importance is given to silence and to a regulation of the word imposed on everyone, women regain equality with men. Above all, they become aware of the cultural meaning underlying language, and the fundamental value of silence: not as a deprivation imposed by male power, but as the freedom to think of themselves and concentrate on their own inner experience. Moreover, singing in the choir not only allows women to learn the epic and poetic contents of the Bible from the liturgical texts, but it also teaches them to exercise control over their voices; for men, such control has always been an indispensable trait of social presence (among the Romans, dominion over one's tone of voice was a sign of virility). In short, in the convent, for the first time women perform a social function through the use of words. The recital of the Divine Office, an official collective invocation to God, puts them on a par with monks, who are not necessarily priests; as monks, they perform the role of "mediators" between the group and God.

Yet an even more important element in monasticism leads to the liberation of women, the initiation to *knowledge*. An initiation which, once again, makes female monasticism a totally different historical and cultural phenomenon from male monasticism. We can affirm, if only on the basis of what we mentioned earlier, that monasticism introduced knowledge to women — the kind of knowledge that had always been denied them: first of all, an awareness and reflection on their own role in the world, and then the discovery of the organization and values, no longer obvious and blind, that mark the forms of human society. This is the first, fundamental step to "knowledge": the assumption of an "I" which is historical and not alienated, valid in itself, an end in itself, together with the learning of an objectifying cognitive category that is indispensable for understanding any experience, above all, one's own. Through the centuries, up to the scientific theories of Bacon and, later, Galileo, many were those who thought they could draw all pertinent knowledge from theoretical reflections on their own personal experiences. This conviction still accompanies both men and women, especially with regard to the female experience. If practical life were sufficient for "understanding" and for "theorizing" the facts of experience, no one better than women — in every era and culture — could have elaborated the hypotheses and theories of physics, medicine, chemistry, and even religion. It is women, in fact, who have always cared for the sick, been present at deliveries, brought up children, and watched over the dead. It is women that have practiced all the laws of physics by keeping the fire lit and cooking foods in every possible way, from baking to boiling; who have used water for cleansing the body and objects; who have gathered plants, using them for nourishment, for lighting the fire and keeping it lit, for making bandages, plasters, and juices to cure all sorts of wounds and illnesses, and for sewing garments suitable for the heat and cold. (The examples are virtually countless, since it has always been women who have occupied themselves with physical survival.)

Yet experience serves only if one is capable of asking the "why" of a given phenomenon; and it is precisely this which has been denied to women's intelligence (as it has been to all the lower classes; indeed, the same observations could be made about slaves and servants, or today's "proletarians," to whom — on the basis of an epistemological error — Marxism has attributed group-saving wisdom). Women have picked, and continue to pick, billions of ripe pieces of fruit, but they have never asked "why they fall," as one of Newton's anecdotes recounts, since no society has given women the task of "understanding," "theorizing," or "reflecting" on the meaning of the laws governing the world. The same can be said about religions. If what religious historians, ethnologists, and anthropologists say is true, that is, that it was the primary, unacceptable awareness of death that gave rise to the belief in the survival of souls, survival of ancestors, cult of the dead and, finally, religions— there is no human group that has not assigned women with the task of caring for the ill; of preparing and watching over cadavers. This because women have been attributed with a contamination analogous to that of cadavers (such an "obvious" phenomenon that the ethnologist Ernesto De Martino could write his *Morte e pianto rituale nel mondo antico* without realizing he was speaking only about women).[35] And yet, no religious theory has been invented by women. Women are the "object" of religion, not the "subject."

So monasticism offered women this first "male" experience: that of *needing* and *being able* to reflect about themselves and the world. This first fundamental cognitive moment was followed by another: learning to read. Most women entering the convent were illiterate. Female education, just learning to read and write, has never been considered a "right" for women until today; and even in our times it is still not considered to be so for most women outside the Western world. Indeed, the female illiteracy rate accounts for about 70 percent of the global one. Even in the early convents of Pacomius, nuns were taught to read in order to recite texts from the Scriptures and liturgical prayers. The mental "leap" made by learning a written language is incommensurable. Not only does it provide an instrument for further learning, but also for the discovery of forms underlying language itself. In other words, discovering language in a conscious form also means discovering the existence of the symbolic and collective forms of thought.

Therefore, when women entered the convent, their existence totally changed; even though they took "vows" of self-deprivation, obedience, humility, poverty, and chastity, they became actively aware of their place in society. Their hold on the world became stronger. At a given moment of their history that hold would lead them out of the convent, as they dedicated themselves to teaching: putting at the disposal of the "poor" that instrument of reading and writing whose revolutionary force they had understood from personal experience. In fact, strange though it may seem, religious women were the first ones to throw themselves into "work": not secular women, be they rich or poor, noble or bourgeois. It was monastic life that first made women aware they were active subjects, albeit in absolute isolation, whereas laywomen continued to "belong" to others both mentally and physically.

The convent, then, took shape as a "room of one's own" which, after many centuries, Virginia Woolf still longed for as a woman's supreme condition of freedom.

The Realm of the Mother, Realm of Hate

One of the most grotesque things about the false analogy between female and male monasticism is the placing of a woman, the so-called abbess, in a role corresponding to that of the abbot. In the Rule of St. Benedict "*abbas* means father" thus, the term "abbot," and, as such, he represents God. How anyone can possibly imagine that a mother is a father, and that she represents God, remains a mystery, given the silence which, in this case as in all others, accompanies the history of women. At any rate, we might refer here to that mental inertia marking the social, cultural, and psychological indifference of men toward women's lives (and it is men alone who possess the authority to define and establish "institutions"); this inertia is shared by women as well, since they have always been kept from thinking. The relationship of power in a women's convent between nuns and the abbess is a false relationship: as false as any hypothesis of "matriarchy"; communication among women is really non-communication in a social sense; it is an exchange based only on a positive or negative affectivity between individuals. In other words, power is power only when it is based on the existence of a group. Among women, on the contrary — precisely because no woman possesses any social authority — no "group" forms except in numerical terms; and the power of the mother, whether in the domestic or monastic family, is only a relationship of psychological and emotional domination over single members, and not a relationship of true authority.

The more or less silent jealousies and emotional conflicts that break out within a group of nuns rarely reveal themselves as such; but this does not prevent them from being a violent, destructive force. The levels of false pretense that consequently develop in a female monastery can barely be described in their concrete or symbolic reality. In fact, a convent is not based on any existing, recognized social model. Until very recently, any kind of authority copied the model of the *pater familias*, and the family was such only if a male authority existed as a point of reference for all the family members, women, children, and slaves. When all is said and done, dependence on a father, even as adults, has been a model that was imposed and accepted by society; dependence on a mother, instead, is socially and psychologically intolerable. The only way to adapt to it is to regress to childhood and make oneself a child. This explains the exasperating infantilism of many nuns, their recourse to the mother figure for the slightest disturbance, the disproportion between the anxious care given to an ill "daughter" and the harshness with which the others are subjected to the most burdensome sacrifices. Historians, anthropologists, and jurists have always maintained that "matriarchy" could not exist as a real organizational stage of society because the power of the mother has no extra-biological foundation, and female monasticism furnishes undeniable proof of this. Mothers and daughters have been victims of one another; they have loved and hated each other to the point of destroying one another psychologically, and physically as well, mutually exhorting one another to achieve the supreme level of sacrifice with a ferociousness and absoluteness that finds no similarity among the monks. They were unable to produce anything valid until they bolted outside, into social action: It was this

I. Christianity: A Religion for Women

action that finally broke the closed circle of the maternal reign. The mother became the "Superior." Even though some ambiguities typical of the maternal role have remained, we refer with the "Superior" once again to the hierarchic categories normally foreseen by society, and the conflicting relationship finds justification in the inevitable dynamics of power.

Cohabitation in a convent is more or less a cohabitation among co-brides who vie with one another to see who is more of a "bride," favored by the divine bridegroom in his harem; and they vie, above all, in hating the one who is formally the most "bride-like" of brides: the abbess. The psychological dynamics operating on that true stage of socio-psycho-drama, the female monastery, are so ambiguous and elusive that, in the great majority, nuns can honestly say that they do not know them. But in reality, the conflicts breaking out in relation to the abbess, both in order to conquer her affection more securely than the others and to contrast her orders, bear witness to the impossibility of any "realm of women." Moreover, one can never precisely tell what the divine bridegroom's will is, since he is absent; one can never know which co-bride he loves the most: the most recently-arrived novice, who represents a "young woman," a most dangerous rival, or else the abbess, the first and foremost of the brides; the one who, on the basis of the power she exercises, is necessarily the nearest to the husband-master. From one occasion to the next, the dynamics of deprivation, a positive value underpinning the entire monastic life, thus become proof of the bridegroom's predilection toward one or another of the brides. The contest in this area is indescribably cruel and pitiless. The younger the novices are, and therefore the more "beloved" and more "beautiful" rivals of the older women, the more perfectly they must obey all the precepts of penance and sacrifice. In this respect as well, a contradictory challenge is created, full of jealousies and real hates. The novices must show themselves worthy of the bridegroom by observing to the letter, not only the official rule, but above all the tacit, yet extremely burdensome precepts, which accompany each gesture, each monastic form of behavior, in never-ending, harrying examination and control.

In this area women have always been experts. It is almost as if a hypersensitivity to all the tiniest details of living were written into their genetic code: The weaker and less powerful they are, they more alert they are to everything surrounding them. They have learned to live in the world like animals hounded in a thick forest, where every rustling leaf, every reflection of light, even the softest variation in hue, signal hidden dangers.

The conflict with the novices, who fruitlessly try to deserve their status as "young brides," and as such beloved by the bridegroom, is counterbalanced by their conflict with the abbess. Though elderly, she in turn must prove worthy of being "chosen." Naturally, the revealing mirror will be obedience, "perfection" in everything: perfection, that is, in what is not achievable except through self-annihilation in death, whether one continues a living death, or (and this is the final goal, the true one) hastens to perish. A sacrificial spirit dominates the cloistered life, reaching nearly unimaginable limits. A novice who wears her belt a bit more tightly than an unwritten tacit law rigidly dictates is not a thoroughly bridelike bride. For this reason she arouses a subtle kind of satisfaction in the other nuns, together with the pettiest criticism. Similarly, a novice who is not the first to arrive at morning choir will be an object of blame as much as an instrument of consolation for the elderly nuns. In fact, when the young bride is not even dying to run up to the bridegroom, the indolent fatigue of the others finds some justification. The same can be said of the Mother Abbess. She cannot and must not grant herself even the smallest exception to the rule; an exception that is up to her to make for her underlings when necessary: This is the only way her so-called "daughters" can take revenge for her power. Each nun's surveillance over the others' faithfulness to the rules—above all those who, for one reason or another, arouse the greatest jealousy -is relentless and ferocious, since it seeks justification in the desire for "perfection" before God which monasticism proposes. Such perfection actually implies deprivation of pleasure, both physical and psychological, so that nothing eludes or can elude a value judgment. For example, since each nun must keep her gaze lowered, and use her sense of sight negatively so as to humiliate any curiosity, the time will come when she is caught with her eyes raised, inasmuch as she will raise them sooner or later. And if each nun must conform until she disappears as an individual into the group, sooner or later someone will be scandalized when succeeding to "recognize" her voice in the choir, for it is impossible to hold back the power of one voice when it is stronger than the others.

Moreover, competition in relation to the abbess proceeds on two levels. On one level, she painstakingly controls the justifiable exceptions to the rules that her office foresees, exceptions that cannot be established with any precise measure. The abbess's relations with the outside world, for example, are always the cause for a scandal, for the simple reason that only she is allowed to have them, and they represent the supreme sacrifice imposed on the others, such relations cannot help but become the object of harsh criticism, inasmuch as they always appear excessive. In addition, there is an attempt to be loved by the abbess in a privileged way, with a particular friendship; something no one can free herself from unless she is substituted by another. After all, in no family do the daughters love the mother: both because she is the father's wife, and because she possesses a false power, a pseudo-authority whose weakness the daughters well recognize and which, in reality, they despise. Nor can the nuns love one another as "sisters," for they are not sisters, and in no family do sisters love one another; suffice it to recall all the fables based on the hatred of the "stepsister." What is a "stepsister," if not a false sister? At any rate, the lack of blood ties that recurs constantly in fairytales as an explanation of hostility and the mortal struggle within a family is only a fragile screen placed in front of reality. Stepfathers, stepmothers, and stepsisters demonstrate, through this small, ever-present psycho-linguistic "deviation," that the unmentionable family secret is one of hate.

The falsity of relationships in a monastic group thus reaches extremes that exist in no other group except the family. Everyone "pretends," both outside and inside the family. Outside: those spiritual directors, confessors, theologians, relatives, and friends, who proclaim the happiness and perfection of the brides of Jesus. Inside: the nuns with each other, with the abbess, and with the novices, since none can reveal the failure of her marriage to the others, her falling out of love, her fatigue in the face of an unachievable romantic perfection, her hate for the silence of all the nuns about their common failure and the great lie about the divine lover. No "earthly" wife confesses that she has been betrayed by her husband because, in one way or another, she knows that this betrayal would reveal she is lacking something in order to be loved; she knows that in any case, she would be to blame. All the more so when the husband is God: the one who, by definition, never "betrays" and who, conversely, betrays at every moment, eludes all accusations, fails to keep all his vows, always chooses someone to favor — abandoning to the obscurity of routine those who are empty and worn out by the effort to "believe." Everyone "pretends," then. The mother with her daughters, from whom she cannot take away the illusion that their marriage is better than the others'; the nuns with the novices who, though hated, are nevertheless indispensable for the survival of the group. Everyone keeps the "secret" of a failed marriage, both inside and outside the convent. Moreover, what real possibility of communication subsists in a group consisting only of women? It is precisely because they themselves are the "word," an instrument of communication among men that women can never truly "speak." But when there are no men in the group, women lose even their function as "word," and their coexistence is the coexistence of "mutes" — letters of the alphabet without sound.

Thus, hate breaks out silently among women gathered together for the rest of their lives in a group which (until the advent of active nuns having a common social goal) is not a "group": women forced to "represent" themselves before each other on that stage *par excellence* which is the cloistered life. Such hate can have no other outcome than to drive representation to its highest perfection. Even the lattice window and the curtains opening on a great scenario in the parlor confirm the nun's role as a complete "actor," an actor who carries within herself and incarnates the drama of the world at its origin, when the "sacrifice" of the victim was real, concrete, and yet lay the foundations of the "spectacle": a spectacle unleashed in and by Greek tragedy in an impulse of traumatic but liberating awareness, a "rupture" of the sacred.

In the anguish of a falsity that can never be revealed, monasticism slowly lost its historicizing power for women. However, even after the 11th century, women continued to pour into the monastic and para-monastic life; and apart from those women whose fathers forced them to enter the convent as a form of life imprisonment, the value of monasticism as self-affirmation for women has continually waned, seriously threatening the mental sanity of those who have continued to believe in it and wished to practice it at any cost.

Nuns are thus forced to find symbolic motives and projections analogical to their own existence (in this sense, the cloistered nun's statement that "praying for the salvation of the world is her world" is significant and moving). The poignant, heroic force vibrating in every image and every word of the famous book, *The Story of a Soul*, resides in that tragic effort. In this perspective, Thérèse of Lisieux is the last nun. Her life clearly reflects the reasons leading to the exhaustion of a contemplation that anxiously struggles for action; of a monasticism which, in order to find achievement as evangelical reality, forces those who live it to make a heroic effort at symbolizing their lives: a continual, obsessive effort at transforming and sublimating their existence. Little Thérèse is shut up in a world in which the values of contemplation, offering, and the re-founding of time and space are now extinguished at the community level, and wholly entrusted to the individual who might give them substance. Moment by moment, day by day, she dedicates herself to discovering hidden meanings and symbols analogous to her inner life: a life rich in the desire for love, even in the pinched, arid desert of her convent. The story of a soul thus appears as a giant, mortifying effort to make use of the poverty of everyday life, by continually turning its objective meaning upside down in order to transform it into an inner reality: a private one, which can only assume value from within. Thérèse of Lisieux's intelligence and creative richness are thus exercised in an immense and tragic struggle to find realization as a woman and a person in liberty and love, despite and by way of what monastic life offers her. In a desperate attempt to actuate what she perceives as being true in the Gospel, and in order to rediscover herself as an efficacious presence, as action in the world, she cries: "I shall be the heart!" But the existential pretense, the harrowing game of a life which is true only when it recognizes itself as symbolic, can only lead her to an early death: a death which, despite her striving toward love, is desperate.

Thérèse of Lisieux represents the symbolic limit of reality, beyond which a woman cannot go. The future of women's religious life is now tied to their capacity to express themselves in the world as they creatively participate in the formation and development of new values. Women, however, are not yet ready, despite feminism and the cognitive instruments they enjoy today, to abandon the premises of Judeo-Christian values: those which have hampered the work of Jesus by rebuilding the roads of the sacred, and consequently the need for a "victim." This touches on the error and illusion of feminist theology.

Why Aren't You a Man?

As social institutions aiming to absorb non-marriageable women from the 11th century on, monasteries increasingly widened the sphere of their functions. While some orders specialized in taking in the daughters of noblemen, others slowly admitted illegitimate girls as well, who until then had not been allowed to accede to the monastic state (and this fact marks the diminishing of the "sacral" prestige of the nun). They also received girls lacking a decent dowry, who, like the illegitimate, were excluded from finding a husband. Social organization was based so inseparably on the sending of non-marriageable women to the cloistered life, that we must once again note that making religious history a "separate" history has kept us from knowing reality; it has kept society's major crime secret from the conscience of Europe.

It is impossible to know how many girls were in convents simply because they were illegitimate; both the statistical and historical research in this area are still in the early stages. Still, the number must have been enormous, since this practice lasted until 1800; not only was it extremely widespread, but it was also encouraged by the Church authorities. In his own times, Thomas of Aquinas had affirmed with absolute certainty that "A woman who has given birth to children after adultery, would be committing theft if she let them have part of the inheritance; she should strive instead to have them enter religion."[36]

In this perspective, scholars of Church history always speak of the men who were certainly victims of forced entry into the monastery as well, often as victims of the institution of oblation; that is, the father's "offering" of his children to God. Still, although the injustice was the same, we cannot make a true comparison with the suffering inflicted on women, because of the cloistered imprisonment imposed on them, and the privation of any comfort in society outside the convent. Even when men were illegitimate, they often succeeded in performing an important social role as monks, and in obtaining particular prebends from the Pope. Moreover, and this is the key fact, they could enjoy the highest degree of learning and prestige possible in society of the time.

Of the vast majority of illegitimate girls condemned to become nuns, we know nothing. However, one important name has reached us: Galileo's daughter, Virginia. Together with her sister, she was sent to the convent of the Clarisse at Arcetri, since her father had never wanted to marry Marina Gamba, the woman with whom he had lived *more uxorio* for a long period, and who had given him two daughters and a son. Though illegitimate, the son had been sent to study, and introduced to an ecclesiastical career, but the daughters, as custom dictated, had been sent into the cloistered life.[37] Having become a Sister of St. Clare with the name of Sister Maria Celeste, Virginia had an enormous love and admiration for her father. Galileo, in turn, loved his daughter deeply, yet never had the slightest doubt that his daughters might have been wronged, given the "obvious" way in which social institutions are accepted by those who live in them. Galileo went to the convent each day to visit his favorite daughter, to speak of his ailments, and, above all, of his studies: what he contemplated, meditated, understood, and calculated on starry nights. Sister Celeste, in turn, understood, meditated, and reflected in a complete exchange of intelligence that, had she been a male, would perhaps have been recognized by her father as "his own." And so it was Sister Celeste who wrote down and recopied the *Dialogue on the Two Principal Systems of the World*, who kept an archive of his correspondence, answering the letters Galileo received from all over the world. And when the terrible period of his Roman journey arrived, when he was called by the Inquisition tribunal to justify what he had declared in the *Dialogue*, Sister Celeste continually wrote to him, trying to comfort him in every way, sending him linens, sweets, and his medicine with attention and care, convincing him with the sweet pressure of one who, as the official herbalist of the convent, perhaps knew a bit more about medicine than he. But above all, she incessantly assured him that his thought and work would not die, whatever abjurations he might be forced to make by the inquisitors. Her fear was that Galileo would resist, and be tortured and killed. At the same time, the certainty that she could spare him such an end by convincing him that his discoveries would remain, reveals her extraordinary sensitivity and intelligence. The Inquisition had burned all the copies of the *Dialogue* that it could lay its hands on, and prohibited the spread of the theories contained therein both in Italy and in foreign universities, but a scientist — she continually repeated to him — must never doubt even for one moment that one of his friends or students had safely hidden away his own copy which would be passed along to friends and future scholars.

Some hundred letters written by Sister Celeste have remained, addressed to that father of whose greatness she was absolutely certain, despite the Church's condemnation, and which, according to her monastic vows, she was to believe and accept. When Galileo finally returned to Arcetri, condemned to house arrest for life and to the recital of the Penitential Psalms once a week, Sister Celeste was ready to care for him and, as far as possible, alleviate his punishment, above all, the recital of the Psalms. Who but a woman would have thought to ask the Cardinal of Florence, whose duty it was to control the execution of the sentence, to transfer this obligation to her, dispensing the condemned man from fulfilling it? The Penitential Psalms were certainly not the gravest penance imposed on Galileo; but only the intelligence and delicacy of this daughter could understand how dearly it cost him to submit to a prayer of penitence, for a scientist cannot repent, since he knows his calculations are correct.

Sister Celeste died in April 1634, at the age of only 33, a few months after her father's return from Rome; and Galileo wrote in sorrow to his friend Elia Diodati that "she was a woman of exquisite mind, singular goodness, and extremely fond of me"; and that there was no doubt that she had fallen ill and died "because of the melancholy she suffered" as a result of the Inquisition trial against him.[38]

How Florence Put Off Its Enemies

Besides being condemned to the monastic life, non-marriageable women, including the illegitimate, very often intensified one of the most ferocious aspects of the "sacredness" assigned to women. We can only briefly mention here the phenomenon of the "recluse," which would require a deep psychological and social study, but which still eludes any objective analysis, probably because it would shed too strong a light on the meaning of "victim" that has been projected onto women. In fact, we must point out that after the 11th century, and increasingly during the centuries that followed, the great majority of recluses were of the female sex. At first glance, it almost seems impossible that such a physically and psychologically terrifying life would have been taken up by women; it is even more surprising that it was not only allowed, but even exalted and supported by society. In any case, we once more find here that constant, fundamental aspect of Christianity that dates back to the earliest times: the "victim" *par excellence* is the "woman." The wish, the will to kill her is so strong that culture drives a woman in every way possible to satisfy this need by herself: something that the collectivity cannot acknowledge in a concrete, explicit manner. However, the facts prove that the group appreciates the "sacrifice"—in the technical sense of the "killing of a victim to offer the divinity"—when the woman requests to be "walled up" for the rest of her life; that is, shut up into a tiny space, at the mercy of those on the outside, on whom she depends for her food.

For she will never get out again.

When this "social" invention first began, the small room reserved for the recluse was usually contiguous to the chapel of a male monastery, which guaranteed material protection and a certain spiritual assistance, but later it was located in different and highly significant places.

In any case, above and beyond the institutionalization that society made of "reclusion," we must still delve into the question of why it was women who chose to be condemned to this type of death. In fact, at least as far as we know now, it seems that the first people to be "walled in" were two women, Marana and Cyra, to whom Theodoretus of Cyrus dedicates a chapter in his *Historia Religiosa*, written around 440. Born into a noble family in Syria (today's Aleppo), according to Theodoretus's account, the two sisters had themselves walled into a small room near the city. Instead of a door, they had a small window through which they received enough to survive on, and they spoke only to the women who came to greet them during the Easter holidays. They spent the rest of the year in total silence, partly because Cyra never uttered a word; and they made their suffering all the more painful by carrying heavy chains on their backs, and fasting for 40-day periods.[39]

Interestingly enough, we already find here a detail that was to become typical of the "recluse": the choice of settling at the entry of a city, as an "apotropaic object," defending the group from outside dangers. Often, the recluse settled on bridges as well, following the same principle of "magic" protection for the inhabitants living on the other side, in a manner analogous to the custom among many ancient populations that placed the bodies of sacrificed children at the bases of bridges.[40] In Italy, where this phenomenon was widespread, the places of reclusion were called "*carceri*" or prisons, and the imprisoned recluses were called "*carcerate*." They were often kept alive by the town from which they came, as well as by those asking for their prayers, who left donations in their wills for this purpose.

Incredible as it may seem, the walling up of women became a way of finding them "accommodation," when for social or economic reasons they could not be shut up in some monastic order. For example, many were widows, to whom the monastic order often forbade entry into a convent for the obvious motive that they could not "mix" with the virgins. Many were the illegitimate as well, or girls who did not possess a dowry or the required nobility; indeed, these impediments ceased only when the monastic state began to lose prestige.

As it typically happens in cities, the designated "walling in" places became known for these presences. In Florence, for example, the Ponte delle Grazie has remained famous, because for many centuries numerous women lived walled up in cells on the bridge pylons; only in 1500 did the municipality decide to move them to a bridge in the neighborhood of Santa Croce. In Rome, instead, there was the Contrada delle Incarcerate in the parish of Santa Maria in Traspontina. Its aim was similar: to magically protect the bridge over the Tiber River. The entry of the imprisoned woman into her cell, whose door was solemnly closed by the bishop with a lock or wall, was celebrated with a Requiem Mass and liturgical chants for the deceased; so that it was very clear that a death had occurred.

In the still fragmentary story of women recluses, the prostitute, Thais, has remained famous. Converted to a life of penance by the exhortations of the abbot Paphnunzius, she inspired one of the Dramatic Dialogues by Rosvita of Gandersheim. Another famous case is that of Wiborade, the daughter of a noble German family. In 916, she was walled up in a cell by the bishop and abbot, Salomon III, near the church of St. Magnus. Wiborade lived in the reclusery for 10 years until she was killed in 926 by the Hungarians who devastated the country. Pope Clement II canonized her as a virgin and martyr in 1047.[41]

In concluding this overview of such a terrifying phenomenon, it remains to be seen why Christianity manifested itself with such forms of annihilation and death in life, and why women, above all, were induced or forced into embracing them. Undoubtedly, society held them to be "perfect" institutions for reaching sanctity, accepting and desiring their presence. At this point we must delve into the matter of the victim's role, which was so wholeheartedly assigned to "femininity," rather than trying to hide it from our own eyes. This role inevitably finds expression in the concrete sacrifice of women. Only by understanding this role, can we also understand the profound structures of the mechanism of the "appropriation of guilt"; structures underlying and overwhelming a Christianity that has become increasingly destructive of the "human factor."

4
The Religious System of Fashion

The Irrepressible Difference of the Female Body

There exist various essays and articles, scattered throughout encyclopedias and catalogues, concerning the style of dress of consecrated persons in the various religious orders and successive congregations.[42] However, we find few reflections of an anthropological nature. Above all, these writings barely take into account how different women's experience of their bodies is from men's; nor do they take into account how different the public image of the female body is, when dressed in one way rather than another. In any case, starting from a premise that scholars usually take for granted, the design of the religious habit requires that the body be hidden as much as possible for reasons of sexual modesty; and that the dress endow the person with a special "supernatural" dignity. These premises, however, are never totally explicit. The explicit element is to indicate that the wearer of a given costume belongs to the consecrated life. Moreover, with the birth of the orders and congregations, the habit had to function as a uniform and signal the collective identity of the institution.

Silence over the sexual implications imposed by the monastic rules in nearly every detail, including dress, of course, would be surprising if it did not reflect both the obvious nature of the sexual motivation, and a more or less conscious desire not to *emphasize* the defense from sexuality; this defense is so strong and obsessive because it pertains to the decision to separate oneself from the other sex. In other words, the fundamental rules, particularly the Rule of Benedict of Norcia, adopted by a great number of institutes, or taken as a basis for successive rules, were written by men; and the force of sexuality in everything men think, feel, and do, is so obvious and conscious that it need not be illustrated.

Furthermore, the fear of the homosexual significance of the separation from the female sex has led men, we do not know to what unconscious level, to remain silent about the fundamental and truly subversive aspect of monasticism: that "family" life among men which eliminates women from their "society."

Another rather surprising element is that women have accepted the rules written by men without making virtually any change. If we did not know to what extent women have been included in the Christian model of life from the very beginning, this total acquiescence might be hard to believe. Therefore, the same regulations were adopted, even regarding the habit, since nearly all the male monastic orders were imitated by women, who formed female groups subject to the same rules (and often, with the creation of the second order, there was membership in the first one). Only with the birth of the institutes of active life, which had no male model to imitate, did customs become different from one order to the next; and indeed, totally autonomous, at least in appearance, from those of males. We must add this qualification: "in appearance," since it was often the confessors and spiritual directors who advised the founders how to dress. At any rate, even the regulations regarding habits are silent over the meaning of defense from and refusal of sexuality, which the religious life implies, and, above all, over the difference of the female body.

Despite the enormous mass of documents, statutes, minuscule regulations, precepts regarding customs, and reflections of all kinds that mark the female religious life, there is a total silence about the existence of monthly hemorrhages, and how to stem them with tampons. Perhaps it is no mere coincidence that the topic is confronted openly by that extraordinary nun, Heloise, in a letter to Abelard. Before becoming the abbot to whom her convent referred, he had been the lover she had abandoned herself to with total dedication, becoming the mother of his son. A woman, then, who had enjoyed a physical and psychological intimacy with the abbot, something no woman or nun could experience with a spiritual director. Heloise, who founded the Convent of the Paraclete according to Abelard's wish, complains, writing him her reflections concerning the Benedictine Rule and the wool tunic it required, that it was an unsuitable garment for women because it was soiled by blood. It is clear — says Heloise — that the Rule was written for men, and "it can be observed only by men. What sense is there for women in what it says regarding hoods, stockings, scapulars? What do we women care about tunics and the woolen garments meant to be worn on the naked skin if, because of menstruation, we cannot wear them at all?"[43]

Still, Heloise is wrong in thinking that "those who made up the rules for monks not only deliberately kept silent about women; they also fixed norms that they knew women could not observe." She is wrong because everything that men had conceived, organized, and achieved was in relation to themselves, and not for women. Women have never been taken as the free subjects of any culturally real action; they have only been passive objects. Christianity introduced them to the same life as men, but by inertia, and not out of any conscious or premeditated male will. Therefore, as in the case of martyrdom, women have found themselves on a par as nuns, but assigned diversity as women. When we think how much of the day in a Benedictine monastery is spent dedicated to the recital of the Divine Office — the primary aim of the monk's life, according to Benedict — we realize that women were excluded as *subjects* from this activity, since the Holy Scriptures forming its very framework consist of accounts written by men, and they project values, thoughts, feelings, and duties that are exclusively male. Women have always had to seek self-identification in these accounts analogically, but have done so without being aware of the fact, and without ever mentioning it; since both for them and for society as a whole, it was obvious that they should identify with male creations. (Were it not necessary for clarity's sake to use the adjective "male," the author would not add it, since it is obvious that both creations and actions are only male.) Heloise herself, though highly aware of the existence of an intellectual reality as such, does not realize that the wearing of a woolen tunic is a much less dramatic condemnation for women than the absolute closure of cloistered life: an imprisonment that drastically distinguishes female from male monasticism. Indeed, the Abelard to whom she turned moved with total freedom outside the monastery in order to teach, preach, study, and meet friends; but for Heloise, the cloistered life of women is so "obvious" that she is unaware of the difference: It is a disparity not prescribed in the Rule. Just as she is unaware that the Rule does not require a veil to cover her face or those of all nuns—for the simple reason that Benedict's Rule was conceived only for men.

The fact remains that the word "menstruation," pronounced with such nonchalance by Heloise, is surprising. In fact, it was a taboo word, as was the corresponding physiological reality. In Europe, this taboo lasted virtually until World War II. In Italy, for example, grotesque euphemisms were used to allude to this "embarrassment" of female life, while the generalized use of a disposable sanitary napkin was not introduced until the 1960s, together with many other practices and simple customs from America. Incredible though it may seem, European women failed to invent a device for stemming the flow of blood during the menstrual period; Denise

I. Christianity: A Religion for Women

Malmberg, a scholar of Swedish customs, tells how even up to the early 20th century one could make out the passage of women who had gone to work in the snow, by following the line of blood they left in their path.[44]

Such total passivity was induced by a society that left no initiative to women, and above all, categorized menstruation as part of a guilty destiny. In reality, women did not even invent underpants, a garment that might have helped obviate their physiological problems. Underpants only began to appear in the last centuries of the Middle Ages, as an extension of male "femoralia": a kind of trousers that monks wore only during journeys for reasons of modesty, since they habitually gathered up their tunics around the belt so as not to muddy them along the way; they were usually naked underneath the tunics. Francis of Assisi himself advocates this garment only for friars who must undergo long trips.

Referring again to the matter of the habit then: The entire female body receives and sends out messages as signs and symbols relating to sexuality. Thus, clothing is always considered in relation to sexual signs and symbols, both when it emphasizes them and when it hides them. Here, we can take only a rapid look at the most important aspects of what we might call the "religious system of fashion," expressed as a constant through innumerable variants; starting off, of course, from the simultaneous meanings linking the personal experience of the woman and that of society regarding her "dressed body." The first thing that strikes one when looking at a nun is the *impossibility of nudity*: practically everything must be covered, and covered repeatedly. In the second place, the way in which the body is covered denies, and must deny, any femininity, any feminine attractiveness, both as a sexual element and, perhaps even more, as an element of "beauty." In fact, we realize when observing the negative effects of their habits, which make all nuns appear terribly ugly, how intrinsically attractive, graceful, and beautiful every form of the female body is, and how it has been forced to take measures not to reveal the slightest part of it. If one part is covered, the eye is attracted to another part, which, given that the first has been dulled, seems to have a greater force, an extraordinary capacity for concentrating fascination. Consequently, almost nothing remains uncovered, except what is indispensable for moving and acting: the eyes, which struggle to peek out from under the veil; the hands, which struggle to emerge from the long, cavernous sleeves and half-gloves; and sometimes, the feet.

While the entire religious system of fashion is meaningful, the most important aspects regard the head and hair, which are "confronted" in the most varied and complicated ways; and the feet, whose adventures and misadventures pervade the entire history of Christianity.

The Power and Impotence of the Feet

In considering the feet, we immediately recall that as a sign of poverty and humility, the ascetics of the earliest centuries went barefoot, as did slaves and other lower-class people. Sandals were generally used only when one had to make a long journey; and this is hardly surprising since, in all countries where the climate is not exceedingly rigid, shoes were (and are) a luxury for the poor. But as early as Cassian's Rule, around the year 400, the monk's apparel had concrete and symbolic meanings. According to Cassian, monks had to wear "sandals" in order to obey the Gospel precept which, indeed, mentions only sandals as footwear. Later, early movements contesting the wealth and decadence of the church, the Waldense, in particular, would once again take up the custom of wearing sandals, thus recalling the ascetic movements of Christianity's early centuries.

Indeed, this is one of the "errors" that the Waldensians were accused of; but later, "unshoeing" became the mark of the reformed monastic orders as well, beginning with the "discalced" Carmelites. Ascetics and hermits signaled their renunciation of the "world" by divesting themselves of any garment, and going about covered only by their beards and hair, as texts narrate in a rather legendary context. Nudity has a sacral potency to which many peoples recur in particular rites. However, it is hard to believe that ascetics went completely naked (though in the early centuries the "stylites" and "aquatics" reached extreme forms, even "psychotic" ones, in their refusal of society). First of all, because the beard and the hair never reach lengths capable of covering the sexual organs; then, because of the cold which, particularly in desert areas inhabited only by hermits, is very bitter at night, and contrasts harshly with the heat of the day. At any rate, we must also take another factor into account: it is extremely rare for any people, even the most "primitive," to completely expose the sexual parts, both because they must be protected from insect bites and contact with anything that can injure them, and because of their "numinous" nature which obliges people to hide them; an obligation which, contrary to common belief, need not be attributed to modesty.

Legends concerning ascetic and penitent women like Mary of Egypt, who appear naked, covered only by their long hair, cannot be taken as true. Women's hair, though longer than men's, can hardly grow long enough to cover the pubic area. In any case, women more than men need to defend their most delicate parts. Among primitive peoples, women generally cover the pubic area with entwined leaves, held above the hips by a string, which also function as a tampon during menstrual and postnatal hemorrhages. The tales and paintings showing Mary of Egypt or Mary

94   I. Christianity: A Religion for Women

Magdalen covered only by their hair are thus products of the imagination, but this renders them all the more meaningful. First of all, because of the contradictions they reveal: On one hand, the ascetic returns to a condition preceding the fall of Adam, and is therefore no longer oppressed by modesty which, according to Genesis, is a consequence of original sin; on the other hand, male fancies regarding hair that is supposed to favor modesty by covering parts which it really cannot reach. Furthermore, punishing women by stripping them naked was one of the many ways excogitated by the male fantasy, in relation to the sexual connotation, which was (and is) unavoidable in condemning them, whatever crime they have committed. In verdicts against women martyrs, the *expositio* appeared (we earlier discussed the legend of the martyr Agnes, who, when condemned to be stripped naked in the square, was covered by her long hair). In the Middle Ages, adultery was often punished in this way as well; and of course, the famous episode of Lady Godiva, wife of the Count of Chester who, in 1104, rides on horseback through the city, covered only by her hair, was inspired by the "potency" of the link between nudity and female hair.

At any rate, the problem of women's hair is so complex that we shall need to come back to it later.

The difference between men and women is enormous in the detail of bare, sandaled feet; whether one is wearing sandals or looking at them, no analogy is possible between the sexes. Women's feet have always been an erotic object, a mark of a social condition that up to now, for women, has depended exclusively on sexual appearance. Bare feet or sandals for women slaves and for freed, poor women; luxurious shoes decorated with precious pearls for rich matrons in the late Roman period: In his *Natural History*, Pliny complains that Romans "walk on pearls." Later on, shoes had higher and higher heels; the rich Venetian women during the Renaissance were forced to lean on their maids in order to walk. And now there are a variety of shoes for different occasions, from "sports" shoes for daytime wear to modern "evening" shoes. Even today, however, with unisex fashion appearing in the West, shoe store windows still present men's and women's shoes separately.

Women's feet, then, have never been "neutral." Men have not only "looked" at them, but also forced them to "resemble" (or, as in China, concretely assume) the specific symbolic meanings assigned to them: erotic qualities, lightness, elegance, beauty, purity, transcendence. The dance of the Nymphs and Sylphs, which has inspired some of the greatest musicians and choreographers of the West, is associated with this lightness and transcendence, as is women's desperate, impossible aspiration for liberty, symbolized by the "little red shoes" (from the film *The Red Shoes*) which nonetheless bring death to the maiden who has worn them. Even the extenuating, mortal nocturnal dance meant to save the beloved, as in the famous ballet *Giselle*, reveals the link with the transcendental, with the "above," assigned to women by the male fantasy, by way of the marvelous lightness of female feet. We might note here that through the feet, the function of forming a "link" to the transcendental — and not the "transcendence per se" assigned to women — finds its opposite in the power of men's feet. Powerful men, in fact, from the Pharaoh to the Pope, make no effort to raise their feet in the air; their feet simply "do not touch the ground," since such men are carried on special chairs by their subjects. A trace of this transcendence of the powerful can still be made out today in the custom of unrolling a long red carpet at the feet of the authorities, as a sign of their "detachment" from earth, trampled only by their poor inferiors.

How then, could we possibly imagine that, in stark contrast to men, it makes no difference whether women expose their bare feet in sandals, or wear the heavy stockings and thick black shoes, ostentatiously devoid of grace, required by the religious habit? Such footwear, more than any other detail of dress, seems to signal a refusal of femininity, of any erotic attraction: whether the feet are completely covered or, instead, bare in sandals. Indeed, when they are bare, this negative message appears even more strongly, for the nudity itself then contradicts the erotic signal. Today Western women wear sandals on their bare feet with absolute nonchalance during the hot season; and in dressing their feet in some way, they emphasize the fact that it is not only the heat that leads them to show them bare. The particular care shown by women for their feet during the summer "dresses" those feet with an unnaturalness; nail polish in varied colors applied to the toenails seems to cover the feet more than the sandals themselves. In one way then, the humiliation of religious women in showing their bare feet while denying their sexual attraction at the same time, is much stronger than the humiliation felt in covering them, and it has nothing to do with the meaning of poverty which is supposed to motivate that exposition; a meaning valid only for males.

The potency of women's feet is always somewhat in contrast with the potency of men's. *His* feet have a particular potency in that they signify the possession that man has taken of the earth on assuming the erect position; his standing up on such a narrow base, at the same time dangerous and powerful, towering on high just as his potent organ towers, that unit of measurement and symbol of every power. (The thought comes to mind that the September 2001 attack on America and its highest towers also had a meaning of radical destruction.)

Ever since the human species came up with a "covering" for itself, challenging nature which had given all animals but man an encasement suitable for survival, nudity has a more potent meaning than apparel. This meaning can be used both to raise the force of the human element and to lower it. In any case, nudity is not, nor can it ever be, neutral. Countless times in history, the winners have reduced the losers to the lowest degree of humiliation ("humiliation," from the Latin *humus*, is indeed "a lowering," putting oneself on a level with the ground); the losers have been forced to strip down, go naked. Thus the Nazis made Jews take off their clothing, before shooting them; thus Mussolini's body was exposed naked in Milan; and thus the Romans—the people who most acutely perceived the dynamics of the plan of potency—condemned Christian women martyrs to the *expositio*. The sexual implication of nudity pertains to the transcendental ambivalence of everything belonging to potency. The male sexual organ is always covered because it is too "tremendous," too "numinous," to be looked upon, or seen; consequently, its nakedness signifies that it is no longer potent. The ambivalence of nudity is manifested precisely by the fact that only in its apotropaic function is the erect penis also naked, thus adding potency to potency. For example, the enemy is totally conquered when he is without a penis (it is often cut off before or after his death, and thrust into his mouth, as is done today by the Mafia — which unconsciously represents a sort of deposit of all "primary" cultural meanings in much of its behavior); or else he is totally conquered, when the penis is uncovered; that is, when it has lost all its potency, so that it can be "looked at" or "seen." Its "mystery," which is always associated with potency, is no longer a "mystery," no longer "secret."

In an oppositional system of thinking, the "savage" one so acutely described by Lévi-Strauss, the feet and the head belong to the opposing poles of meaning. Therefore the Christian man-male will keep his head "uncovered" in church because, as St. Paul says, this signifies he has regained dignity before God, he has been "saved." The Jew, instead, wears a skullcap because he bows before God. But what does "bowing" mean if not a renunciation of the most potent act, that of "erection" par excellence? Paul states that a man must keep his head uncovered before God, because, as demonstrated by so many of Paul's affirmations, he has "become" God in being *alter Christus*. Men's feet participate in the same oppositional complex, and will be covered or uncovered, shod or bare, on the basis of the meaning of potency that they assume with respect to the head. Muslims therefore keep their heads covered, but they remove their shoes when entering the mosque, because no male completely annihilates himself before God. Even the Great Priest of the Hebrew temple went barefoot when sacrificing. The Christian, on the contrary, does not take off his shoes, because he uncovers his head. Naturally, at this point, the hair and beard come to the fore; they, in turn, acquire meaning in relation to nudity or covering. The long hair and beard of the ascetics and Christian monks signify potency when assigned the meaning of nature against culture, therefore virile sexual potency, restored by baptism to the fullness of the human element that is no longer weakened by original sin. Or, as in the case of the priest, the tonsured head, whose hair is cut short only in part, signals the virile potency of the uncovered head, but at the same time, the "femininity" of the priest/bride-of-God, with its partial, circular shaving.

Extreme Despair: What Shall We Do About Hair?

It should be clear by now that female nudity and apparel assume meaning only in contrast to the male significance, to male sexual potency. The woman's head is always " covered," both before and after Christ (in Judaism, in Islam, and also in Christianity up to the modern deconsecration and liberation in the West), for the simple reason that a woman does not possess a penis. Her head therefore signifies that she is always "bowed down," devoid of "erection," low, humble, impotent, weak (the female sex is "weak" not because of its physical makeup, but because it lacks *vis*). A woman's uncovering her head is a sign of subversion, of wanting to put herself on a par with a man (the feminists in the early 20th century who bobbed their hair were considered "boyish"). Meanings associated with the woman's head can thus be correlated only with those linked to sexuality-virginity-possession, as used by males. In such a play of meaning, the hair comes to the fore, first of all. In fact, women's hair is endowed with an importance that is generally absent in men's hair: beauty. It is female beauty that Christians associate with the transcendental: i.e., with what they "visibly" imagine as transcendental. In the iconography of saints, indeed, male portraiture undergoes a kind of "sweetening" of traits which actually amounts to feminization: even in the case of those characterized, like Ignatius of Loyola, as a concentration of virility: black hair, aquiline nose, dark skin, harsh, authoritarian gaze.... Thus the religious habit, by inexorably making women ugly, loses its primary intention the aim that was to mark transcendence, so that now it is a common conviction that women "become nuns because they are ugly." At any rate, it is women's hair in particular which expresses the beauty of youth: verdant, elusive youth, and sexual attraction, that of a virgin ready to be plucked, and yet never-to-be-plucked, whose beauty is the beauty of a spring flower, fixed forever just as it "appears" as something that is promised, a hope that can never be satisfied. Therefore, the fascination and the potency of female sexuality are bound up in hair *without a head*, because the head of a woman symbolizes impotency and passivity; her head is bowed, sad, like a person destined to be possessed, destroyed, or killed. It is meaningful and, at the same time, appalling, in this perspective, to see paleolithic statues with faceless women; or rather a face which is all "hair," rather than being "covered" with hair (see, for example, the famous prehistoric Venus of Brassempouy).

It is practically impossible to review all the multiform meanings and customs surrounding hair. One thing is certain, at any rate: As part of the head and as an element that grows, hair takes on a meaning everywhere, according to the circumstances: When shaven off or cut, it signifies a lessening of potency; when let down or left to grow, an increase in potency. In the area of the sacred, cutting the hair clearly represents a deliberate diminution of potency before the divinity who is therefore recognized as being more potent than the person offering up his hair; in terms of Christian ascesis, this lessening of potency has been translated into a "penitential" custom. In Rome, those maidens chosen to become vestal virgins between six and 10 years of age were subjected to a cutting of hair, which was then hung on a sacred tree. The shaving off of hair on the occasion of marriage, whether to a man or to a divinity, is almost a cultural constant, one that scholars describe but never explain.[45] But on the basis of the charge of potency attributed to female hair, it is not difficult to imagine that the custom of shaving hair off on the wedding night, before the arrival of the bridegroom — both in the case of Jewish and Greek women — was meant to diminish the potency of virginity by way of a form of defloration, thus "magically" assuring the husband's capacity to deflower the bride.

Throughout the centuries, shaving off women's hair instead of raping them, as a sign of scornful violence, has remained an almost spontaneous gesture among males, because of its meaningful cultural implications. It is well known that during World War II soldiers of both factions punished women who, rightly or wrongly, were considered traitors, by shaving their hair off in the public square. The meaning is clear: Betrayal by a woman is always "sexual"; she is so horribly repugnant that she is not even raped, except in a form that is even more violent than true rape. (Males have always talked very little of such behavior, as they are wont to do concerning any war action that they prefer not to remember in peacetime.)

Among the Romans, again, the potency of women's hair emerges visibly during the supplications women addressed to the divinity on their knees with their hair loosened. In order to drive away harmful insects from the crops, women walked around the field three times, their hair let down and feet bare, during the menstrual cycle. (Columella's "recipe" against

The Religious System of Fashion

caterpillars in *De Agricultura*, XI, 3-64 is supposed to date back to Democritus.) And in Rome, once more, the professional weepers at a funeral wore their hair loose as a sign of desperate grief and fear of death's transcendence.

In Palestine, long, loosened hair, uncovered by any veil, marked the sexual disorder and contamination of a prostitute (a famous example in the Gospel is that of Magdalen who dries Jesus' feet with her hair). The theme of women's hair has so fascinated artists that we find Magdalen's long hair in many depictions of the crucifixion; the beauty of her hair leaps to the foreground and seems to fill it up, summing up all meanings (suffice it to recall the golden-blond hair depicted by Masaccio in his *Crucifixion*, at the Carmine church of Pisa).

Even in many representations of martyrdom, the gesture of a woman martyr, who gently gathers up her hair as she offers her neck to the executioner's sword, seems to sum up feminine grace in all its fullness, in contrast to the horrid hardness of the executioner's blade. Loosened hair, then, signifies the potent fullness of virginity at the moment when it is about to be "plucked." We can make out an attenuated form of the hair cutting before marriage in a custom that reigned in Europe for many years: Girls wear their hair loose, while married women wear theirs gathered and tied in a bun or something similar; or else the girl's head is uncovered or merely adorned with ribbons, while married women always wear a hat in public. Undoubtedly, we find here the last remaining traces of the "covered-uncovered head" issue, which has dogged us since antiquity, throughout the history of Christianity; an issue that is clearly discernible in the history of consecrated virgins. The fact that hair had become a sign that distinguished the consecration of virgins is clear, for example, in the Gangra Council's condemnation (mid-fourth century) of those women who "go so far as to exchange their women's clothing for men's garments, and cut their hair under pretext of piety."[46]

The prohibition against cutting one's hair like a nun's is found much later with the "beguines," or at least those who called themselves beguines, though not officially recognized as such by the bishops. It was forbidden for members of the monastic orders, as it was for the Waldensians, to perform rituals for women that included the shaving of the head. And yet we see that at a certain point, Francis cuts Claire's hair. In theory he was not supposed to do so, not being a priest. But what strikes us in Francis is not so much this apparent transgression, as the fact that a man so innovative in everything else, so contrary to any violence, failed to realize the terrible violence that monasticism was committing against women. Indeed, he seemed to accept it as "obvious." Not only did he himself cut Clare's hair, forgetting all his admiration for the beauty of created things, but he shut her up in the strictest form of cloistered life, quite aware — he, who had made birds' freedom a reflection of men's — that no death was crueler. Perhaps the only explanation we can find is in the fact that, like all founders of monastic orders, Francis repudiated the female sex with horror, and kept silent on the subject, like Benedict, Dominic, and so many others. In any case, his harshness toward Clare (and consequently, toward the countless women who followed her in the institution of the Sisters of St. Clare) can only have been dictated by an obsessive refusal of sex. This refusal finds, in silence and in the long persistence of the cultural unconscious, its most efficacious symbolic-concrete expression in the cutting of hair: I possess you at the very moment I refuse to possess you.

Why had this terrible custom been introduced into the consecration of virgins? By marrying God, the virgin was expected to behave toward Him as she would toward any other husband. With an extremely simple, yet pathological, form of reasoning, the bride of God was obliged to signal her belonging to a bridegroom who deflowered her perennially but never deflowered her, by keeping her head shaven for the rest of her life, and not only on the wedding night. There are groups of religious women in the East, the Melchites, who make a belt from the hair cut at the moment they take the veil, which they wear on particularly solemn occasions, such as receiving the Eucharist, or on their deathbeds. The *belt*, inasmuch as it is connected with the "waistline" or the fecund sexuality of the female pelvis, pertains to the same complex of meanings as women's hair, meanings that flow together once again at the moment of death.

Veils and Mystery

We must not abandon the topic of hair without briefly mentioning the very intricate one of the "veil." Starting with St. Paul, the problem of the veil has been so deeply felt by the men of the Church that one might think that the achievement and preservation of Christianity depended on it. The importance assumed by the *velatio* of the virgin ever since the earliest times cannot be completely attributed either to the Eastern custom that requires all women to keep their heads and faces covered, or to the Roman marriage rite during which the bride wore the *flammeum*. Intertwined though the two customs may be, we can find no explanation for the violent dispute that arose concerning the problem of covering "Christian female heads." We must note first of all that when Paul orders women to keep their heads covered in church (*First Letter to the Corinthians* 11:6), he is probably referring to an innovation introduced by Christian women who were much freer than other women of the time, both in the East and in the Roman world. Roman matrons, in fact, covered their heads with a flap of their long tunics, leaving their faces uncovered, so that the veil was not a separate garment, nor a true "veil." An abundant, transparent fabric, separate from the dress, was, however, indispensable for Eastern women who struggled to see through the long cloth hanging down to chest level. But surely, the imposition of a veil on consecrated virgins implied meanings of transcendent potency and death that went well beyond the simple coverings of head and hair. In various Roman rituals, the actor of the rite "veiled" his head with a flap of his toga (the formula *velato capite*, used by historians, hints at a certain, still-to-be-clarified ambiguity in relation to the concept of covering). The priest did the same when sacrificing to the gods according to the Roman rite (though when officiating in the Greek rite, his head was bare except for a crown of flowers); and in the *devotio*, self-immolation was performed by throwing oneself into the Tiber with the head "veiled." Similarly, Caesar, when mortally stabbed, covered his head with a flap of his tunic, as did the consul, Publius Decius, who had taken a vow for the sake of his army's victory. A woman giving birth "veiled" her head as soon as the labor pains came on.

Briefly said, the *velatio*, unlike the normal covering of the woman's head, both in the East or West, indicated a particular contact with transcendence, with the mysterious potency of the transcendental, of which death is everywhere the strongest and the most dangerous signal. Through the imposition of the veil, the consecration of virgins thus testifies to the fact that they are sacrificial victims, offered up — in the symbolic-concrete death implied by renouncing fecund sexuality — to the divinity; and that through this sacrificial death, they participate in the potency and mystery of the divinity itself. Moreover, the allusion to a potency which can hide and at the same time "reveal" itself, is already present in the "veil" of the Temple which hid the Holy of Holies from the sight of the Jews, and which probably underlay the very concept of "revelation," thus giving rise to the diversity and strength of Judaism. A revealed religion, in fact, never knows with certainty what has been "revealed" by the divinity. Like the "veil," it "hints at" and simultaneously "hides." Therefore, despite the Revelation, the "mysteries" of revealed religion subsist since, without mystery, there would be no tremendous and numinous potency superior to man. Consecrated virgins thus can do anything *but* free themselves of the "veil." It is the veil that testifies to the "mystery" of their belonging to God, so that even in the modern reformation adopted after Vatican II, the veil has remained as an absolute sign of the nuns' mysterious participation in the transcendental. Once more then, we are forced to observe that in Chris-

102   I. Christianity: A Religion for Women

tianity, women are both the symbolic image of men's relationship to God, and the concrete achievement of this image.

The "theme" of the veil and veiling pervades psychological, philosophical, and poetical reflection in the West, from Augustine to Pascal;[47] it is so dense and meaningful that we cannot even sum it up here. In any case, the task which remains to be done is to illustrate the cultural ineluctability of passage from the symbolic to the concrete: the only path capable of explaining the history of women.

Despite its importance, there never seems to have been any specific research on the "veil" as a fabric, not even to establish when the particular technique for producing it was invented, so that it is difficult to understand whether its very existence first suggested the image — and the theological concept — of revelation. Nor have scholars confronted the medical consequences for women, both physical and psychological, who are forced "never to see clearly," to see the surrounding reality only through a haze. Their experience might even lead one to deduce that this *is* women's way of perceiving and understanding, that this *is* their "world vision": uncertainty.

As an additional comment on our brief tour around the problem of the woman's head, we can point to the "masculine" will of such a famous, authoritarian visionary as St. Bridget of Sweden, who ordered her Bridgetines to wear five red arrows standing straight up on their veils. Officially these are a symbol of the Bridgetines' devotion to the Passion of Jesus; however, these surprising, distinctive little arrows seem to mark, in their erect position, a desperate attempt at subversion against the "bowed head" assigned to women.

II. The Tragic Game of Mysticism

5
Mysticism and Culture

The violence perpetrated against women by choosing a husband or convent for them lasted throughout most of European history from the time Christianity became the state religion up to the full-blossomed development of secular thought, and the weakening of family power (or rather, of the male authorities in the family, including fathers, brothers, and uncles) over the lives of daughters in the early 20th century. Telling the story of this violence is an arduous task, as it belonged to the *normal* structure of a society, in which the religious class not only was an integrated part, but a guiding one. All the aspects of monasticism we have examined up to this point, in their function of subjectively liberating women, of opening up knowledge (albeit only liturgical and devotional), of recognizing the autonomous responsibility of the person or the self; these little by little became instruments of oppression: an oppression that nonetheless is much more conscious than that of matrimony. In marriage, in fact, the woman is subject to the husband; virtually an eternal "minor" together with the children. Yet the performance of her normal sexual, procreative role not only gives her some degree of gratification, but even prevents her from considering herself oppressed despite the fact, fundamental though it is, that the many pregnancies following close on one another, the nursing, the care demanded by children and home, the frequent premature deaths in childbirth, leave her no time at all to think or look into herself.

One Sole Possibility: Marriage to God

With the first heretical movements developing after the year 1000, and then with the battles for reform and counter-reform, people begin to doubt (though with only partial awareness) the *obviousness* of a culture and social organization that is completely based on religion. Thus women can begin to realize the violence inherent in condemning them to the incarceration of cloistered life, to the deprivation of a loving sexual relationship, to the refusal of their own femininity, the violence of forcing them to embrace the symbolism of "God's bride." At any rate, at this point we already find ourselves at an early distancing from the global sacral model: Italy is at the center of the humanistic Renaissance, and secular movements of liberation from the absolute authority of the ecclesiastic hierarchy: movements attracting women, on a par with men. We shall soon find as well a face-to-face battle between Luther and the monastic vows, whose echo even reached the women closed up in monasteries, for nothing circulates with greater speed and greater force than culture.

Before and during this upheaval we find two deeply contrasting tendencies. On the one hand, some religious women attempt to work in the social environment outside the cloistered walls; they include the beguines, women adhering to the heretical Albigensians and Waldensians and, later — with pronounced success — the followers of Angela Merici and the first institutes of active life. On the other hand, within the convents we find an ever stronger codification of the nun as the bride of God, one who has fallen in love with God in a romantic Passion of fusion with the divine lover, giving rise to what will be called "mysticism": a phenomenon surely influenced by, even in symbiosis with, the secular movement of courtly love.

The new monasteries and orders that arose after the year 1000 particularly through the action of itinerant preachers were not reforms, but transformations of a religious movement that began and developed outside the monasteries as a refusal of traditional monasticism. Since this religious movement held a particular sway over women, it became necessary to channel the numerous followers of the itinerant preachers into some convent.

Two points should be strongly emphasized here. The first is the ready, attentive willingness to actuate the Gospel message in a form that corresponded more closely to the thought of Jesus, despite the deformations wrought by history. Such willingness has always been present in some groups, much more pronouncedly in women than men. It implies trust in the single person as such (giving rise to the value of equality, which put women on a par with men), the spirit of freedom of the "person," and liberation from the structures of power, be they family or ecclesiastic. Such willingness also implies the urge toward poverty as a value: an ever-present urge, for only a person who is truly poor can free himself from the ties of social power. From the beginning, women had been the most convinced advocates of this message; and they have remained so on all the occasions of renovation and "return" to the origins that have constantly emerged during the development of European Christian history.

This is the first point, then, an indispensable one for understanding what occurred later on. But there is a second aspect, in the attitude and action of women, which somehow contradicts and contrasts with the first. That is the fact of having, in greater or lesser awareness, reinforced the fundamental cultural model, even while appearing to contest it. This has been the fate of every revolution during the two thousand years of Christian Europe. For example, Luther, though meaning to transform the organization of religious society by undermining ecclesiastic power at its base, through elimination of the priesthood, the sacraments and monasticism, nonetheless renewed the tie with Judaism. He thus reproposed the dramatic logical contrast inherent in the *choosing* of a people by God, though this was transferred from the choosing of a group to the even more severe election of single individuals. The consequences were and are terrible. In addition, women were closed up more severely than ever by the walls of the cloister, as they sought self-achievement in the identity of *she who loves*— the Virgin, the victim, assigned to the "female element" by culture — deluding themselves that this was the supreme form of liberty. (Perhaps, after all, it was and is impossible to elude the base meanings of one's culture.)

The followers of Robert of Arbrissel, one of the first "prophets" to propose preaching by the poor itinerants, included a great number of women; and because they were women, Robert could not take them along on his wandering journeys, since in medieval society respectable women had to remain at home, much like cloistered nuns (Bernardine of Siena would later prohibit them even from looking out the window.)[48] Despite his rebellious spirit, Robert ended up by founding a convent at Fontevrault for women where they were subject to the most rigid kind of cloistered life. And at the moment of his conversion in 1179, i.e., of his rebellion against the exclusive theological power of the clergy, not even the merchant of Lyon, Waldus, had the slightest doubt as to how women should lead their lives. He sent his daughters into the closure of the Fontevrault convent.

People have often claimed that the women who let themselves be fascinated by preaching of the "apostolic life"— a poor, wandering kind of existence — were ignorant and poverty-stricken; but aside from what we have just observed about the presence of Waldus's daughters (Waldus being a very wealthy man), we have now found abundant proof that the new convents were crowded with rich, noble girls and widows. It seems that more than ten thousand of these were closed up in the convents at Premontré, founded by Norbert of Xanten, where they were ruled by an even stricter cloistered discipline.⁴⁹

The problem which emerged by that time and which was solved, albeit only in part, by the end of the 15th century with the first institutions of active life, was that of the incapacity and impossibility of both men and women to conceive a social life for women that did not end either in marriage or the cloistered life. In the "mixed" monasteries (so to speak: the monks lived isolated from the nuns in any case) which sprang up through the work of Robert of Arbrissel and Norbert of Xanten, the female element was preponderant (a constant phenomenon throughout Church history: even today, consecrated women are two thirds the total number of the religious). Furthermore, the presence of monks in double convents was due only to the nuns' liturgical and sacramental needs. It represented an attempt to obviate the reluctance that all male orders had always shown (and would show later on) when dealing with the female branch. An interesting phenomenon, this reluctance, both from a psychological and a social point of view: Though repeatedly pointed out by historians, it has never been studied in detail, perhaps because it arouses some embarrassment when it comes to proving the absolute self-sufficiency of an exclusively male society. But double monasteries, in which it was the abbess who theoretically governed, remained intrinsically fragile, and they were eventually dissolved. Society, organized according to male power, could not help but fracture, albeit implicitly, an institution that, to all appearances, contradicted it. Moreover, female monasteries, when not connected to a strong male order, never succeeded in sustaining development over any length of time. Yet in all the religious movements that began to evolve after 1110, with the intent of reproposing an "apostolic" life (similar to what people believed to be typical of the early Christians) through poverty and preaching the "pure" Gospel, and later through the mendicant orders and monastic reforms, the presence of women was always massive and surprising. Women's sensitivity in perceiving the deepest, most subversive aspect of Jesus' message has always been eager and keen. The fact that such a sensitivity actually served to promote and ratify the worst aspects of Christianity, as theorized by men/males, the holders of power, remains one of the most tragic historic phenomena in the life of women.

Sexuality and the Experience of the Divine

By "mysticism" we usually mean an *experience* of the divine — either an "immediate" one or one that may be fulfilled by following a gradual ascetic pathway — which should or could (the outcome is always uncertain) culminate in unity with God, a deification of the subject or, at any rate, his "salvation" for the afterlife, acquired through the liberation from "evil." In Christianity the concept of evil as guilt, as transgression against divine laws, and as sin intersects with the personification of evil in a rebel spirit or angel, Satan, so that one seeking the divine finds oneself combating not only with oneself and with the sinful desires distancing one from pure good, but also with Satan, who contends with God over possession of one's soul by tempting one, and by assailing one in one's effort to "deify" oneself. In the New Testament, with St. Paul, we find the premises of a deification which is the union with Christ: that is, with a man-God who is the bridegroom, and who dies. Therefore, nuptial sexual possession, which is possession by masculine potency "over" the bride, appears simultaneously with the annihilation brought by death, and is analogous to that of the woman's body possessed by the male. Sexual possession as death, annihilation of the one possessed, thus establishes "femininity," the womanly identification of the person — whether man or woman — who wants to belong to, unite with, merge with God. It is the male who perceives the act of sexual penetration (significantly designated as "possession") as the annihilation, death, and destruction of the one possessed; and it is therefore the male imagination that sets up the base of "femininity-annihilation-death" of anyone, male or female, who wants to be possessed by and united to God. This premise also implies the exclusion of the sex act by a person who is the "bride of God," and his/her wanting to experience death as the only possibility allowing him/her to achieve union with the divinity. In the male, in any case, the pursuit of self-destruction in merging with God is the act of supreme delirium, that of the "possessed" being (analogously to the condition of the woman who, once she is married, belongs to her husband, or rather, lives through her husband, assumes his name, becomes the container of his essence/sperm), so that the "femininity" of the male-mystic marks his "diversity": a diversity found, after St. Paul, in many other mystics.

With Paul, the message of Jesus as the "fulfillment-overcoming" of Judaism is totally overturned, that is, his message of man's salvation "down here." Moreover, there is no pathway to travel in order to "know" and "touch" the divinity, since one who is baptized already finds himself in this state: He/she is a bride (therefore woman), possessed (therefore he/she sexually belongs, is symbolically and concretely tied to the flesh of Christ), and *sees*. As Paul says in the *First Letter to the Corinthians*, he is "raised up into the third heaven." There is consequently no progression: ecstasy is already given. This fundamental point serves to understand the entire phenomenology of what is called Christian "mysticism" from the Middle Ages to the modern era, and up to the present. Many "paranormal" aspects mark mysticism (this adjective only defines the will *not* to define them, like many other allusive, deliberately confusing terms, it should be eliminated). Ecstasies, visions, voices, revelations, "stigmata," the exchanging of hearts and nuptial rings, all belong to pathological forms of consciousness that the great majority of Christians never reach, whatever their ascetic efforts may be; all the fasts, wakes, sexual abstinence, hours of prayer and meditation to which they submit themselves. However many spiritual "itineraries" have been proposed, attempted and followed: first, with the immediate, total *experience* of unification with Christ through *martyrdom*; then, gradually, with a definition and description of the spiritual "stages" of "ascesis" (images of "stairways," "mountains," and "steps" multiplying with the passage of centuries); those who pursue a psycho-physical union with God resign themselves to remaining in the condition of perpetual wanderers, pilgrims on earth, putting off the nuptial ceremony until death. Or else it is monasticism itself, as a "state of perfection" or "contemplation," which becomes a surrogate for deification; nonetheless, it does not demand ecstasies and visions, since indeed, *not* having them and *not* desiring them becomes a dutiful act of humility.

Naturally it is men/males who pose the theoretical problems implied by unification with the divinity. First of all, they ask whether the experience of the divine is "expressible," tellable, recountable: Toward the end of the fifth century, with his *De Mystica Theologia*, Denis the Areopagate set the point of departure from which this query has unraveled with its innumerable answers until today. With Bernard of Clairvaux (1093–1153) the question emerged of whether love itself, rather than intellectual reflection or meditation, led to the "wedding." Bernard was a man of his time: a time of romantic love, of the woman-as-angel: that is, "femininity," passivity in love, in union, in marriage. Once more we find ourselves facing the problem posed by Paul of Tarsus of men/males who "identify" themselves both physically and psycho-culturally with the sexually-possessed woman, the bride. This female component in male mysticism is decisive if we wish to describe and theorize it. Precisely because he knows what "possessing" is, since he has the necessary instrument, he also knows what "being possessed" is much better than one who, like the woman, is only its object. In fact, it is always the person who acts—the physician with his lancet on the patient's body, the artisan with his drill on wood—who, in controlling his action and its effects on the object, truly realizes what the object experiences, how it is modeled, how it is transformed.

To Possess and be Possessed

The male who simultaneously possesses and is possessed finds an explicit cultural current in the *dolce stil novo* which, however, has always been present in Judaism and Christianity. With one single but decisive difference: The historic pathway of the European West has experienced this psycho-cultural desire as a value[50] more intensely and consciously (which explains why the priest must remain chaste only in the West), so that after the year 1000, the movement of ideal love developed simultaneously in the "secular" world and in the religious one. The theme of love is so interchangeable between the two areas that poems dedicated to the beloved apply with hardly any variation to the Madonna as well.

But this is not all. Eminent French historians hypothesize that behind the image of the ideal woman hides a male partner in reality; this would explain why the identity of the beloved is kept "secret," a secret exalted as a necessary ingredient of courtly love. And yet, we are not so interested here in revealing a concrete homosexuality, as much as a "mental" one which, as such, inevitably implies a psychological "identification" with a "masculine femininity" on the part of the subject.[51] In the male conception, the only one that has created cultural meanings, coitus is always an aggression-appropriation, so that the woman is the object-victim — as the bride is, an object of exchange among males in any pact of alliance. According to this conception, the process of identification with the "victim" of sexual possession leads all victims to assume a "femininity," so that Jesus is perceived by those in love with him as having "feminine" traits: sweetness, meekness, non-violence, obedience to the Father until death, non-use of sexuality. Later on, we find the martyr Sebastian, who with his countless piercings, gradually became an emblem of the adolescent as an object of erotic desire, of male penetration. Finally, the great theorizers and experimenters of mystic "passivity" appear, from Bernard of Clairvaux to Phillip Neri, to John of the Cross who, in one way or another, reveal their "putting themselves in a female position" in the amorous, unifying encounter with God. For a male, to put oneself in a female position means to "be underneath," to lower oneself, humiliate oneself, let oneself be invaded.

In any case, our problem is to separate, as far as possible, the attempt to comprehend and unite oneself with the world of the transcendental by way of the so-called "mystical" itinerary sought by countless Christians of both sexes ever since the early centuries from the abnormal phenomena that arouse in the course of this itinerary in some men, but above all, in women. For once again, we must note how erroneous it is to narrate the history of women as if it were included in that of men, or as if it could be added on to male history. Whereas in martyrdom, as mentioned before, the sex of the "victim" totally changes the psychological, social and cultural meaning, the sexual identity of the "victim" in mysticism as well obliges phenomena to assume forms that in their logical coherence necessarily become different.

"Do You Love Me? How Much Do You Love Me?"

So then, starting with the early attempts at reform made by the heretical movements, female monasteries became a place, not for the liberation of women, but for perfecting their function as the brides of God. Urged on to fall madly in love with someone who is neither seen nor heard, they must demonstrate instead to themselves and the world that this bridegroom exists, and that they, His chosen ones, "reveal" what no theologian or sage of the Church could ever succeed in imagining through study or knowledge concerning his life as man and God, the world where He reigns with the angels and saints, and above all, his love for the souls that give themselves up to him. Who, then, is more potent than these women who have access to the divine secrets in a direct, immediate form; a form which cannot be reached by will or by study, since it depends exclusively on the embrace of God's unifying possession; on that "you shall become one flesh" which defines coitus? But on the other hand, how is it possible to convince the world, the powerful of the world, that this unifying belonging, these secrets "revealed" only to one who, as bride, takes part in union with the bridegroom are *real*? The need for proof leads to a multiplication of concrete "testimonies" of union, testimonies that must necessarily be "miraculous," since only as such can they demonstrate their divine origin. The "logical" mechanism underlying the phenomena of so-called "mysticism" is so elementary as to be exemplary, as is the will for power to which women cling in order to "exist." This is a tragic "game," an infinite circle, from which there is no escape: The more you want to be someone, the more you want to make positive the annihilation to which you have been condemned, the more you must annihilate yourself.

The "machine" of Kafka's penal colony could serve as an emblem of the entire history of women, but it is above all in women's union with the divine bridegroom that it finds its supreme expression.

Ecstasies, divine seizures, conversations, images, which only the extrasensory capacities of the lover, raised to the heights of the divine mouth, can perceive: the wedding ring visible only to the favored bride, the rays of light shooting out from the wounds of the God-bridegroom-

Crucified One which provoke on the hands, feet, chest, forehead of the beloved, the "stigmata" of her absolute participation, homology, and total union with the divine body, suffering an agony that is never consumed. Finally, more and more frequently, the heart becomes an object of exchange between the one and the other, so that you no longer know which of the two hearts burns more with love and Passion; nor how the lover can live without the heart of the beloved woman, and vice versa.

We shall mention this "body language" repeatedly during our journey through the extraordinary lives of some of the most famous visionary women. In any case, as soon as it starts speaking of the "body" as if it were separated from the totality of the person, our culture deceives us. (The difficulty in finding a different term for "body" is experienced daily by scholars in all the human sciences. We, too, are forced to use it.) What strikes us most dramatically here is that, despite the passing of centuries, the phenomenology accompanying these women's efforts to "resemble" what they imagine to be a perfect bride and lover of a God-Man-Crucified-King of transcendental potency, remains more or less constant and similar. Thus, the bride attempts to participate in the suffering of his Passion, to annihilate herself in the presence of His Majesty, and at the same time, to become the most intimate and privileged confidante of his divine secrets, called in a most exceptional form (indeed, for each bride, "the only one") to "reveal" these secrets to the rest of the world, which, without her — the instrument of love — would never be capable or worthy to know.

Wrapped in a mantle of prejudice concerning their recognized "sanctity," these women have eluded detection throughout history in what would otherwise have leaped into view for everyone: *they lower themselves so that they may rise* in such an ingenuous way that they arouse compassion, given the absolute injustice pervading their lives. Their inventions of love, similar to those typical of so many romantic girls, project onto the divine bridegroom emotions of adolescent love; they utter the words that all lovers have repeated an infinite number of times in order to be reassured as to the fullness and the totality of being loved in turn. In short, there is such a romantic "femininity," unsatisfied and insatiable, in everything they say and have others say, in what they do and have their God-Prince Charming do, that one might well marvel at the credulity of those who have lauded them, declaring them examples of sublime sanctity, were the praisers not those very men who have fabricated the prototype of the ideal woman who bows, adores, lives, suffers, and dies for her beloved man. This man is a God-man-male to whom men/males offer up their own women as brides, reserving them to Him; the brides become eternal prisoners, in love until death with a Him who, in reality, represents all males. That is why men cannot help but ratify and exalt what they themselves have desired and desire: to be adored, loved, served, listened to, obeyed to the point of annihilation.

The story of this tragic and terrible annihilation that has persisted through the centuries without a single voice being raised to point out its existence as one of the most coercive, pitiless cultural and social institutions ever invented and actuated, will only be rapidly sketched here. We hope to point out its most relevant, meaningful aspects. To do so we must follow the road that certain human beings have managed to trace, to dig and travel little by little in the desperate effort to elude the inescapable concreteness of their psychological and social death, once they are shut up in their concentration camps. In some ways, life imprisonment in the convent has been even more hopeless and atrocious than the Nazi extermination camps, for the women have had no "enemy" to blame for their fate; they have not been able to find a motivation, however absurd and unjust it might be, such as hate for a religion or race, to explain the *non-written* law with which their *own* society, their *own* families, their *own fathers*, foresaw their cancellation from "earthly" reality.

A Nun's Story

It was not until late in 1871 that a man/male, Giovanni Verga, a writer with an extraordinary capacity to understand the silent "non-being" experienced by women, finally described the cloistered convent in its reality as life incarceration, as death, as the mad annihilation of an innocent being who can do nothing but bow to the *obviousness* of the institution. This obviousness is such that, even in a recent edition of Verga's *Storia di una capinera* [*The Story of a Blackcap*], Giovanni Croce, the critic presenting the novel, judges it to be the pathetic fruit of the burning sentimentalism of the Romantic age, the story of disappointment in love. He is not alone in such a vision. In an essay about Arcangela Tarabotti, the famous Venetian nun of 1600, Emilio Zanette also chooses to attribute the rebellion of a nun against her destiny, a true nun this time, not one invented by a novelist's fancy, to an unhappy love story.[52] The anguish over the privation of liberty that drives Arcangela to write (the title of the text itself, *L'inferno monacale* [*The Nun's Hell*], is a demonstration of its courage): "Whoever has lost her liberty loses everything,"[53] "touches" neither the thought nor the feeling of those who listen. It does not touch them because it is expressed by a woman. These are words that would be exalted as the most sublime ones a human being can cry out to the world were they pronounced by a man/male. But a woman *must* correspond to the image that has been glued onto her once and forever: If she cries, if she shouts, if she becomes desperate, there can be no other reason but the "stupid sentimentalism" that has been built up on her person. She is thus not only a prisoner of the towering walls and iron grates whose likes have never been constructed even for those serving life imprisonment, but also of that closed circle forcing her to be in love until death with a man who, in any case, will elude her because he cannot help but elude her. Whether it is an earthly lover or a divine lover, both of them have been invented by men/males in such a way that a woman will be lost in him, annihilated.

But before we discuss the emergence of the monastic institution as life imprisonment, we must examine the long centuries that from 1100 on saw women "specialize" in their task as brides of God, in love with the Man-God-Jesus to the point of madness.

The only, or nearly only, Catholic historian who openly recognizes how deeply women have influenced the way of "feeling" and "recounting" "mystic" spirituality, the emotional relation experienced in union with God, is undoubtedly Henri Brémond, with his *Histoire littéraire du sentiment réligieux en France*.[54] Brémond's history is indeed a surprising work, in its effort to approach the female personality, its open-mindedness toward the phenomena of religious life which almost go beyond the borderline of Catholic orthodoxy, and finally, its attitude of sympathy and admiration toward the woman's world, for it is almost completely lacking in the prejudices usually shown by males and the male religious.

Brémond moves with great agility in the mine-strewn field of female mysticism, even when speaking of the most problematic centuries, those marked by the Reformation and by the decrees of the Council of Trent. His treatment of the French foundations of the Oratoire, the Ursulines, and the Descalced Carmelites, for example, is sincere and rich with sensitivity. We could perhaps say even more. Brémond refrains from condemning the decadence of the monastic institutions in its social aspect; and in particular, he refrains from condemning the decadence of women's convents. Perhaps aware of the fact that failure to observe the rule and the vows was a consequence of the monasteries' role as prisons full of innocent victims, he acknowledges some positive aspects of the reform revolution which extended the sphere of Catholic theology in the direction of an "individual" experience with God, a personal one.

In fact, this is the point of convergence between the demands for religious freedom marking the Lutheran and Calvinist movements, and those marking the movements involving the monastic "experience" of the Catholic world: so-called mysticism. It is the mystics, the empirical knowers of the divinity, those of the female sex, who arrogate the right to penetrate the intimate being of God apart from any theological teaching or official knowledge, thus liberating themselves from the control and power of the hierarchies. Women mystics even claim they possess a "knowledge" superior to the academic one of university theologians, since it is "revealed" by God himself, through his will, to those like women who are not furnished with scholastic instruments and so cannot achieve knowledge of certain truths by themselves. The more ignorant a woman is, the more her type of knowledge is "revealed": revealed in a contemplative form, through emotional and intellectual union with God. Confessors, spiritual directors, theologians, the wise, cannot interfere with this knowledge, since they do not know its "code" of communication. This is the line followed by Brémond: a very thin line, even a dangerous one, since (as he himself repeatedly admits) he is obliged to rely on his literary, aesthetic, "poetic" sensitivity in evaluating the authenticity of this inner knowledge.

Moreover, observes Brémond, the Church *knows* that a true mystic easily conforms to the role that the Church itself demands of her:

> The mystic is saintly: her "voices" preach to her, advocating renunciation more than boldness. She is a woman: therefore she knows the art of saying without saying, of gently attenuating resistance, of gaining her ends almost without appearing to do so. Ignorant or not, it does not matter; but God never chooses vulgar ones.

The little picture painted here corresponds positively to what males have always attributed negatively to women. That is, success in pursuing their aims in an indirect way, with that sort of "dissimulation" which, in all situations and in all eras, has characterized female behavior. Such dissimulation is, after all, similar to that used by whoever is a slave or a servant, whoever is inferior or a child, and therefore always forced to conceal something from his master in order for his will to be satisfied.

In other words, it seems that "femininity" goes arm in arm with mysticism, given the psychological gifts that all males "acknowledge" in women, and because, despite their exclusive contact with God, they do not put the authority and power of the Church at risk. Brémond writes again,

> Apart from the very rare cases in which the mystic immediately addresses her ecclesiastic superiors on behalf of God, as Catherine of Siena did, for example, her action only touches on those directors who are the official delegates of the Church near her [...]. Usually subject to confessors who know little about such matters, the mystic asks herself in anguish the true name of the spirit that threatens to invade her or begins to invade her (it might be the devil). Both in the family and in the convent, opinions are divided about the mystic. Like the Hebrews in the presence of Moses, some immediately pros-

trate themselves before the man who has seen God. The prudence of
the others leads them to be suspicious, and to consider the use of
showers [a therapy for hysteria] or exorcisms. But as cruel as such
agitation may become on an external level, it is only a light breeze
compared to the inner storms and moral doubts lacerating the seers.

And again:

The spiritual director at first simply represents God's envoy in the
presence of the mystic's grace, but later, once he has received the
secrets of his penitent, the director discovers himself through the
revelations that are made to him. It is she that *directs* him, dominates
him, *reigns while kneeling*.[55]

Brémond, then, is well aware of the intellectual and emotional dynamics underlying the relationship between the woman "invaded by God" and the priest representing the authority of the Church, that is, male authority as such. But though Brémond is the most open-minded of scholars in attempting to understand this relationship, he does not distance himself from the "virtuous," orthodox, Catholic judgment, on the basis of which he describes, understands, and interprets the event.

On the contrary, seen from the outside as objectively as possible, the "mystic" and her directors "represent" themselves to each other according to a previously codified script that "the woman" and the male hierarchical authority *must* follow. The woman is in any case the mediator, both with hell and heaven, a mediator who communicates with the transcendental as "woman," given her *nature*, and not out of any priestly role of power recognized by society, which pertains only to the male.

Of course, she, too, performs a role foreseen by culture, one foreseen in an *implicit* way, because it is acknowledged on the basis of the nature of her sex: Predestined as if it were biological, it explains her task both as Eve, an instrument of communication between the devil and the male, and as the Madonna, an instrument of communication between God and the male. The danger inherent in her nature is considered extreme because she is free and not codified by hierarchic power. The Church, in fact, reserves the right to judge all "mystics." Moreover, in modern times, it has tended to reduce those small fragments of authority enjoyed by abbesses and women famous for their visions during the Middle Ages, aware that, as Brémond says, "the woman is particularly subject to the special action of God that 'creates' mystics."

The eagerness to return to the Gospel of the origins and to reform the monastic institutions, which had by now become normal structures of the social organization, gave rise to various religious movements centered on wandering preachers who spoke of poverty as a value. But when women did not accept the condemnation of the Albigensians and Waldensians and faced trials and the stake together with men, they found a wholly original way to reactuate the Gospel message of love. This term, this concept, has always been ambiguous throughout the history of Christianity since sexuality and the individuation of a single object of love were not included in its meaning of *charitas*; whereas in reference to the theme of courtly love, its meaning is identical in the sacred and profane areas.

The bride of Jesus becomes the most passionate of lovers, uniting with him almost to the point of detaching herself from earth; she speaks to him, sees him, hears him, and is loved in return, in a concrete, ardent exchange of "hearts" which even the most passionate of earthly lovers can achieve only in an imaginary form. Female monasteries thus became places of extraordinary adventure where heaven seemed very near and God within easy reach; the limits of the senses were annulled and the borderline between the human and the transcendental destroyed forever. "Mysticism," indeed, is none other than a falling in love, in which the union must seemingly be so total as to place the body between parentheses. In coitus, the individual learns above all to become aware of his own body, of the borderline limiting his body at the very moment he tends to cross it. On the contrary, in the union with God, this limit is annihilated. One who tries to transcend oneself in a reality surpassing the self finds nothing but oneself. He or she can never find anyone else in the illusion of going beyond the self. And indeed, in the end, the woman mystic is forced to return brutally to her body, in order to have something to say to herself and to others.

The contents of what she "brings back" to men as knowledge of the transcendental, is extremely poor, both from an intellectual and an emotional viewpoint, since it fails to *create*. For the woman abandons herself to a self who, because it declares it wants to empty itself in order to fill its self with the other, cannot create. The woman mystic's attitude here is the opposite of that of the artist and the scientist, in the global meaning of the terms. The genius, be he an artist or scientist, makes a supreme effort to understand reality and the continuous interaction between what lies within man and without in a tension of "asking" and "understanding" that always involves re-elaboration and growth: the maximum "principle of reality" that is also included in invention and the creative fantasy of poetry. In other words: absolute trust in man. With "mysticism," instead, we find ourselves face to face with a phenomenon that has accompanied the history of women beginning with our earliest efforts to follow their traces: Women create nothing, invent nothing; not even in their extraordinary experience of the divine and mysticism where they so greatly outnumber men. Society has never expected anything creative from them; therefore they have no self-confidence, not even in the things they have always done: tending the sick, caring for children and women giving birth, bringing up and educating the girls in their institutions. We find the same void when speaking of women held to be "heroines." Heroines, yes, that's it: those who have not silently bowed down to their destiny as lifelong prisoners, as the living dead; who, just in order to feel alive, have absolutized their role as lovers of God, running with all their might toward annihilation. They have exalted the ideals fixed for them by society and by male power to the highest degree and so, quite justly, have been declared "saints," which means "heroes." Like all heroes, they have served the fundamental values of society and culture, without the slightest doubt, reconfirming the validity of those values, and thus rebuilding the towering walls closing in the female image. And together with it, all women.

Socially and psychologically, in the amorous relation with Jesus, Man-God-Bridegroom, women find themselves in a more "realistic" condition than men, because the sexualized or male-female individuation is the "normal" one, even though it is transferred to God, and the role of the bride of God is assigned and recognized by the collectivity as a social status. And yet, because of this, because they are walking down a "normal" pathway to all appearances, the nuptial one, it is women who reach limits that inevitably appear as abnormal and pathological once they have crossed the borderline of the symbolic to reach the concrete.

A mine-strewn field extends before us now, that of the relation between personality and culture. Even more perilous, perhaps, is the matter of the relation between divine love — being in love with the divinity — and madness. We are not called upon to reduce such a complex whole to the level of pathology. As notes Alfred Kroeber in *The Nature of Culture*,[56] the global cultural pattern, and single levels of analysis, even while presenting some temporary usefulness, must always be readmitted into the total "process." In this process, consecrated women given over to the concreteness of their "belonging" to the divine bridegroom, confirmed the pathological aspects of the male imagination which, through the invention of cloistered life, had achieved the symbolic-concrete goals inspiring the offering up of one's women to God. In conforming to these, some women have doubled their pathological aspects. There has thus been a passage from the concrete-symbolic reality of the cloistered wedding to the concrete-real one of ecstasy, with the exchange of hearts, wedding rings, piercings, penetration by fire, unifying stigmata, and divine "rapture." From the Latin *raptus*, this term has always indicated the violent appropriation of a women for sexual purposes.

6
A Custom-Made Lover: God

Though no proper statistics have been made on the matter, it is clearly women who excel in visions, ecstasies, raptures, exchanges of the heart, stigmata, and who become the heralds of messages from Jesus, the Madonna, angels or saints. We need only make a superficial list in order to demonstrate the overwhelmingly female presence in the history of ecstatic phenomena. During the cruel suffering inflicted on them, the early women martyrs found consolation in celestial visions and in the visitation of angels. We find it hard to doubt a testimony like that of the *Passion* of Perpetua, in which the martyr herself recounts her visionary dream. One remains perplexed, however, at the abundant visions and similarities described in so many hagiographic legends. At any rate, we must not forget that legends are passed down and repeated in the course of centuries merging with the cultural material in which the women are immersed, material that often stimulates them to follow a certain direction. Surely, the frequent pictorial representations of a tranquil but blood-curdling realism, of the tortures and deaths inflicted on martyrs like Agnes or Cecilia, to whom the Christian West was extremely devoted, led people to believe that an "absence" and "detachment" from the surrounding world similar to truly ecstatic experiences was possible, like those illustrated in the scenes of martyrdom. Nevertheless, after the year 1000, it was the emergence of the love theme, and of women as lovers-brides of God, that sparked the growing explosion of female ecstasies and visions.

Some of these women lived during the same period and were friends, such as Elizabeth of Schonau and Hildegard of Bingen. They certainly must have influenced one another, not only because an era of real "mass communication" had sprung up in which a striking abundance of information circulated,[57] but also because nothing is more contagious than the methods used to draw out the transcendent. Because, as Franz Boas notes, invention in this field is difficult and rare, but at the same time, men desire nothing more intensely than to communicate with otherworldly powers; learning possible techniques and suitable attitudes is something one does very quickly, in a way that hardly varies at all from culture to culture or religion to religion.[58]

Why Women?

The long procession of the names of women who had extraordinary visionary experiences is thus not surprising. We shall stop to consider several cases in particular to demonstrate how much certain biographies resemble one another, and even more, the similarity of these women's "experiences" of the divinity, above and beyond the historical context.

Were we to use a computer to analyze the contents of the visionary accounts given by most of the women "mystics," we would know for certain what an approximate glance already leads us to perceive. The accounts say nothing and "reveal" nothing. They narrate what is already well known and absorbed through the connective tissue of explicit and implicit information furnished by the culture in which they live: sermons by priests or itinerant friars, prayers and liturgical passages, tales from the lives of the saints even in their most clearly imaginary aspects, church iconography as presented in paintings and sculptures, popular legends, pious and edifying readings. Because this material is experienced on an hallucinatory level of ecstasy, it lacks any critical re-elaboration, and thus can provide us with reliable information concerning the standard concepts and judgments of the society.

Hildegard of Bingen, for example "sees" the cosmos as an egg with an earthy globe in the center, inert and squeezed by elements in contrast with one another, water, fire, air.[59]

At the height of the black plague, in 1348, Marguerite Ebner "received confirmation from God that the Jews were to blame."[60] The béguine, Marie de Oignies, not only advises and urges her spiritual director, Jacques de Vitry, to preach in favor of the crusade against the Albigensians, but in her visions "she sees descending from the sky a multitude of crosses upon those who go off to fight against the heretics."[61]

Again, such data could easily be classified by computer, as is done in all scientific and literary fields today. But who could have any interest in destroying, or at least reconsidering, what is considered a kind of patrimony, not only by believers, but literary historians as well? Moreover, the banality of the contents in visions is a logical consequence of that scarce capacity for invention and intellectual reflection marking women who, unable to leave the prison, "chose" to make it become a supreme "liberty."

If this were not true, we would find that assertive, liberating divergence that prevents artists from losing contact with reality, and permits them to re-elaborate the fantastic material of religion by developing its irrational aspects symbolically. In other words, because the artist *gives reality* to the delirious element in art, making it reach, through the filter of his sensitivity, a beauty which only man can perceive and draw out, he does not "dispossess" himself in the artistic work but, on the contrary, recognizes and confirms himself in it. That is why the artist, in using the symbolic code, can never fall into psychosis, for psychosis, as far as we are able to define it, can be taken to mean the passage from the imaginary and symbolic to the concrete and real (or what is believed to be real, as in hallucinations).

The terrible "penances" inflicted upon nearly all the women mystics whose lives we know, can also be seen as a psychotic passage from "penitence," preached in the Gospel as spiritual and moral conversion, to the concrete, almost destructive frustration of the body.

In reality, the borderline between the symbolic and the concrete is often unstable; and, particularly in Christian-Catholic culture, it is difficult to fix a norm defining it, since the "symbolic-concrete" hallucination is institutionally foreseen, not only as possible, but indeed, as certain, true, guaranteed by dogma.

If we consider, for example, the sacrament of the Eucharist, tracing the event of the host which bleeds, we note that once the first step has been taken (the bread and wine are *really* the body and blood of Christ sacrificed on the cross), it is easy to take the second step: I see blood dripping from the communion wafer.

As it did in the Bolsena, the Church confirms that this is a true miracle, that the host really did bleed, and women do nothing but follow the Church in this direction.[62] In fact, it is women above all, the "mystics," who concretize the theological truths with their visions, who see blood gushing from the wounds of Jesus, who drink it from his side. It is they, women, who intensify the desire for frequent communion (some to the point of believing they can live on that alone), driving the Church to ratify its need as "grace." Aside from the numerous cases recalled in the biographies of the "saints," we find one pertaining to the 19th century in Italy, exceptional in that it regards a lay woman, Maria Domenica Lazzeri, who according to a physician, lived for 14 years without ever partaking of food or drink, except in weekly communion.[63]

A Custom-Made Lover: God 123

Again, the question emerges: why women? No answer is sufficient to fully explain the ease with which women predominate, thought-wise and experience-wise, on the level of imaginary concreteness. This is perhaps why religious women have not succeeded in creating anything, even though they have employed nearly every hour of their lives in repeating and participating in religious themes. Even when she has written or voiced her feelings, or her emotions in the "mystic" experience, not even the most impassioned woman mystic has been capable of suggesting anything but very poor images, if by "poor" we understand the *immediate* reference of the fantasy of one's inner life to the concreteness of one's physicality. This concreteness appears conscious only because women desperately want to describe it to others, to make others believe in it. But not even the worst baroque painter, not even the most pallid imitator of Proust, has managed to do better.

Very few women have been recorded by history, among the millions and millions who, down through the centuries, lived a cloistered life of "contemplation." Those who have remained in history are there because the Church removed them from anonymity by declaring them "saints," and proposed them for the group's admiration. If there had not been, and if there were not this prejudice, all those who in one way or another have met up with such figures would easily have seen the "void," the "nothingness" of which they are bearers. But the Church has declared them to be "saints" because they were "women" above all, in accordance with the idea that men, both laymen and ecclesiastics, have always had of the insufficiency of female "greatness." After all, it was they who theorized and inculcated the idea of such scarcity. Innumerable men and women have remained trapped in this vicious circle; even today they dedicate countless words to magnifying the elementary fantasies of "wedding rings," "wounded hearts," and "divine knowledge," to which these prisoners of non-thinking and non-knowing have been condemned. After all, the Church itself declares and confirms this at its canonization hearings. As regards the "true" mystic recognized as such by the sages of the Church, nothing of what a "mystic" says or reveals can contrast with what the Church already explicitly knows or what it is already able to implicitly know.

These great "geniuses" then, are, by definition, not geniuses, since they ask nothing, they discover nothing, they create nothing and invent nothing in the technical sense of *invenire*. That God to whom they attribute their own "knowledge" through visions, ecstasy, rapture, voices, does not actually *reveal* anything to them, for He is a God whom the Church has defined as consigned to its power and knowledge, inculcating "faith" as the supreme virtue. Only this faith nourishes women, even, or more correctly, *particularly* when they think they are distancing themselves from it.

I do not know whether we can claim that religious women who have experienced ecstasies and visions are practically the only ones occupying a place in the history of consecrated women, given the fact that they wrote about their experiences or recounted them in such a way that others could record them. Certainly, the link between "canonized sanctity-ecstasy-narration-writings" appears with striking frequency. We have already encountered Hildegard of Bingen. Though her writings are not restricted to the story of her visions, she certainly drew from her mystic experience the psychological confidence necessary to confront topics usually excluded from women's knowledge, not to mention the assertive demeanor (can we say "masculine"?) with which she addresses her readers. In any case, the list of saints who are visionary writers is not only long, but also extraordinarily characterized by a consonance of themes, images, and emotions, linking them down through the centuries and through varying historical contexts. Many of them knew no other life than the monastic one, since they were placed in the convent as little girls, sometimes as pupils in preparation for future marriage, sometimes as future nuns. (Earlier, we noted this aspect, common to many mystics, surely a determining factor for their future as the extraordinary lovers of God.) This means, among other things, that they have had no relationship of any kind, either physical or mental, with men. Their confessors and spiritual directors, the only persons of the male sex with whom they communicate at all, are, however, a peculiar type of men, for whatever their social, psychological or economic motivation may be, they have refused sexuality and with it the female reality.

Excluded from the Marriage Market

Elizabeth of Schonau, one of the most famous visionaries, was born in 1129, probably in Bonn, of a noble family. According to the custom of the time, she was shut up in early childhood in the Benedictine monastery of Schonau, not far from her city. She never emerged from behind these walls again. It is useless to wonder about her will in the matter, since the monastic life was almost more obvious for noble girls than the matrimonial one; in any case, it was always established by the father. If anything, it is her long and frequent ecstasies, whose visionary content she describes in her writings, that enables one to understand her silent rebellion and her attempt to give personal meaning to her imposed condition of bride of God, as if it were a matter of choice. Her ecstasies began several years after she took her vows (at the age of 18 in accordance with Benedictine cus-

A Custom-Made Lover: God 125

tom), and after suddenly being cured of a serious illness. The event of illness at a significant moment is a common phenomenon in the biographies of "mystics"; it clearly marks the appearance of a decisive crisis in the face of one's fate. We find it, in fact — to name some examples at random — in Hildegard, Gertrude of Helfta, Frances of Rome, Teresa of Avila, and many, many others. A global comparison would prove intriguing.

Elizabeth's manuscripts were turned over to her brother Egbert, a monk, and later the abbot of the nearby male monastery. As was natural, given the uncontestable superiority of the monks' culture and their authority in judgment, Egbert took on the task of correcting the literary form, and often the contents as well. In 1157, at the age of 28, Elizabeth was chosen as "magistra," that is, the direct superior of the nuns, who were not entitled to being governed by an abbess (as was normally the case in Benedictine convents) because the Schonau monastery was a "double" one and thus depended on the abbot of the male sector. True, historians often claim that in double monasteries it was the abbess who wielded power; but in reality, this was hardly ever the case or else it was only a formality.

Liturgical texts were almost the only source of Elizabeth's thought, as in the case of any other nun at the time, both in compliance with one of the precepts of the Rule of St. Benedict, and because it would have been difficult for her as a woman to accede to other readings. Thus her visions almost always occurred during the choral recital of the Office, during Mass, on Sundays and other festive days. Her visions yield no other teachings than the well-known, obvious ones dictated by the theological theories of the time which circulated in the convents and were inculcated by confessors and preachers. For Elizabeth, as for all men of the penitential culture, the ascetic life was a "way"; life itself was a path leading to experience of the divinity. The person who has purified his heart of all uncleanness, who walks toward God, will be "filled with divine light"; he will be similar to the angels in the contemplation of God's essence. The image of "light" dominating Western European culture in all its manifestations from the year 1000 onward, with the stained-glass windows in Gothic cathedrals, the first spectacles using glass, with the rejection and taboo of the blind, who were considered incapable of salvation because they were incapable of "seeing God," is also the only image enabling all visionary women to somehow describe what they believe they have seen. But there is clearly no need for personal "revelations" in order to speak in terms of "light" in a culture where light is the fundamental theme underlying the construction of all values.

Moreover, theology itself claims that the beatitude of Paradise will be "seeing God"; thus ecstatic women signal the fact that they are already "holy" with their visions, and are admitted to the life of the blessed from their earthly life. Their more or less conscious will to affirm themselves as "winners" in the eyes of those who have predestined them to union with God, is elementary, moving and, at the same time, frightening. It would be interesting to verify both on a neuro-cerebral level of consciousness and on the phenomenological level of their biographies, whether the choice between a hallucinatory "seeing" or "hearing" (as would appear from even a general analysis) corresponds to a voluntary, if unconscious, aptitude for acting in a more or less "passive" way. When a "voice" is heard, the premise is given for "acting," much more than occurs in the case of seeing. The light-oriented theology of the beatified life does not presuppose any activity, since the blessed "enjoys" God fully, and nothing is lacking in this fullness. At any rate, a qualitative difference of the senses appears here which is cultural as well as biological. The human species has placed vision over all the other senses; consequently, it has projected this specialization onto the supreme cultural value: God, and life with God.

As always, we discover nothing from the visions of our "mystics," we learn nothing. Elizabeth, though, like all religious women possessing ecstatic capacities, adopted the force and authority drawn from her exceptional relationship with God, to influence, and severely admonish bishops, abbots and other powerful men whom she held responsible for the problems for the Church. Her story is related in the *Liber revelationum de sacro exercitu Virginum Cononiensium*, the umpteenth fantasy on the legend of the eleven thousand virgins of St. Ursula, which if anything, confirms that she knew nothing of the event which went beyond or differed from the absolutely absurd body of beliefs circulating in the cultural knowledge of her time, reflected in *De resurrectione Beatae Virginis Mariae*, the *Liber viarum Dei* and the *Libri tres visionum*.[64]

What we have said about Elizabeth of Schonau could be repeated concerning many other women who, imprisoned in a convent from a very young age (often at four or five years), traveled along the path of marriage to a man-God. This "way" was assigned by society as a "condition," with the same, normal certainty dictating that male sons were born to occupy the social status or profession of the father. In reading today the writings of "experts in mysticism" of both sexes from the 12th to the 19th century, we become aware that such writings pertained to an "official," "specialized" field, and wholly corresponded to a given social status, more or less like medical texts for doctors or law texts for jurists. True, there are sporadic cases today as in the past of people living an intense kind of religiosity as laymen, outside of the organizational structures predisposed for a contemplative life; for example, the famous Marthe Robin, who died in

1981, is said to have nourished herself only on the Eucharist[65]; but these are always exceptions. The monastic state of the bride of God is one of the bases on which European society, from the Middle Ages on, has constructed an organization for the absorption of marriageable females, who became more and more numerous because of various factors. The population increase in Europe after the year 1000 led to a greater numerical disparity between the sexes, since neonatal mortality (at least according to today's statistical averages) is higher among males. The male-female ratio was also influenced by the Church's increasingly rigid, intolerant exclusion of ecclesiastics from marriage, ecclesiastics then forming a very numerous group; finally, the secular arm began to exercise a severe repression of abortion and female infanticide; whereas these means had always been used in Europe (as they are today in African and Asian countries) to reduce the number of females.

Naturally, everything possible has been done to find a compelling spiritual significance in the deportation of daughters not placeable on the marriage market to special jails; this spiritual significance has responded to and reinforced the logic of the entire cultural model based on sacral structures. In the *Acta Sanctorum* we even find tales describing the obstinate wills of little girls who want to become nuns at any price; such accounts represent an absurd attempt to prove that there was no imposition, only holy aspiration. No one has ever found much to criticize in these tales. Agnes of Bavaria, the daughter of Emperor Ludwig IV, was led at the age of *four*, together with nine other little daughters of nobles, to the convent of the Sisters of St. Claire in Munich. To oppose those who wanted to take her back to the world of the court, she is said to have clung weeping to the tabernacle. Wounds appeared on her hands, feet, and side that were considered "stigmata" (this is 1350, when the "fashion" of stigmata had full sway), so that her will was respected in the end, and Agnes died surrounded by the fame of sainthood, at the age of *seven*.

Many such cases can be recalled, since the monastic imprisonment of women is considered normal, and accepted as a wholly voluntary religious choice. The fact is that a society always creates points of balance for its survival; where it was impossible to think of women except as "wives," and earthly matrimony had to be discouraged in order maintain an orderly status quo, marriage to God became an instrument functional to the scarcity of earthly husbands. Furthermore, the urging of widows not to remarry gradually became increasingly pressing, so that it was perfectly logical culturally to establish that widowhood was a greater state of perfection than matrimony. This "perfection" is meticulously quantified at 60 percent, against the 30 percent assigned to married women (as claimed with absolute certainty by popular preachers, including St. Bernardine of Siena).[66]

Widows, in fact, were numerous in times of war, of crusades, of continuous local battles, of great danger for traveling merchants, and when there was an enormous difference in age between elderly husbands and child brides; and so they too overburdened the shrunken marriage market and the distribution of family patrimonies. It thus became a "saintly custom" for widows to shut themselves up in convents as well, where they could calmly prepare for an early death: a psychological, social one, before physical death befell them. However, no one thought to ask (and the Church still does not, since it rarely tends to look at its own history) why this type of "perfection" was not applicable to widowers as well, since it was considered obvious that the social organization in heaven corresponded to that on earth. From antiquity, "widowhood" as a state of loss only implied a female condition. Moreover, we have already seen that from the earliest centuries, the Church welcomed widows to its ranks by way of a particular consecration, considering them in some way dead to the world after their husbands' deaths, even though it did not expect them to be physically buried along with them.

At any rate, the parade of women endowed with prodigious visions, with exceptional eucharistic devotion, with physical participation in the Passion of the Crucifix, and those who become "writers" exclusively in order to leave a testimony of their extraordinary experiences, continued uninterruptedly from the 12th to the 19th century. We can trace here only a thin thread that allows us to observe not only the particularly symptomatic analogies in their psychological stages, but also those analogies which society, in a perfect feedback mechanism, constructed for them, with them, through them, and upon them; so much so that their presence has ended up constituting much of the history of the Church, of devotion, of popular beliefs and of the "values" pertaining to women. A simple list of these analogical stages is, in itself, overwhelming. It includes fasts, wakes, crowns of thorns, wounds on the hands, feet, and chest, sometimes visible, sometimes invisible, but always terribly painful; wedding rings, exchanges of hearts with Jesus, ecstasies and raptures lasting for days at a time, encounters with angels, with saints, with Our Lady, revelations of the most intimate thoughts and plans of the divinity; miracles; the emanation of perfumed aromas and extraordinary luminosity from their bodies both when alive and after death; cadavers uncorrupted after centuries which release therapeutic oils and "mannas."

Though some of these phenomena are found in male biographies as well, they characterize female ones with absolute predominance. To establish whether they are the inventions or illusions of those who lived through them and described them has little importance here; what matters is the continual interchange between and among expectations, social "values" and the construction of the individual life. Suffice it to consider, for example, the associative chains forming virginity-purity-flower-perfume-incontamination-light-incorruptibilty: How can we not help but notice that these characteristics are attributed by society to "femininity" in a valence which is simultaneously physical and moral?

The uncorrupted cadaver is thus an almost exclusive element in the history of female canonization. The *Acta Sanctorum* never fails to refer to it, even though it is never explicitly assigned a miraculous meaning as confirmation of purity, and so of sanctity. A random list of uncorrupted bodies includes those of Margaret of Cortona, followed by Rita of Cascia, Elizabeth, Queen of Portugal, Catherine of Genoa, Catherine de' Ricci, Gemma the virgin-recluse, Catherine of Bologna, Teresa of Avila, Laura Mignani, Bernadette Soubirous, Maria de Jesus Lopez Rivas, Anna Maria Redi, Beatrix I and Beatrix II of Este (I shall stop here because a systematic study seems never to have been undertaken); all of them "mystic" figures. This, of course, corresponds to the idea of "surphysicality": participation of the "flesh" in the celestial non-contamination of the soul.

Who "Invented" Stigmata?

In any case, if we go on to the other characteristic traits among those listed, we shall find that it is nearly always women who, in one way or another, have to do with the "heart." Devotion to the Sacred Heart is an almost exclusively female chapter of Catholicism, so long and complex that we can point out here only its most relevant traces. The problem of devotion to the Heart of Jesus, propagated from as early as the 13th century by nuns and women mystics, is nearly always connected to that of the stigmata and the "wounds in the ribs."[67]

The problem is very simple: The rib wound caused by the spear thrown at the crucified Jesus *must* be on the right, otherwise, it would have fatally pierced his heart, and the Messiah's death had to be due to suffering on the cross. Instead of breaking the legs of the crucified man in order to assure his death, as was usually done, the soldiers threw a spear at his side. In the early 13th century, Bishop Luc de Tuy considered the opinion of those who thought Jesus had been pierced by the spear on the left instead of the right as heretical, and something to fight against. Through Francis, said the bishop, God wanted to re-establish the truth, since Francis's dead body resembled that of one deposed from the cross, and bore a wound on the right side.

For the lovers of the Passion, instead, the wound and the opening in the side coincide, because what counts is the heart: the heart as the source of love; so that not only is the heart visible, but it is easily movable in the exchange between Jesus' heart and that of his favored brides. All the "devotions" centered on the love of the divine heart, pierced for the sake of man, thus associate the wound in the side with the heart; and therefore, the "stigmata" imply the wound in the side lying on the left.

In her study, *Francesco e l'invenzione delle stimmate*, Chiara Frugoni traces the iconographic development of St. Francis's stigmata, demonstrating that the wound in the saint's chest shifts from right to left, just as the "rays" striking the body of the saint, starting from the body of the crucified Jesus or the crucified cherub that is said to have appeared to Francis in a dream or vision, follow an inclination from right to left. Stigmatization by means of burning rays of light persists then in nearly all the tales of ecstatic women, confirming the fact that it is difficult to invent anything new, once an imaginative path has been established.

At any rate, as far as our "lovers" of the Passion are concerned, the wound always lies on the left. They drink the sweet liqueur-blood oozing out of it, they kiss the heart appearing from it, they sweetly lean their heads there. On the left, then, upon their own heart, a wound takes shape; the name of Jesus appears there, as do the symbols of the Passion, all deliberately imprinted by knife or fire (Marie d'Oignies and Frances of Rome, for example), or miraculously found inscribed on them after their death.

Marie d'Oignies, a Belgian beguine, became famous thanks to her exceptional biographer, Cardinal Jacques de Vitry, who had been her confessor and spiritual director. She so closely identified with the suffering of the Passion that she wounded her hands and feet with a knife, in order to suffer the same pain as the Crucified One. Her case is considered significant because it preceded that of St. Francis; consequently Francis's stigmata do not really possess that "uniqueness" and "priority" that were supposed to make him the "second Christ" par excellence.

In any case, remaining within our area of inquiry, two fundamental points remain difficult to clarify. The first: It seems probable that the passage from the symbolic to the concrete, i.e. the creation of wounds similar to those of Jesus in order to suffer like him, is a "female" idea, signaling that crossing of the borderline between normality and psychosis which is manifest in so many cases. Since the *Vita prima*, on the life of St. Francis, was written by Tommaso da Celano after the death of Marie d'Oignies (published by Jacques de Vitry in 1215, whereas Francis died during the night of October 3, 1226), some say that Brother Elia drew the idea of the "stigmata" from the biography of the Flemish beguine. But the central problem regarding Francis's "stigmata," which has deeply influenced the entire history which followed, is the "miraculous" nature of these wounds; that is, his having received them directly (during an ecstatic vision) from the wounds of the crucified Jesus. In other words: To deliberately carve wounds on one's body similar to those of the Crucified One is a "psychotic" gesture, though easily conceivable by a person who totally identifies with the suffering of the Passion, especially if she is a woman. Regarding St. Francis, instead, the question is quite different. No matter whether there were truly "stigmata" on his body or only wounds caused by his illnesses, it is certain that Francis's mentality and evangelical feeling were not consistent with his wounding himself deliberately. A similar gesture, in fact, presupposes an aggression against oneself, a will to self-destruction, which is alien to his entire behavior. Even in "poverty," the central point of his view of the Gospel, Francis urges his followers to accept what is offered to them; for instance, to eat meat on days of abstinence if meat is set before them.

For Francis, being poor is above all "not choosing" what one prefers, but accepting the condition assigned by God in total tranquility of spirit, in the certainty that it is somehow "beautiful." When we consider what was "right" during his time, it was virtually unthinkable that one could fail to observe abstinence from meat in order to accept anything coming from God. Furthermore, if we are to give just recognition to Francis's decision to take the Gospel among the enemies of Christ exclusively by way of the word and without weapons—whereas this, too, was unthinkable in a world convinced of the "holiness" of the crusade—then we surely cannot believe that he exercised similar physical violence against himself. (In the *Regula non bullata*, in fact, he still exhorts men to convert the infidels in a peaceful way.)

Well then: Were there or were there not stigmata on his body? And how did Brother Elia succeed in imagining, or rather "inventing"—if invention was involved—the fact that wounds similar to those of the Crucified One could be presented as a miracle signaling Francis as the only second Christ, if he took the idea from Marie d'Oignies's deliberately self-inflicted wounds?

Apparently, in England there had been a few other cases of this kind; it seems that the Church had even condemned to death those who had wounded themselves on purpose, because no one should ever attempt to resemble Christ. Saving oneself by the effusion of one's own blood was widespread culturally from 1200 until the end of the 15th century. It is reflected in the institution of the "flagellants," which the Church forbade once people began to look on flagellation as a new type of baptism, a baptism by blood that made the one by water superfluous.[68]

The dilemma of passage from the symbolic to the concrete, as exemplified in "washing oneself with blood" instead of water, has always been present in the history of Christianity because it is central to the cultural structure of "sacrifice." Two essential factors are implicit in "sacrifice." First, the *victim's* desire to be a victim and his acceptance of death; a death, however, that cannot and must not be self-inflicted, for this would eliminate the other essential factor, the *sacrificer*. Whether he is a priest, infidel, or enemy, he represents God; God, as the "giver of death." Suicide is condemned by the Church for the same reason that it is often exalted in other societies, both ancient and modern: It represents absolute dominion over one's self and one's body and negates God's power, the power of death.

"Martyrdom" constitutes the supreme form of "faith" because the martyr is one who *recognizes and testifies* that God exists as the giver of death, by accepting a death inflicted on him. Therefore a Christian must desire death to the extreme limit, as our women "mystics" do; but he must not perform the gesture of killing himself. Francis, instead, more or less consciously refused the sacrificial structure, as we can see in his refusal to become a "priest"; that is, a "sacrificer." Though his renunciation of priesthood is presented merely as an act of humility, we must also remember that being a "priest," a sacrificer of Christ during the Mass, was incompatible with the personality of Francis.

The distance, indeed the psychological, but even more, the conceptual leap between the pathological banality of wounding oneself in order to suffer like Jesus, and, conversely, imagining that the wounds have been created miraculously as a sign of God pointing to Francis as the new Christ, the refounder of the Gospel and the Church, is too great to have been conceived and decided by Brother Elia only a few hours after the death of the saint. It remains probable that Francis's stigmatization was a psychosomatic result of his ecstatic concentration on the Passion of Christ that we can consider as the first and "strongest" stigmatization, since, unlike many stigmatizations manifested after him, it was not due to a suggested imitation. From the nature of stigmatization itself, we can deduce a certain "femininity" in Francis's personality that we have already observed in other forms of his behavior. In the forms assumed, it characterizes a capacity for compassion and an identification with suffering that is typical of women's sensitivity.

Even in the "creation" of pathological phenomena, we must suppose that there exists an "inventor" who, as such, is gifted with an imagination superior to that of his imitators. If anyone ever "invented" in the history of stigmatization, it was probably Francis himself. In the context of penitential culture, which focused on the identification of Jesus as the Man of Sorrows, it came quite naturally for Elia and his religious brothers to recognize in Francis and his wounds his perfect conformity to the Crucified One: a man marked by Christ himself. At any rate, after Francis the history of stigmata is almost wholly female, and is linked in an increasingly "impassioned" way to the adoration of the heart.

In the history of a culture there is nearly always a "first," an inventor, and at least as far as we know, the signs of the crucifixion seen as "miraculous," that is, not deliberately inflicted (at least concretely) by the individual, appear only with the story of Francis. The very term "stigmata" indicates the miraculous nature of the wounds:

> Around 1224, in coincidence with the mysterious apparition at Mount La Verna (Francis had received the vision of a luminous seraph), which was mentioned vaguely, Francesco's companions began to conceive with greater and greater intensity the idea of a supernatural explanation of the wounds, later confirmed on by the sight of the unclothed cadaver.[69]

In any case, the biblical affirmation that man was created in the image of God, in His likeness, implies that in reality, no man can say that he truly *is* His image; and the only legitimate likeness, even if miraculous, will refer to the Crucified One: that is, to God-Man.[70]

In the biography of Francis, two new episodes are presented as miracles, unknown to any previous hagiographic model: the sermon to the birds and the stigmata. Elia was the first to spread the news of the "unheard-of" miracle of the stigmata: unheard-of, not only in being new, but also because it was a prodigious event *contra naturam*, in derogation of the normal course of events, and proper to the realm of the *super naturam*, events directly wrought by God.

With his *Legenda maior*, terminated and approved in 1263, Bonaventure of Bagnoregio combined the three biographies written by Tommaso da Celano in one, definitively identifying Francis as the saint of the stigmata. His conformity to Christ *in the flesh*, through the wounds of the Passion, make him partake of divinity, raising him to the heights of a sanctity unattainable by others. In accordance with what Paul states in *The Second Letter to the Corinthians*, that God has "marked us with Christ's seal, giving us as pledge the spirit in our hearts," the stigmata were a seal making Francis similar to the living God, Christ crucified.

Chiara Frugoni is inclined to attribute to Elia, the thoughtful companion who watched over Francis during his last illnesses and was present at his death, the decision to transform into a miraculous process the friars' grief over Francis's dead body, its wounds now visible (Francis had always kept them covered). Now the wounds were "changed" into "stigmata," and now the brothers would spread news of the miracle, making it resound to the highest degree. "The pious, surgical sisters in the monastery of Montefalco would behave similarly," says Chiara Frugoni, "successfully finding in Chiara's heart all the signs of the Passion, which the saint, while alive, had said she carried within her."[71] However, it seems difficult here to speak of true analogies, since Chiara of Montefalco died in 1308, whereas Francis died in 1226. The cultural invention of the "possibility of stigmata," interpreted as miraculous signs of participation in the Passion of Christ, had meanwhile become something "obvious," in the banal sense of the "obvious" which actually impedes critical thought.

Aside from the extraordinary credulity with which everyone recognized in the heart of Chiara of Montefalco certain "little nerves"—the cross, the whip, the three nails, the point of the spear—one fact appears clear: The difficult thing is inventing and being the first to propose a miraculous fact; after which anything becomes possible, once the pathway has been pointed out. Indeed, repetition becomes easier and easier. The crucial point of the problem remains: the mental leap necessary in order to pass from self-inflicted in order to suffer like Christ, a belief that these wounds occur "miraculously," as God's extraordinary response to the love of his favored one. Once taken, it is this mental leap that makes possible what seems totally impossible: from the first "stigmata" on the body of Francis, to the increasingly numerous ones later marking the bodies of so many women devoted to the Crucified One and to the Passion. The evidence of the Passion in the heart of Chiara of Montefalco pertains to this successive possibility, which her religious sisters had conceived after Chiara's death, remembering that "the saint had lived in constant contemplation of the Passion of Christ, and during her last illness, she had repeated these words: I hold Jesus Christ Crucified within my heart." But the idea would never have occurred to these same sisters had they not heard of the stigmata of Francis, and remained indelibly struck by the account.

However, we note here a considerable shifting both in devotion and image. First of all, the "heart" of which Chiara speaks, the center of a person who loves, in which she carries the Passion of Christ, is surely a verbal expression, a symbolic image similar to that used by millions of lovers who, from the love songs of ancient Egypt to the madrigals of courtly love, until today, have always said: "I carry you in my heart." In any case, the ease with which women, nuns especially, pass from the symbolic to the concrete, is so well-known by now that we cannot be surprised at the exploratory autopsies carried out by the Saint's religious sisters.

It is the same ease with which, from the beginning of Christianity, the body of the martyr and saint has testified to salvation through its miraculous manifestations. This conviction accompanies the entire history of Christianity, especially Catholicism. The Catholic cult of saints is primarily the cult of their bodies and tombs, the cult of the "relic."

It was widely believed, both among women mystics and those who surrounded them, that the heart of the saints, a burning furnace of love, was enlarged by amorous inflammation. This was seemingly confirmed by examinations made after their death (for example, in the autopsy of St. Philip Neri, the cardiac dilatation was indicative of problems that had nothing to do with love).

Moreover, it has always been easy to mix concepts of physical pathology with those relating to "spiritual" pathology. Thus the heart of Chiara of Montefalco was "as big as a baby's head"; in the spasms of love it had taken on the shape of the cross of Christ, its nails, the whip of his flagellation.

A Parade of Imitators

It seems that the first woman to receive stigmata after Francis was the Fleming, Elizabeth of Spalbaek, who lived from 1248 to 1316. Elizabeth did not belong to any religious group, but her lifestyle was certainly similar to that of many other women "recluses"; although a laywoman, she never left her house in Spalbaek which was situated in the immediate vicinity of the famous Cistercian abbey of Herkenrode in the diocese of Lieges. (The location probably explains why it was later widely believed that Elizabeth had been a Cistercian nun.) Her *Life* was written in 1268–72 by the Abbot of Clairvaux, Philip (who died in 1273); he claims that his story is based exclusively on what he and many others saw with their own eyes. What he saw was stigmata, which he describes in extremely realistic detail. For example, a great deal of blood gushed from the wounds; he further states that Elizabeth is the first person (though a woman) who was stigmatized after St. Francis: "in persona beati Francisci dudum revelavit idipsum: ut sic uterque sexus" (*Acta Sanctorum*). It is superfluous to point out that Elizabeth spent her entire life in sickness, filled with mystic graces and particular visions; and that her devotion was centered on the Passion.

Catherine of Siena was wounded by rays of light emanating from the crucifix painted by Giunta Pisano, while she prayed before it. These stigmata, which providentially remained invisible to everyone but her, gave occasion to a ferocious dispute between the Dominicans and Franciscans, since doubt was cast on the uniqueness of Francis's stigmata.

With Catherine we find the unification of the wound in Jesus's ribs, caused by the spear, with the heart, which according to the lovers of the Passion lies on the left: The heart wound is the source of divine love, assuaging their thirst. We can see here the aforementioned passage from the symbolic to the concrete, which characterizes the thought and emotional makeup of women much more than men, even those in love with God and considered great "mystics." The passage from the symbolic to the concrete transforms the wound in the ribs, located in correspondence with the heart, into an imaginary love object possessing a truly daunting physicality. Moreover, even the exchange of hearts between Jesus and his lovers now seems possible, albeit absurdly so, seeing that we are in the area of the transcendental. The spear opens a wound in Christ's breast and precious blood flows out, that sweetest of liquors that many women say they drink. The devotion to the wounds of the Crucified One and his blood grow stronger and stronger, along with the disputes of theologians, who have trouble admitting the authenticity of the relics of Christ's blood which numerous churches are proud to possess (for example, in Bourges and Mantua). Thomas Aquinas claimed that the Christ's blood had united with his body immediately after his death, but many preachers disagreed, and popular fantasy was stimulated by such disputes which circulated the idea of the potency of blood. It is therefore no coincidence that the famous shroud of Turin, Jesus' winding-sheet, made its first appearance at this precise time, around 1389. The shrouds now multiply, as do the miracles linking the Eucharistic host to blood: from the famous one at Bolsena to an amazing number of other bleeding hosts. Similarly, it is no coincidence that after the end of the 15th century, hosts no longer bleed.[72] At any rate, it is women in particular who more or less consciously find the profound meanings implicit in the link of blood-life-soul-potency in the blood of Christ and in the desire to nourish themselves on it.

Starting from the invocation, "blood, blood!" launched by Catherine of Siena, we shall find countless examples of women "mystics" who thirst for divine blood and contemplate it ecstatically in their visions as it drips from the face and heart of the Crucified One. Almost from the very beginning, the story of female mysticism is tied to a devotion to the "heart" and blood, and thus to the Passion and the stigmata. We can draw out only a few names from the long parade of women mystics in love with the heart.

The biography of St. Liutgard, the patron saint of the Flemish, was written by a contemporary, Thomas of Cantimpré. We know that she lived during the first half of the 13th century, and that at the age of 12 she was interned in the monastery of the Benedictine nuns of St. Catherine at Saint-Trond. From there she moved to various other communities where the peculiar mystic life of Julienne of Cornillon and Ida of Nivelles flourished, but above all, where an intense, confidential bond with the "heart" was growing. Liutgard became the protagonist of this bond, and is famous for the images depicting her as she exchanges her heart with that of Jesus, as she drinks the blood pouring forth from his ribs and just before her death as she approaches the Crucified One, who extends his arm from the cross in order to embrace her.

The "heart" theme is so closely tied to that of the blood and the crucifixion that it must be discussed in this context: context that emerged with increasing clarity and reached its highest expression in the "revelations" of Marguerite-Marie Alacoque. More importantly, the mystic "visions" allowed the nearness, the love and the understanding of the "heart." Woman-vision-heart, and, finally, stigmata are inseparably linked because they are based on the physicality of this heart. Because it is a heart of "flesh" even while divine, and it cannot be reached through prayer or reflection, however contemplative, but only through ecstasy: that is, in a "pretended" separation and sublimation of the body. This then is the fundamental nucleus of psychosis, that is, of what we have defined as the concretization of the symbolic.

Give Me Your Heart!

Margaret of Cortona (1247–1297) also concentrated on the Passion at the same time as the heart. She desired to enter the heart more deeply than in the rib wound, saying to Jesus: "If I am in your heart, I shall still be in the wound in your ribs, in all the nail holes, in the crown of thorns, in the bile and in the vinegar, and in the cloth on your venerable eyes."[73]

Ecstasies and visions are thus so closely tied to the "heart" theme, and depend so strongly on the female emotional makeup, that we can continue our list (even one limited to the most famous names) with another woman who was condemned to being a "mystic," Gertrude of Helfta. In 1261, having just turned five, Gertrude was shut up in the Saxon monastery of Helfta, which observed the Benedictine Rule according to Cistercian custom where she remained until her death in 1302. The events of her biography are common to most women mystics: "imprinting" as the bride of God from earliest childhood, the inevitable crisis at the age of 20 which, when not a physical illness, goes under the name of "spiritual darkness," which "Jesus cured her of when he appeared to her in the form of a very handsome young man." From that moment on "she always remained in

138   II. The Tragic Game of Mysticism

the company of her divine husband," narrates *Book II* of her "revelations," with tranquil certainty, "except for eleven days when she was punished for having excessively enjoyed a mundane conversation."[74] Only when we recall that she had been closed up in a convent from the age of five, can we perhaps explain the infantile fantasy to which her relation to God had been reduced.

Gertrude had begun to write her "revelations" in 1281, as she puts it, "driven by the Holy Spirit"; and later, again by divine commandment, she dictated them to a religious sister. It is here that Gertrude speaks of receiving the stigmata (a phenomenon now famous outside Italy), and a wound in the heart from a golden arrow of love. In *Book II* we also find the usual claim of modesty, the "mystic's" incapacity to describe certain manifestations of divine love to others. Jesus, who would later address Teresa of Avila with nearly the same words, tells her that such "small souls might be scandalized" by the accounts, but he promises to suggest what she must write. The level of awareness-unawareness is obvious here with regard to the earlier mentioned "pretending." What is surprising is thus not the ingenuous psychological trick of the visionary woman writers, but the fact that it is not immediately perceived as such by readers and commentators.

At any rate, women's devotion to the "Heart" and to the Passion of Christ took an important step forward with Gertrude: "*In Corde Gertrudis invenietis me*," declares Jesus through Gertrude's lips when she is in a state of ecstasy, thus revealing to the world the holiness of our saint. Two centuries later, the certainties of women mystics concerning "hearts" would be such that Teresa of Avila would take the extreme step toward her own exaltation and overturn Gertrude's image: Jesus assures her, in fact, that it is "in his heart that Teresa will find herself."

Angela of Foligno (1247–1309) was a contemporary of Margherita of Cortona. She represents a restricted but important category of Italian women mystics who experienced marriage and maternity, but who nonetheless fail to say a single word about this aspect of their lives: not a word about sexuality, their relationships with men or, much less, motherhood, despite the physical, psychological, and emotional demands of maternity. Influenced by Franciscan spirituality, Angela interprets it exclusively as the concrete quest for penitence and poverty and thus reaches limits of self-abnegation that are clearly "psychotic" and totally alien to the message to Francis. In 1291, during a pilgrimage to Assisi, Angela thought she experienced the reality of the divine Trinity during a "mystic" crisis. Her confessor, a Friar Minor by the name of Arnaldo, according to custom, began to write what Angela narrated to him; it became the first part of the *Liber* of the blessed Angela, or the spiritual autobiography or *Memoriale* of

A Custom-Made Lover: God 139

Brother Arnaldo.[75] There is no need to spend time discussing the linguistic analyses of the *Liber*. The question that arises is: Just when does the will to reach the aim of penitential culture—yet free oneself from it at the same time—become an absolute in the female experience, without everyone thinking that it looks like "delirium" only because the group believes in it and confirms it?

The most meaningful moments of Angela's spiritual journey are already familiar to us: love as death, union with the crucified Christ, experience of the void as the supreme knowledge of God. Angela joins Christ in the tomb, kisses and embraces him until his death-stiffened body loosens up and becomes alive in order to caress her. Countless times, certainly, in the madness of mortal desperation, a lover who has lost her beloved has dreamed that this could happen: that a cadaver could come back to life. But are we not here again in the presence of a delirious abyss, a wholly human delirium on the borderline of psychosis, which has nothing to do with the transcendental? And when Angela tells her confessor she has seen "the beauty of the throat and arms of Christ just as she sees it in the Eucharist," and that, indeed, she sometimes sees the host as "the eyes of God, so large that only the edge of the host remains," how can we help but realize the "pathology" of such fantasies? In any event, our problem remains that of tracing a rapid picture that might exemplify the central theme, aside from its countless variations.

Let us thus rapidly proceed, with a brief mention of Agnes of Montepulciano, born in 1274, and sent at the age of nine to the Dominican convent at Sacco. She was a "mystic" endowed with extraordinary powers, including the famous one of covering with manna the altar on which a bishop was celebrating mass in her presence. Catherine of Siena was devoted to Agnes; having gone to venerate her remains in 1377, she was present during a miracle, when manna formed around the cadaver. It is, indeed, with Catherine of Siena (1347–1380) that the Passion for Christ's blood takes on a clear shape, along with her passion for the "heart." In her ecstasies Catherine saw this blood dripping for the sake of the Church: "may I be granted the grace of bleeding and may the marrow of my bones run in this garden of the Holy Church."[76]

The corporeal nature of her fantasies might perhaps be called "baroque" had we not noted some time ago that all excesses are "naturally baroque" in the emotions and affections of women. What sense is there in this definition, "baroque," anyway? The fact is that the violent physicality in which Catherine immerses herself is both shocking and revelatory of a delirious experience, in which the symbolic is lost to a terrifying concreteness. She writes to Fra Raimondo of Capua, her spiritual director:

140   II. The Tragic Game of Mysticism

> "My very dear father, dear son in Jesus Christ, I, Catherine, servant and slave of the servants of Jesus Christ, write to you to recommend you in the precious blood of the Son of God; wishing to see you suffocating and drowning in that most sweet blood of his, blood soaked in the fire of his ardent love. This is the wish of my soul, to see you in that blood [...] Sweet father, your soul, which has become my food [...] would not reach the small virtue of true humility, if you were not drowning in the blood [...] Thus I want you to close yourself up in the open rib of the Son of God, which is an open shop, full of smells, so that sin becomes something smelly to you. There the sweet bride rests in the bed of fire and blood[...]."[77]

In the account that Catherine herself wrote of the famous episode in which she accompanies a man condemned to death to his execution block, the celebration of blood is such that even the one transcribing it here does not feel up to dwelling on it for long. We shall therefore quote only her concluding words: "Once laid to rest, my soul rested in peace and quiet, in such an odor of blood, that I could not stand to remove the blood from myself which had come upon me from him."[78]

Her ecstasies lasted so long that the Dominican friars were often forced to drag her out of the church by the arms, leaving her unconscious in the church courtyard. Besides the wedding ring given her by Christ— this, too, a must, an exclusive constant for women mystics (it is the man who takes the bride: the cultural unconscious is not to be deceived)— Catherine presents the phenomenon of the invisible stigmata that provoked a bitter dispute between Dominicans and Franciscans for two centuries. The dispute was not settled until 1630, when Pope Urban VIII decided that Catherine's stigmata were authentic, but only luminous, not cruel, and prohibited painters from representing them. In any case, the "fact" that the stigmata were impressed on her by rays of light while she was absorbed before the crucifix, once more exemplified the fantastic effect that the story of Francis's stigmata was to have for a long time on those who followed.

In any event, we are appalled to consider the list of these fantastic effects, which are so similar from one century to the next and which mark the lives of some women, almost all of whom are considered saints by the Church, with abnormality, with a flight from reality, and in any case, with intolerable suffering, even from a physical point of view.

Bridget's "Non-Revelations"

After Catherine of Siena, the next major name on our list is Bridget of Sweden, an influential figure in the political and religious life of her time. It was the imposing phenomenon of her "visions," in any case, which brought Bridget lasting fame. Raised in a highly religious family, related to the reigning family of the Fonkulgar, Bridget began her ecstatic life at the age of seven, in 1295, with a vision of the Virgin placing a crown on her head; three years later, deeply moved by a sermon on the Passion of Christ, she saw Jesus wounding her heart. At the age of 13, despite her all-too-foreseeable desire to remain a virgin, she was given in marriage to a nobleman, a friend of her father's, Ulf Gudmarsson, and became—here, too, in compliance with a traditional hagiographic *topos*—an exemplary wife, giving birth to eight children. The second child, Catherine, accompanied her for many years on her pilgrimages to Rome; she, too, became a "saint." After her husband's death, Bridget dedicated herself even more intensely to prayer and meditation on the Passion, while voices and visions became more and more frequent, and the divine Bridegroom crowned her with a tiara of seven precious jewels.

As with nearly all the women mystics we know, we can read the contents of her "revelations" through the account that she herself gave, at the end of the ecstasies, to her secretaries, and later submitted to the judgment of her confessors. Often, Bridget narrates what she has heard and seen concerning Our Lady, and everything corresponds so perfectly to what a woman of her time could imagine or know that the most surprising thing is the exaltation which through the centuries, the widest range of readers and commentators have accumulated around these naive imaginings.

Our Lady presents herself to Bridget saying:

> I am the Queen of Heaven, the Mother of God. I told you always to wear the necklace on your breast. Now I shall show you in a better way; how I, by hearing and understanding that God exists ever since childhood, was always attentive and anxious concerning my salvation and obedience [...]. I also vowed, in my heart, to remain a virgin, and never to possess anything in this world [...]. Having then reached the time when by law virgins had to be presented to the Lord in the Temple, I was present among them out of obedience to my parents [...].[79]

Aside from its paucity, such a "revelation" reflects certain pious legends told during Bridget's time about Our Lady: legends having no historical truth to them (they are mentioned in the apocryphal *Proto-gospel of James* which was very well-known in the Middle Ages). The vow of virginity did not exist in ancient Judaism, and no presentation of virgins ever took place in the Temple. Furthermore, in Bridget, as in so many other women mystics, great attention is given to the "heart." In *Book I* of the

Celestial Revelations, Jesus says to her: "You, then, my child, chosen by me and to whom I speak in spirit, love me with all your heart [...]. Your heart will be in mine, and will be inflamed with my love."

On repeated occasions, Jesus speaks to Bridget of his justice and, as usual in the case of such sweet lovers, her imagination is full of ferociousness. To the divine tribunal such women transfer all their hate, all the feelings of guilt and punishment present in society and in the culture in which they live. Is there any need for particular "revelations" in order to imagine a "Hell" like the one described by Bridget, wholly similar to Dante's, which she surely was acquainted with? Men who will not recognize their Creator,

> like those who hang from the gallows, are devoured by devils, and never consumed. Like impaled men who find no peace, so these will suffer pain and bitterness everywhere. A burning river runs in their mouth; nor will their belly ever be satiated, but from day to day their torture will be renewed.

Clearly, this is an *elementary* kind of imagination, characteristic of autistic thinking, the only type of thinking active in the ecstatic *absence*.

In any case, what must be emphasized here is that men who have come to know these Revelations, who have meditated and commented on them, have been full of enthusiasm; and certainly, they have considered them valid, in their conceptual poverty, only because they came from the female realm. Thus speaks the bridegroom to the bride:

> I myself want to live in your heart. To this degree I love You. The heavens and the earth and all things contained in them cannot hold me: and yet I want to live in your heart, which is only a piece of flesh [...]. In the heart, then, my tabernacle, there must be three things: a bed where we can rest, a chair where we can sit, a light to illumine us. Let there be in your heart, then, the bed to rest in, that is silence, so that you will find rest from bad thoughts and worldly desires [...].

What can we say here? What need is there for any comment?

Many of Bridget's vision takes shape as "trials" of the deceased person's soul before God; psychologically childish trials, revealing the many medieval images depicting the moment of judgment: the angel and the devil who present the sins and virtues of the deceased person to God, each reading a list from his own book. From 1200 on, Church teachings increasingly exalt the protective function of the Virgin Mary, who intervenes with mercy in favor of the condemned. But it is precisely when the figure of Our Lady appears in the visions of our mystics that the level of their thought is lowered further. Perhaps, having to deal with a "woman," whom they somehow perceive as being similar to them, induces, or rather "authorizes" them to lower their defenses in the face of the transcendental. Once again, we are forced to note that the enthusiasm of readers for such accounts would never have been possible had the protagonists not been of the female sex. In the presence of ecstasies we find ourselves facing an autistic type of thought, an elementary one, lacking in any possibility for critical reflection, and it is for this very reason, even though we are dealing with *women*, that we cannot help but be disconcerted by the fame and exaltation surrounding them, which seems to reach its apex in St. Bridget.

The Angel and I

Frances of Rome (1384–1440) lived in a rich, aristocratic household during a highly turbulent period for Rome during the struggles between the popes and anti-popes. It was a period of strife when the Italian kingdoms and duchies fought over territories and dominions, while the great European monarchies never ceased their interminable clashes and wars (Joan of Arc died in 1431). Frances's tale begins with the usual theme of the little girl who from early childhood wishes to remain a virgin and become the bride of Jesus, but whose father forces her to marry, at the age of 12, the man predestined for her. Frances gives in to her father's will, urged to obey by her confessor, Father Antonello of Monte Savello. Confessors have always upheld women's duty to obey the constituted authorities, their fathers and God, with one variation: Some gave precedence to obeying the vocation of God's bride. It would be interesting to analyze the absolutely personal, unquestionable criteria that spiritual directors observed in favoring one type of obedience over the other, without any concern about which choice might be more suitable for the girl. *She* was merely obliged to believe that the confessor's will was God's will. And to obey.

In accordance with the usual path followed by "mystic" women, Frances falls ill with a mysterious disease, but suddenly recovers after receiving a vision of St. Alexis. An exemplary wife and mother, as her contemporaries attest, she had three children. Her life, however, is dedicated to prayer. Her husband, Lorenzo Ponzani, sides with the Orsini family in defending the Pope's rights against the Colonna family. In 1409, he is wounded in a battle taken up by the Orsinis against the Neapolitans under King Ladislas. They take his brother-in-law prisoner and, in substitution of the wounded man, carry off his first-born son. The episode is narrated as an offering by Frances to God, one similar to Abraham's sacrifice. Later, the plague kills her two other children, and Frances is totally free at last to dedicate herself to works of charity for the poor of Rome.

As she herself narrates, an angel always accompanies her in visible form (visible only to her, of course); furthermore, she enjoys the particular protection of St. Paul, Mary Magdalen, and St. Benedict. She dresses like a poor woman and begs for alms in the most derelict neighborhoods of the city (which puts her on a level with prostitutes and serves to demonstrate her humility). She also cares for the sick in the hospitals in Trastevere, and it is narrated that, in order to hide her miraculous capacity to cure the sick, she uses a simple ointment to justify the good results she obtains.

In 1433, the friends that collaborated with her in works of charity join together as Oblates in her famous house of Tor de' Specchi, where Frances dies in 1440. Some say that the Oblates of St. Frances of Rome were forerunners of the modern congregations of the active life, since they went out of the convent in order to perform their good works; however this interpretation seems a bit forced, since assistance was not the declared purpose of the institution.

Despite her outside activity, Frances remained in ecstasy many hours a day: Her visions are remembered thanks to the work of her last confessor, the priest Giovanni Mattiotti who, like all diligent spiritual directors, had obliged her to tell him everything that "went on daily between her and Heaven."[80]

More Ferocious than Dante

As narrated, Frances's visions (like those of so many other women mystics who have described orally or in writing what they have "seen") translate the contents learned from theology into concrete images, inevitably reducing them to their flat, elementary external reality, the only one remaining, once we have eliminated the logical obscurities of a language invented ad hoc, the language of theology. Angels and archangels along with various saints come and go around the high thrones where Francesca sees, or obscurely perceives God, Jesus, and Our Lady in a splendid, crystalline light; and nothing can be learned from her visions except that life "up there" is more or less what Dante or St. Thomas talk about. The only difference, if any, is the extreme ferociousness that characterizes her fantasies concerning the punishments of sinners. Though the punishments she envisions are similar to those of Dante in *The Divine Comedy* in that they represent the *contrappasso*, the correspondence of the punishment to the type of sin committed, she seems unable to find a suffering equal to what her imagination strives for, in accumulating torture on torture, crushing on crushing, fire on fire.

In the deep and terrible place there were the souls of the miserable men and women with the sodomite sin, and the one against nature. The devils tormented them in the same way and form they had committed such a disgraceful vice. So they impaled them from one end to the other with big spits that they made come out of their mouths. They lifted them up and then they turned them over, as one often does with meat roasting on the spit. They tore such souls apart from head to foot with fiery hooks, while they continued to impale them and extract the spits from their mouth. For greater torture, the devils then always abused them in accordance with the sin that they had committed [...]. I saw the souls of blasphemers undergo many forms of torture. With fiery iron hooks, the devils cut out each soul's tongue and put it on burning coals, then took these coals and stuck them in their throats. Then the soul was set in a tub of boiling oil, which was made to pour down their throats as well [...]. The souls of traitors also underwent infinite torments. The devils scraped their hearts out with fiery iron hooks, then forced it down their throats with all the flesh surrounding the heart. Then they immersed them in a basin of boiling tar, reprimanding them [...], and dragged their hearts over burning coals.

Frances, then, invents almost nothing beyond what has provided material for religious preaching concerning the torments of the damned from Dante onwards. However, we perceive here something totally lacking in Dante: enjoyment, the pleasure of physical torment for its own sake; an enjoyment that seeks out ever new, impossible satisfactions in the torturing of the flesh. Not one thought is given to the sins mentioned: They are "sins" that are defined as such by the ecclesiastic authorities; she believes in them as "absolutes." Her "justice" makes absolutely no attempt to understand or pity; her only satisfaction is an intense pleasure in the violent physical suffering she is able to imagine.

At any rate, just as she is incapable of inventing anything but an unlimited ferociousness concerning the cruelty of her God, so is she incapable of imagining anything new concerning her amorous exchange with Him.

Her mystical experience is one of the most fabulous or "fable-like" and also one of the most hallucinatory. Frances claims that she is *always* in the company of an angel that she sees in the form of a young man. She has frequent visions during her ecstasies in which, according to her confessor's narration, she is sometimes "mobile"—that is, she speaks, walks, and accompanies what she sees with dances and hand gestures—while other times she remains rigid and immobile. This type of symptomatic manifestation is typical of hysteric "absences," but the priest describing them to us thinks he is witnessing supernatural "states," and so we are not to doubt their mystical authenticity.

II. The Tragic Game of Mysticism

But what can we draw from Frances's visions? An ingenuous, even "regressive" confirmation of what she has learned from religious instruction; one at a childish intellectual level (especially when compared to the intelligence she showed in her practical life): the Passion of Jesus, the exaltation of the Madonna, hosts of angels and cherubim, all immersed in different strata and bands of splendid light. In Frances's visions, as in those of so many other women mystics, Paradise is naturally imagined as a beautiful garden.

She has the usual intense relationship with the wounds of the Crucified One; she "sees" the number of his wounds; she drinks the water or sweet liquor gushing from them; she reproduces the famous "rib" wound on her own breast with the flame of a candle, a gesture, surely suggested by the hagiographies of women who preceded her; that raises a question we have discussed on other occasions: Can a type of behavior that copies the behavior of others be considered psychotic when the latter are exalted as heroes by society?

> I was later led in three lights, until I saw a beautiful round tabernacle, on which stood a dazzling white Lamb, and around it were three stools. Three rows of lambs came in, all white. Each row took its stool and, in great joy, leaped about in front of and around the Lamb, and passing in front of it, bowed graciously [...]. I saw that the Lamb turned its breast toward the other lambs, kindly and graciously inviting them to drink. On its breast, in fact, it had a wound toward which I was led, and I saw inside it a very deep sea of infinite light[...]. The more I gazed into it, the deeper the sea of light appeared, and the more I wished to immerse myself in it [...]. The Lord showed himself to me in his glorified humanity, with his arms crossed upon his breast; rays came forth from his wounds, dazzling beyond expression. As great as the light was that emerged from the wounds of his feet, the one emerging from the hands was greater; and greater still, the one emerging from the wound in the ribs [...]. I saw that these rays even reached creatures living in the mortal flesh, and these, too, were irradiated, some more, some less. Some of them had the rays of the wound on their feet, others those of the hands, others from the wound in the side, according to the love they had [...].

This idea that rays emanate from the wounds of Christ and strike the souls of women in love with him is part of a narrative tradition, and an iconography that Frances certainly knew. What can we say though — what adjective can we find to describe a fantasy of the transcendental which conserves a negative image of "feet," though they be the feet of the Crucified?

> I was raised up to a high mountain on which there stood a very large, very shiny column that reached the sky. A burning fire came

out of the top. It was divine love that, coming out of the column, spread to different places [...]. Over an immense fire stood a very fine tabernacle in which there was the Lord in his sacred humanity, in such reverberation and splendor that I could make out nothing else but his height. From his most holy wounds lights were lit that reflected on the multitude of souls [...].

In virtually all of the visions referred to us by ecstatic women, the play of light serves to "reveal" everything that they are unable to describe in any other manner. The theme of "light" which dazzles, which gushes from the wounds of Christ, which pours over angels, cherubim, and saints remains constant down through the centuries. But surely, this very constancy demonstrates that the theme was handed down and learned by tradition; and above all, that these "visionaries" actually see and know nothing except what theologians, poets, and philosophers have always claimed. Light illumines but conceals, because we know nothing and can say nothing about God: Fire is the light that conceals God from the eyes of Moses; fire and light remain the constant images of Christianity which has defined "seeing" God as the fullness of otherworldly bliss, and not seeing Him, as the condemnation of earthly existence.

Naturally, Frances of Rome also exploits her ecstatic "absence" in order to report the praise that her God lavishes on her:

> You have kept discretion even while knowing the secrets of vile, evil souls, and I have fortified you against the malice of the devil. I am pleased that you have been wise, you have kept a clear eye, you have looked upwards and put the world beneath your feet; you have done everything out of love, for you have not been afraid of hell, and you have been content with pure justice [...]. Your intellect has greatly helped you; it is clear in discerning the truth [...]. You have kept your soul pure, you have not submitted it to your sensuality; you have kept it as precious silver and have preserved it to give me pleasure; you have placed all beauty in it [...]. You have done everything out of obedience; you have never stained yourself, and it was I that gave you the guardian [angel] that always accompanies you [...].

In leaving Frances of Rome, we shall rapidly go on to Liduina, a Dutch woman mystic (1380–1433). Her story shows to what extent these women's paths in life were predetermined and similar: the vow of virginity at the age of 12, a long serious illness spent in union with the Passion of Jesus, and extremely painful but invisible stigmata. Then, again choosing at random among the most famous, Catherine of Genoa (1477–1519), with her extraordinary mystic graces, which she reports in the *Dialogues*; the search for penance and humiliation in curing the sick and, like so many other women driven to conceive penitence as the pathological dereliction of their own life, the sucking of pus from their wounds. Extremely long ecstasies during which she seemed to be dead except for a rapid heartbeat: The extraordinary heat emanating from her body is a manifestation of the inner fire of her love for the Lord, narrates the *Life*. It is perhaps superfluous to add that her body has remained uncorrupted.[81]

A Simple Technique for Self-Elevation

We now come to someone who is, perhaps, the most famous figure of all: Teresa of Avila. We shall discuss her in greater depth only because she represents a kind of paradigm of the phenomenology of the woman "mystic."

Born in 1515, died in 1582, Teresa thoroughly belongs to that period of European history, the Renaissance, which has remained unrivaled in its capacity for intellectual and cultural innovation. And it is on the basis of this observation, namely, Renaissance humanism, that we cannot help but wonder why she has been so exalted: as a person, first of all, and then as a thinker and writer. We need only read a few pages of her famous *Life* to notice that we are in the presence of certain classical *topoi* of the life of "mystics" that have already been pointed out, but that nothing is said of her as an individual or of her true psychological experience, so dominant is her will to conform to the model of perfect uniqueness constructed for the Woman-God's bride by her cultural and historical environment.

As one might have expected, a serious, mysterious illness marks her "conversion," and by overcoming that conflict the nun sets out on the road to absolute compliance with divine marriage. A declaration follows, one similar to that of mystics, that she is a terrible sinner; however, no concrete information is given concerning the types of sins, because her confessors "have forbidden her to speak about them" (how incredibly easy it is to appear "humble" at the height of pride!). Finally, there is a continuous invitation to obey the ecclesiastic superiors and God as she narrates the extraordinary events regarding her. Events, of course, that cannot help but leave her readers bewildered but which, in a childish psychological game, are invoked in order to demonstrate how poor Teresa is a "nothing" in the hands of Almighty God.

The simple mechanisms of humiliation-elevation which ascesis provides her, and through which she tries to explain the "knowledge" that God grants her, are so typical of many other woman mystics that they are easily interchangeable. She always *sees* only what theology has taught her; indeed, finding herself in the era of Reformation, she sees only what the

A Custom-Made Lover: God   149

Catholic Church at that moment obliges one to believe, more strongly than ever, in order to check the dangers of Protestantism.

> I was seized by such a strong spiritual rapture that I could not resist. It seemed I was in heaven, where the first persons I saw were my father and mother, and other great wonders, in the time it takes to say an Ave Maria.[82]

The fact that a saint's parents are "saints" is one of the traditional themes of hagiography, and Teresa sets it aside for herself, attributing its certainty to a vision. The "time" to say an Ave Maria, like that of a Pater or a Credo, is the usual way of measuring time in the Middle Ages, and testifies to the naiveté and the elementary nature of visionary thinking, far from being any otherworldly innovation.

> On Pentecost Eve, after Mass, I went to a very solitary place where I used to retreat in order to pray, and I began to read about that festivity in the Cartulario. I read the signs by which beginners, the proficient and the perfect can know whether the Holy Spirit is in them, and after considering those three states, it seemed to me that thanks to the goodness of God, as far as I could judge, the Holy Spirit was in me as well.

Here we are presented with the "grades" of perfection foreseen by ascetic theology, which Teresa confirms by her divine vision, and, in passing, she informs her public that she is on the road to perfection in the presence of the Holy Spirit. We see here again everything that was questioned by the Lutheran protest. But if we proceed, we find nothing but the usual leitmotivs:

> As I stopped to make these considerations, I was surprised by a great rapture without understanding why. My soul being incapable of containing itself, it seemed to want to go out of my body in its eagerness to reach that goodness [...]. In this state, I saw a dove over my head that was quite different from ours, with no feathers, and wings like scales of mother-of-pearl that gave off great splendor. It was bigger than ordinary doves, and I seemed to hear the fluttering of wings [...]. Another time I saw the same dove over the head of a father of the Order of St. Dominic, but this time the rays and splendors of the wings seemed more diffuse. I understood from that that he would lead many souls to God [...]

It is superfluous to point out that the Lutherans contested the work of the preachers, along with that of all the monastic orders, whereas the Church had given the preaching order of the Dominicans the task of renewing obedience to its teachings, in particular by way of the Inquisition. It is impossible to cite all the "visions" in which Teresa has God confirm the principles of the Catholic Church; suffice it to recall her continual reference to the force of the Virgin's intercession which, indeed, was one of the main points contested by the Reform.

> I saw Our Lady cover with a candid mantle the one presented from the same order whom I have mentioned other times. And she told me that she was giving him that mantle as a reward for the services that he had done for her in contributing to the founding of this monastery, and with which she would always defend the purity of his soul, as a sign of the protection, keeping it from every mortal sin [...].

The Madonna's "candid mantle" marked her protection and was a commonplace in Marian devotion and iconography.

Or consider this:

> Great things have I also seen concerning that father's order, which is the Company of Jesus, whose religious I have often seen in heaven, holding white flags in their hands. Yes, wondrous things have I seen of that order, and I venerate it deeply because, having been in contact with many of its members, I have seen that their life complies with what the Lord has given me to understand about them [...]

Need we go on? Every image that Teresa relates serves to confirm the Church's teachings against the Protestants; moreover, in this case, as in many others, her vision includes an exaltation of the Jesuits, who had been assigned the task of reconquering the primacy of Catholicism. In her accounts, the level of thought is clearly "primary"; we could easily define it as childish and ingenuous were it not proof of hallucinatory ecstasy, and an impossibility to "reflect" in any other way. In this perspective, the neurobiologist Gerald M. Edelman questions whether this is not what mystics are seeking: namely, an abandonment of superior consciousness, which is the only one that enables a person to realize the activity of the primary consciousness.[83]

Defense of the Jesuits was one of the strong points of the Counter-Reformation: to say that "their life complies with what the Lord has given me to understand about them" hardly explains much. The self-referred confirmation on the basis of what God has led Teresa to understand, seems so naïve and only because so many readers, scholars, or simply, Christians, have believed her throughout the centuries, can we say that Teresa saved her prestige and her presence in the world and in history with this system. And in spite of everything else, we can also conclude that, from her own point of view, she acted correctly.

As always happens with women mystics, Teresa "sees" only what she already knows or believes she knows, having learnt it from her environment. Even when she thinks she is "revealing" new things, she always

A Custom-Made Lover: God 151

adheres strictly to the same terms adopted by those around her, so great is her fear (whether conscious or not), or her incapacity, to create new ones: "In a clear and wondrous way I saw Christ in the bosom of the Father, but I cannot say how, because I seemed to be in the presence of the divinity without seeing a thing." Had she only explained to us the meaning of the oft-repeated formula, "In the bosom of the Father"! But naturally, she does not know it, as we do not. Let us proceed a bit further in order to clarify the mechanism sustaining all of her visions:

> One day, as I was going to communion, I saw with the eyes of my soul, but more clearly than with those of the body, two devils of an abominable aspect that seemed to be squeezing the throat of the poor priest between their horns. As he came to offer me the host he held in his hand, I saw in it my Lord with the majesty of which I have spoken. I understood that that soul was in mortal danger: his hands were those of a sinner. What horror, my Lord, to see your ineffable beauty among such abominable figures! The devils seemed afraid and trembled in your presence, and one could plainly see that, had you let them, they would gladly have fled. I was so disturbed by all this that I do not know how I managed to take communion, not to speak of the fear that seized me concerning the origin of the vision in believing that God, if it came from Him, would not have allowed me to see the condition of that minister of His. But He told me to pray for Him, adding that He had allowed all that in order to let me know the virtue that the words of the consecration have, and that He does not fail to become present in the host, despite the unworthiness of the priest pronouncing them.

Aside from the usual self-exaltation, openly hidden behind the "humble" doubt that God would not have allowed her to perceive the unworthiness of the priest, there is a clear intention to confirm the official, positive conclusion to the old and bitter debate over the validity of sacraments celebrated by priests in mortal sin (which often meant married ones); a debate that had torn the Church ever since the middle of the 11th century.

What can we say, then, of Teresa's vision of devils? There is another amusing passage in this regard:

> A person died who, I heard, had lived quite badly for a long time. He had been ill the past two years, but in some respects seemed not destined to be damned. As they were preparing him for burial, I saw a large number of devils take that body almost as if they wanted to play with it. They beat it and cast it about with big pitchforks [...]

As if that were not enough, in order to demonstrate Teresa's strict obedience toward the precepts of the Catholic Church, we find, at last, another "revelation" regarding her own order of the Carmelites: "A friar of our order, a religious of great virtue, was very ill. While I was listening to Mass, I began to meditate and I saw that he had died and risen to heaven without passing though purgatory. I later heard that he had died the same hour I had seen him." (Another casual revelation of Teresa's participation in the transcendent life). "Since I was very surprised to see that he has been spared purgatory, I understood that having faithfully observed his Rule, he had obtained this favor through the edicts of the order." It is superfluous to point out that this too is a "revelation" confirming the saving power of the monastic life in opposition to Luther. The fact that her own order is under discussion, one she herself reformed, is naturally pure coincidence.

There is nothing "revealed" in all this of course, just as there is nothing that was not declared by the Church, particularly after the Council of Trent. In addition, even at a first glance we can see the schematic, conceptually scanty nature of the fantasy dictating these tales: tales corresponding to those little images of hell, purgatory, and paradise that women themselves love, especially religious women. Images nourish emotions and affections devoid of thought and any concept except that primary awareness, that concrete-symbolic realism characterizing the conceptual representations of medieval art.[84]

Moreover, the horns and pitchforks of the devils constituted one of the most widespread themes of church iconography; they were vulgar tools of terrorism wielded by the ecclesiastic authorities against the "people." Like nearly all women "mystics," Teresa has not an iota of creative fantasy, even in those areas that, being revealed to her by God, she claims to know best. Hieronymus Bosch does a better job without "revelations."

Despite the praise that has been lavished on her strong personality, the first certain point is that Teresa *voluntarily* complies with what men of the Church say; she does not do so to elude the dangers of the Inquisition. The latter hypothesis is advanced by some of her most attentive admirers in order to justify the banality of her thought and to claim that in reality Teresa rebels against the orders of the ecclesiastic institution.[85] But if this is true, why, instead of remaining silent, would she have recounted "visions" that do not correspond to what she actually believed she had seen, unless to exalt herself? At any rate, whether or not Teresa is deliberately lying, the result is that she was right, for she did attain her goal: Teresa has remained a "saint" in history and, by confirming the God-given origin of what the Church in its infallibility defines as true, she has become a doctor, the first female Doctor of the Church. (Much later, Catherine of Siena would become one too, and just recently, and ironically, considering her intellectual and emotional martyrdom, Thérèse of Lisieux has been made a doctor as well.)

Teresa and Her "Pretending"

At this point a revealingly significant question comes up around the figure of "Teresa," a question argued by scholars of various psychological, cultural and scientific backgrounds: the "falsity" of Teresa's writings. While doubt about the sincerity of her written works was raised even in the minds of those who read them with sympathy, indeed, with devotion, the answer remains very complex. It cannot simply refer (as is usually done) to the difficulty of slipping her ideas through the filter of censorship, for this woman was under the strict control of both confessors and the Inquisition. There is practically no consecrated woman, whether mystic or not, who fails to claim that she "obeys her confessor." This affirmation is to be understood in the strict sense of its meaning: permission has been asked for and granted, because a nun *has made a vow of obedience.*

We have no reason (nor any right) to believe that Teresa was not faithful to her monastic vows: She herself had worked to renew them in their vigor as a form of "perfection," in contrast with the relaxed practices of her time. Moreover, her rigor is reflected in her pages regarding the system of authority in the convent, formulated by herself in the *Constitutions*; it gave primacy to total obedience toward those who lead the community, the prioress and the mother superior.

Teresa believes in the necessity for such obedience as strongly as the leaders of the Counter-Reformation. Any word or act against the prioress is discussed in the chapter, "On the gravest fault"; disobedience toward a prelate or superior in the chapter, "Extremely grave fault," and punishable with "monastic prison during the period which shall be deemed suitable by the prioress or visitor to the convent." We shall soon have a look at the reality of the "monastic prison" that Teresa finds justifiable for use in her rule, without stopping a moment to reconsider.

Having established this much, however, the fact remains that an "obedience" in function of one's own desires was quite easily obtainable, as is well known not only by all nuns, past and present, but also by all women, both wives and daughters, who never having been held responsible for their decisions, *compos sui*, have done their utmost to get permission to do what they wanted from the authority on whom they depended.

This is the first instance of "pretending," to which many commentators unconsciously refer, but whose complexity cannot be resolved by simply considering it a form of deception in the face of the Inquisition. Its complexity is caused, instead, by the fact that the "make-believe" is experienced as "obvious," implicit, and inevitable not only by women, but also by the men holding power over them: be they biological fathers, spiritual fathers, or husbands who are eternally suspicious about their wives' faithfulness. As we saw before, Henri Brémond is well aware of the "anomalous" relationship of reciprocal deceit; he is neither surprised nor scandalized by it, since he considers it "natural." The never explicitly exposed psychological, social, and cultural aspects of the "self-representation" required of women drives them to live in the uncertainty of their own "being," even, and above all, at the deepest level of the self.

Today, it is highly difficult for us who live in an era separating secular society from religious society to realize what it meant to live in a society whose religious structure was total and obvious. Except for the personal behavior of single members, whether they were men of power, political leaders, ecclesiastics, or scholars in the sciences and arts (who in the 16th century of Teresa were laying the foundations of a culture based on man and his free creations), the area of "faith" was never questioned by anyone. One could ridicule popes and bishops, one could deny priestly and sacramental powers, one could sing to the beauty of a life free from the burden of bodily mortification and penitence; but no one, neither Leonardo da Vinci, nor Michelangelo, nor Galileo, ever cast doubt onto the truth of Faith, the Christian ideal as the highest one achieved by humanity. Luther's ferocious criticism of the ecclesiastical institutions further strengthened this conviction. The Christian God upheld the basic network of human co-existence, despite all the errors committed by men themselves, including ecclesiastics.

So, then, Teresa chose God, the God of the Catholic Church, who makes women become His brides. In reforming the Carmelite Order, Teresa reinforced the structure of the divine marriage of women to the highest possible degree. She is so subjugated by this model that one of the gravest faults in her *Constitutions* is the nun's leaving the confines of cloistered space, since Teresa more or less consciously considers the cloistered life to be the highest form of the sacred-taboo of the God's bride. Moreover, not being aristocratic, during her lifetime there was nothing else for her to do except become a famous nun in order to attain the primacy that she herself required. Furthermore, given her very personality, she could not become one unless she stretched the behavior allowed by theology and Catholic society to the maximum by really becoming God's bride physically and intellectually, therefore with ecstasies and visions, implying the divine possession of her body. While working like a "male" all the same in the most important social area of Church reform; "founding" convents (being a "founder" is the strongest form of male power that a religious woman can reach); writing a *Rule* of her own; imposing her authority and her power over the only group willing to recognize them — the most adamant, the most easily subjugated believers: women; and a few rather "effeminate males" who were psychologically averse to any sexualized relation with women: John of the Cross and Jerome Gratian.

Both in her desire to be "God's bride" and in her ecstasies and visions, Teresa actually conformed to the greatest model of faithfulness to the Catholic Church. In the Lutheran Reformation, "God's bride" does not exist because not only is Protestant theology less "sexualized" than the Catholic, but phenomena of "unifying mysticism" are kept to the sidelines of a faith that is as respectful as it can be of the transcendence and inscrutable nature of God; in particular, the openly erotic-sexual phenomena of women "mystics." In rejecting "miracles," God's direct, contingent intervention in earthly affairs and the anomalous, semi-deified figures of the saints, ecstasies, visions, and stigmata are rejected as well in total tranquility.

But it is also true that, like most women "mystics," by exploiting and absolutizing the highest goals allowed her, Teresa thought she was rebelling not only against the authority of males in general, but also against everything that her culture and society imposed on women as "inferiors." The potent word has always been prohibited for women, whether written or spoken; and Teresa, like so many other women "mystics," has taken up the word as the "voice" of God.

At this point, another level of "pretending" springs up. Was it not perhaps the Church that claimed that God reveals himself to the humble, more than to the powerful? Fine, then, here is where the tug-of-war begins: first of all, with the ambiguity of the concept, "humble." Who are the humble? The alienated, the poor, the ignorant, peasants, indentured servants, women? No, this affirmation is to be overturned. It is because all these persons are somehow linked to the "part of femininity" that they are "humble." Femininity is the paradigm of any "inferiority-lowliness" because woman is unmistakably, by nature, devoid of "elevation." What is humble is what is "lowly," declare Horace and Cicero, what "creeps on the ground"; but this literal meaning immediately becomes metaphorical and much more explicit: "*Oratio humilis et abjecta* " is "low" speech, speech that is not "raised."

Here we clearly find ourselves in the primary area of meanings and values constructed on the functioning of the penis, which is totally negative when it "is low," when it is "vile"— etymologically, "devoid of *vis*"; when it cannot "rise," "eject" (see Part I, Chapter 3 of this book).

Therefore Teresa, as a woman, can claim to know something only when she denies herself as a thinking, knowing subject. What she knows is revealed to her by God, the only possibility that the Church has left to the "humble." Like all holders of power, the Church grants its subjects (like parents playing with their children) what they can never truly claim as their right. This situation gives rise to the struggle that women "mystics" have to wage so that their words will be believed, but above all, so they will be endorsed by ecclesiastic power. Another result is that mechanism of "testing" through which, in a gradual crescendo of clarification proving that these visions are not the false inventions of insignificant little women (*mulierculae*), or deceits of the devil to be rejected by all possible means (penances, fasts, exorcisms, etc.), the Church finally "discovers" that the ecstasies and visions of the most "humble"—women—are highly useful to it. In fact, they serve to confirm on behalf of God the truths that the Church itself asserts. At this point the interests of Teresa (of women "mystics") coincide with those of the Church. The women "mystics" become powerful because they side with the powerful, with men. As we have already seen, this is the tragic, ineluctable destiny of women under Christianity.

If we read Teresa's writings objectively, one point among the many whose interpretation is debatable appears the most interesting. We are led to ask: In moments of normal consciousness, to what extent does Teresa deliberately "help" her visions to penetrate coherently her own cultural, social, and religious world? The fact that she does so is impossible to doubt, given the very obviousness of her hallucinations, which are based on an incontestably accurate theological logic (verified and acknowledged by the Church in declaring her a "doctor"). It is also impossible to doubt because of the paucity of those revelations that are "so marvelous that I cannot describe them," to which she alludes when she is incapable of inventing anything new or different. At least in part, here, we are in the presence of that level of falsity/non-falsity that until today women have always been unable to escape, prisoners of the role assigned them, a role invented by males that they have been forced to "perform." Still, Teresa may have been content to choose the monastic life of her own will (she was not forced, at least when we speak only of a concrete constriction and not a generalized cultural one); she may have been content performing such male works as the founding and reforming of monasteries, and becoming the leader of women who consigned themselves to her power by entering her convents and submitting themselves to the most rigorous obedience toward a rule written by her. Writing a rule not only meant arrogating the right to the highest kind of wisdom, that of leading others to "perfection," but also becoming equal to the most important men/males in Church history: Augustine and Benedict.

Moreover, Teresa had managed to elude possession by a male, a husband and master, without losing — indeed, even while intensifying — her relations with the world outside; a privilege of all "founders" and "superiors" who are the severe judges of any transgressions on the part of their subordinates. Indeed, in her *Constitutions*, Teresa, too, takes care to impose the prioress's censorship over everything that enters or leaves the convent. Finally, Teresa succeeded in maintaining relations on a basis of equality — when she was not on a superior level — with many "top-quality" males including John of the Cross and Jerome Gratian. But this did not satisfy her aspiration for absolute domination over men and women, an aspiration that could be satisfied only through intimacy with the only one who was equally dominant and absolute. When the "voice" tells her not to "search for me within yourself," as so many lovers of God, beginning with Augustine, had believed, thought, and theorized as possible; but rather to "look for yourself in me," her deification is complete. Her ego has expanded identifying itself with omnipotence, and the reality principle is lost. The commentaries written by Teresa, apropos of "look for yourself in me," on the interpretations attempted by many of those around her are full of scorn for all these individuals, because the only one who can understand is the one (she, of course) who has received this order from God. God gives this grace that is attainable only through love to those whom he chooses.[86]

Once again, we are amazed at the blindness of all those who have read and commented on the thoughts of a woman who found the simplest way to boss others: that of the impossibility of explaining. Such readers have been unaware of the vulgar mechanism of humility-elevation that Teresa set into motion. Indeed, there can be no doubt as to Teresa's absolute certainty of her own superiority.

Waste of Intelligence or Lack of Intelligence?

From one century to the next, and from one scholar to the next, Teresa has been painted as a highly intelligent woman, possessing an acute "discernment of spirits" as well as concrete good sense. But even in her case, one must recognize a complete lack of intelligence, if by "intelligence" we mean a capacity for autonomous, creative reflection. If we accept the premise that she is not lying, then we must admit that Teresa understands nothing, not even of herself. Indeed, everything she recounts is extrinsic and lacks profundity, even when she describes ("describes," not narrates) events that would be extremely problematic for anyone else.

Teresa is a "woman," and as such an actress of the poorest quality; she knows her part by heart, she recites it but does not live it, nor does she make it live. And she is so convinced that her audience is ready to believe anything she narrates, that we can draw two conclusions. First: Teresa lacks true intelligence, the sense of critical doubt. We have observed this trait in many other women visionaries, and it probably facilitates the abandonment to visions as a loss of the reality principle. Second: This lack of intelligence allows her to speak and to write as if what she has learned from the surrounding society and culture, even unconsciously, were new, and hers alone. The "aplomb" and "nonchalance" with which she writes (and which have always been highly admired) thus depend only on her own conviction that all those who listen to her are her inferiors, since she — woman — experiences at the highest levels what only women are allowed to experience: participation in God through the total psycho-sexual union of the bride; knowledge of the divinity which only the transcendental sexual union permits; and finally, the authority deriving from it, since it is endorsed by God in the manner established by society itself.

Teresa provides the world with the most convincing proof of this sexual "union": the vision of "transverberation" (the capacity of the theological sciences to invent terms capable of expressing unthinkable phenomena is nearly unlimited), where a cherub pierces her heart with an arrow making her die of love, is the definite response to what the world expects of the perfect bride of God. But control by Teresa's ego over everything that could "lower" it, putting it on a par with normality, is powerful; therefore Teresa never speaks of sexuality. Teresa's highly praised concreteness disappears in the face of her silence over one of the major problems of the monastic life: the management of sex. That is why it is very difficult to decide whether the "piercing" so often mentioned can be understood as analogous to any sexual type of perception, because Teresa's ego is stronger than any unconscious sexual impulse. In psychiatric terms (we are, indeed, speaking of hallucinations) it may seem strange to refer to control over the ego; but here, we find a subject that acts under a form of self-hypnosis, doing exactly what it has been commanded to do by the ego in its conscious state. As in many other cases of women visionaries, in fact, Teresa's behavior clearly presents itself in terms of self-hypnosis, facilitated by the repetition of thoughts and gestures.[87]

Moreover, the inexhaustible confirmation of her primacy is so overflowing as to provoke a sense of malaise in the reader: "In thinking over what might be the cause for my almost never having any more raptures in public [so despite her expressed will to 'conceal,' she was worried that someone might be surprised by them], I heard said to myself: this is not fitting for now. You already have received enough credit for what I intend. One must also beware of the weakness of those who interpret everything maliciously." Aside from the fact that, in the lives of many women "mystics," it is common for ecstatic phenomena to become rarer as the personality stabilizes and is reassured by consensus from people surrounding them, allowing them to attenuate the anguish and waste of energy required by the flight into otherness, the response that Teresa has herself given by God is totally in line with the pseudo-craftiness of her reasoning. She blames the maliciousness of others, once she becomes aware that she can no longer exaggerate in her demands on people's gullibility. Were it not considered improper for the writer to make overly personal comments, this would be the moment to cry: "Poor woman! Poor women!"

In the tortuous circles that mystic thought forms with such appalling abundance, one senses a complete waste of intelligence. A waste of intelligence, because mystic thought discovers nothing and can discover nothing: There is no possibility of verification. It fails to construct upon itself, in the eager hope that the divinity will fill up the space left free by the ego, corresponding to what the woman — in the *non-being* of ecstasy, vision, self-abandonment, and self-depletion — believes is revealed to her. The concreteness of "emptiness/fullness" that those who are considered the greatest experts and theorists of mysticism claim to be the mechanism leading to contact with the transcendental is shockingly vulgar. The human being is imagined as a kind of "storehouse," a body, thought, and soul, which is opened and shut, emptied and filled, so that depleting it of earthly food by fasting serves to nourish it with God, and emptying it of earthly images and affections makes it capable of visions and divine yearnings. This conception reveals such intellectual grossness that perhaps only the indispensable concrete participation of the body in mystic phenomena can serve to justify it. In fact, people think that mysticism is above all, the concrete phenomenology, *experience*, and perception of the divinity in oneself.

Indeed, people believe that only the man or woman who has had such an experience can speak about it, communicate it, explain it, theorize it. (One reason why women achieve first place as mystics is that they generally have no knowledge outside of experience.) This is an old conviction. In all eras, in all areas, it conceals and protects "non-verifiability"; it always re-emerges when someone wants to establish the mystery and form of an "initiation" (as in the case of psychoanalysis). The same old conviction protects and defends the possibility of *knowledge* for all those — the majority until today — who have been kept from theoretical, cognitive, or speculative knowledge. In so doing, it fools the very persons it seems to be benefiting. Even today, people refuse to accept the idea that "experience" is or constitutes a very limited form of knowledge, one that is nearly always erroneous and illusory, which in turn can be transmitted only through experience, and therefore prevents both accumulation and progressiveness. Such a refusal, indeed, would deny the value of life as such.

It is women especially, and the feminists in particular, who claim that life is knowledge; a kind of knowledge gained by experience. But as we shall see in our discussion of the social activity of religious women, their "experience" unfortunately has not served to change the structures of domination and oppression over those they meant to help, nor to construct any knowledge capable of combating the diseases of the most unfortunate, whom they nonetheless have assisted for hundreds of years. Finally, and this is perhaps the most tragic evidence, despite their experience, religious women have not learned to liberate themselves and other women from the prison men have constructed on the foundation of "femaleness."

We thus find ourselves inevitably facing another factor that explains the overwhelming presence of women in "mysticism." Excluded from any speculative knowledge—from theology, philosophy, jurisprudence (indeed, from all those forms of thought that even before the development of science at least allowed one to construct a "method" for knowing)—and, at the same time, from any social power, women seek within themselves, in their own body-as-container assigned to them in a biological-transcendent role by masculine culture, a knowledge which, in compensation, must be stronger than the knowledge denied them: that is, the knowledge of God. The "emptiness-fullness" corresponds in the highest degree to the female body, which becomes "impregnated" (that is how many women mystics express their being invaded by the divinity). In this perspective, therefore, "mysticism," understood as an obsession or "plenitude" of God, presupposes a certain kind of "femininity" even in those men who have theorized and experienced it.

The concept of "emptiness-fullness" implies an opposite type of thought process, marked by those elementary cognitive structures that anthropologists have analyzed so acutely among the "savages" (but which they have had trouble discerning among us). We thus find here one of the clearest pieces of evidence that the product of visions and ecstasies, and of the effort to form mystic concepts, is minimal; it is absolutely unequal to the capacity for reflection attained by the Western European culture to which our women "mystics" belong. At any rate, we need only glance at certain passages written by John of the Cross (whose "femininity" might well be discussed in greater depth than has been done up to now, despite the enormous bibliography concerning him) in order to observe how effectively oppositions serve to render thought only apparent; or rather, null. The pedagogy of "annihilation," which only women have carried to such extremes inasmuch as they have done so with their bodies, works like this in the *The*

Ascent of Mount Carmel: "Since I was reduced to nothing, I have found that I lack nothing [...]"; "In order to be something in everything, one must be nothing at all [...]." What can we say here? Perhaps these ingenuous little games, these words or non-thoughts seem strange in the mouth of a male religious, and would be judged more praiseworthy on the lips of some woman "mystic." But it is not our task here to delve into the feminine element of many male "mystics." We must therefore leave John of the Cross to some scholar who desires to look into the problem with greater attention.

7
In Love Until Death

There is an uninterrupted thread in the religious experience of women, running from their first encounter with Jesus up to the early years of our century (with St. Gemma Galgani): This thread is usually defined as "mystical." It is an absolute enamoring. Beginning with Mary's silent listening at the feet of Jesus in Lazarus's dwelling, it stresses the forgetting of oneself in order to concentrate on knowledge of the other. This experience is possible in Christianity because God is man in Jesus, and for women, He is the bridegroom whom society presents to them in marriage. It is therefore right—indeed, necessary—to seek total union, both sexual and intellectual, with this God-bridegroom. An abandonment of one's body and mind is allowed, in fact, desired by the group, only for the feminine part of humanity.

The term "mysticism" covers, under an apparent technicality, a set of behaviors that could, and often do fall into the category of psychic abnormality, when society decides they should. In this study the term will be "dissolved" into different meanings and actions as far as possible, for two reasons. First, the term runs the risk of preventing readers unfamiliar with theological language to really understand what we are talking about. Second, because this type of anthropological analysis aims to eliminate "technical" terms pertaining to separate sectors of knowledge (terms which create false realities at the very moment they define them) in order to make the most varied behaviors circulate in the reconstruction of a "normal" cultural model that will not cross the boundaries of the laws of physics.

Life as Death

The history of Christianity presents numerous examples of visual and acoustic hallucinations, lack of consciousness, paralysis, and all kinds of "miraculous" phenomena, beginning right after the death of Jesus. Such phenomena appear in Paul's Letters, in the Acts of the Apostles, and in the acts of the martyrs and saints. However, the consciousness of a particular religious experience — the absolute enamoring of those women who have been assigned this enamoring, the brides of God in the monastic life, seems to arise as a desired, sought out experience and, in appearance, a creative one, only in the 11th century.

It develops parallel to that progressive, increasingly accentuated identification with the Man of Sorrows, with the "human person" of the Savior, which manifests itself and takes definite shape, above all, in the culture and society of central Europe. A "penitential" culture, whose contours become increasingly clear as the expectation of the millennium is overcome: the expectation of Christ's glorious return, to close the history of the world. A number of factors, though varied and distant from each other, flow together to form and stimulate a Christianity in which there is a greater awareness that, if Jesus is man and condemned to die by the Father, then all men like him are condemned to die by the Father, and existence on Earth *is this death* which must be experienced and consumed to the utmost.[88] No longer considered, as in the early centuries, a rapid passage to salvation brought by Christ-God which found its culmination in "martyrdom," this life-death is reality per se, and the only mortal time granted to man as man. No one better than Thérèse of Lisieux succeeded in expressing the sense of life as death that, however, "finishes" or "passes": life "is the only night that is not repeated."[89]

All human forces — psychological, social, and cultural — are thus concentrated around the life of Christ as an itinerary of suffering that hastens toward the fixed goal of the cross (the repeated utterance of the Gospel writers: Whoever loves me must "take up his cross and follow me" is surely not attributable to Jesus, given the reference to the cross). Such human forces form a perfectly coherent, interrelated picture. Journeys to the Holy Land become more and more frequent, dictated by the wish to "touch" directly the life and Passion of the Savior; and eventually, by the conviction that this land, Jerusalem, a concrete symbol of paradise, cannot belong to anyone but Christians. This situation inevitably sparks efforts to take over the land by means of the crusades — the frightening articulation of Christian violence in which men face a new type of "martyrdom" in which the victim is simultaneously also the "sacrificer," the killer of God's enemies.

True, there had already been episodes of serious violence beginning with the early "heretical" disputes over Arianism and iconoclasm, but only with the crusades is the concept of "martyrdom" turned upside down. The

Christian martyr, he who had been praised for his acceptance of death, as humble and obedient as Christ, who "bore witness" to his faith with the "scandal" of his non-violence in a world where failing to combat and defend oneself represented the lowest "vileness" and "dishonor," now becomes a martyr twice over. For he *kills* in addition to being killed in bearing witness to his faith. Instead, for women, who are no longer "martyrs" as during the anti-Christian persecutions, their individual lives take shape in the quest for suffering and martyrdom. This is the core of the female religious experience: union with the crucified Christ.

As journeys to the Holy Land become more frequent, so does the cult of relics, especially those allowing men to concentrate their devotion on the earthly, human existence of Jesus. First of all, such relics concern the Passion: cross, nails, blood, Veronica's veil; then little by little, the Mother and Child, the milk with which the Virgin nursed him, the little gown and swaddling clothes in which he was wrapped, the prepuce of circumcision, and so on.[90] As in the case of the early relics of the martyrs, we perceive here a particularly feminine kind of sensitivity. Concrete relics cede to an explosive growth dictated by fantasy; the history of events regarding relics is elaborated until we reach the symbolic-concrete presence of relics in the experience of those who most intensely concentrated on and identified with Jesus-Man, and his body. In the great majority, it is women who, shut up in convents where there is hardly any intellectual stimulation, can abandon their imaginations to the earthly life of Christ. They need no theoretical "knowledge" in order to examine, both mentally and emotionally, the decisive events of Jesus' life as a "human being," passing from those of his infancy to those of his agony and death, for women have been (and are) always present in such "events." They are assigned to look after children, the moribund, and the dead.

The so-called "devotions" thus develop (a term which, like "mysticism," should be "dissolved" into its emotional and imaginary reality). As the experience of and search for a Christianity to "live" rather than "theorize," devotions are "effeminate" in themselves (and are always considered somewhat minor, if not inferior forms of religiosity).

With the Catholic Counter Reformation and the "path" theorized by Francis de Sales (whose most famous work is his *Introduction to the Devout Life*), devotions became a recognized system for spiritual exercise. We are dealing here, as always, with transference of sensitivity from femininity and women's emotional world to a vaster audience that includes all the faithful. Indeed, does not Francis of Assisi's impulsive gesture of affection toward the leper seem a bit "effeminate"? Or rather, does it not strike us as a gesture of potent sanctity, since it is performed by a male? How many lepers, wounded, plague-stricken, or moribund people have been assisted, washed, and cared for by women, without their presence and dedication ever being taken into account by history, much less exalted as a virtue? Is that Francis whom tradition credits with the first manger scene, not a bit effeminate? A manger scene which, indeed, will be prepared each year with such care and tenderness, above all, by women, nuns in convents or mothers with their children at home. And finally, is that *Hymn to the Creatures* not a bit effeminate, when it calls water "sister" and fire "brother"? Francis's "femininity" manifests itself as a sign of his diversity, both with respect to monasticism (Francis, in fact, wanted neither to found an order nor write a rule), and with respect to all those who thought they could imitate him even during his life, beginning with Clare who, shut up in the hermitage of St. Damian, forced herself and her nuns to do violence to themselves in the most rigid penitence, and whose life expresses none of the sweetness and freshness of Francis.

A Romantic God

The names of so-called "mystic" women continue uninterruptedly down through the centuries. Expressed in images and words similar to one another, their passionate, intimate, face-to-face encounters with the bridegroom repeat an absolute, radical enamoring which carries the experience and insatiable desire for love to its extremes. "Romantic" love of which, with few exceptions, only women are capable.

True, at least until today, it has been men/males, the artists and the poets, who have imagined, sung, and theorized romantic love, as they have all cultural creations. But it has been, and still is women who believe in romantic love absolutely: living it, concretizing it, consuming their life in the effort to achieve it. Romantic enamoring is always desire, dream, the unachieved and unachievable, for in "fusion" the "you" is annulled. But the "I" of "you" can only be annulled in the simultaneous death of the two "Is."

"Mysticism" in women is romantic love and absolute passion that finds a means for perfect fulfillment because the you, the other to be loved, is God in a "game" that never ends and can never end, since the "you"-God sets no limits; it conforms to what the lover wants, in a union that reaches total fusion. For the body of the other is imaginary, the fruit of fantasy, and is projected onto it by the subject who loves.

Says Thérèse of Lisieux: "I need someone who, having assumed my nature, will love me without ever changing. What happiness to know that God *cannot* change."[91]

II. The Tragic Game of Mysticism

Naturally, it is not true that the God spoken of by the woman "mystic" does not change: He changes continuously, in satisfying response to the "I" of the lover, which grows immeasurably until it loses consciousness of itself, its own reality, the I of the God it has constructed. Catherine of Siena, Angela of Foligno, Chiara of Montefalco, Maria Maddalena de' Pazzi, Bridget of Sweden, Teresa of Avila, Marguerite-Marie Alacoque Though we could name some male "mystics," the women outnumber them to the point of eclipsing them.

But why women? The answer can be found, aside from everything we could say and have said concerning female psychology, in the "nuptial" construction of Christian, and especially Catholic theology. (The passage from an ideal desired, imaginary union to that of the woman with a potent male is not reversible; it is the male who takes the "bride," and God is the prototype of this male.)

Femininity and masculinity are necessarily present in a "nuptial pact," which make no sense unless it is understood as a pact between male and female.

In Christianity, males find themselves in a sexualized position which tends to feminize them; for they truly become what the Jews have never succeeded in being, except symbolically, because of original sin: the *brides* of God. This femininity of the nuptial bond with God has made the lives of male Christians extremely difficult in relation to women and the use of sexuality (for sexuality implies the supreme risk of the betrayal of God, adultery). And it has made their personal identity in religious life even more difficult, since no "I" is conceivable without a sexual identity. This situation gives rise to ascesis, monasticism, the negativity of the use of sex, and the renunciation of concrete marriage, which becomes incompatible with the female identity of one who is the God's bride. In other words, males must experience a "female" life in Christianity, constructing it *ex novo*, somehow copying the life of women by putting themselves in a *passive* position in the presence of God, for this is the position assigned to the female sex. The concrete-cultural position of the sexual act, as lived by males who possess the instrument capable of penetration and possession—to be subject, to "be underneath"—has become a standard image for any "lowliness," be it physical and concrete or psychological and social. Humility, the supreme virtue of the Christian, alludes (albeit unconsciously) to that "staying down," "staying on earth" (*humus*, the root of humility, indicates earth), which is the opposite position of the "high" one of the erect penis.

Naturally, not all males can accept a similar reversal of psychological and social roles. Indeed, the profound division between those who can and those who cannot gives rise to the distance between common Christians and a social class unto itself that finds fulfillment in monasticism and the priesthood.

From the very beginning of Christianity, it has often been asked whether Christianity was a religion for the few, for the elite, and almost impracticable in its essence on the part of the masses. The query has made us realize (albeit without any awareness of the deeper causes) that "true" Christianity — not the "Christianity" indicated by Jesus, but the one constructed by St. Paul and men who came after him — is in itself subversive toward any social establishment; many perceived its more or less distinct danger and so fought against it.

The Femininity of Males

In reality, the history of Christian Europe has been one of continual psychological, social, and political conflict, because of the need to find compromises between the radical anti-sociality implied in the logic underlying the marriage to God, and the concrete necessities of life. Only with the recognition of a secular state that was separate from the ecclesiastic one, which followed on the heels of the Enlightenment and the French Revolution, have men succeeded in settling the conflict with any semblance of logic. Still, in a subterranean form, it continues to pervade the difficult co-existence between civil and religious society.

The problem, then, was *marriage to God* on earth, with all its attendant emotional, intellectual, and sexual implications. First of all: "knowing" God in a nuptial way — that is, as a bride. This is the point which most clearly reveals the mental homosexuality of males: God is the only true male, and males must assume a feminine role in order to approach Him, to let themselves be possessed by Him, to love Him and be loved by Him. To overcome masculine sexuality to the point of "becoming eunuchs" for the kingdom of heaven, as the Gospel puts it, is the most difficult battle; in any event, homosexuals have an easier time of it, for the psychological exchange between male and female roles is not only understandable to them, but pleasing.

By shutting themselves up in a monastery, men satisfy a primary need: to live, eat, sleep, and work among other men, and eliminate the "domestic," daily presence of women. They then slowly construct an ideal object, a pseudo-feminine one, on which they can project all their aspirations: the Madonna. The true bride of God, fecundated by God and the Mother of His son, the Madonna is what they would like to be: brides of God, possessed and fecundated by Him (the virginity of the Madonna represents, indeed, the masculinity of this fecundation, which has no need to come in contact with a hymen in order to be effected).[92]

The road along which this "object" has been constructed is highly indicative. The Madonna was said to be the "Mother" (*theotokos*, the first dogmatic definition referring to Mary, was established in 431 at the Council of Ephesus), who is, sexually speaking, the least dangerous figure for males, and the only one admitted to the male homosexual horizon (in the film, *The Gospel According to Matthew* by Pasolini, a homosexual director, the actress representing the Madonna is the director's mother); and in addition, the least "scandalous" one to be presented theologically to society. There follows the virgin-mother, and gradually all the most scabrous and, at the same time, most contiguous attributes of the ideal object that men dream of: conceived without sin and therefore devoid of any sexual temptation, both as regards herself and men; devoid of menstruation, free of labor pains, "closed" into virginity even in childbirth and after childbirth; and finally, assumed into heaven, and hence untouched by the corruption of death.

It is those males who are most bridelike in relation to God, the most "mystical" ones, who are in love with Our Lady. It is they who emphasize the feminine elements of their own personalities in the loving relationship with God, that is, those in whom we might legitimately suspect at least a mental form of homosexuality, one intensely experienced on the emotional level as well. Suffice it to name Bernard of Clairvaux, who receives in a vision a few drops of milk from the breast of Our Lady; Francis of Assisi, the first to reconstruct in the manger scene the tenderness of birth and the loving relation between mother and child; Bernardine of Siena, who never ceases to say that the Virgin is the only woman on whom he can gaze.[93] Bernardine's sense of repulsion toward real women is so strong that he blames them for all wrongdoing, even accusing them of driving their husbands to sodomy; he refuses to have anything to do with them, even when required by his ministry as confessor.

And then, among those enamored of the Madonna, how can we forget Philip Neri, in whose arms the Madonna places the Baby Jesus in a vision? (He is so depicted by Guido Reni in the painting over the altar containing his body in the Roman church of Santa Maria in Vallicella.) Philip's passion for sexual purity (a trait marking all those in love with the Madonna) has remained so famous that he has been attributed with the capacity to recognize the presence of "sinning" women by their odor, and it is said that he covered his naked penis with his hand during his autopsy. Who was more passionately in love with Our Lady than Grignion de Montfort, who totally consecrates himself to her as a "slave of love"?

His praises and devotions to the Virgin seem to gush forth from attacks of delirium.[94]

However, if we look at these same men, we realize that they are in fact "mystics"; their relationship with Christ is full of concrete, personal affection, and the images with which they address the bridegroom are very similar to those used by Christ's women brides.

John of the Cross's comment to the *Song of Songs* is famous. Entitled *Songs of the Bride*, it contains the lyrical effusions of a wholly real lover, who exalts the erotic qualities of the body of the beloved woman, with whom John identifies.

Naturally, this female identification has been hidden under the guise of symbolism. It is the soul that is loved, and yet, the femininity of the "soul" re-emerges precisely in the fundamental nuptial image of Judeo-Christianity.

If God is the Bridegroom-Male, the soul is necessarily feminine. And yet the lives of these enamored males are so different from female lives that there can be no comparison. Men's enthusiasms, visions, and ecstasies never totally absorb their capacity for action in the world. Bernard of Clairvaux, for example, worked with overwhelming zeal for Church reform; he brought with him into the monastery dozens of friends and companions who had previously shared his adventurous life as a rich knight; he did not hesitate to preach with violence the need to fight in the Crusades against the "infidels." In short, he was one of the most active, committed personalities in the political life of his time and he did not need to recur to visions (as women have always done) in order to be sure of his ideas and actions.

When we then think of the origins of Christianity, of everything done and imposed on his followers by such a man as St. Paul, who nonetheless claims he was moved to action because of a "vision"; and who proclaims "passionate" forms of identification with Christ, perhaps the strongest ones held by any of the male "mystics," then we realize how psychologically different women were, and how socially fragile, despite their raptures and their ecstasies.

At any rate, there is another fact that profoundly distinguishes the love of women for the divinity from that of men: a quest for physical suffering that is pushed to nearly inconceivable extremes. The instrument of ascesis and bodily suffering, however, is authorized and guided by confessors and spiritual directors, who never would have even thought of a similar "lowering" of male dignity. In any event, the forms of penitence imposed on women (lack of sleep and food, long nightly meditations) facilitated hallucinatory phenomena; indeed, this behavior may at least partially explain the prevalence of hallucinations in women.

Historians of Christianity have long wondered about the so-called "women's movements" of the Middle Ages, when there was a great flourishing of women "mystics" beginning with Hildegard of Bingen and down to the less famous, such as Elizabeth of Hungary, Bridget of Sweden, Catherine of Siena, Chiara of Montefalco, Angela of Foligno; and countless others (all "saints" of course). The movement has not undergone significant changes in form during the modern era, although we find specialized studies concerning the period of the Reformation in particular, for example, regarding quietism and victimism. The woman-bride's love relation with the God-Man, Jesus, is always the same: the knowledge of this Man-God's privileged love for his bride-lover; the sensation of his physical presence and ardor in the exchanging of hearts, and in an outer or inner voice, which reveals his most intimate thoughts to the favored loved one, so that she shares in his earthly suffering and heavenly glory. What changes is not the feeling or the desire for union, possession, or participation, but the psychological, social, and cultural context nourishing them. It is a context formed by the historical moment, by the themes and values in which the woman defined as a "mystic" finds herself living, be she inside or outside the convent, and by the theological-political facts pervading and unifying the center and the south of Western Europe.

We have mentioned the influence that the cult of relics had on the religious life of the faithful during the Middle Ages. In particular, this cult was a source of material for the imagination and affections of women, the brides and lovers of God. Undoubtedly, the great search for the relics of the Passion vivified devotion to the details of the crucifixion and death of the Savior. Suffice it to recall the name of Catherine of Siena, who never stops crying: "Blood, blood!" as she contemplates the face of the crucified one; and the visions of the Passion experienced by Maria Maddalena de' Pazzi, Angela of Foligno, Catherine Emmerick ... until we reach Gemma Galgani — she too a bearer of stigmata — who cries: "How good your blood is to drink!"[95]

Moreover, the iconography has always focused on the instruments of the Passion in increasingly realistic detail, isolating them from one another to the point that each nail, thorn, whiplash, bruise, or wound seems to assume an autonomous meaning, an essence.

Therefore, women "mystics" often turn to the rib wound which lends greater and greater force to devotion to the Sacred Heart, not only as a loving heart, but as a bleeding one; they turn to the crown of thorns which seems to pierce their heads as well, making them bleed; and finally, they turn to the rib wound, giving rise to the phenomenon of stigmata.

The quest for suffering, or even the "mystics of suffering" as it was defined in the late Middle Ages (which, as far as women are concerned, has lasted from the beginning of Christianity to the present), is present in all the manifestations of Christ-Man of Sorrows, from whose pierced heart that blood gushes which so many mystics yearned to drink, and which triumphed with Marguérite Marie Alacoque. The love relation with a Crucified Bridegroom is completely revealed, with its true, easy-to-grasp, correct logic, in the relationship between women and Christ; because femininity has no need for any concrete or symbolic transformation to achieve this marriage. That is why marriage is explicit in the fantasies of possession of women who reach the extreme limits of desire for and mental "experience" of erotic yearning. It is only our habit of transferring the amorous adventure implied in a religion founded on marriage with God to a symbolic level that allows us to ignore these limits or to overcome them.

Imprinting: God's Bride

In order to understand certain aspects of the life of transcendent female love, we might consider one of the recurring themes of these women's biographies: the fact that they were sent to monasteries in early childhood. In itself, it offers numerous clues concerning the psychological and cultural paths that religious women were almost obliged to follow.

Consecration to God occurred in earliest childhood, in the years in which an individual absorbed everything uncritically from the environment, and nearly always only on the basis of the customs that accompanied European society from the early Middle Ages until the end of the 19th century. Shutting them up in a convent served to protect them and mold their childhoods and youths, both in view of future marriages or their passages from the status of pupils to that of brides of Christ, and thus never to leave the convent again. In both cases, it was according to the father's will.

However, in the *Acta Sanctorum*, as in their biographies, this deliverance to a convent is not presented as a daunting social constriction, but rather as a sign of early divine favor. Bona of Pisa (12th century) was blessed at the age of seven by the Crucified One as she passed before the Church of San Sepolcro; Colette of Corbie (14th century) prayed continually at the age of four, and had her first revelations at the age of nine; Matilda of Hackeborn (13th century), taken to visit a convent at Rodersdorf at the age of seven, was so conquered by it that she gained permission to stay; Catherine of Genoa (15th century) was already performing acts of penitence at the age of eight, smitten by the Passion of Christ; Maria Maddalena de' Pazzi (16th century) entered a convent as a pupil at the age of eight, and had her first ecstasy at 12; Agnese of Montepulciano (13th century) entered a Dominican convent at nine; Bridget of Sweden (14th century) had her first vision at the age of seven, and at 10, the Crucified Jesus "wounds her heart"; Marguerite-Marie Alacoque (17th century) took a vow of chastity at the age of four (none of her biographers shows the slightest surprise in reporting a fact like this, which reveals the kind of environment in which little girls were raised), and enters the convent of the Sisters of St. Clare at Charolles as a pupil at the age of eight. All these verbs: "entered," "took a vow," etc., habitually used by biographers as active expressions of the subject, should obviously be understood in their passive sense: the little girls "are turned over" to convents, "are induced" to take vows....

We could go on at length. These are only some of the sporadic details that confirm, with due allowance made for the typical, inevitable themes of the "legend," that most of the women canonized for their "mystical" gifts had childhoods that were marked by a strong presence of the sacred. They were placed by their fathers in convents as pupils, and they themselves were deeply influenced by the religious fabric of the culture of their times. It does not interest us so much to emphasize the sociological fact — important as it is — as the qualities sharply differentiating female childhoods from male ones. Together with other factors that we shall attempt to highlight, this difference can partially explain why so-called "mysticism" is a prevalently female phenomenon.

The limited scholastic knowledge imparted to women forms totally obedient personalities, not only in their behavior, but also and above all in their mental development, in the learning of logical thought. Their thinking is forced to move and mature in association with the ideas furnished by theology. It is a theology stripped of any philosophical or theoretical format, as it is taught to women, and therefore it does not allow them to understand what "thinking" is. What little girls, and then women, learn is the worst in religious culture, since theological logic, which lacks a systematic theoretical base, does not allow anything to be perceived of its absurdity and irrationality. On the contrary, it lends itself to an affective, emotional adjustment, the only element allowed women. Indeed, it becomes the only element in which they can grasp or recognize anything of themselves within a construction which totally adheres to male fantasy, and to the male will for domination.

It is there, then, in the emotional life that women "produce," for that is the only area in which they are called on to produce. But if this is the inevitable neurobiological result, since only this type of neuronic path has been activated, the question we must still answer concerning the interchange between personality and culture is this: Why have some of these women identified with and followed such paths to the point of absolutely believing in what they needed? Undoubtedly, among the countless number of women who have been subjected to monastic acculturation, those who emerge with phenomena bordering the "limits"—visions, ecstasies, rapture, voices, stigmata, exchanges of hearts and wedding rings—remain exceptions. And yet, compared to men, they are too numerous and too similar to each other to be considered simply "ill" (aside from the fact that the Church presents them as role models by canonizing them); especially since their "delirium" never transgresses beyond the logic of the religion in which they move. Later, at any rate, we shall more clearly see how a number of factors combine to make up the social, cultural, and bio-psychic dynamics accompanying the lives of these women. We may then be able to understand, at least in part, some of the most surprising, obscure phenomena that emerge even today.

Their spasmodic quest for "true" life cannot help but be confirmed as hallucinatory, since it originates from the individual relation with an otherworldly reality, and eludes any possibility of verification. What are the limits of reality for a person who from early childhood has been taught to believe that such limits do not exist? Since no ideal goal has been proposed to such women, except that of going further and further along the road of the invisible, transcendent world, some of them finally choose the "adventure." They are women whose egos will not be annulled without some compensation: the most self-aware, and at the same time the least intelligent (from a critical point of view); those who have the greatest passions and who, in having to choose between the emptiness of a lifetime in a convent, and the psychic, physical adventure of an encounter with Almighty God, presented as Man, Male, Bridegroom, and Lover, cast themselves into an unreality that must be reduced to the real, since it is up to them and them only to concretize it. In the condition of absolute impotence in which the world has put them by assigning them to the life "beyond" during life on earth, they choose absolute omnipotence.

The Adventure of Hallucination

On the basis of the most recent inquiries into biology, it now seems certain that the environment or external stimulation is influential in the selection of neuronal groups; it influences their "specialization" and their "development" in "specialization."[96] Setting off from this premise, to what degree does such pressure—be it from the global cultural environment, the family environment or the monastic one—contribute to making the

II. The Tragic Game of Mysticism

brain of God's women brides "specialize" in its tasks? Such women, remember, lived a cloistered life from childhood on, one without any confrontation with a different kind of reality. Perhaps there are particular subjective conditions that lead certain women to absolutize to extremes the role assigned to them (those who are subject to ecstasies, visions, hallucinations, and stigmata always represent an exception).

The question always remains the same: Are they "ill" even though their symptoms are totally adherent to the culture? And would they be so, albeit with different symptomatic manifestations, in other cultures as well? At least for now, this is impossible to answer with certainty, since research in the field of ethno-psychiatry is still in its early stages. The responsibility of the group, in any event, is always the predominant one. Following the road indicated by Gerald Edelman, perhaps we can better understand the mechanisms of this responsibility since, with primary monastic acculturation (that undergone in childhood), they imply the stimulation of exclusive neuronic associations, according to the theory of neuronal group selection. This leads to the formation of a particular (individual) type of "consciousness," both primary and superior.[97]

Undoubtedly, the phenomena of greatest alienation from reality developed in the religious environment (the area of religious thought), and in the period from the Middle Ages to the end of the 19th century, in Catholic thought in particular. In no other society, in fact, has imaginary thought — thought unhinged from reality — been established as a "science," of a logical certainty. Theology has forcefully claimed primacy over all other knowledge (and we have not sufficiently reflected on the astounding fact that it has officially "obtained" this). In this perspective, we need only recall the role performed by theology in the most important medieval universities; one performed even today (though not in an explicit declaration of primacy) with the existence of theological chairs at the leading universities of many Western countries. In logical terms, the result of the trial against Galileo can be summed up as showing the supremacy of imaginary thought over perceptive thought. And this occurs because with the development of theology, Catholicism has theorized the "normality" of delirious thinking.

In Christian Europe, because of the intersection and overlapping of cultural themes centered on the meaning of being a "woman," women have undergone pressure to conform, lacking any instrument for self-defense. For even when they possessed some knowledge, it was acquired from within the ambit of religious thought. Therefore, it was already based on a premise of detachment from reality. (In order to have an analogous scheme of reference, consider the function of the mother tongue in the individual's learning of all knowledge.)

In order to make the unreality of their reality "true," women could do nothing but commit themselves. Because of the meanings assigned to femininity, this meant passing through their own body. Moreover, the continual feedback between women's emotional fantasizing and the Church which ratifies or rejects it, creates a circle of "normality-abnormality" and of "perdition-sanctity" that women cannot escape. Only the Church (men of power in the Church) can assign them to one or the other category. If their visions, ecstasies, and revelations are recognized as originating from God, then society in turn will exalt them as heroines. And they really will "be."

After all, history (the history we are trying to write here) demonstrates this: Of the infinite number of women who have lost themselves in the non-being assigned to women, the only ones of whom we are speaking, whose memory we have somehow crystallized, are those who have chosen unreality. Only until yesterday, moreover, the alternative was that of diabolic possession, heresy, and condemnation.

A Simple Little Woman: Joan of Arc

Joan of Arc is exemplary of this "logical" mechanism. She was a simple young woman, a "maiden," a "virgin"; an extremely important fact, for had she not been young and equipped with the intrinsic potency of female youth, virginity, a "woman" would never have succeeded in dragging armies and men of power along with her. Her weapons, besides that of youth-virginity, are "the voices"; communication with the world of the transcendental. Could any male have managed to lead men to war or to the Crusades by the force of his ecstasies, of "voices"? Certainly not. Even the greatest saints—Bernard of Clairvaux, Peter Damiani, John of Capestrano—with all their ecstasies and visions, never used them to preach in favor of wars against the heretics, or Crusades against the infidels, although they *did* preach those themes very strongly. Their strength was that of the "potent word," that of earthly authority. Joan, as a woman, can convince men only because she is in direct communication with the transcendental, and because everyone believes her claim (there are no witnesses) that a "voice" inspires her, a simple voice that says, "*Va, fille Dieu, va.*" The trial leading to her condemnation tragically and logically confirms this fact. What do her judges ask of her in order to make sure she is not a heretic who has been inspired by the devil? To recite the "Lord's Prayer" and the Creed, which is all she knows, for Joan almost proudly affirms this in the presence of the greatest sages of the time, the theologians of the University of Paris: "All I know, I know from my mother."[98]

It is an absurd trial, given the disparity of knowledge between the accusers and the accused. Knowing nothing of what her accusers know, elements that they use against her, Joan nonetheless speaks their same language, following the logic of unreality that they too accept. What can they do, seeing that in any case, even before the trial, they know they must find her guilty? They make an initial attempt: despite her claims to the contrary, Joan cannot be a virgin, for her non-virginity alone would suffice to prove that it is not God who is speaking to a maiden. But the horrible midwives who ascertain the fact confirm Joan's claims. So it must be the devil that inspires her, all the more so since Joan refuses to take off her masculine clothes, which she wears as a coat of mail, moving around alone among the violent, lecherous men of an army at war. Her judges even hint at the possibility that she might be saved from burning at the stake if she agrees to take up her feminine garments once more. Here it is truly difficult, even for us, to understand why she does not give in, if we did not again recall what "dress" means for women (see Part I, Chapter 4 of this book): their social identity, the strongest means that they possess in order to "represent" their role in the world. Their dress is their body and their spirit, just as their body is body-and-spirit when they inscribe it by using fire, the knife, or the unifying ardor of the Passion, marking it with the name of Jesus, the signs of the nails, the wound of the spear, the bleeding scratches of the crown of thorns.

Passage from the symbolic to the concrete re-emerges in all its possible gradations; where is the borderline delineating imminent delirium? Moreover, in what sense can we state that Joan is "in delirium"? She is in delirium when she is under the impression of acoustic hallucination, when she hears "the voices," but she is not in delirium when she follows the most logical military strategies, leading her men into battle. And yet, it is not her victories that prove to the inquisitors that God inspires her. This would be the only "logical" thing; it is the only thing instead that does not count.

As we have seen before, what counts is virginity, obedience to the Church commandments, dress. That is, the "world" that "femininity" has been assigned to by men. Joan, who dies at the stake murmuring the name of Jesus, will be declared a "saint," but not a "martyr," because she is perhaps the only woman that men (though unable to do so) would like to believe died exclusively "for the faith," and not in defense of her virginity. According to the logic of the culture, then, Joan should not exist. But as always, the exception confirms the rule.

With the end of the 19th century, with the development of psychology and psychiatry, the Church increasingly adapts to the hypothesis of "madness" as an alternative to "diabolic possession" in cases where it does not recognize the intervention of God. Instead of the stake, the "false" visionaries will end up in an insane asylum.

At this point we come up against an historic example that might have been deliberately invented by the scholar, given the ways in which it corresponds to the mechanisms that we are attempting to describe. Gemma Galgani was born in Lucca in the same year that another victim of visions, the famous visionary of Our Lady, Bernadette of Lourdes, died at Nevers in 1879. Of course, neither knew anything about the other, but their lives burn out in the same way, with the violent haste of one who is "dear to God." Gemma is so poor that out of compassion a well-to-do family of provincial traders takes her into their home as a maid. She is even poorer intellectually than she is materially; hardly able to read and write, she has had no mental stimulation apart from religion, and she recurs to that in order to survive in life's desert. However, she possesses such great strength, such a will to love and to "exist," that whoever approaches her is daunted. Like Thérèse of Lisieux some years before, she cries: "Who can satisfy my immense desires?"

A "different" world presents itself to her: This one is infinite indeed and limited only by the borders she chooses to establish. But while these borders depend on her, nothing else does: Like all the other great lovers we have met, Gemma cannot and does not create anything; nor does she invent anything. Everything is predisposed for a member of the female sex by the environment in which she was born: a culturally defined "sex" which the individual nevertheless experiences as if it were biological, instinctive, and as predetermined as the language learned from birth. Gemma therefore lives out her only adventure in life as the "bride of Jesus." She unites with him, she becomes one with him, in the only form that truly reflects her personality, that of victim. Ecstasies, visions, stigmata: Has she not perhaps been "crucified" ever since she opened her eyes to the world, to herself and her destiny? Who is more "nailed" than she (we shall find the term "nailed" countless times in women's language; as with stigmata, it "represents" their destiny)? She can do nothing, she must know nothing, except that being a servant is a blessing granted her by the charity of her extremely Christian masters; and that she cannot even claim ownership of the only possession that she tries to grasp with her force alone, her force, the wish to love and be loved.

The Church has inculcated this idea in her, as in all those who are and must remain "humble." The gifts that she possesses are not hers. If they do not come from God, they come from the devil; and all the more so if she chances to think that something might belong to her. Only if she obeys, only if she suffers all the tortures that the usual tuberculosis—the inseparable companion of poor people like her — imposes on her, without letting a single complaint come from her lips; only then will she be a victim pleasing to God and to his representatives. Tuberculosis has slowly attacked Gemma's entire organism, spreading from her lungs to her spine, pelvis and feet, the so-called "Pott's disease," causing extremely painful abscesses, and killing her at the age of 25. Until the end, however, and despite the continual coughing up of blood, there were those, even among the physicians, who denied that Gemma was "tubercular."[99] For the negative aura accompanying this disease, as with AIDS today, seemed incompatible with the "purity" of a young woman chosen by God.

Gemma thus proceeds further and further into a world she cannot control; a world not of her own invention, though highly similar to the one she believes to be real. The circle that forms around her as a true victim — lacking everything, nailed to the female duty of non-being — and the image of the Crucified One presented by those who know everything with the absolute authority of power. The Crucified One is actually the only person who resembles her, nailed as she is, bleeding victim as she is. She lives in a frightening logical labyrinth from which she cannot escape, except through the painful death of her 25 years of Passion.

Is it Gemma who is outside the reality principle, with her ecstasies, her stigmata, the blood she sees running from the wounds of one crucified like her by the same institutions that crucify her? Or is it the world surrounding her that is outside reality? This is the crux of the problem. Her confessor incites her to put her ecstasies to the test, ordering her not to fall into them, in order to make sure they are not provoked by the devil; he exhorts her not to be a sissy, to be "virile." But why should she? Has she not perhaps been taught that the only way she can be somebody and exist in the absolute nothingness belonging to her, is to become a saint, a perfect bride of Jesus? In order to "be virile," in order to obey the orders of those who hold power, Gemma is forced to run continually up and down the stairway of the house, her breath faltering, her lungs consumed by tuberculosis, forcing herself to remain "alert." But again, why should she? Who more than she adheres to reality, seeing that the only way offered her to "live" is that of non-reality? Who is more delirious: Gemma, who feels attacked by the devil that wants to "possess" her (as we have seen, this term implies sexual possession as defined by the male), who covers the diary she shows to her confessor with black spots, or else the confessor and the group that invented the devil and so believed in it that this notebook is displayed as miraculous proof of the devil's existence in a Roman church? No one can be psychotic if the group is psychotic. Or *no*? Or perhaps, our problem remains that of the difference between an individual with altered perceptions and the group which believes in the hallucination, yet continues to see and hear nothing?

Seals That Are Symbolic and Concrete

Yet, is it not the group that is psychotic, since the group decides that Gemma is not psychotic, and that Madeleine is? Who is Madeleine? She is a girl who has ecstasies and stigmata who, during Gemma's lifetime (1903), is under the control of Pierre Janet in the Salpetrière insane asylum. In 1904, Janet describes her "religious delirium" as a clinical case.

Madeleine, too, wanted to escape her destiny, the poor, arid destiny of one given in marriage to a man; she aimed to achieve a much higher, richer destiny instead as the bride of God. She runs away from home. But what can she do in the streets of Paris, alone, a young woman with no money, no work, no education, except become a prostitute or a "madwoman"? Faced with her ecstatic estrangement, the police haul her off to the Salpetrière, a place for all those alienated from the true world, the one recognized by society, where countless women fleeing from "reality" have consumed their lives. It is a reality that is too tragic, too coercive, too repugnant in its bestial concreteness, to escape denial. So Madeleine is an "hysteric." Janet, being neither a spiritual director nor a theologian and believer, is forced to diagnose the hysteric symptoms of ecstasies and stigmata. As an honest, scrupulous psychiatrist, he is the first to acknowledge that Madeleine is sweet, obedient, helpful, and full of good sense; that she speaks with an eloquence and linguistic correctness surprising in a person with so little learning. Above all, she does not "pretend" during her long periods of ecstasy. An important observation, Janet's, since the problem of "pretending" is one of the most controversial aspects of the female mystical experience. At any rate, Madeleine's ecstatic rapture toward the Crucified One is no different from that of Gemma, her contemporary. However, her destiny is different, because she finds an eminent psychiatrist near her, an honest, loyal scientist, who diagnoses her "hysteria," and not a confessor and spiritual director who is convinced that a "woman" must communicate with the transcendental since a "woman" is the bride of God. However, he can do nothing to "cure" Madeleine, much less "cure" the group that has created the true "delirium," the institution of the bride-victim of God.

What is certain is that the hypothesis of hysteria is accompanied by the cultural symbolism that obliges a woman to "be" only if she "belongs," if she "gives of herself," if she "offers up herself," and so it obliges her first of all to "pass" through her own sexualized body in order to put herself in communication with the rest of the world. It makes little difference whether this world is the earthly one or the supernatural one, since communication, in any event, is made possible to her only as a "union" which, as nuptial, is always physical and sexual, even when it is proposed as abstinence from sex, virginity, and "closure." The Catholic Church celebrates the feasts dedicated to Our Lady, exalting her with the famous lines that describe her a "closed garden," a "sealed fountain." (The majority of scholars argue that the *Song of Songs* is an ancient Egyptian love song. We should stop to reflect then that it originated in a land where infibulation has been practiced from time immemorial.) Madeleine adopts the same image when she tranquilly explains to Janet, who questions her on the subject, that during her ecstasies, however long they last, she cannot urinate because "a seal has been set on the opening."

But is there really any difference between a symbolic "seal" and a "concrete" one? Let us recall the millions and millions of women who, from the remotest times until today, in vast parts of the Islamic world in Africa and Asia, have been subjected to clitoridectomy and to the almost total sewing up of the vulvar opening (infibulation). In this perspective, we cannot help but realize that the problem of the "opening/closing" of the female body is one of the most evident "obsessions" of male thought; perhaps, even a true and proper "cerebral state," to use K.M. Pribram's terms.[100]

It is superfluous to repeat once more that cultural inventions and their relative institutions are all products of the male mind and will; therefore, it is the latter which must still be studied. The attempts made up to now to understand the reasons for vulvar closure are not only limited and superficial, but they are always linked to removal of the clitoris. On the contrary, we are considering two different operations here that, though performed in the same context, are not necessary to one another unless we emphasize "closure" rather than the removal of the clitoris, which facilitates closure but is not necessary to it. In any event, up to now, observers have failed to emphasize closure, revealing their "resistance" against recognizing its true meaning.[101]

The motivation usually given, both by persons directly involved and by ethnologists, missionaries and anthropologists (who in any event, until the arrival of women anthropologists, maintained a discreet Victorian silence on the subject), is that of a rite preparatory to marriage. But this motivation so blatantly contradicts the real "result" of the act, which in itself proves that it is the husband who needs to find his wife "closed"; and that this need once again puts us face to face with meanings implicit in the cultural structure. By "implicit," we intend those profound meanings men are unaware of, rather than "unconscious" meanings in the Freudian sense.

Vulvar closure, in fact, obliges the husband to take up a hunting knife on the wedding night — or, in more modern usage, a razor blade — in order to widen the opening sufficiently to introduce his penis; without considering that the tiny aperture does not allow the complete outflow of menstrual blood, which causes serious psychic and physical consequences, marking the woman for the rest of her life. At the moment of childbirth, surgical opening becomes necessary in order to allow passage of the baby's head; but punctually, on request by the husband and other relatives, shortly after delivery the woman will be sewn up again till the next birth. Considering that the populations involved have high birth rates, this plainly aberrant operation will be performed over and over again with devastating consequences.

As we have already observed, no one is psychotic if the group is psychotic. But doesn't this symbolic-concrete cultural pressure on the body of a woman and on the collective significance of her closure-virginity, force her to live outside reality as if it were "real"?

Group Logic: Delirium

Perhaps it is possible to assign a kind of gradation to the different phenomena accompanying the detachment from reality in women totally in love with the transcendental bridegroom. On the basis of this gradation, we may better understand to what extent their personalities ends up almost totally alienating themselves from the life of human relations, making them incapable of following the rhythms and tasks normal to the majority. Naturally, the fact that they nearly always lived in a convent saved them from the most traumatic social impact. Nonetheless, the long, frequent fasts almost to the point of starvation, the physical penance that cruelly tested their health, and cruelly tested those around them as well, made them "different" even inside the convent (Maria Maddalena de' Pazzi crawled around the garden at night, crying and moaning, with an enormous wooden cross on her back; Gemma Galgani struggled for days at a time, shouting at the devil who attacked her in bed...).

We must take into account another very important factor here: the duration of human life. Many of the ecstatic women we have encountered so far died at a very young age. This early death prevented both them and those around them from having to create a *modus vivendi*, having to adapt to reality; it also prevented them from having to force things or perhaps "fake it" more or less consciously when the voices, ecstasies, or visions failed to emerge. Or, as clearly appears in the biography of several "great lovers" who lived long lives, it prevented them from having to fill with "relatable" contents, what they perceived obscurely or what, at a given point, they perhaps failed to perceive any longer at all. In fact, ecstasies and visions rarely last in time; or rather, they tend to become very rare at an advanced age.

Life expectancy also influenced the prestige and power created by their "diversity." Outside, people eventually heard about the miraculous phenomena and this was advantageous to the entire convent. These women were therefore encouraged by the entire society to proceed further and further into delirium. Once again, we find ourselves facing the initial problem. If there were not a group sustaining the reality of a God-Man, claiming that he is the bridegroom, that there are angels, devils, and saints; if other women whose mystical experiences are exalted were not proposed as wondrous examples to imitate, would anyone identify with them to the point of transferring herself to the realm of delirium?

True, even within a religious environment, visionaries find themselves in a condition of "abnormality." It is "positive" abnormality, however: This is the first premise we must accept in order to attempt to find any order in the highly intricate problem of psychopathology. If one sees or hears things which do not exist in the physical reality outside of the organism, one has surely lost connection with this reality *at the moment one sees or hears them.*

The contents of what one thinks he sees or hears are always, however, sustained by and correlated to everything one has learned during the process of acculturation; that is why in the West today, we have "saints" and "mystics," as well as "hysterics" and "paranoiacs." In other cultures, instead, we find the woman who is the "mare of God"; in still others, the "shamanic flight," and so forth. In other words, detachment from reality is never true detachment, or total detachment, because it is always accompanied by the contents sustained by the logic of the group to which one belongs, and by a greater or lesser adhesion on the part of the group itself.[102] It is such adhesion that determines the progressive evolution, at least to some degree in one direction or another, of the "paranoid" process. "In one direction or another," in this sense: If the group exalts the individual and thus drives him toward hallucinatory phenomena, *it is the group itself that constitutes the link with reality.*

Then to what extent are we correct in speaking in terms of detachment from reality? Is not the group responsible for it? We always find ourselves facing the unsolved problem of the substantial difference between one who produces hallucinations, and one who does not produce them, yet loses the sense of one's own self's boundary. This has occurred and very often occurs with many of the powerful in the world. In these cases as well, however, it is the group that follows and encourages the individual in the abnormal expansion of his own ego. The inflated ego then sets itself up as a link to reality, pushing the individual into the delirious abyss of omnipotence which, given the presence of the group encouraging, no one perceives (except, on a few occasions, as an historic afterthought, after his death).

In any event, it is the relationship with the transcendental that "forces" the "paranoiac" personality to develop hallucinatory phenomena; the transcendental *is* transcendental, and cannot be drawn out on the basis of the normal laws of physics. This explains why hallucinations are much more frequent in the pathology of a religious context, rather than that of political power.

From a scientific point of view, therefore, the problem emerges on two interconnected paths: that of cerebral neuropathology, which must explain how visual or audible "perceptions" are formed without a stimulus corresponding to the external reality of the organism; and simultaneously, that of the adherence of these false perceptions to the contents expressed and institutionalized by the culture in which individuals with this "pathology of consciousness" find themselves living. The "devils armed with pitchforks" that we have found in the visions of many famous lovers of God are one of many examples proving the paucity of "mystics'" inventive capacity, but also proving the persistence of mental associations perfectly in line with the "logic" of the group nourishing them.

8

If This Is a Woman

In convent life, women are nearly always needy of emotional comfort because they lack any kind of social relationship (a monastic community is a particular kind of group, not a "society"), so that the stimulation implied by "marriage" to God leads to sexual thoughts associated with the giving of the body. Such thoughts can sometimes only find an outlet in the object of another woman. Furthermore, in convents, persons of a mature age nearly always live with novices or pupils who are much younger, and who easily become the objects of particular tenderness. Usually this danger has been hidden behind terminology that avoids the problem, but at the same time alludes to it with "particular friendships." These are closely monitored, impeded and indicated as transgressions that are to be shunned, however, the sexual dynamics underlying them are never explicitly mentioned. Indeed, the taboo on sexuality in the female world probably prevents women from gaining a true awareness of the erotic desire that incites them toward such "particular friendships."

Censorship and Sexuality

Silence regarding the problem of female sexuality is such that even Teresa of Avila, known as an extremely sensible, concrete woman, not only fails to hint at the problem that concerns her, but also fails to mention it in general terms. Is it possible that, living in a rigidly cloistered convent, she never encountered this drama and all the conflict it provoked, not even in her conversations with the nuns entrusted to her care, or with the confessors, spiritual directors, and priests with whom she exchanged opinions on virtually everything? The censorship which Teresa imposed on this topic is all too evident. What does her fleeting hint at "natural movements" actually conceal? For males, this definition could be an allusion to the nocturnal emissions or "pollutions" which, beginning from the early centuries of hermitage and the Pacomian monasteries, were obsessively discussed and combated with fasting, prayer and penance, but which were, at any rate, considered normal inasmuch as they were "physiological" and almost totally independent of the will.[103]

But for women? Without any physical stimulation of some kind or other, it is extremely difficult to reach orgasm. On the other hand, if male monasticism clearly implies refusal of the other sex, and the more or less conscious choice of a homosexual type (living among males), for women, monasticism presents itself with psychological, social, and cultural characteristics so complex and varied that with the passing of time it is impossible to make even the tiniest comparison. To flee from men, fathers, brothers and husbands, represents a form of liberation that highly compensates for the renunciation of the use of sexuality. In this respect, even the process of canonization, which, by adopting the usual lifeless, brainless analogical mechanism, considers the heroic virtues required of males and females equal in order to declare them "saints" is quite distant from reality. We have seen forced comparisons such as these in operation right from the beginning, in one direction or another, with female martyrdom transformed into martyrdom for the sake of virginity, and with the "consecration of virgins," an autonomous institution, highly different both from priesthood and from male monasticism.

In any event, sexuality is always present in any interpersonal or group dynamics, among women as well. The silence regarding this fundamental aspect of monastic life concerns only female communities, since in male ones, sexual sin in any form, from masturbation to erotic fantasizing, affectionate manifestations between two individuals, up to a conscious homosexual relationship, is the greatest worry of abbots, confessors, and superiors. This silence is partly due to the taboo on sexual "knowledge" which has afflicted women up to modern times: all women, young and old, rich and poor, married and unmarried, with the exception of "bad" women, and even more, virgins and the brides of God. But such silence is also due to the near impossibility for women, psychologically speaking, to recognize in the presence of an erotic sexual attraction in themselves. This fact is easily explainable by the transference to the symbolic, to which the nun's whole life is subject. The habit, for example, is extremely important among nuns, as much and even more than clothes are for other women; but the prohibition against thinking of it as a meaningful enrichment of the body allows them to tie their belt more or less tightly, keep their ears more or less covered by bands, let their hair escape from under the veil more or less freely, and yet remain totally unaware of the sexual-aesthetic pleasure such tiny variations imply (even when they themselves confess it in the "chapter," as established in their rule, as if it were a sin).

We mentioned such mechanisms in a paragraph dedicated to clothing; in any event, what we need to emphasize here is that body language — even in its erotic aspect — subsists in a female community, without ever being explicitly acknowledged. The abbess, mother superior or the director of novices will point out to the nun that her hair is visible beneath her bonnet, or that her belt is knotted too tightly around her waist, but why this should or should not happen is never up for discussion. Elsewhere in this book, we consider the emotional dynamics among nuns; what we wish to underline here is that women "mystics" — those who theoretically should delve most deeply into self-knowledge and knowledge of the world surrounding them — keep silent regarding this fundamental topic, almost as if it did not exist. Still further proof of "pretending": the pretending that voids the mystics' writing of any true introspection.

As occurs in all closed environments in which heterosexual liberty is impeded — military barracks, prisons, boarding schools, and hospitals where patients remain for long periods — the homosexual relation explodes as a consequence of deprivation, or it brings a latent homosexuality to a level of awareness that would probably never have come to light in normal conditions, perhaps because of a certain biochemical stimulation among bodies. In this respect, we must take care not to consider male and female monasticism as equivalent (as occurs through that principle of historic-analogical inertia that we have repeatedly denounced). Monks have nearly always "chosen" to become ecclesiastics (even though their families were urged to place them in monasteries in order to let them grow and study at little expense). Surely, the fear and sexual refusal of women was (and is) an important motivation in this choice. Furthermore, the cloistered life as total imprisonment has been imposed only on female convents. Moreover, as is well known, female homosexuality has always been blanketed in silence for a number of reasons that have yet to be thoroughly analyzed. Given our specific area of inquiry, we need only mention the most obvious ones. The main reason is inherent in the very concept of female sexuality that has virtually accompanied the history of Christian Europe until modern times.

Fathers and Daughters: Female Concentration Camps

Once the burden of original sin was loaded onto the shoulders of Eve, whatever definition it assumed, it has always been directly or indirectly

If This Is a Woman 187

linked to sexual sin. Since the advent of Christian salvation, chastity has become the greatest virtue for women, who must know nothing about sexual needs, except what is indispensable for procreation. And even in this case, it is supposed that a woman puts up with the "conjugal duty" without drawing any pleasure from it. At that point, the taboo involves not only the act, but any discussion of sex as well. Certainly, only prostitutes can dare touch certain topics. In addition, the scant attention paid to relations among women is also due to the fact that there is always more than one woman in the same house — mothers, daughters, sisters, sister-in-law, aunts, women friends; and female domesticity implies affectionate gestures, an intimacy of language and behavior that are, indeed, made possible(without this ever being explicit) by the exclusion of eroticism and sexual desire. In short, the cultural message imbibed by women — that their own sexuality has nothing to do with them — functions just as smoothly as their nuptial union with Christ.

In any event, only in rare cases has history left us precise documentation concerning female homosexuality. A book giving interesting accounts, but at the same time reflecting the general paucity of information about cases of lesbianism (information that exists only because the cases mentioned were criminally condemned), is *Immodest Acts*, by the American historian, Judith C. Brown.[104] With material from the archives in Florence and Pisa, together with other material from the secret archives of the Vatican, she reconstructs the story of an Italian nun of 1600, Benedetta Carlini, who was condemned to life imprisonment in her convent for having committed "impure acts" with another, younger nun (the institution of prisons in convents was foreseen as early as the Rule of St. Benedict in the fifth century).

The most relevant fact in the case of Benedetta Carlini, from our perspective, is that the inquest concerning this nun started off for reasons that had nothing to do with her sexual sins: Her judges meant to verify the authenticity of her visions, her miracles, her "stigmata." Benedetta had been born in 1590 in Vellano, a village on the slopes of the Apennines; and according to a custom formally approved by the Church, she was offered with a "vow" on the part of her father soon after her birth. This father, who today is described as a particularly devoted man, was actually not much different from the majority of men of his time and social status (he was a small landowner), since the values and customs he had inherited included the formal "oblation" to God of one's own children. This act was foreseen as early as the first monastic rules and required a precise ritual: the offering of the child on the altar together with the bread and wine during the celebration of the Mass.[105] The man highly valued a crucifix before which he recited his domestic prayers (this habit probably left its mark on Benedetta's fantasy of identification through the stigmata). In his will he stated that after his death, his house should be converted into an oratory dedicated to the Mother of God.

At the age of five, Benedetta had already learned the litanies of the saints and other prayers from her father, which she recited several times a day. At the age of six, she learned to read, studying the most elementary notions of the Christian doctrine and, perhaps, even a bit of Latin. This education was superior to the one most girls of Benedetta's social condition would have received and it undoubtedly helped her in her psychological experiences during monastic life, and in the ascendancy she managed to assume over others.

In this respect, we must consider the substantial difference between one who knows what writing is, and one who does not (a fact which in today's mass-media society is all too easy to forget). We think of illiteracy as a situation of cultural poverty which nonetheless does not exclude the individual from a certain type of popular knowledge, a situation in which the notion of psychological "reflection" is somehow present. On the contrary, in the past illiteracy was not only the privation of knowledge imparted by reading, but, above all, the inability to master symbolic thought; indeed, the inability to imagine that any objectifying projection of thought could be possible. Therefore we must remember that when speaking of Catherine of Siena, Hildegard of Bingen or even Teresa of Avila as "unlettered," we are alluding not to illiteracy, but to the lack of regular scholastic studies to which only males had access.

The distance between these "unlettered" women and most women of their time, who really had no instruments to know what "thinking" is, is enormous. It is most likely that this distance was one of the factors that enabled them to assume power, and nearly always become abbesses of their convents, or teachers of novices, a "guide" for others. And it also enabled them to reflect on their own inner experiences, and describe them not only to others, but above all to themselves, through that form of self-awareness which only writing provides.

Returning to Benedetta, we must add that in her home great devotion was shown to Catherine of Siena; indeed, the day of the saint's "mystical marriage" to Jesus was celebrated as a feast day. This is an important detail, which probably marked Benedetta's future identification with the Passion through the stigmata, and the magnificent marriage to Jesus imposed by her on the convent, with a pompous, symbolic ceremony.

The frightful life of Benedetta Carlini serves only as testimony to a "whole": a tragic itinerary that countless numbers of women have been forced to follow. As with most women "mystics," her destiny is marked from childhood: At the age of nine she is turned over by her father to the Theatine convent of the small town of Pescia; her life "experience" — psychological, social, sexual, cultural, historical — will be this. A group of women, more ignorant than she, less intelligent than she, shut up from their earliest years as she is in a monastic world that is presented as the only world: This will become the group over which to gain primacy, the horizon on which to stand out, the futureless time in which she must invent a "becoming" for herself, that up to now has been excluded by the never-changing repetition of the liturgy. A "becoming" which only the "fantasy of the sacred" allows one to invent. At the age of 23, in 1613, Benedetta begins to have visions. Like so many women mystics before and after her, Benedetta sees a "garden": "a fine and pleasant garden with an abundance of flowers and fruits; in the center, a fountain of perfumed water, and near that, an angel...." Fantasizing about the "garden" as a place of supreme beauty and delight accompanies the history of Europe from the Middle Ages to 1700,[106] and demonstrates — should any doubt remain — the impossibility for the individual to withdraw from the cultural fabric in which he lives, even in such a seemingly subjective, personal, private aspect as "visions."

At first, the biography of Benedetta Carlini seems to highlight only the long-term mechanisms underlying the ideas and actions of millions of women whose individual characteristics we do not know. However, in the life of Benedetta we find an additional aspect, a range of behaviors that change in time, both her own and that of the surrounding group, and the ecclesiastic authorities as well, obviously (which in her era also included the civic authorities). This range touches the crucial nerve centers of the entire cultural system so explicitly that it may have been invented for our purposes of exemplification. Benedetta has been "promised" to God from birth, and is turned over by her father to the convent when still a child. The only world she has known is that of the nuns. Everything she learns in reading, listening, and acting is centered on religious meanings and on the level of "taught" prayer that is locked into formulas and reflects no theoretic knowledge. Furthermore, as always occurs in those who must remain ignorant, the imagination is stimulated almost exclusively through "visual" channels; painted images are all the more striking, when no other possibility of knowledge exists.

Therefore, one of the main characteristics of female "visions" is their presentation as "pictures," as compositions of images; whereas in the Old Testament, on the contrary, the "revelations" received by men were prevalently auditory. We noted this earlier: the "voice" is a hallucination that incites one to action, and therefore it is specific to men. In the Old Testament, God "speaks," God "reveals" through words: The Judaic culture refuses iconographic representation; it is not based on "seeing." Christian European culture, conversely, is dominated by the search for "seeing." Despite the traditional imagery and edifying tone of her visions, like nearly all visionaries, Benedetta was aware of the danger of visions, as well as their power. Of course, the explanation given then as now (and which visionaries themselves give) of their fear at their first experience of visions is that these might come from the devil instead of God.

This was a very real fear, because no one at that time doubted the need to struggle against the devil, and the entire surrounding culture, including Church authority, confirmed it. But aside from the fact that there has always existed a certain idea of "illness" or "madness" in the presence of manifestations that differ from the norm — scarcely developed though it might be, since the demonological explanation is easier and more convincing — in no culture is detachment from the reality of the senses an experience immediately perceived as positive, either by the individual or the group. Man depends on his senses for survival. A blind or deaf person is always considered the most cruelly deprived of persons because man no longer knows how to live without the help of these guiding senses. Therefore the illusion of seeing or hearing — in short, any form of hallucination — is in itself terrifying whether it is called an illness or not. Indeed, the ease with which people in Europe have believed for so long that something was really seen or that something was really heard, attributing it to the devil's deceit, is also due to the fact that one hoped to avoid jeopardizing the "certainty" of the senses.

The question of whether visions originated with God or with the devil protected people from the truly terrifying, unsolvable phenomenon of seeing and hearing what does not exist. In any event, ecstasies, rapture, visions are an absolute way for women to acquire a kind of primacy of subjectivity, totally inculcated by the authority of fathers, confessors, and the community in which they live. All they need do to escape the proposal of society and culture is to absolutize it: They need only use the same instruments that are adopted to subject and condemn women to obedience, sacrifice and non-being, in order to master the instruments themselves and turn them against the very society that imposes them.

Moreover, that is why the Church has always kept mystical phenomena under its control: No one must evade the ratification of its authority, since only the men of the Church are the "right" channel of communication with the transcendental. But the system of confirmation is always the one established with the complicity of the Church: miracles. What miracles, then, can prove that the bride of God is truly a most beloved bride? By complete belonging, by conformity to the bridegroom.

A Desperate Embrace

On the second Friday of Lent in 1618, Benedetta receives the stigmata. Having discussed the problem of stigmata earlier, we can now confirm what we observed before: Although stigmata were inaugurated as an absolutely extraordinary, unrepeatable miracle, and held to be the sign that Francis was truly the second Christ, immediately after Francis's death, stigmata actually become an almost exclusively female phenomenon, like everything else regarding the body and the participation of the body in mental suffering. A woman cannot become a "priest"; that is, one who, as a sacrificer, repeats the sacrifice of Jesus for all the faithful; she thus becomes a priest-as-victim, sacrificed as Jesus was on the cross. We find ourselves dealing here with the passage from the symbolic to the concrete, which we have already considered a number of times, and which in itself signals the loss of the reality principle.

As had already occurred in the case of other women mystics, in the same way that Francis's stigmatization was portrayed by painters, Benedetta sees "a ray come from all the wounds of that crucified one who was before me. And it seemed to me that those rays that he had in his wounds, were impressed on my hands, feet and side." Bartolomea Crivelli, a figure who was to become extremely important later on, was present at that miraculous event. She was a nun who slept in the same room as Benedetta because, as an exception to the norm, she had been assigned a companion to help her in the physical and psychic sufferings brought on at night by her ecstasies. Nuns normally sleep one to a cell, according to a rigorous rule that probably — despite the silence that has always accompanied the possibility of sexual transgressions on the part of women — springs from the intention to prevent such transgressions.

Everybody believes in the marks of the stigmata and, shortly afterward, Benedetta's primacy is ratified by her appointment as abbess. Time goes by, and a new miracle occurs, one that is predictable among women mystics: the exchange of hearts with Jesus. First, Benedetta is deprived of her heart, and no one is surprised that she manages to live for three days (as her favorite saint, Catherine of Siena, did); then Jesus puts his own heart where hers had been, even though Jesus' is bigger than normal (Bartolomea sees it sticking out of her chest, and pushes it back inside) and topped by three arrows symbolizing Benedetta's love for him. The exchange of hearts, like the gift of the wedding rings, is a dominant, exclusive trait of women's mystical experiences. I know of no male case (though it cannot be excluded) since, as usual, no comparative research has been done in this area.

Certainly, Benedetta must have been aware of what had happened, not only to Catherine of Siena, but also to a woman who was nearly her contemporary, Caterina de' Ricci, who died in 1590 in Prato, a Tuscan town near Benedetta's.

On the occasion of the exchange of hearts, Jesus assigns to Benedetta the company of an angel, whose name is revealed as Splenditello. He is a good-looking youth, with long, curly hair crowned by a garland of flowers. He holds a green wand in his hand, with flowers on one side and thorns on the other; he strikes her with this wand when she is good, using the flowered side; when she is bad, with the thorny one. The flowering staff often appears in images of male saints, a phallic sign of their transcendental potency; so that this representation, too, is void of any originality on the part of Benedetta's fantasy. Finally, the expected moment arrives of her marriage to Jesus. A vision reveals to Benedetta how the ceremony must be conducted (though the details are extremely significant, we cannot stop to describe them here), but no one—neither her confessor, nor her sisters—is surprised at that. Indeed, everyone hastens to obey the heavenly orders that Benedetta transmits by preparing a pompous nuptial ceremony, with flowers, carpets, decorations, tableware, and food sent from outside the convent as well. Everyone in town believes and participates in the event. The procession advances as Benedetta walks in a trance: Jesus puts the ring on her finger, assuring her that no one will see him but her.

The system of "signs" that exist but are not seen in order to safeguard the humility of the favored women who are marked by them has always been considered credible, and ratified, to what extent of naiveté, we cannot know, by the Church authorities. For example, the Dominicans had sanctioned this "prodigious" mechanism with regard to Catherine of Siena's invisible stigmata and wedding ring. Still, we are not authorized to claim that Catherine, and so many women after her including Benedetta Carlini, were actually lying: The problem of awareness-unawareness in women is almost impossible to solve. In any event, the ease with which the group around them allows itself to be convinced is not only confirmation of the reality they presume to be true, but also reflects the "need" of the group itself to see the system of meaning constructed around women re-enforced by means of transcendental potency. At this point, we can well understand how impossible it is to separate the "pathological" phenomenology of a woman-individual from the context in which *she is forced* to "represent" herself. But we can also understand how dangerous it is to let a delirious

If This Is a Woman 193

logical process like the one "established" by theology crystallize around the base of the cultural edifice.

Benedetta notifies the public that now God is speaking through her; He "reveals" himself through His faithful servant. This is the most dramatic moment of the interaction between personality and culture. A nun is no one; she is socially and psychologically annulled unless she demonstrates to herself and the world that God has truly favored her as His bride-and-lover. When she does not agree to be annihilated, when she wants somehow to be someone in the world, the woman can do nothing but conform to the supreme ideal to which society and culture have assigned her.

At this point a new and even more dramatic level emerges: that of the "make-believe" accompanying the life of the woman/bride-of-God. She deludes herself that what society has taught or imposed on her is true, and therefore that she is truly God's favorite lover-bride. So much so, that this predilection manifests itself *concretely*. It will be she, then, who will know Him better than anyone else, because she is joined to Him in total "union": a sexual-matrimonial union, the only one assigned to the woman. For women, to be "possessed" is always being possessed sexually, since this term-concept springs from the male experience of possession: appropriation of the woman by means of the penis and, by analogy, by all other things. It is thus the female body that is possessed. In this way psychosis is ready and waiting for the woman, much more than for the male, because the woman is always forced to pass through her own body to reach her goals.

In psychiatric terms, participation of the body is called "hysteria." For the woman, the strongest level of make-believe presents itself as a necessary, absolute "choice": to abandon herself intellectually to what society has inculcated in her, and therefore to speak truly to God, to be concretely possessed by God, to unite "visibly" with Him. Consequently, the "signs" of the transcendental must appear: visions, ecstasies, exchanges of hearts, wounds on the hands and feet; crown of thorns, voices of Jesus, the Madonna, the angels, the saints who speak to the bride of that world that only she can reach. Or to put it differently: to pretend to herself and the world that all this is really happening. In a form of make-believe, however, that is not entirely conscious, since the make-believe state is "normal" for women: They never know whether they are pretending or not, and the border between reality and make-believe is extremely hazy for them. The only thing that can prevent them from abandoning themselves to psychosis is intelligence (and knowledge). That is, a reality principle that dominates that of the emotions and the sentiments; these, on the contrary, induce women to conform to the strongest will, that of the group.

It is the group that verifies its convictions and assumptions through the woman's life. If the woman conforms, her life as bride of God not only makes sense, but allows her to achieve the only priority, the only primacy destined to her and acknowledged as possible for her. If, on the other hand, she does not conform, if her intelligence (since knowledge, the other factor, is nearly always denied her) prevents her from doing so, she can do nothing but declare herself defeated and accept her desperation, accept the absolute solitude. Their impotent rebellion that has made so many nuns the most malevolent, intransigent and tyrannical of persons, and the least capable of love, both for themselves and for others, or rather, for the "others" with whom they happen to have any relationship, orphans or pupils, the ill or the criminal, servants or peasants, or their "co-sisters" who are condemned to share the same prison.

At any rate, the exaltation of Benedetta's virtues now begins. Through her mouth, Jesus condemns those who dare not to believe in them, and commands that everyone be informed of the miracles that he has performed for her, even the most important civic authorities, including the grand duke. Here, however, Benedetta has "overdone it," even in the eyes of a society like the one surrounding her that is ready to believe anything. God's praise of her has contrasted with the supreme virtue required by the Church in order to believe women: humility, the acknowledgment of one's nothingness. So the inquests begin regarding Benedetta: inquests that are supposed to establish the truth about her visions and which, instead, lead to a truth that no one ever would have expected, the revelation of sex among woman.

Since the stigmata are the only visible proof, the examination naturally starts with them. After numerous checks and the testimony of three co-sisters including Bartolomea — who was present both when Benedetta received the stigmata and when she had exchanged her heart with Jesus — the inquisitors are unable to prove that the "signs" on Benedetta's body are not authentic. The inquest thus terminates positively, and Benedetta once again becomes abbess.

Homosexuality: Life Imprisonment

Despite her material and spiritual commitments as abbess, Benedetta continues to have visions in which she often foresees her death. She communicates this to the nuns, exhorting them to take good care of her, since they can enjoy her company only for a few days longer. Punctually, in fact, on the day of the Annunciation in the same year, 1621, the nuns are present at her death. But the confessor, who has immediately been summoned, orders Benedetta to return to earth in a thundering voice, and Benedetta comes back to life. Naturally, she recounts what she has seen in paradise, but although everyone believes in this resurrection, the presence of such an abbess becomes more and more uncomfortable for the nuns, and the Church authorities become suspicious.

This situation gives rise to a second inquest. It departs from a premise that contrasts with the first one: the objective now is not to prove that the stigmata are authentic, but that they are false. There are many reasons for resentment and fear on the part of the nuns concerning Benedetta; nothing can be concealed from an abbess who is in direct communication with the Almighty, no infraction of thought or feeling. We have already seen that living with a "saint" is an extremely uncomfortable destiny for anyone. Moreover, Benedetta has overplayed her part in the "representation": Some have seen her incise the scars of the stigmata so that they bleed; others have seen her use saffron in order to accent the yellow mark of the ring around her finger. Then, there are those who have found discrepancies between her visions and the theological affirmations of the Church; so it slowly becomes clear that she is obsessed by the devil, and not sanctified by God. But what Bartolomea reveals this time is absolutely unforeseen. When Benedetta calls her for help at night, in reality, she makes her lie underneath her until both of them reached an orgasm.

Benedetta's abandonment to sexual desire, the orgasm reached through the mutual rubbing of bodies with Bartolomea, suddenly topples the whole castle of visions forming a union with the "divine Bridegroom": The stigmata become false, the ring does not exist, the sacrilege is all the greater in that impure acts have been performed even during the most sacred periods, on feast days or during the liturgical rites. Sexuality is the dividing line defining the "true" bride of God; and this proves, beyond any shadow of doubt, that the woman is a sexual gift from men to their God: a sexual gift exclusively, a real, concrete one.

Benedetta is condemned to spend the rest of her life in the convent prison. It is a terrible condemnation, but much lighter than burning at the stake, which was also foreseen as punishment for "sodomy" (the concept of sodomy at the time was much more extended and polyvalent than today, since it concerned any sexual act "against nature"). We have no documents regarding the motivation of the verdict, which we learn of only from the convent chronicles that inform us that "Benedetta Carlini died on August 7, 1661, in penitence, having spent 35 years in prison." In *La religieuse*, Diderot, as well, has his sinful abbess die in the convent prison; she has gone mad. When he wrote the novel, a century had passed since Benedetta's real-life term in prison; a century dense with historical, psychological,

II. The Tragic Game of Mysticism

and scientific events; but the nuns' convent had evidently remained the same, for Diderot is not obliged to make the slightest effort of fantasy in order to tell his story. Women do not speak, they do not rebel; they change nothing, not even that which is entrusted to their care, and could change. Benedetta's co-sisters lived for 35 years beside her, opening and closing her door each day to bring her the prescribed food of penance, but not a gesture of pity for her or themselves induces them to disobey or reflect upon what is fair or unfair—not only in their own eyes, but also in the eyes of that God to whom they dedicate infinite impulses of love. Teresa of Avila, so wise as to be declared "doctor," foresees "prison" for the sins of "sensuality," in her Constitutions; but the women enamored of the crucified Jesus, who cry in pain over his suffering, who identify bodily with his Passion, who sing hymns to the sublime and merciful love of his heart, do not say a single word about justice, compassion, or forgiveness (assuming we must speak of forgiveness) regarding the women—nuns and otherwise—entrusted to them by the civic and religious authorities. Women who, in the harshest way imaginable, must pay for actions defined as sins by the same men who invented and established what women must be and do. For centuries, until the founding of prisons by the secular state, female religious institutes were destined to imprison girls who had been "dishonored"; prostitutes, repentant and otherwise; thieves, heretics, women who performed abortions, old women abandoned to alcohol or begging, adulteresses who had managed to escape capital punishment; but not a single voice about the nun jailers has come down to us concerning this aspect of their lives.

The convent prison is transformed into a prison within a prison. It is the most secret, terrifying dungeon, because, having no communication with the outside world, no political or social identity, no purpose of redemption or recovery, but only that of punishment, as an institution it interests no one; it provokes no reflection. Thirty-five years without saying or receiving a single word (the Rule forbids co-brothers or co-sisters to speak to anyone who is shut up in the jail cell): 35 years without any "open-air hour," without "recreation," without "visits" from relatives or friends, without a gift box containing an orange or two; without any of those things that secular society considers indispensable for the incarcerated person, even the most merciless criminal. Thirty-five years in which Benedetta's "co-sisters" (how ironic the term!), who live together with her, have not left a trace, except to inscribe in the convent chronicles, according to law, the date of her death.

Diderot's Lack of Indignation

In order for the topic to be discussed, society had to wait for Diderot, one of the most intelligent and learned men/males of his time. He did present the topic, albeit with limited efficacy, and then the matter was allowed to drop, and was covered by silence once again. The Enlightenment and the French Revolution liberated women, not because this was the declared purpose, but because in the concept of "subject," in the elaboration of the rights of the "person" and universal equality, women were implicitly included. Another half century passed before the topic of nuns' sexual sins became an object of discussion again; this occurred only because of the historical and literary pros and cons relative to Manzoni's *Promessi sposi*. But though the scandal provoked by Manzoni's nun of Monza was momentous, the sexual transgressions of nuns were more easily believed in the "normal" version, that is, in their relations with men, sacrilegious though they might be. It was still difficult to speak of female homosexuality.

La réligieuse was published in 1796, after the French Revolution, when Diderot had already been dead for 12 years. Nonetheless, it caused a scandal, and has continued to do so until our time; today it is, if nothing else, a disturbing element. Society, men and women who weep so bitterly over the Nazi concentration camps, refuses to consider that other concentration camp, female monasticism and the atrocities committed therein down through the centuries on countless women incarcerated for life, almost from birth. No one has ever defined the institution for what it is: humanity's supreme expression of racism. Apropos of his *La réligieuse*, Diderot said, "I do not believe that such a frightening satire has ever been written against your convents." The text is acute in its psychological description of certain characters, and certain emotional dynamics set into motion by coexistence in a closed environment, devoid of any social or intellectual activity. Nevertheless, it was conceived by a cold man, one incapable of true indignation, as he would certainly have felt in writing about a similar institution for men/males.

The nuns whose characters emerge in the novel, even those who rebel against their condition, such as the protagonist, sister Suzanne, or the mother superior, are driven by sexual passion to the point of madness. But they are all believers, because even for Diderot, it would be unthinkable for them to be otherwise; they pray, they obey, they confess their sins. Sister Suzanne rebels because she does not feel she has a vocation for monasticism, and instead has been forced to embrace it, but her faith in God and her faithfulness to obedience remain intact. In short, as far as women are concerned, Diderot condemns the custom of shutting them up in a con-

II. The Tragic Game of Mysticism

vent with force, when "they are devoid of a vocation"; but he continues to consider their religiosity a beautiful thing; and to believe that there is such thing as a "vocation." In any event, he takes it for granted that these women are intellectually amorphous, and incapable of theorizing a social rebellion.

The sexual drives that perhaps reached the point of concrete sexual relations between the mother superior and Sister Teresa are left to the reader's imagination; the author does not dare speak of them explicitly. Here as well, however, their faith, their fear of sin and disobedience, and the conviction of their damnation that torments these characters are not in the least touched by any doubt, nor does the author shown any compassion, or indignation in the presence of beliefs inculcated in women in such an uncritical form.

In reality, on the eve of the Revolution, France appears profoundly religious in Diderot's text, as least as regards the female world. No question, no true interrogative is posed about the role of women, who are finally forced (as Diderot testifies regarding his main character) to work as washerwomen or prostitutes once they have been excluded from matrimony or monasticism. Everything the Encyclopedists had theorized and discussed concerning the need to instruct women is still very far from reality. Moreover, sexuality is presented obscurely, induced by the totally female environment and closed to any male figures except the anomalous ones of confessor, bishop, or the constituted authorities, that we cannot even be certain that Diderot meant to allude to a true form of lesbianism.

The problem of the borderline between environmental homosexuality and personal homosexuality is hard to establish, but the way in which Diderot presents homosexuality allows us to realize how unworthy and perverse it was considered to be. Unworthy and perverse per se, for the women themselves, not only as a social transgression, since any thought or desire regarding sexuality was considered incompatible with the female world. Moreover, the absolute impossibility on the part of Christian society to think of women as "subjects" of sexual desire is the inevitable consequence of having always considered them ready to accept death rather than the loss of virginity from the earliest "martyrs" onward. Virginity, indeed, is the supreme value to be defended, independently of the violence of an imposed coital act. The exaltation of motherhood as well is always divorced from any idea of sexuality, as if this were not the cause for becoming a mother in the first place. At the same time, the sexual relation is presented as an indispensable burden for procreation, and experienced as such by women. Indeed, maternity is exalted and sublimated nearly to the extent of making one forget the sexual act that preceded it.

Furthermore, the sexual relation between women is hardly ever mentioned, even among the various sexual misdemeanors foreseen by canonical law. In some archival research that was carried out to understand the attitude of both the authorities and public opinion regarding "sodomy" in 17th-century Venice, one case is cited as being exceptional for its rarity. It is based on the accusation made by a nun of the San Sepolcro convent concerning a case of lesbianism between a convent maid and a nun. In the trial documents of the Provveditori sopra i Monasteri, the acts of "libertinage" on the part of the nuns nearly always had a heterosexual connotation.[107]

Both ecclesiastical and juridical texts were hard put to find a common definition for female homosexuality; they often disagreed over whether to attribute to it a level of gravity identical to that of male homosexuality in order to define punishments accordingly. The tendency of the ologians and canonical jurists was to consider sodomy between women less serious, and punish it with lighter sentences. "Lighter," of course, considering the times: decapitation instead of burning at the stake; perpetual exile alone, unaccompanied by the cutting off of the nose and lips; life imprisonment in the convent itself instead of death. As in Benedetta's case, such incarceration was preferred, not as an act of clemency, but in order to prevent the scandal from leaking outside the convent walls, as would have been inevitable with an execution.

It is perhaps superfluous to add that even this minor intensity of criminal alarm depends on the fact that women have never been considered as subjects of history, and therefore, transgressions between women did not put the social establishment at risk. Furthermore, it is of fundamental importance to remember that the codification of sexual acts was thought out and theorized by males who departed from the organ considered to be primary, the penis, with its erection and emission of sperm. Whatever their erotic gestures, women can neither contaminate their own uterus by themselves nor procreate, the only events feared by men.

In the Judaic world, and then in the Christian one, the real sin is the useless emission of sperm. This explains the gravity of sodomy, understood as ejaculation into an unnatural and therefore non-fecundating "vase," whether in a heterosexual relation (even between spouses) or in a homosexual one.[108] Moreover, not even Bridget of Sweden in her famous *Revelations* is capable of indicating any sexual sin more serious than the useless emission of sperm. This is one more proof of the fact (should there be any need) that women "mystics" not only failed to receive "revelations"; they were incapable of thinking anything in their ecstasies apart from what they had learned from the environment.[109]

Finally, although this is never declared, sexuality between women is irrelevant beyond the sphere of sexual sin, because what counts for the future of the group is the penis. While the woman can always be forced to undergo fecundation, the male cannot be forced into erection and ejaculation. He cannot be forced, in the sense that the functioning of the penis is extremely sensitive to physiological-psychological conditions, and there is no force that can take it where it cannot or does not want to go. Whatever Claude Lévi-Strauss may say to the contrary, and the feminists along with him, the "most precious merchandise" is man.

9
Self-Annihilation in Order to Exist

The will and the capacity to achieve that self-annihilation that Christian ascetic and mystical ideals inculcate as the supreme instrument of knowledge and union with God finds points of extreme expression in women. Such extremes upset anyone who approaches them, albeit with the greatest desire to understand or "justify." The impossibility of tracing a borderline between what can still be considered "normal" and what, instead, cannot help but appear "pathological," makes any discussion of these aspects of Christian history terribly uncertain. To define a basic premise from which to start in order to delineate this limit is vastly difficult, even in the case of male biographies. It becomes virtually impossible in the case of female ones.

The pressure exercised by male authorities, spiritual advisors, confessors and preachers, over the intelligence of women and, at the same time, over their belief that they must trust those authorities, can find neither opposition nor limits. For such obedience has been inculcated in them during their entire history: obedience to fathers, brothers, husbands, sons; obedience to the rules of society, public opinion, and every hierarchy and power. *Fear* in the presence of males, physical as well as psychological, leads to abjection, an abjection that no one dares to evaluate as "delirium" when the Church ratifies and exalts it as a saintly virtue; but which, on the contrary, becomes, or rather is considered, "madness" when it eludes male authority. Indeed, it is well to point out that in the system of meanings constructed by society, a woman is "mad" only when she fails to obey; and her "delirium" is inevitably connected with and consequent to her disobedience. In fact, according to what has been claimed down through the centuries, as a "woman" she cannot conduct her own life, either intellectually or emotionally, without falling into the error of her mental and psychological weakness.

This mentality is emblematically reflected in certain relationships between the penitent and the confessor, in which the tie between the penitent's desire for self-annulment and the director's pursuit in annulling her, lead both to delirium.

Spiritual Advisors and Torturers

Although there are numerous examples, we must limit ourselves here to defining the problem. At any rate, besides the more or less famous figures to whom we have referred and shall refer in the course of our story, it will be useful to analyze an exemplary case of the virtue/madness of *annihilation*: that of Louise de Bellère du Tronchay, a French aristocrat who became a nun in the Order of St. Vincent de Paul. An exponent of the most frightening kind of "mysticism," she wrote to her spiritual advisor when she was confined in the Salpetrière insane asylum because of her terrible crises of "furious anguish."[110] Louise signs her letters from the Salpetrière "*Louise du Néant*": Louise of Nothingness.

How was it possible to so totally overturn the thought of Jesus of Nazareth, transforming it from the redemption of the human being to the annihilation of the human being? And why have women, above all, been the ones who recognized their own reality in this annihilation, and tried to carry it to such extremes? This question virtually sums up the entire history of women *in* Christianity, *under* Christianity, and *for* Christianity. But aside from the developments given to ascetic and mystical ideals and practice by men/males, by thinkers and those who actuated their theories in society, they were undoubtedly driven not only by their convictions and a desire to prove their validity as regards women, but also by a more or less conscious thirst for a destructive dominion over the woman entrusted to them. In fact, in the name of God, they could exercise absolute power over her with a cruelty and gratification that only a paroxysm of hate can explain, and which no Marquis de Sade would have ever imagined. Spiritual advisors have used this power to spontaneously induce women to annihilation, abjection, and death, hiding behind the screen of their self-attributed knowledge of God's will.

The typical relationship between victim and sacrificer-torturer is thus formed, between the spiritual advisor and his penitent. Much more than in physical torture, this relationship manifests itself in the enjoyment of seeing the victim reduced to abjection. Such abjection knows no limits, because the enjoyment consists in keeping the victim alive; in giving him or her the hope of remaining alive in the transcendental life, providing that he or she accepts increasingly inhuman degrees of dereliction. Moreover, the fear — since it is fear of God's justice — is limitless as well; so that it is only the spiritual advisor, God's representative, sacrificer and mediator, who can establish at what point of annihilation the victim can and must halt. But in practice, the sacrificer — he himself an inventor of this type of God created in his image and resemblance — hardly ever halts the victim; or at any rate, he halts him/her only at the point where the victim might just escape his power if the advisor did not put him or her to the test by forcing the victim to stop.

In this respect, certain episodes highlight extremely well both the absolute dominion exercised over the victim, and the "limits" that the male advisor perceives as insuperable, since they are insuperable for males. Such limits nearly always concern the contact with feces. These so-called women "mystics," who eat garbage of all kinds, lick pus-filled wounds, eat up others' spit, devour others' vomit, do not stop even at the feces of diarrhea (Marguerite-Marie Alacoque); these women usually meet the advisor's prohibition in the presence of feces. Perhaps feces are more repugnant, and require a greater degree of abjection? Surely not, since the greatest abjection is pursued and desired both by sacrificer and victim.

In reality, as in so many other cases, it is their being women that qualifies even the exercises of abjection. Pus, menstrual blood, and vomit are perceived as *beyond* nature more than *against* nature (as one could perhaps say in the sense indicated by Lévi-Strauss)[111]; and so they are "female" and analogical to the female element. Feces, instead (like urine), are potently ordered according to the functions of nature, and are therefore "male." As such, they are unsuitable for the abject instrumentation of women. Furthermore, there are no known cases of true and total abjection of this kind among males; the only case recorded (with some reluctance on the part of hagiographers) is that of Benedict Labre, who nonetheless remains firmly on this side of the ferocious abyss reached by women.

Louise's biography was published by her last confessor, Jean Maillard, in 1732. Maillard explains that the crises of "furious anguish" which determined her commitment to the Salpètriere insane asylum — the "frightening screams," the "shouts of a damned woman" that his penitent uttered — were due to Louise's certainty that she had been rejected and condemned by God. This point clearly indicates how women have been imprisoned in a labyrinth without an exit, constructed by a person holding absolute power over their intellectual and emotional life, once they sought escape from the brutal concreteness of the fate assigned to them by fathers as wives and mothers, by fleeing to that seemingly freer fate of "God's bride."

What vicious circle was (and is) created by the holders of ecclesiastic power? God, the Almighty, the absolute Master, gives a woman the possibility of being His bride, of uniting herself with Him. A woman, that most repugnant of human beings, is full of faults, impurities, and weaknesses. A woman surely plays no active role in this concession, given the abyss separating the greatness of God from the female creature. Nevertheless, she has the possibility of making a quest, according to the dictates of the Church, as represented by confessors and spiritual advisors. The quest will not be an effort to grow toward God, but to "diminish": to humiliate her body and soul. In fact, the only thing possible for a being that can do nothing positive is to increase its own abjection; to make its own body and passions reveal their true level of lowliness. In this annihilation, God will recognize the face, sunk in turpitude, but "justly" derelict, of something belonging to Him. Nonetheless, God can always reject any soul, even one seeking the extreme degree of humiliation. Thus, the other task confessors assign their women penitents is that of trusting completely in God's love, abandoning themselves to the prayer of "union" characterizing the bride's love of the bridegroom. Once again, the woman comes up against something that overwhelms her: She must "empty" her mind, and not think or concentrate on anything else outside of a bridegroom she does not see nor hear. Thus emerges the other end of the labyrinth: The mind is distracted, it is attracted by concrete thoughts, and so "fails" before God; or it abandons itself to dreamlike, hypnotic concentrations. The woman mystic, in fact, hypnotizes herself. She convinces herself that she has had amorous relations with God that "fill" her (terms referring to the "void" and to the "fullness" of so-called mystical life are crucial, and even more so for women who are the bearers sexually and physiologically of a void that must be filled). At the same time, she is afraid of being deluded; she fears she will be considered a saint; she is afraid that the devil will convince her of falsities ... because she lacks an intellectual instrument that enables her to think and "judge" for herself. By definition, women are considered incapable of "judgment," both because they are "empty-headed" and because judging, even on an intellectual level, presupposes an authority that is denied to them.

The Victim Must Not Die

Thus once again, the vicious circle emerges: the quest for self-annihilation, abjection. From this point of view, the letters written by Louise du Néant are exemplary. She hints at her condition as a sinner, but never mentions any actual sins, which is typical of nearly all the writing of women mystics. At most, she refers to some generic "temptation" in the area of purity or pride, yet she speaks of herself as being the worst of sinners.

> I am a miserable being who deserves infinite punishments without any consolation; none of the creatures on earth could console me enough for the loss I have suffered; the fact is that God no longer wants me, he has been obliged to abandon me to my enemies and to myself, because I persist in my guilt without worrying about correcting it; yet I tremble with the fear of committing some grave sin.

Therefore the idea of God's justice has been so inculcated that she claims God *has been obliged* to abandon her. No male would have been permitted to express a similar idea, if for no other reason than that it is theologically incorrect. But a woman is a "woman" in the eyes of the confessor; her "diversity" in guilt is as absolute as it is in her sexual makeup. Louise, then, is convinced she is guilty, and yet she trembles at the thought of sinning. With no possibility for rational verification, she is trapped in the lack of logic provoked by theology, which wraps itself up in unsolvable contradictions, since it means to *define* and circumscribe God. Her dependence on what she has been taught by priests is total:

> I can assure you, before the Divine Majesty, in whose presence I write you, that the illnesses, insults, effrontery and humiliation that are inflicted on me and which I myself cause, though they greatly afflict nature, are pleasing to me, and I enjoy the fact that God is thus satisfied. But it is not enough, my good Father, I beg you to favor *your interests against me and vindicate* ... [emphasis added].

This is the logic of sacrifice and the victim in the presence of a vengeful God like the Judaic one, whom the Christians have "improved" by establishing a "law of accountancy between God and men which is even worse than the law of retaliation, for it is impossible to respond to the infinity of God, and the books *can never be* "balanced." Annihilation of the victim, then, by definition, can never end. Only two possibilities remain: to commit "suicide" by becoming sacrificers, their own priests, as many women have done by seeking out their own death, with the help of confessors and those surrounding them (the name of Thérèse of Lisieux suffices); or else—as in the case of Louise du Néant, Marguerite-Marie Alacoque, Madame de Guyon, Margaret of Cortona and so many others that it is impossible to name them all—by eluding a rapid final conclusion, since death would remove them from the increasingly burdensome suffering that they inflict upon themselves.

The borderline between the sense of reality and delirium is extremely hard to draw, perhaps impossible. But this borderline does exist, and can be discerned, albeit vaguely, in the "absolute" pursuit on the part of certain individuals of the union between the symbolic and the concrete. Therein lies the greatest danger in a society like the Christian one (though the symbolic-concrete mechanism that is set up in the dialectical relation between society and the individual that drives him to delirium is similar in all cultures). Ever since the death of Jesus of Nazareth, the foundations were laid for a vital experience based on a particular "game" through the works of the disciples, especially Paul who, having been converted by means of a "vision," was the first to unite the symbolic with the concrete. Possible at all times and in all situations, it is a game of passage that allows one to place oneself either within symbolic or real action from one occasion to the next, according to the need. This danger has frequently become a reality because it points to the symbolic, and so prevents those who experience it from seeing its hallucinatory foundations, thus putting the logical system at risk. To concretize the symbolic is obviously a road without limits; that is why a person who believes he can and *must* succeed in following it, ends up by performing delirious actions. The very concept of concretizing the symbolic includes a logical error, the loss of the reality principle.

As we shall see apropos of Louise du Néant, women in particular have been the ones who strive to travel down this road in Christianity, even though none of those who have studied the phenomena of so-called "mysticism" has ever considered this detail. But it is no mere coincidence that it is women who try to achieve the symbolic by moving along roads that tend to lack the reality principle and are increasingly "annihilative" of the person.

At this point, I shall attempt to list the main reasons for this behavior, though the problems involved are so complex that they need separate studies. The techniques of so-called ascesis, the techniques of humiliation and self-dominion actuated ever since the early centuries of Christianity, were invented by males (as clearly emerges from the fact that the only subjects who are "theorists" and endowed with the right and power to theorize are men/males). Such techniques are centered on food and sex, and so on dominion of the "body." But in reality, food-centered ascesis functions in relation to dominion over sex for men, since it is the only true, terrible problem for them. Chastity is preserved by depriving oneself of food, and gluttony, in turn, foments lechery.[112]

The usual failure on the part of spiritual advisors to take into account the substantial difference with which food and sex are perceived by women in comparison to males (see Part I, Chapter 3 of this book), prevents them from understanding virtually anything. Furthermore, "spiritual" direction for women, who have no function or activity outside the convent, is actually direction *tout court*, total direction, so that the obviousness with which the concept of "spiritual" direction is applied to women pertains to the usual error of historic inertia that I have often underlined. Religious women's relation to themselves and to God virtually constitutes their whole lives, since they lack both work in society and any exchange or real communication with people having "normal" experiences," relations with people of both sexes.

Through spiritual direction, men spur women on to extreme abjection with a pleasure and insistence that in themselves are enough to reveal an intensity of hate and sadism driven to shocking limits. The difference between males and females in their perception of their own bodies and their function in the world is radical. Women *are* their own body, because society and the culture have always convinced them of this. It is on the basis of her physicality that the woman achieves shape and significance in the eyes of the world. But not in function of any active enjoyment of sex: This is forbidden for women, at least "respectable" women, since until today sex never presented much of an attraction for them anyway, inasmuch as it implied submission to the brutality of males whom they had not chosen and may not even have known, because they were assigned to them by their fathers. Moreover, for women, sex has inevitably been linked to procreation, which often represented a possible, even probable death sentence. As we have seen, these were some of the fundamental reasons for women's adhesion to Christianity in the early centuries.

Ferocious Abysses

Within the area of the ascetic practices of "mysticism," placing men's abstinence from sex on the same level as women's means blinding oneself to practically everything concerning the penitential life of women. It is not the desire for sexual pleasure which drives them to grinding penance, but being perceived as a "body" that leads to temptation and corruption, not of oneself, but of others: men. To oppress one's own body is not a virtue for women then, but an unlimited obligation for justice that must reach the point of destruction, since only it can lead them to God. The female body is not redeemable, because it is not a source of "temptation" for the woman herself, but for the other; *by its mere existence* it is a cause of perdition for men and for the world.

Furthermore, the female body is a container of "filth": that is how males think of it and theorize it. True, the theme of the body as container

II. The Tragic Game of Mysticism

of filth has been present from Augustine onwards, in reference to mankind in general; but the female body is execrated as "filth" from birth, from the uterus to the feces among which one is born. In all societies, including the Judeo-Christian one, the tabooing of menstrual blood, supreme paragon for males of everything that is dirty and filthy, inculcates in women a horror for this product of their body. This horror takes a shape that cannot be compared with the horror humans in general — male and female alike — feel for their own excrement. Menstrual blood is not considered excrement which "regulates" the physiological fullness-void; it is therefore not a "natural," but a potent, supernatural poison, a revealer of "death," because the mechanism of female sexuality is the consequence of original sin and condemned by God.

Many theologians and thinkers in the Church are convinced that before the expulsion from Eden, menstruation did not exist, and that coitus was not necessary for procreation. Bernardine of Siena, for example, is so sure of these facts that he maintains that women can give birth without losing their virginity.[113]

In short, the penitent woman finds herself face to face with her own body and not just the desires of her own body. The horrid gestures women force themselves to perform have no counterpart even among the most famous male ascetics. A fundamental passage is made in moving from the privation of food to the assumption of filthy foods. This "leap" in meaning, typical of femininity, indicates the tendency to identify the symbolic with the concrete, and consequently, a form of psychotic pathology.

Women concentrate on food instead of sex, and on eating and drinking the most repugnant pseudo-foods, because they are food-linked, linked to the ineluctable fate of "becoming food" for others. The woman feeds the newborn with the same breasts that are instruments of sexual enjoyment. The connection between pleasure giving and breastfeeding is one of the factors driving women to self-directed ferociousness, in seeking their own annulment by means of the negation of food as pleasure. This probably explains many cases of "puerperal psychosis": the numerous psychic disturbances often developing during the nursing period, as well as anorexia in adolescents.

Louise du Néant licks and sucks the purulent wounds of her inmates at the Salpêtriere insane asylum; she eats the food left by others, mixing it with the most nauseating refuse; she drinks liquids contained in a human skull, and vomit gathered from the floor where it has been thrown up. Marguerite-Marie Alacoque sucks the wounds of the sick women in her care, and eats the vomit of others. Madame de Guyon would have eaten the feces of the dysenteric patients had the director not forbidden her to do so. However, Marguerite-Marie Alacoque recounts in her autobiography that "she sinks her lips into feces, she fills her mouth with them and stops short of swallowing them, because it is forbidden to eat without permission." Or else she wipes up and devours the vomit of a sick woman, and for this act, Jesus rewards her "by keeping her mouth stuck to the wound of his Sacred Heart for two or three hours."[114]

Examples of this kind (humiliating to recall, even for this writer) are countless. They all revolve around the search for abjection by female subjects through the ingestion of abject materials. In his essay commenting on the letters of Louise du Néant, Mino Bergamo analyzes such behavior by referring to Marguerite-Marie Alacoque and Madame Guyon as well, but not once does he point out that he is speaking exclusively of the female sex. Perhaps he is not aware of the fact, it being obvious to him. He speaks generically of 17th-century "mysticism" when he is dealing with women, above all, women who throughout the centuries (and not only in the 17th century) repeat the same acts of dereliction and annihilation authorized by males.

Bergamo links food "refuse" with Louise's feeling like "refuse," claiming that her marginalization exemplifies the condition to which the Christian aspires. But nothing could be more deceptive, indeed false, than this type of analysis, which bundles men and women together in a generic "mysticism" and in the search for self-annihilation, defining such phenomena as typical traits of Christianity. In reality, feeling like "refuse" is certainly not a condition the Christian aspires to. The Gospel instead emphasizes the importance of Christians' *being yeast* in the world, on their being chosen to be the flame that lights up the world from on high.

The guidance of directors and confessors to whom these women submit their will, inasmuch as these men are invested with the authority and knowledge of the male hierarchy, does not in the least perturb those who write about this type of women "mystics." Our scholars waste not a word, not a thought, on the behavior of male torturers. The enjoyment of such torturers in witnessing the achievement of female abjection, extinguishes in them any memory of Jesus' message concerning the dignity of the human being. The gradual passage to psychosis, a passage whose limits are very hard to establish, occurs synchronically, in any case, and through the reciprocal action of confessor and the woman entrusted to him. Obedience and humility, virtues stressed by the religious vow itself and obligatory for the nun, make everything the penitent thinks and does subject to approval of the male authority directing her. Yet this potent male is often incapable of maintaining the necessary equilibrium, because he expects the woman-victim-Godlink to carry him along with her into the vortex of divine passion, even if this passion takes a female form and so excludes him by definition. However, since the exclusion of women from the life of a religious man and priest constitutes the more or less conscious basis of his choice, he himself is a judge that any earthly, non-ecclesiastic tribunal would consider unsuitable and eliminate as prejudicially hostile. In fact, the spiritual advisor hates the woman entrusted to him more than any other woman, because any other one ratifies his hate by eluding him and throwing herself into the arms of another man, and by using that sinful sex so that the priest considers her a "sinner." So the more the woman obeys him, humiliates, lowers, and tortures herself, while asking his authorization to do so, the more the spiritual director spurs her on in this work of destruction. He projects onto her the entire burden of guilt that has made him, a male, an "impotent" being in continual struggle against his own unsatisfied and unsatisfiable sexuality.

Margaret of Cortona, for example (1247–1297), oppressed by guilt for having lived with a man and given birth to a son out of wedlock, is so clearly the fruit of Catholic teachings on sexual sin that none of her biographers are surprised by the fact, including a man seemingly endowed with delicate spirituality, François Mauriac.[115] For such men, she is the sinner, as Mary Magdalen has been from the beginning. The woman's sin is the sin of sex, she leads men to sexual sin, their worst, or rather, their only sin, the sin that sums up all other sins in the eyes of men.

So, then, Margaret of Cortona sees herself with these same eyes: The eyes of men are the eyes of God. She condemns herself to the most ferocious penitence because nothing can be equal to her guilt. And she condemns her child to the same penitence. But even this behavior, which would normally be considered unjust and abhorrent, is exalted instead as a sign of her extreme quest and capacity for violence against herself. Did not God condemn his Son to die? Did he not ask Abraham to sacrifice Isaac? The child of sin will expiate as well, from the earliest age, enveloped in the horror with which Margaret sees herself; and he will be submitted to the same destructive fury: without a house, without food, without clothing. It is her confessor who relates her virtuous words: "My son, when you take possession of the little cell that will be your home from now on, you shall eat in silence the raw food destined to you. It is not right for me to waste the time destined to praising God in preparing food...." "The child was lacking in everything," Brother Giunta adds tranquilly in his diary: "she no longer took care of him, as if she had not been his mother." As we now know quite well, confessors have never "stopped" their penitents until they crossed the extreme abyss.

Having succeeded in joining the Third Order of the Franciscans, Margaret finds herself living in that period of furious struggle over the way of conceiving "poverty," which shook the world of the Mendicants immediately after the death of Francis. The town of Cortona lay at the center of these struggles, being home to Brother Elia, Francis's first successor, and an enemy of the absoluteness of Lady Poverty.

There is nothing of Francis and his gentleness in the violence that Margaret uses against herself or in the ferocious penitence to which she submits herself. Often covered only with the rug on which she sleeps naked, having given her few garments to poor people, with a rope around her neck, her head shaved (instruments of condemnation used by the civil and ecclesiastic tribunals to punish the errors of heretics and criminals), she crawls around town so that everyone can see the dereliction in store for a sinful woman. She hardly eats any longer, only raw plants and a few nuts from her land. She does not sleep, she weeps and wastes away in the desire to destroy her body, the beauty of that body that led men to sin. She decides to cut off her nose and lips, as the law foresees for prostitutes, thieves, criminals; but here Brother Giunta stops her, as always happens when destructive gestures are about to become extreme. The torturer keeps his victim alive as long as possible. But what good is this annihilation? Margaret's ecstasies and visions are similar to those of so many other women who are madly in love with God and despise themselves.

The descriptions handed down to us by their confessors repeat exactly what the Church teaches, and what the autistic thought of the individual absorbs and re-elaborates from those teachings. We find here the most schematic, elementary form of ideation, detached from the interdependence and limitations of any external context. Margaret's ecstasies define the periods in which she "sees" or, as she says, Jesus "shows" her how horrible her sins are, and how she must suffer in order to expiate them. In any event, it is before the crowds at Cortona, gathered in the church to witness these wonders, that Margaret sees a Jesus that no one sees, and shouts words of love that everyone can hear and so appreciate her extraordinary adventure.

Though seemingly solitary, the "experience" of the woman "mystic" is concretized into a spectacle because there is a group around her which believes in it. Above all, it believes that the woman's task is to make that experience act according to the dictates of the group.

Nailed

The need to be loved, to be favored; the romantic longing to be the "only one" for the beloved, re-emerges from one century to the next and from one vision to the next. In no male ecstasy does God express such intense, abundant effusions of a unique love. To Margaret, who suffers over his Passion, Jesus says:

> You have soothed my wounds with the balsam of your tears, you have taken me down from the cross.... Daughter of suffering, glory and greatness.... Daughter of perfect faith.... Star ... my chosen one ... my companion, my sister, Margaret, my martyr ... living sanctuary of my grace....
> White rose of innocence, red rose of love.... Love yourself because I love you.... You are my daughter because you obey me. You are my bride, because you love me.... I love no one more than you on earth....

But how many times has this lover lied, since so many women have heard these same words: "I love no one more than you"? During our examination of visions and ecstasies, we have often asked ourselves whether these women are lying, and we have been persuaded every time that if we are in the presence of lies, they are the same lies that all women have found themselves forced to pronounce in one way or another for themselves and for the world. Such lies vary in their degree of awareness; they are nearly always mixed with the truth; but they have saved women, albeit in extremely cruel ways from a definite realization of their own annihilation. Often, a low level of intelligence has allowed affections to prevail and a series of gratifications regarding female pride, power over others, need for love, evasion, and flight into the unreality of ecstasy in the face of the pitiless, irremediable realization of her condemnation to non-being. Some women have "pretended" more, some less. Some have resigned themselves to the convent as one resigns oneself to prison: floating through life in the routine of obedience, with the little joys of a feast table, visits from relatives, the unexpected sermon of a passing confessor, the appointment of a new mother superior.

After all, it is not much worse than obeying a violent husband, facing pregnancy and childbirth, caring for the house each day, the children, the ill, and the elderly. Society has celebrated the vows of the new "nun," just as it has celebrated the oath taken at the altar, by that other sacrificial victim who pretends to feel joy, the bride. Both of them wear a white gown, a veil, a tiara of flowers on their heads, exalted by the "representation" of an absolute, eternal love to which only women are called.

Pierre Fauchery grasps the isomorphism between matrimony and the taking of the veil as sacrificial killing, as death. Highly sensitive to the "fate" of women, he observes:

> The veil, with its sculpture-like draping, swallowing up the living being in a superhuman plasticity, petrifies and dissolves the corporeal

mass that it sanctifies. The orchestration of this moment thus necessarily implies an ultimate "presentation" of those beauties rendered so precious by the imminence of their disembodiment; it is, if you like, the equivalent of the last image one has of a person before he is buried.[116]

But when a woman's intelligence does not permit her to believe and live out the falsity, and no other escape is possible, she remains "nailed," as a young "schizophrenic" studied by Ronald D. Laing expressed it, nailed down and unable to move. This is an acceptance of helplessness by a person who does not want to give in to make-believe, a kind of make-believe imposed by the cultural meanings assigned to the woman by the historical conditioning that these meanings imply.

In their study, *Normality and Madness in the Family* (1970)[117], the psychiatrists Ronald D. Laing and Aaron Esterson present 11 stories of women who have been patients in a psychiatric hospital for a long period. They attempt to give a phenomenological explanation of these women's "schizophrenia" which will render it intelligible. While aiming to cancel out the category of schizophrenic "abnormality," by leading it back into the vast framework of family interrelations, these authors do not seem to perceive the continual dramatic references of the family environment with the vaster, more conditioned environment of cultural and social systems of meaning. But above all, they forget, and so neglect to emphasize to the reader, that the hospital ward in which they study and work, is a "female" ward, and that their clinical cases are all "cases" of women, Western women. We can assume that the crisis takes shape as "schizophrenia" more frequently in the Western woman than in those of other cultures, because, given the historic-social context and more "literate" acculturation, it is easier for the Western woman to become aware of the "conflict" in which she lives, the conflict of make-believe. At the same time, she is more easily aware of the impossibility of escaping it.

In the Blair family, studied by Laing and Esterson, the "mother" represents the average Western housewife in all the most concrete and symbolic elements that have been assigned to her by society throughout the centuries. The drama is concentrated on her because, given the pettiness and misery of her existence, her daughter Lucie cannot and does not want to identify with her. Lucie rejects identification, not with Mrs. Blair, not with her own mother, but with "the Mother."

Of the poorly expressed, yet clearly tragic accounts that Mrs. Blair gives of her daily life and her relations with her husband and other family members, at a certain point, Laing and Esterson observe that

> we must be careful to distinguish between the facts and what we infer

from them. At the moment, Mrs. Blair is clearly expressing in a coherent manner, and with a wealth of detail, these opinions about her husband and family. The opinions may or may not be true. If they are not true, Mrs. Blair is probably psychotic. If they are true, her husband is probably psychotic, or both of them are.

Laing and Esterson thus refuse to see that the institution of the *family* in the West today is "psychotic" (and not Mr. and Mrs. Blair). The condition of the "woman" (and not the mother as such) is in a phase of transition or passage from what it once was, without knowing it, to something that is still unknown. Not even today have psychiatrists fully understood the reality of the Western woman's daily life and the values that she now recognizes as false and alienating, but in which she is trapped; the constant repetition of gestures that are actually gestures of sacrifice and service, but which communicate hate, repulsion, and scorn. Mrs. Blair, observe Laing and Esterson, depicts her life as a continual battle against many enemies, one of whom is her husband. This is true. Except that what Laing and Esterson consider as the psychotic vision of the individual, "Mrs. Blair," is the condition of any woman, wife and mother, whose life is consumed as an instrument for others, but who today *knows* (at least in the West) that no one can or must be an instrument. *Not even* the woman.

It is this reality of female life that Lucie refuses: not as a daughter, but as a "woman" who sees her own destiny perfectly incarnated in her mother. Rather than accept this destiny, she "prefers" schizophrenia. "There seems to be no solution, complains Lucie, no further move is possible, no hope. It is like a game of chess. One remains nailed, and no longer able to move." Lucie, then, like the majority of 'schizophrenics,' is a women submerged by an extraordinary gift of sensitivity and intelligence; she even claims that she is convinced she must do something special with her life. "Everyone must. Everyone is destined to do something in life...."

To this affirmation, which would be considered just and true for any male, the woman, "Mrs. Blair," a mother like all mothers, can answer only with the same reply of a countless number of women: The only solution is in renunciation, the acceptance of one's state of hopelessness. But it is the perception of this solution as "false" that drives the woman toward "schizophrenia." All psychological and psychiatric interpretations, like all psychoanalytic ones, push the role of the woman's intelligence into the background; they de-emphasize her capacity to compare the ideal contents of the culture with those that are concretely experienced and, in particular, to perceive the "falsity" of the woman's position, as one called upon to objectify herself, to deny herself as a person in order to recognize herself exclusively as an "instrument."

"Woman's malaise in experiencing civilization" is completely different from man's. It expresses the tragic, absolute impossibility of accepting, or identifying herself with, symbolic contents that have been built up around the woman, objectifying her and reducing her to being a sign. Western women today have become conscious of this objectification with a growing awareness of each person's right to be a "subject." This awareness acts in such a way that women are now forced to become symbols of themselves, while still embracing the symbolic contents assigned to them,. But no one can accomplish this without falsity and fear. That is what Thérèse of Lisieux did, through what she herself called a "giant" effort.

A Crime Outside of History

The conclusion of this lengthy part of our journey through the history of women may be summed up in only one way. The silence, indeed, the consent and exaltation on the part of both religious and secular historians concerning the most atrocious crime that has ever been committed: The torture and slow killing — the physical, psychic, intellectual, emotional, social killing — of an incalculable number of women in the name of the value of "sacrifice," is a reality, a "fact" that must be studied in depth inasmuch as it is "history."

By itself, the history of history, of the way to make history, testifies better than any other document to the psychological and cultural reality of a people. The two thousand years of Christian Europe, studied in a thousand ways in their most recondite aspects, still conceal (in the very admiration often shown by scholars toward certain "values") the darkest, deepest male certainty regarding women. Women are instruments that serve to gratify a God that, despite the Christian exaltation of love, is a male God: violent, jealous, ferocious, vindictive, and hungry for victims. It is from His behavior toward His brides that we can understand what the traits of this God are. But it is also from the way men goad women on to waste away in suffering, to despise themselves, to annihilate themselves for Him, that we can understand how men have constructed a God totally similar to them. Similar in hate, in scorn for women as human beings, as persons.

A document of this hate is the life imprisonment imposed on women, concrete imprisonment in the cloistered life, but above all, the psychic imprisonment of "sacrifice." There is one more thing that is never mentioned. Men have driven women to hate life as much as they themselves hate women. Men have convinced them that everything human is ugly, repugnant, and despicable; something to "sacrifice" until it is no longer recognizable as "human." They can never be absolved of this crime. Men have driven women toward the world of unreality, delirium, hallucination, the sphere of the self, forcing them to "produce" where it is actually impossible to produce: in the loss of reason. They have convinced women that they must hate themselves, and as themselves hate man as humanity. They have convinced women that they must reject everything that is "beautiful" for humanity, everything beautiful that people can create: music, poetry, art, philosophy, science, for everything must be "sacrificed." The "heart of flesh" of Marguerite-Marie appears as the last, desperate "fruit" of women shut up in their physicality, similar to those cage-maddened animals that devour their own legs in hopes of nourishing themselves. To know the poor thoughts of women mystics, lost in an impossible invention, leads to compassion and rebellion against absolute injustice. But above all, it leads us to ask a question, which would violently emerge as the only true *given* of history as we have traced it thus far, if the blindness of habit did not consider the quest for extreme suffering and self-detestation as obvious and "right" and the very essence of Christianity: The question is: Why do men hate women to this extent?

The Triumph and Victims of the Sacred Heart

If we could sum up in a single trait (difficult and dangerous though it always is) what has been called the "mysticism of the heart," we should say that this has been a "psychological" way to experience Christianity, one that has accompanied Christian history from Augustine to Pascal and Bernanos. It is considered a "psychological" method; in reality it has also been, at least for men, an intellectual and philosophical method principally: a cognitive reflection concerning oneself, though seemingly a reflection about how to know God. In following this path, one actually reaches the extreme limits of human annihilation, for in order to know God, humanity should do nothing but let Him emerge and act within it. Instead, humanity reaches not only the certainty of its absolute solitude, but also the annihilation of God, together with its own. It is a pathway parallel, but only seemingly so, to that of female mysticism that results in psychosis. It is the itinerary that philosophers, thinkers, literati, believers, and non-believers follow between *esprit* and *coeur*. Along the road leading from the consciousness of Descartes to the unconscious of Leibniz, from one occasion to the next, *mind* and *heart* become the source of the intuitive knowledge of self, or of absolute non-knowledge, which eventually culminates in the Freudian unconscious.[118]

Self-Annihilation in Order to Exist 217

Women, however, never bother to theorize their inner states through thought. On the contrary, they make that immediate leap from the theoretical to the concrete, which appears as a kind of female curse. Women seek out in the "heart of flesh," that of the Crucified One and their own, all "truth" in which to believe, without making the slightest reflection apart from an affective, emotional kind. It is to this level that Catholic theology falls as well, once it adopts the female experience, as occurred in devotion to the Sacred Heart and in "victimal" spirituality (as theology defines it).

The path followed by women does not lead to any "knowledge" except the evident projection of a boundless need — dictated by total deprivation — to be loved, recognized, and exalted, at least by that God whom everyone praises because He has let Himself be tortured, humiliated, and killed, as women are tortured, humiliated, and killed. When the Church takes possession of women's devotions, and their vision of divine love, it does so because that is exactly what it needs in order to keep the so-called "people" at the supreme level of obedience, fear, sacrifice, and ignorance. Women mystics who have immediately been made "saints" are exemplary prototypes of that "people." Indeed, the most dramatic aspect of the history of women — from the early centuries of Christianity, in martyrdom, up to our times — has always been this: Whatever women have done has served to establish or re-establish power, ecclesiastic, family, social or cultural power. Through the exaltation of the virginity of "God's bride," for example, the value of virginity as the supreme female value was strengthened and lasted up to the mid–20th century. Every woman were to possess the virtues of purity and modesty, whether her husband was God or man — since earthly marriage was only a sub-product (lamentably inevitable for procreation) of marriage to God. Therefore, the male-husband was to be honored, served and obeyed as the substitute of God on earth. Only now that he sees that the Catholic principles dictating woman's role have been put at risk, has Pope John Paul II begun to canonize simple laywomen. However, these new "saints" have done nothing outside of what all women have been forced to do for two thousand years, without anyone exalting their heroism, obeying husbands and dying of childbirth.

The history of devotion to the "heart" has lasted for a long time. In any event, it is with Marguerite-Marie Alacoque (1647–1690) that we find an extreme emotional concentration on the physical heart of Jesus, and the popular development of this devotion, which has aroused passionate debate, and equally passionate feelings of love. Indeed, it has characterized the three centuries going from the 18th to the 20th.

Aside from any discussion concerning the "revelations" of which Marguerite-Marie — like so many other women mystics we have encountered — was both a psychic victim and a conscious inventor, the way in which this kind of devotion was presented and practiced has lent itself to objections of all kinds. The Jansenists accused adorers of the Sacred Heart of idolatry and fetishism, calling them ironically "*cordicoli*" or "little cords," because they worshiped a flesh "viscus" detached from the person of Jesus. Another point subject to argument was the fact that this devotion was presented as an anchor of final salvation, an absolute, certain system for saving oneself from the wrath of God.[119]

It was easy to counter this "apocalyptic" function by responding that it could still quite properly be done without, since it had not been activated until that moment. In the early 18th century, the Jansenists' objections were too strong to be ignored, and the Roman Curia was rather cautious about officially recognizing this new form of devotion. This results from its refusals, repeated until 1765 when Pope Clement XIII decided to approve the feast of the Sacred Heart.

But theological subtleties had nothing to do with the historical reality experienced by all those who had become enthusiasts of this form of devotion. A woman, a "mystic," takes it upon herself to "save" the world with her revelations, no longer by exhorting popes or spiritual advisors to act as God suggests through the visionary, but by her own suggestion of a theological-concrete way of behavior. Later, in following her example, other women and children would tell the world what the Madonna wants, as at Lourdes and Fatima; at any rate, the "inventor" had already appeared; furthermore, using the Madonna is much "weaker" than using the "heart" of Jesus the Savior. Whether Marguerite-Marie is in good or bad faith in claiming that they depend on a revelation from Jesus, the practices that she proposes (for they are precisely this: "practices"): perpetual adoration of the Most Holy Sacrament, expiatory communion on the first Friday of the month, consecration to the Sacred Heart and the scapular become a synthesis of all Christianity. Therefore, in 1928, Pope Pius XI, in the Encyclical *Miserentissimus Redemptor*, declares that "in this form of devotion one finds a summary of the entire Catholic religion": thus, the total vindication of a woman in the presence of ecclesiastic and theological power.

In the history of Catholic Christianity, "femininity" has always influenced the "magic" affectivity, and therefore the popular affectivity of devotions; women have contributed decisively to the *presence* of the Church among the masses of the faithful, keeping themselves and the faithful in general at the "lowest" levels of religion: the "lowest," but the most "authentic," those that underlie the cultural structures.

Marguerite-Marie Alacoque assigned to the Company of Jesus the task of spreading devotion to the Heart; obviously, this task, too, was "revealed" by Jesus. And though Ignatius Loyola had always opposed any activity on the part of the Jesuits in relation to religious women, the great majority of institutions dedicated to the Sacred Heart were co-founded by Jesuits (together with a woman). Similarly, most of the advisors, spiritual directors, and writers of constitutions that have urged women to sustain institutions dedicated to the Sacred Heart, have been Jesuits. It would be interesting to study the strange contrast between the Jesuits' intense relationship with mystical, feminine "devotions," and the intellectual rigidity and search for power marking their will to influence the world. Herein probably lies one of the reasons why "Jesuitism" has been opposed and so deeply hated: the absolute masculinity of the *ratio studiorum* and political cynicism, together with the obsessive, infantile "abacus" of spiritual practices. There are decidedly feminine, infantile aspects in the devotions which the Jesuits have instituted and encouraged: the institution of the Noble Guard of the Madonna, for example, the Eucharistic devotion, and finally, devotion to the Sacred Heart.

Moreover, from the very beginning, women, perhaps deceived by this emotional devotion, have shown a real passion for the Company of Jesus. Not only was this passion not in the least returned, but it was also opposed in every way possible. On the basis of his supreme scorn for women that, as a good soldier, he reserved for female inferiority, Ignatius went so far as to manifest a harshness and ingratitude toward them that were truly abnormal, besides being morally unjustifiable. Sustained for many years in his studies at the University of Salamanca, and then in Paris, by the generosity of Spanish women friends who had placed the greatest trust in him and his religious aspirations, Ignatius impatiently awaited the money, woolen sweaters, and flavorful sweets which, like all women who love, they sent him, challenging the perils of that era's naval expeditions. The sweet friends, however, acted thus in the expectation that, once having established his great enterprise in Rome, he would institute a female branch of the company, as had occurred in the other religious orders. For a long time, Ignatius let them go on hoping, fudging through with the most varied excuses, but determined that he would never fulfill their expectations.

But after waiting for many years, after selling their property for the construction of the marvelous Collegio Romano, his benefactresses realized that Ignatius was biding his time. So they decided to give him a surprise by reaching him in Rome in order to found the women's branch of the institution. They thus found themselves facing the bitter, eternal fate of women: fooled, exploited, abandoned.

Ignatius's inflexible refusal and "male" cruelty toward women lost in an unknown country, who had been deliberately deceived and who now, devoid of everything, could not even return home, find no justification outside of that authentic male hate for women of which we have already encountered abundant proof. In any event, falling for the umpteenth time into the error of naiveté, and unaware of the superior "justice" founded on invincible male solidarity, his old women friends turned to the pope in exasperation. They meant to sue Ignatius. It was a useless gesture, of course, and no female Jesuits ever saw the light of day.[120]

The suppression of the Company of Jesus in 1773 (whose task, according to Marguerite-Marie, was the diffusion of devotion), and Clement IV's unfavorable attitude toward the "little cords," hampered its development until 1804 when Napoleon's regime began to authorize the reopening of female religious institutions, but only those dedicated to useful social activities, such as the hospital orders.

At that moment, the first institutions dedicated to the Sacred Heart appeared with the purpose (a secret one, of course) of working toward the reconstitution of the Company of Jesus. This desire, again, was due to the female passion for the Jesuits, a passion that we might jokingly liken to a desire for forbidden fruit. Who but a woman could have "sacrificed" herself with this aim? In 1800, Sophie Barat founded an institution in order to spread the devotion to the Sacred Heart, a devotion disapproved by everyone because it was too closely linked to the activity of the Jesuits. Her nuns added a fourth vow to the three foreseen by the rule: They would be "victims" of expiation for sins against the "heart," even though they were not permitted to bear the name.

With the advent of the Restoration instead, and with the reinstatement of the Company of Jesus in 1814, what the Revolution had deemed a symbol of regression in its implications of elementary affectivity and feminine magic, became a symbol of progress and peace. The development of foundations dedicated to the Sacred Heart is striking. Between 1810 and 1830 we see 39 new foundations, and except for an interval during the Italian Risorgimento insurrections, this number continued to grow. Indeed, the 19th century would be defined as the century of the Sacred Heart.

Moreover, the cultural pattern of the 19th century explains the many elements connected to the spirituality of the Sacred Heart. Love for one's country, love for the beloved and love for God are tied by a single thread, and nourish one another.

In its miserable pettiness—pettiness toward man and God—the vow to become a "victim" in order to "pay for" offenses perpetrated against the

Heart of Jesus could only have been conceived by a woman like Marguerite-Marie, closed in the ghetto of her cloistered, mystical self. Nonetheless, it served to inflate the spirit of sacrifice in 19th-century heroism. On a symbolic level, we find its most significant cultural concentration in poetry and music, and, above all, in opera, which sums up all the themes of the romantic model in a way that can only be defined as unique. There is no operatic heroine who is not a "victim" who is destined to die of love. The "heart"—a heart of flesh, whether human or divine—sums up all the characteristics of the model: heroism, fatherland, and victim ready to sacrifice himself for ideals in war, in liberty, or in obedience to divine destiny, in the victory of the beauty of death.[121]

Even tuberculosis, understood as a romantic disease, seems ideally connected to the "heart" rather than the lungs. (In fact, although they are more indispensable to life than any other organ, the lungs have never assumed a significant symbolic meaning in cultural history.) The symbol of "heart," therefore, includes the idea of a "total" human society in the presence of God: the Catholic Church and the nation, or rather, in its ancient but renewed ideal force: the sacredness of the "kingdom."

It is no coincidence that the two most Catholic nations, France and Italy, where devotion to the Sacred Heart developed more intensely, were the ones where people sang with the most passion about the regality of Christ: *Christus vincit, Christus regnat, Christus imperat*. It is superfluous to point out that, despite the eagerness of a number of priests to found institutes consecrated to the Sacred Heart, it was only the female ones who made a vow of "victimal" reparation. In fact, there are no male institutes entitled or dedicated in this sense. The few attempts made in this direction almost immediately burned out. The two institutes that did arise in France, the *Priests Victims of the Sacred Heart of Jesus*, founded in 1850, ceased to exist in 1882 with the death of the founder. In France, again, another institute was founded with the same title by Caroline Lioger, a rather naive woman. It was her intention that it be exactly like its female counterpart; but of course it lasted very briefly (1875–1880). After all, one cannot invent, much less give life to anything that goes against the basic cultural meanings. As for the need for a "victim," this can only be the woman-bride of God in the consecrated life. Therefore no male institutes of "repairers" and "victims" exist. In any event, aside from the vow of reparation, in the ambit of the Sacred Heart as well, a devotion in itself sacrificial, the preponderance of female institutes is significant. Male institutes dedicated to the Sacred Heart of Jesus number little more than 16 percent of the female ones: 36 as opposed to 228.

We cannot end this brief journey among the victims of the Sacred

Heart without mentioning Sister Victoire Conen de St-Luc, a member of the Institute of the *Nuns of the Retreat* at Quimper, who was guillotined in Paris in 1794, accused of having spread the devotion to the Sacred Heart.[122]

III. Religious Women Out to Conquer the World

10
Acting So As to Exist

Goodbye to Cloistered Life:
The Struggle for an Active Life

Schools were soon organized in convents, with the aim of enabling women to recite the liturgical office. At first, the majority of pupils could neither read nor write. Of course, learning to read totally changed the mental condition of women by putting them in a world, the world of symbolic knowledge, that surpassed the one limited to reading the scriptures (theoretically the only aim of their education). For women, monasticism thus took shape as a way to understand the world, a way toward that social enrichment that would have been excluded from them in a normal life as laywomen. The Benedictine convents in particular were famous for their schools, and they maintained this fame virtually up to the institution of state schools. But in 15th-century Italy, an early attempt to educate girls took form independently of monastic life. This experience drastically broke with what had seemed obvious until then: that women should have no right to any type of learning outside of their traditional tasks as workers, servants, both at home and outside, and mothers. Their participation in the knowledge belonging to "men" was considered socially useless.

The idea of letting the poorest girls—those who remained outside the convents—learn certain prayers and the basic elements of religion, by teaching them to read, was conceived by an intelligent woman, Angela Merici. Determined to be concretely useful in the harsh reality of women's lives, Angela is famous as the founder of one of the most widespread female religious congregations, that of the Ursulines. (Obviously, the Church has declared her a saint, even though it strongly opposed her.) But the force that for centuries has attracted thousands of women to this institute of Angela's is due to her having for the first time concentrated an evangelical interest on improving the female condition upon a globally "human" plane, outside of any monastic or matrimonial objectives.

The details available to us concerning Angela Merici's life are scarce. As always occurs in the case of "saintly" figures, her ascetic and mystic virtues tend to be stressed rather than the social ones. Born between 1470 and 1475, she died in 1540 in Brescia, where she had almost always lived. Angela began to take care of the many young syphilitic women, during the first outbreak of that disease, who were crowded into hospitals deliberately named "for incurables." Here, as she hastens about the tragic wards of a disease condemning women to refusal and social death even before a physical one, she realizes the extreme precariousness of the lives of women. When they are not marriageable or protected by some male member of the family, they have no choice except prostitution or death by starvation. And yet Angela Merici does not think, as was considered obvious for so many centuries, that the only solution for these girls is to flee to a convent. She attributes their social and moral fragility to ignorance, above all, with a vision that anticipates today's psycho-sociological theories. She is thus the first person to occupy herself with the young women outside the "holy places": that great number of women without a destiny, who were bewildered and lost in a world that refused to find a "mental," let alone a real, place for any woman who was not the "wife" of someone, whether God or man. She even establishes what today seems a thoroughly modern experience, collaboration between the parents and the educational structure. From this point of view, her decision to let the young women working with her continue living at home is something new (though inspired by the ancient "consecration of virgins" existing in the early Church). Her "daughters" were to remain in the world in order to act, protected by the shield of virginity itself. This was so far from the prevailing attitude of the ecclesiastic hierarchies that it encountered the hostility of both bishops and pope, who, indeed, refused to grant the statues of "nuns" to Angela's companions (as he would later refuse to grant it to the Visitandines of Francis de Sales, given the absence of cloistered and community life).

The humanistic ferment of the second half of the 15th century in Italy, including the concern to instruct women, most certainly reached Angela, just as, a few years later, she would be reached by the debate regarding the moral laxity and corruption in monasteries, and the Protestants' polemics over the so-called "perfection" of monastic vows. Due to a series of extraordinary historical coincidences, Brescia became the center of heretical and reform movements in the Church during the years Angela Merici lived there.[123]

However, during the last decades of the 15th century and the first half of the 16th, reformers in Brescia attempted to correct the structures of the Church from within, without abandoning it. While Italy had seemingly been on the sidelines of the Protestant polemics, in reality, a reform movement had already been actuated and had failed because of a series of converging phenomena, including the spread of popular preaching and the birth of the mendicant orders. We can recognize the sign of this failure in the pyre that put an end to Girolamo Savonarola's preaching against the "prostitute" Church in 1498.[124] Actually, the entire 16th century, up to the definitive conclusion of the Council of Trent, was filled with attempts — more of thought than of action — to shake off the heaviest burdens that the absolutizing of a sacral vision of life had imposed. The sacral pattern had spread throughout Europe. In Italy, it had taken on a particular configuration, and had become identified with the power of the ecclesiastics and the popes in all those areas that had always pertained to the state during the long history of Rome.

In other words, unlike what occurs in all societies in which religious law includes civil law as well (Judaism, medieval Christianity, Islam), it was civil society that exploited the symbolic-sacral structures, and not the other way around. As things were, no one would ever have thought about teaching women to read, had the Italian language not become widely spoken. Present in Italy in popular preaching as early as 1200, it became the "normal" means of learning and religious discussion for the "lower" classes, together with the circulation of the reformers' texts. The Italian language allowed laymen who knew no Latin to venture onto theological terrain that until then had been precluded for them. Consequently, women had access to this type of learning as well, or would have, had the majority known how to read. It was in this cultural context that Angela Merici decided to occupy herself with women's education, beginning with the essential of knowing how to read. Considering the ferments of the era, it is surprising that Angela Merici not only realized the new educational needs, but above all, the fact that the poorest female "class" had a right to a knowledge of the religious texts that was not simply passive rote learning. Her work represents the first step made by religious women toward the conquest of the world through actions and not through contemplation. The first consequence of this step was a refusal of the cloistered life.

Naturally, the biography narrated to us today preserves all the classical themes of the "saintly" woman, endowed with visions and penitential experience from childhood, who practices "perfection" in total obedience. However, these characteristics fail to hide the absolute newness of her action that actually negates the virtues officially attributed to her.

Angela founded the Company of Saint Ursula which, right from the beginning, was characterized as an institute for the protection of young women before it blossomed absolutely unexpectedly into the highly successful Congregation of the Ursulines. But as has always happened to women who have been pushed by faith to operate in the world, despite the Ursulines' invincible will and the modernity of their actions, the Church exploited Angela in order to reaffirm its own power and hold over society. It accomplished this, first of all, through the fascination that "virginity" has always exercised over women as a subjective, personal form of liberty and conquest. As had already happened in the case of monasticism, Angela Merici, like so many other women who moved ahead of the cultural awareness of the ecclesiastic hierarchy, was eventually betrayed and, at the same time, saved by the fascination of virginity. In fact, in virginity, Angela summed up the value allowing her to carry out her Christian action in the world; even though, more or less conscious of her own intolerance toward the corruption of the Church in her time, she was thinking of the consecrated virginity of the early centuries, which allowed women to become "brides of God" while remaining in society.[125] She was a friend of the Brothers of Divine Love, a group of enthusiastic reforming spirits who inspired the works of Philip Neri, who was also convinced of the need to reform the Church outside of monasticism. Monasticism, indeed, had become the greatest center of corruption of the Gospel message, a center of power over rich and poor alike. Since Angela was a woman, her biographers scarcely hint at her condemnation of monastic corruption. But the issue cannot be ignored. Angela was well aware of the fact that monasticism reflected the corruption of society as a whole, with its ruthless oppression of servants and slaves, and its absolute privileges for the rich and noble that even affected admission to the monastery and important positions within it.

Not a single word has been said about Angela Merici's reflections concerning the Church of her time, whereas biographers speak of her exaltation of virginity, of the perfection included in the virtue of virginity, of her love for poverty and obedience. But the search for poverty is an explicit condemnation of all the wealth of the Church; for Angela, obedience is above all obedience to the Holy Spirit in the secrecy of one's conscience, which is, in itself, analogous to a negation of the need for ecclesiastic mediation. That negation would become one of the explicit crucial points of the Protestant Reformation, and an implicit one in female monasticism in the 17th century.

But Angela is a woman. She does not argue; she acts. Once again, a woman is manipulated by a culture that keeps her from believing she is a leader in society, in her thought and in her theoretic systemizing. And once again, it is virginity that saves her from losing herself in the haziness of works performed by ordinary women. This occurs because — as in the beginning of Christianity — the very refusal of marriage and motherhood implies a supreme protest against society. In proposing virginity outside the monastic context, we find an attempt to recuperate the early Church which, though not explicitly expressed in Angela, from the year 1000 on, the spirits remaining most faithful to Christianity had preached and actuated as the only possible way of purifying the Church of its total immersion in earthly power.

To confirm Angela's desire to return to the primitive virtues of the Church, we need only note her reference to the institution of "consecrated virgins," who remain in the family to bear witness to their faithfulness to Christianity, in an era when monasticism has become merely an institution for social placement, and when the cloistered life is the only way to regulate the matrimonial exchange. But even the devotion to St. Ursula, which dictated the choice of her congregation's name, is proof of Angela's will to return to primitive times: that is, to martyrdom. Ursula is actually a legendary figure whose story, in many ways similar to those sung in the *chansons de gestes* and in the legends of the martyrs, had won the hearts of medieval Europe. Obviously, when women were involved, the accent was placed on martyrdom in the defense of virginity. Briefly, the legend tells of Ursula, a Britannic princess, who had been promised in marriage by her father to a pagan prince, even though she had consecrated her virginity to God. During the long journey undertaken to reach her fiancé, accompanied by 11,000 other virgins, she was killed by the Huns together with her companions. This story, the fruit of centuries of fantasy regarding the martyrdom of virgins, is narrated in the *Legenda Aurea*; Angela had probably been struck by it even as a child. What counts here is the exaltation, not only of virginity, but of martyrdom.

The theme of martyrdom had regained vigor in the era and environment in which Angela lived. It was discussed in a positive or negative light in various proposals linked to the theological rethinking of the sacraments on which much of the church's power was based. The value of "blood," for example, and the need for its effusion for salvation, had long been at the center of the debate. The blood shed by Christ, the object of the greatest "devotion," was identified with the blood of the faithful, who could "baptize" themselves even by penitential flagellation alone: that is, save themselves with their own hands, without the baptismal mediation of the Church.[126] Another highly argued question emerged, as it had during the early centuries of Christianity, because of the Inquisition's persecution of all "heresies": Now that there was a real danger once again of having to die for one's religious convictions, people asked whether it was better to face death, a martyr's death, for the love of Christ, or conceal the theological elements in contradiction with the teachings of the Church in order to escape its condemnation? This was the famous debate over the legitimacy of "Nicodemism" (from the name of Nicodemus in the Gospels) which, in any event, saved the life of many followers of Luther and Calvin.

Angela also lived through the trauma of the sack of Rome in 1527, which many considered God's punishment for the corruption of that city, supposed to be the center of Christianity.

A friend and spiritual advisor of Francesco Sforza II, Duke of Milan, she was therefore perfectly aware of the politico-ecclesiastic condition of her time. The totally new characteristics of her foundation bear witness to this awareness: The condemnation of female monasticism that separated women from concrete action in society through the cloistered life, and no longer served to render them true "brides of God," as they had been in the beginning. A condemnation of any ritualistic, exterior form of consecration of women to God, both because they remained in society and renounced any "sign" of separation from other women, even that of a particular habit. This was an extremely courageous renunciation, since the habit was not only a very potent way of perceiving their belonging to God and the Church, but above all, a defense from the dangers of moving about in society without male support.

Male Logic Must Not Be Contradicted: Only the Dead Woman Is God's Bride

Immediately after Angela's death, the absence of the cloistered life and the religious habit were most harshly contested by the Church that was incapable of perceiving women unless they were married or nuns. Both matters ended up in compromises that weighed heavily on the lives of the Ursulines for centuries, and gave rise to countless versions of Angela's foundation. Absurd as it may seem, the first step toward the abdication of religious women's freedom of action in the world, as the persons solely responsible for their consecration to God, was taken after the authorities required that a particular rope belt be worn over the secular habit, for many centuries a sign of recognition for penitents and monks. It proved everywhere that its bearers were consecrated women. The battle over the cloistered life was harsher yet, but it, too, was settled by a compromise. The Ursulines now gathered in a convent, giving up living a life common to lay people in the world, but they managed to preserve their teaching activity inside the convent itself, thus giving rise to what much later became "secular" institutes with an immense development in all areas: nursing assistance in hospitals; schools no longer connected to convents and dedicated to women's education both for the rich and the poor, vocational training for women, sewing, embroidery, weaving; and finally, the most daring work: the missions.

This commitment to social action was sustained by those in the Catholic world who, like Cardinal Carlo Borromeo in Milan, realized that the doctrinal tempest that Luther and his followers provoked could be effectively opposed only by the practical action of "charity," and not by theological lucubration. The activity of women thus became decisive once again, as it had been in the beginning, and as it continued to be thereafter, with the spread and penetration of Christianity.

Not "word," but "presence"; not the imposition of ideas, but the practical demonstration of a perennially valid message: assistance of life on earth, the care of the body in all its needs from birth until death. In short, the Christianity of women now reached its culmination in the Catholic version. For in the Church of Rome, the theological dispute over the Reformation was resolved by the practice of "charity." Even "men" in a state of desperation over the impossibility of responding to the all-too-just accusations of the Protestants, turned to concrete actions that until then had always been the precinct of women. The faithful friends of Philip Neri put aside their study of history and music, and began going to hospitals to care for the sick, bringing them food, besides the sacraments. Camillus de Lellis was later inspired to found the congregation of the Ministers of the Sick which, at least in the beginning, was meant to deal with the physical needs of patients, as well as spiritual ones. What could the masses care, wondered Philip Neri, along with many spirits anguished by the condition of the Church, what could the masses understand about lucubration over the Trinity or the Holy Spirit? When one realized in the past, as one realizes now, the ignorance of the people about the so-called Christian doctrine, the fact becomes all too clear: Catholicism has managed to survive so many historical vicissitudes because women have translated it into the essential gestures of help for the needs of life, which is why it still cannot be eliminated in the poorest countries. The theological construction remains alien to the majority of people who, indeed, put up a resistance against theoretical indoctrination. For example, in spite of the teaching of Catholicism in school, which until recently was compulsory, Italians know almost nothing about Christianity, because of a kind of instinctive defense against a religion they want to believe in, but which would be irreparably destroyed by an abnormal "knowledge" of theology. This constitutes a fundamental difference with respect to the reformed churches that, having abolished the orders and congregations of consecrated life, lack female armies ready to help everyone.

Thus, for such a profound believer as Carlo Borromeo to try to defend monastic life from the attacks of Lutheran theologians was a lost battle, since no one could ignore the disastrous condition of the monasteries. The male ones had become places of libertine laxity, enrichment, and absolute privilege; the women's convents had become terrifying prisons in the service of society. Together, they furnished undeniable proof in support of Luther's accusation. The sack of Rome, with its irrepressible hate toward any Church representatives, saw the killing not only of nobles, clergymen, and monks, but also the rape of nuns in the convents. In the eyes of all, it appeared as a terrible but just punishment by God against the Church, a Church which, only a few years before, had been condemned by Girolamo Savonarola as a "prostitute." It was no coincidence that all those who most strongly believed in a need to return to the purity of the Gospel were convinced that the awesome Florentine friar was a saint, and wanted to initiate a process for his beatification.

Therefore, the key idea became to "save the Gospel through works," much more than through theological subtleties, whose sterility was now clearly perceived after centuries of Thomistic rumination. The usefulness of works was a concrete response, above all, to Protestant theories concerning salvation through faith alone. The Brescian "virgins" had hit the target in the eyes of Carlo Borromeo, who was involved in the nearly impossible work of reforming his diocese, and it was he who called upon Angela Merici to found a company of St. Ursula in Milan. He encouraged her to work in all fields, no longer following only the common sense that had guided her until then, but with a strategy now consciously theorized from above. The work of educating girls through the teaching of reading and catechism in parochial schools became an institutional task, but all other activities in the service of the poor, begun by Angela, were encouraged and helped as well: assistance of the sick in hospitals, the care of orphans in special institutes, the foundation of "conservatories" for young women "in danger," that is, without any means of subsistence in a society that offered no possibility to work, thus driving them to prostitution. The activity of women who were taken by the work of Angela appeared so important in the eyes of those who hoped to save the Church that Cardinal Borromeo, through his immense authority, persuaded all the bishops to found companies of St. Ursula in their territories. Thus began the long parade of various congregations dedicated to St. Ursula. Their fame as "educators" of girls has never left the Ursulines, despite the obstacles and changes in history. With the exception of religious women, no one has ever believed that any form of teaching was necessary for women *as well* until our era.

Of course, the work of religious women is of a strictly practical nature, even in teaching. As in all other fields to which they have dedicated themselves, women have never assumed theoretical or "political" leadership. The reasons are quite clear. They have not assumed leadership because society has never assigned it to them; and this obviously seems "right" to everyone. More importantly, they themselves lack knowledge of what is not practical or concrete. Consequently, education in the convents and schools of the Ursulines has often remained at an almost elementary level, one suitable to tasks socially attributed to women. Moreover, as time passed, the Ursulines have always conformed to what the authorities expected and imposed on them, educating girls exclusively in religious morals pertaining to all the aspects of life that awaited them; total obedience toward the husband, care of the house, and sacrifice for the children. If there was any exception to this program, it was reserved for the daughters of aristocrats. For them, special classes were organized, with courses in calligraphy, music, and dancing, painting, etiquette … indispensable for their future participation in high society. "Reflection" was excluded in any case, both for the rich and the poor. Furthermore, the pupils led a monastic life, identical to that of their teachers. They remained in a strictly cloistered regime, never leaving the convent, not even for the holidays. It was not until the second half of the 18th century that they were permitted to leave the convent during the summer period, but they were required to remain with their parents.

Therefore, even in the variety of forms assumed by single institutes, and making allowance for differences owing to cultural and social factors in the various countries where they developed (Italy, France, Spain, Romania, Hungary…), the Ursulines never questioned the structure of society, which assigns women the sole task of being good housewives in noble, rich families, or else clever workers and servants when they are poor. In any event, rich and poor were all kept safe from any curiosity or danger in the area of sex. How can women who are consecrated virgins and brides of God understand the problems of marital life, sexual life, motherhood, relations with men, or that personal identity and autonomy that women in the "world" need even more than religious women? No one has asked that question, not even the religious women themselves. At any rate, the fundamental historical fact that remains is the immense effort performed by religious women to become useful to society, even when forced by the Church to be prisoners of the cloistered life, physically, psychologically, and intellectually.

The state-oriented policies of Emperor Joseph II and, shortly afterwards, the French Revolution, established a kind of dividing line in the activities of the Ursulines, both because of the forced closure of many of their institutes, and because of the different direction taken by women's education in the modern era. The suppression of numerous Ursuline houses began in Italy a few years before the French Revolution. Lombardy, annexed to Austria in 1713, and Tuscany, governed by Peter Leopold I, were dominated by sociopolitical policies tending to integrate the Church into the state, which thus submitted all activities of religious institutions to its control. In 1785 a decree of the Grand Duke of Tuscany proclaimed the passage of the "conservatories" to the state, and the conservatories constituted the majority of the Ursuline colleges. In 1789, in Milan, we find the first lists of convents to be suppressed: 15 of them are of the Ursulines. In the same year, with the Revolution, all the Ursuline houses in France, around 350, are sacked and confiscated. Pursued, imprisoned, dispersed, the religious even faced the guillotine at Valenciennes and Orange.[127]

Moreover, the destiny of all religious women, under pressure both from society and the Church, emerges with great clarity in the story of the Ursulines. As time went by, the urge to occupy themselves with the problems of the world by sacrificing themselves, annulling themselves as persons, and renouncing any explicit "judgment" of the very evil they were striving to alleviate, became an *institution* that the all-male hierarchies of the Church defined as such, and which they took over and put under their own jurisdiction. By acting this way, the men of the Church slowly eliminated all those aspects they considered subversive in their image of women. Whatever they do, women must remain prisoners of that image.

The transformations that the work of Angela Merici was subject to by these continual adjustments, both theoretical and concrete, are in many ways exemplary. The main problem tormenting the ecclesiastic hierarchies remained their incapacity to accept the idea of women's life in society, free from family ties and so from male authority. "Private" virginity, that is, non-institutionalized virginity, had virtually no precedent in church history. True, Angela had dreamed of a return to the early Church, in which there was a form of consecration for virgins who continued to live in the family. Even then, however, the Church imposed its seal through public consecration, the shaving of the head and the obligation of the "veil." But above all, we must consider that the very existence of "brides of God" in a society not yet officially Christian was revolutionary in itself, so that their particular status was easily recognizable, even though they did not live in communities separate from the family. Now, instead, after approximately 1,500 years, virginity for non-married women was such an obvious obligation that virginity "offered up to God" had to be marked by "separation" from the group, and by submission to a "rule" officially approved by the Church. This gave rise to a multitude of branches springing from Angela Merici's idea, which invaded not only France and Italy, but practically every region reached by the Church. All these branches can all bear the name of "Ursulines," a synonym for teaching nuns. In the early years of the 17th century, the Ursulines in France were forced to shut themselves up in cloistered seclusion. Those who opposed came into conflict with the authority of the bishops who were endowed with an infallible weapon for reducing women to obedience: interdiction from the sacraments. Moreover, the priests, who guide the religious life of women, now came to practice with increasing frequency the old, never-abandoned game of constructing a ladder with grades of "perfection." Concerning women, the step-by-step division no longer regards only virgins, married women, and widows, but all types of "virgins." The top level of virginity pertains to women who consecrate themselves to God, remaining in perpetual cloistered seclusion. Those remaining outside the convent must be content with the second level. If the Ursulines went outside the convent, theirs would thus be a second-class virginity. Of course, none of this lucubration has anything to do with religious males, who—though afflicted with dramatic problems regarding chastity—are nonetheless not identified socially (and so "objectively") on this basis. On the contrary, the problem of female virginity is of a "public" nature: concrete, objective, externally visible.

During the second part of the 17th century, however, the expansion of the Ursuline orders and their work as teachers for girls had a remarkable development. In Paris, the convent in the quarter of St. Jacques became the most famous boarding school for the aristocracy and upper class, and many other Ursuline schools rose to fame as well. The Low Countries and the German provinces of the Empire had a thick network of Ursuline convents that extended as far as Eastern Europe. After 1639, the year in which the Ursuline Marie Guyart became the first woman to cross the ocean as a missionary to the New World, the missionary work of the order flourished: not only in Canada, where Ursuline convents multiplied so fast as to form the Ursulines of the Canadian Union; but in Brazil as well. The religious women never doubted the legitimacy of carrying Christianity to such different peoples; similarly, they never doubted anything relative to the theories elaborated by male theologians and hierarchies. Their very real sacrifice is in their "works" as the supporting column of Christian expansion; something never acknowledged by lay or religious historians, nonetheless officially it serves to convince everyone how useful the action of the Church is. In any event, how could that fact be denied, in the presence of such a highly organized army? Even today, in the period of decline that has affected all institutes, the Ursulines number around 16,000 throughout the world.

11
Religious Women Invent the "Welfare State"

Reading and Writing, Each Person's Right:
Little Schools for the Poor

Angela Merici's work gave rise to countless foundations of Ursulines, all dedicated to teaching, After the French Revolution, they became hospital foundations as well, since the only Catholic foundations allowed by the French state were institutes for the sick. But teaching and nursing care have nearly always been the activity of religious women. This aspect of their work points to two factors: their absolute lack of preparation in participating in society in any "technical" or professional form; and the basic motivation inspiring them, that of charity and dedication to the poor, both in teaching and healing. This condition logically arose from their having been perennially excluded from membership in the "working" world as women. They felt their love for God authorized them to do anything, independently of the need for professional competence, since they were guided by the "Hand of Providence," by the "Wisdom of the Holy Spirit," by the "protection of Our Lady."

In spite of this situation, only the work of consecrated women was dedicated to looking after the needs of the poor, the marginalized from society, until the 1900s when the secular state decided to take this task upon itself. And yet, at least in countries with a Catholic majority, the state has not succeeded in totally substituting its own ministrations for the works of religious women, either in teaching or in caring for children and the ill.

Hampered by the Church's diffidence toward any "exit" by women from their cloistered seclusion, the great majority of religious women have had to concentrate their works inside the convent. This has led to considerable psychological, social and cultural dysfunction, but it has also enabled nuns to help a great number of people. The hospitals they opened in convents became reference points for all needs; convents were transformed so as to educate young girls and women inside their walls, without obliging the religious to go out and seek them as Angela Merici had done in the beginning. The Ursuline schools slowly substituted for the old Benedictine convents where the daughters of rich and noble families had been enclosed, but with one important difference: Poor girls were taken in to be educated as well, even though they were kept separate from the nobles.

However, the shortcomings caused by the teachers' separation from society reached such a point that in these schools the young girls destined to marry actually failed to benefit from any true preparation for life. For they were excluded from any discussion concerning sexuality and procreation, as the religious themselves were. Thus, at the wedding ceremony, marriage represented the way out of one prison into another, final prison. Total silence enveloped what these young women would meet as their ineluctable destiny. In any event, it was society itself that considered the girls' exclusion from external reality indispensable, especially regarding sexuality and procreation, so that there was a continual feedback between the figure of the cloistered nun and that of the "respectable" woman. Eventually, the religious women were wiser, more mature and expert about life than the wives and mothers, even those of high lineage.

The paradoxes accompanying the collectivity's expectations of women virtually up to our time can find no satisfactory explanation outside the absolute incapacity and refusal of men to create a true relationship with them.

Early Communication Networks for the Protection of Women and Children: Boarding Schools, Asylums, Convent Schools for Abandoned Children and Girls in Danger

Despite the serious limitations hampering their work, the presence of religious women in the life of society, through the myriad of initiatives they undertook, was undoubtedly decisive in meeting the needs of the most unfortunate: women, children, and all those marginalized from civil life. Tramps, beggars, the plague-stricken, the victims of cholera or syphilis, the blind, the mute, the elderly, even criminals wanted by the authorities found silent, comforting help from the religious women in hospitals and shelter from the harsh, often mortal condemnation by the law authorities of the time. Suffice it to recall that the death sentence was often expected for petty thieves who were recidivists and, during certain periods of the 17th and 18th centuries, even for those who begged for alms.[128] At this point, we cannot stop to discuss the countless institutions founded by religious women between the 17th and 19th centuries. But the brief outline that follows can at least serve to indicate main contributions of women to the survival of society in those areas crying for assistance.

Until today, historians have always almost exclusively highlighted and magnified the names of men committed to works of charity, forgetting, or at least putting aside, the actual historical fact that hardly any of them really worked in the field of social care. Some who are famous for their charitable works—such as St. Philip Neri or St. Camillus de Lellis—gave assistance in hospitals out of a need to reach personal "perfection," but took no interest in diseases or the sick.[129] They carried out their roles as priests, ready to preach, confess and prepare the ill for a good death, but it was the religious women who were the real nurses wherever they were, in Europe or in missionary lands. (In Italy, for example, they were not substituted for by lay nurses in hospitals until only a few years ago, while the religious men in the order performed only the priestly role as "chaplains.") Religious men have entrusted women with social care and called them to various tasks of assistance through the foundation of particular institutes. These, in any case, were grandiosely entitled according to the ideas and personal devotions of men: to the "Madonna," the "Sacred Heart," the "Service of the Poor" and so on.

In this perspective, it would clarify things considerably if we made a list of the institutional names that, when given the opportunity, religious women have adopted for their orders. In reflecting the ingenuous but moving desire of women for psychological and social identification, these names also speak of their passions, sentiments, and aims; they are names that, on the contrary, the male religious hardly ever use. If any exception stands out, it is one that reflects the romantic love the religious men have for the Madonna (for example, the "Servants of Mary"), but this is nothing in comparison to the nearly infinite parade of "Maidservants," "Servants," "Oblates," "Repairers," and "Daughters."

While we mention only a few names out of the many from the silence surrounding their work, we must stop to consider one woman who was surprising in her determination to give help to all of society's needs. The story of Louise de Marillac begins like that of many women of her time.

Born in Paris in 1591 of an eminent aristocratic family, she was turned over according to custom at a very early age to the royal convent of the Dominicans in Poissy, where she received the type of education suitable for noble women: a bit of literary knowledge, some embroidery, sewing, music, etiquette, and a great deal of religion. She was given in marriage to Antoine Le Gras, secretary to the Regent Maria de' Medici, and she gave birth to a son, but motherhood did not attenuate the spiritual and religious longing that had possessed her since childhood. She so wished to leave her family that her confessor came to a strange conclusion: He had her take a vow of perennial widowhood even though her husband was still living.

She met the two most famous ecclesiastics in Paris, Francis de Sales and Vincent de Paul, whom she found fascinating and who later became her spiritual advisor. After her husband (finally) died in 1625, Louise became more and more dedicated to caring for the poor and sick. Little by little, the first orders of Les Filles de la Charité formed. In the awareness—surprising at the time—that ignorance increases misery, they joined together to care for people's physical needs by teaching them to read. Indeed, Louise's greatest concern was to find a way to begin teaching seriously; only by justifying this action by religion could women teach, in the same way as Angela Merici. The outcome was that Louise came up with a special catechism that she used as a basic text for learning to read.

The origins of Louise's institute can be traced back to the companies of the Dames de la Charité that had spread to city parishes from the countryside where they had arisen. However, right from the beginning, the "Charités" of Paris had particular problems since, unlike those in the villages, they were composed mostly of aristocratic ladies. The ladies could not dedicate all their time to works of assistance, and often had their maids substitute them in the most humble tasks. Vincent de Paul thus decided to substitute the noble members with poor country girls who came to Paris expressly for the purpose. At this point, Louise took on the task of directing all the works now under way, and in 1633 she took in girls from the countryside in order for them to live in a family community.

As always, the official organization of the Church prevented consecrated women from performing tasks outside the convent, and, at the same time, excluded them from "consecrating" themselves to new activities as religious women. Thus the idea arose of an intermediate form between the secular and the consecrated; and Vincent de Paul did not fail to repeat with pleasure that a type of life binding the "Servants" to the poor was something truly new in the history of the Church. The "Daughters of Charity" were, in fact, the first order of women in secular dress dedicated to caring for the indigent sick at home, as well as numerous other charitable activities. In Italy, the orders of Angela Merici had existed for some time, but in France the Ursulines had been forced into cloistered seclusion.

The Company of the Servants of the Poor was authorized to call itself a "confraternity"; though the problem of the name was not crucial, since at the time, it was almost interchangeable with those of "Pious Union," "Congregation," "Sodality," and countless others.

The Way Women Work: Let the Poor, the Plague-Stricken, the Old, the Mute, the Newborn, the Criminals, Come to Us

All types of assistance to the poor were included in the scope of Louise's institution. In 1655, she became mother superior for life. Gradually, following on home care for the poor and sick, schools opened for girls in the countryside on the basis of the bond between health assistance and teaching that religious women perceived as indispensable. The founding of hospitals and orphanages followed; indeed, orphanages were extremely necessary given the high mortality rate of mothers during delivery. Assistance also began for abandoned babies; then, little by little, after 1638, for those condemned to life imprisonment, the wounded on battlefields, the mentally ill.... In short, there was no social need that escaped the Daughters of Charity's attentive eyes and wish to help. In France, all this represented the earliest successful and approved experiment in which religious women worked outside the convent, after the failure of the Ursulines and Visitandines, whom the church had forbidden to leave the cloistered life, despite the efforts of Francis de Sales and Jeanne de Chantal. The *Common Rules* affirm a point which until then had been unthinkable, and which even today is hampered by numerous obstacles: "As their convent, the Daughters of Charity will normally have the houses of the sick; their cell will be a rented room; their chapel, the parish church; their cloister, the streets of the cities and hospital wards: their seclusion will be obedience: their grate, the fear of God; their veil, saintly modesty."

These affirmations were revolutionary for their innovativeness: not only on a concrete level, but above all, because they threw all the ideas and forms of female life into a crisis, since none of the liberties listed here was even permitted to laywomen. If—as the rule says—women can go anywhere, no longer protected by the habit because their veil will be modesty and their grate and the fear of God, then women are now totally free, not as religious, but as women, relying only on themselves in order to be protected from all danger. It is with religious women then that we see the start of social liberty, autonomy, and responsibility for one's own person, something other women did not conquer until the 20th century. Furthermore, even though the Daughters of Charity take vows—service to the poor, chastity, poverty, obedience—these are annual (and so it is always possible to free oneself from them); and, above all, they are "private": that is, only God is their witness. We realize from this last point, the renunciation of the solemn publicizing of the consecration and commitment of virgins, how much women were now entrusted to their own responsibility, the "subjectivity" implicit therein, and the self-confidence these women gained compared to secular women who were totally subjugated to the authority and authorization of husbands and fathers. The problem of the habit was solved on the basis of the same principle: The Daughters of Charity would wear the dress usually worn by poor women in Paris neighborhoods. (However, along with all the other characteristics of the Daughters of Charity, the conservatism and attachment to tradition implicit in religious life prevented the habit from adapting to the changes of fashion and time. Thus it ended up being one of the most extravagant ones possible in the eyes of modern society—the famous "big hats." It was simplified only with the Second Vatican Council, which proves, in any case, how indispensable dress is for self-identification.)

One of the innovative characteristics of the Daughters of Charity was their freedom in carrying out the religious duties required by their rule. The motto that has always distinguished them (and which still sound scandalous in the official environments of the various mother superiors, who have come to lose one of the most efficacious instruments for controlling their underlings) is "leave God to God": that is, help given to the poor is always stronger than any other act of love toward God, including liturgical acts and prayers. One drawback remains: the consideration of the "poor" to be assisted as "representatives" of God on the basis of the traditional interpretation of "whatever you do to one of these little ones, you will have done to me." This has always been the limit of a religious charity, more or less consciously caused by that value of "sacrifice" which the Church, as a power structure, has never given up. But caused as well, in women, by their love of Jesus, which drove them, like all enamored women, to make the beloved one either the emotional and inner or social and outer center of their lives.

In any event, though Louise de Marillac is exalted in religious literature for her gifts as a "mystic," which so closely approach the spirit of *devotio moderna*, in reality, she is an extraordinary figure because, in a 17th century impregnated with contemplative theory and exercises, she understood that love for Christ must spur one on to act. This conviction was at the basis of all her works. She realized that women who believe in this love must, above all, strive to become more and more present and active in the world. By the time she died in 1660, many other women had understood where the future lay, through her guidance, and had worked alongside her to achieve it: the need for religious women to be active in society by teaching the basics of knowledge to all women in order to lead them out of the beastly ignorance in which they had been abandoned.

Thus, for instance, Marie Lumague consecrated herself to the education of the poorest, most derelict girls, first in the company of Louise, and then by opening a shelter for girls without any support in 1630. She succeeded in arousing the interest of Queen Anne of Austria, who furnished her with abundant financial help and social encouragement. She was therefore able to found the hospital of the "Providence des Filles de Dieu" and the institute of the Ladies of the Christian Union of Saint-Chaumond that was also dedicated to assisting young women.

This same line of assistance for women, the ill, the poor, the illiterate, the exploited, and oppressed working women, would be later followed by a variety of foundations that were aware of their concrete needs. Such foundations have very often preceded the social work of responsible political structures in all fields. Sophie-Augustine de Soubiran La Louvière and her assistants founded family boarding houses for young women from the country, who were lost and alone in the big city, in search of work in the factories. The first sanatorium in France for young tubercular women was established by a religious woman, Julie Richer, a member of the congregation of Our Lady Help of Christians.

The instruction of deaf mutes was first ideated and implemented by women as well. It found a passionate apostle in Pauline di Rosa, founder of the Ancelle della Carità, who were also dedicated to nursing care in hospitals; a scandalous innovation was that this care also included hospital wards for men. Of course, because of this, the opposition shown by the authorities of the Church was very strong, but, notwithstanding their declared obedience and humility, the religious women stood their ground. Convinced of the need to help the poor, they extended the qualification of "poor," with a disconcertingly modern conception, to anyone who had a social need, and refused to be discouraged by any obstacle as they obstinately pursued their aims. The Ursulines and the Visitandines had instead desisted from the active life (largely because of their exaggerated obedience to Francis de Sales), giving in to the will of the Church that insisted on the return of the women to their prison of seclusion and their total subjugation to its power. But, in reality, this surrender was also due to the fact that they themselves did not want to renounce the statue, sealed by their solemn vows, of "true" brides of God. In other words, they were not totally sure that love for the poor was truly the synthesis, in addition to being the basis, of Jesus' message. Only those who were convinced of this, those who followed their "hearts" more than theological theories, had the courage to cast doubt on the affirmations and will of the Church. Certain bold women did so, but history has almost totally forgotten them.

The congregations of the Daughters of Charity enjoyed an almost incredible growth, explainable only by the fact that the order acted as a substitute in addressing society's most pressing needs that the various states neglected. The French Revolution, which had decided on the abolition of this as of all other religious institutions, suddenly cut off one of the most important social works that had every flowered. In sending 14 Daughters to the guillotine, it committed one of its worst crimes. But the killing of religious women — cloistered ones, but above all those engaged in social work outside the convent — is a constant of all revolutions. This fact alone is enough to prove that it is due to religious women that the Church is present in the eyes of the world. They are thus burdened with all the weight used by the power of the Church to oppress men, though they are absolutely innocent and, if anything, victims themselves.

Renewed in 1800 by Napoleon, who was well aware that the social work performed by the Daughters of Charity was too useful to be eliminated, after five years the company already had 254 houses. The first missionary nuns set out in 1839 for Istanbul, Algiers, Mexico, China, Lebanon, and Madagascar. By 1897, they had spread all over the world. In the United States, their work reached its culmination with Elizabeth Anne Seton who, born in New York (1774), became the first American saint.[130] Even today, though the welfare state has developed nearly everywhere, theirs is the most numerous religious community, numbering some 39,000 members.

Fourteen Daughters of Charity were guillotined during the French Revolution, and the Daughters were the target of violent hate against the Church, which they so visibly symbolized, in China as well, where 10 of them were killed in 1870, and in Spain where, during the Civil War, 10 more were ferociously killed. In any event, it is difficult to know how many Daughters of Charity died in helping the ill and poor the world over. Similarly, it is difficult to know how many other religious women have died alongside the poor, killed by their same diseases. The Daughters of Charity were also the first to care for the wounded on the battlefield more than two centuries before anyone thought that this, too, was a worthy social duty. In 1654, they followed the combatants over the bloody terrain of Montmédy and Sedan; in 1656, they cared for the wounded in Poland during the siege of Warsaw by Charles X Gustav of Sweden; in 1658, during the terrible second Franco-Spanish battle near the Dunes; and after that, in virtually every major war in Europe.[131]

How Old Apprenticeship Contracts Are!

Another name among many that must be mentioned is that of Marie Poussepin. A surprising woman, who was born in the second half of the 17th century at the height of "baroque" mysticism, lacking an education except for the elementary instruction reserved for the girls of her time, and armed only with her intelligence and common sense, she succeeded in understanding some of the most serious problems of French society, at that time in an early state of industrialization. From childhood on she had been accustomed to weaving silk, her father being the owner of a modest mill. She soon participated in the direction of the factory, taking care to teach the young apprentices. The time was particularly difficult, given the pre-industrial condition of France where Colbert had striven to introduce the manufacturing techniques that were in use in England. Marie Poussepin immediately realized how crucial it was to adapt to these new techniques if the factories were to survive. More importantly, she realized the need to train the workers to learn the new methods. Therefore, she gathered all the apprentices into an association, sustaining them in this effort, caring for their interests, and guaranteeing them a salary during their apprenticeship in the new techniques. No one has ever thought to classify such action as a forerunner of labor unions and internship contracts. At any rate, sustained by the experience she had acquired during the years spent running her father's factory, Marie had also perceived the greatest social problems in the village of Douran where she lived, especially regarding schools and hospitals.

Marie Poussepin's work, like that of so many other women, again clearly reflects an awareness of the connection, indeed, the strict interdependence, between schooling and health assistance when dealing with the "poor." For religious women, from the 17th century on, the poor no longer included only derelicts who were incapable of surviving because of misery, abandonment by their families, and the chronic, contagious diseases like syphilis and tuberculosis that were so common, but also the young workers of both sexes in shops and factories. Oppressed by grueling working hours, even as children and adolescents, in the hygienically unsuitable conditions of cold, damp spinning mills, the workers were the ones who were now suffering the most. And once more it was a woman who realized that education was just as necessary as bread and good health, just as Angela Merici had done before her.

Only recently has the United Nations realized — during the Cairo conference of September 1994 — that in order to alleviate misery in the Third World, it is indispensable to teach women to read and write. In Islamic countries, the women are the ones who work the hardest (in the Muslim world, many jobs are notoriously "dishonorable" for men). This fact helps demonstrate how ahead of their time an Angela Merici and a Marie Poussepin were in their intuition, and why the work of religious women has always linked health assistance with scholastic assistance whenever possible. In reality, the "poor" are poor both because they lack sufficient nourishment and therefore health, and because they lack the slightest intellectual cognition. Thus a circle of poverty forms that is very hard to break, and only today has the UN decided to deal with it by teaching reading and writing to working women.

Between 1600 and 1700, religious women multiplied their efforts in instructing the ill, while curing them at the same time. As for Marie Poussepin, an occasion unexpectedly arose to favor her activity in the dramatically unstable condition caused in France by the clash between canonical and civil law, which had almost completely halted social assistance in religious institutes. Louis XIV had personally intervened in an attempt to reorder scholastic and hospital legislation by suppressing small hospices without adequate economic resources and by building well-equipped hospitals and, in 1698, by going so far as to lay the early foundations for compulsory elementary school education for everyone. The need for qualified personnel to carry out these projects rendered Marie Poussepin's work more useful and relevant than ever. With state help, Marie began to set up schools and hospitals in the territory of Chartres, together with other women who, like her, wanted to work outside the cloisters, while being "consecrated" by membership in the Dominican Third Order.

There is a particularly moving passage in the *Règles* that Marie wrote for her institute: "This is a community of Daughters, joined together to consecrate themselves in particular to the service of God and their neighbors. Their aim is to imitate, through their conduct, *as far as is possible for persons of their sex* [emphasis added], the life that our Lord lived on earth...." The limitation, the inferiority that society has imposed on the female sex is so fully assumed and accepted, that this woman, who ideated and achieved countless "social safety nets" for the well-being of workers in an era when no one considered it necessary, even working actively with them in factories, as none of the famous union leaders of our time has ever wanted or known how to do, expresses, with modesty and reservation, the aims and behavior that she established for herself and those who follow.[132]

But the fairest thing to do would be to place the history of the religious women's activity in a "normal" context in the history everyone reads and studies, independently of any hagiographic aims that attenuate the social importance of such work. Otherwise, such knowledge is kept from the vast readership whose interest is not confined to religious topics. Furthermore (and this is another aspect pointing to the relative lack of consideration for religious women's intelligence and almost incredible efforts), hagiographic biographies generally present their activity as a result of the ideas and works of men, directors, confessors, parish priests, and bishops, those who supposedly maneuver the works of women. Which of the women named here, from Angela Merici to Louise de Marillac to Marie Poussepin, could compete for fame with St. Vincent de Paul concerning "works of charity"? And yet, what would Vincent de Paul have done if, on returning home in the evening with some abandoned child he had picked up in the street, he had not found the arms of his faithful women ready to accept the waif forever?

Who Has Ever Told the Story of Nursing?

During the early years of the 19th century, another woman succeeded in convincing Napoleon of the validity of her social initiatives: Maddalena Gabriella of Canossa, a descendent of the famous Mathilda, who in the 11th century was at the center of the struggles between the Empire and the Papacy. Born in Verona in 1774, Maddalena aspired to the religious life from childhood, and so dedicated herself to the protection of poor girls without families who were "in danger." At first, however, Maddalena of Canossa's work also involved assisting hospital patients. She was encouraged in this by her friendship with Countess Carolina Trotti Durini, Director of the Ospedale Grande in Milan. Surely, care of the sick seemed to be the most "obvious" charitable work as well as being the easiest to carry out, since hospitals were centers of assistance instituted by the city or state authorities, and so received public financing. Moreover, such work also appeared "obvious" because it was sustained by a long-standing Christian tradition in this area. In addition, people did not think it required much theoretical or specialized knowledge, since women have always been considered—and have considered themselves—"naturally" capable of caring for the ill, so that religious women were not at all worried about starting this type of activity.

However, deciding to teach implied a psychological and intellectual "leap," even though Angela Merici, and many women who came after her, did take this path, justifying themselves in their own and others' eyes with the idea that they were teaching women Christian doctrine and prayer.

Furthermore, through teaching, women were invading a totally male field, that of reflection, which is always present when one intends to "teach," no matter what the subject is, even manual tasks. Religious women were surprised to discover this fact once they began to open up sewing and embroidery workshops for girls.

In 1808, Maddalena managed to have Napoleon give her the building of an old convent of Augustinian nuns, which had been suppressed by the Revolutionary government. Napoleon was well acquainted with the Canossa family, because during the Italian campaign the French had established their headquarters in the Canossa palace in Verona, and often sojourned there between 1797 and 1805. Even though he was highly sensitive about the need for good public administration, Napoleon did not yet think that the state was obliged to look after the social needs of the poor. Therefore, he turned the building over to Maddalena "with the purpose of placing a charity institute there." Here, Maddalena opened a school that became the nucleus of the future congregation of the Daughters of Charity, the "Canossians." Called to Venice as well to assist the poor, Maddalena founded a new house of "Charity" in the ancient monastery of Santa Lucia, and began to write the rules by which her nuns were to abide. In 1816, she founded a house in Milan; in 1820, one in Bergamo; in 1828, another in Trent, after going to Rome for the approval of her rules from Pope Leo XII. She died in Verona in 1835, leaving as a synthetic expression of her life the declaration that "the religious life is nothing but the Gospel translated into works." This declaration seems almost "masculine" in its synthetic inspiration and conviction, but made by a woman, it passed unobserved by history. A prime figure in the passage from the century of the Revolution to that 19th century that saw an intense reorganization in religious life, especially in the social and missionary activity of nuns, Maddalena of Canossa influenced many men of the Church. She went so far against the current as to think of founding institutes, the "Sons of Charity," for boys. That is how Maddalena succeeded in winning over an intellectual as severe as Antonio Rosmini, whom she had met in Verona in 1820. The gelid Rosmini decided to found an Institute of Charity at Domodossola, having been "struck to the heart" by the words and force of Maddalena, as he himself wrote in his introduction to the biography published by Carlo Bresciani immediately after Maddalena's death.[133]

In the work of Maddalena of Canossa we can clearly observe both the will to act that inspired religious women in the 19th century, and the tendency of the orders to differentiate themselves from one other, by inventing names, accentuating particular "devotions," and linking them to the aims of their activities. The number of female institutes with a particular name and new rules and habits that differed even in their charitable aims is incredibly high compared to the male institutes. Undoubtedly, this phenomenon can be explained by the women's capacity to understand concrete everyday needs and, at the same time, by their desire to "specialize" in given tasks, distinguishing themselves from all others even in name. But this almost incalculable division of names and activities arose, above all, from their need to emerge in some way from a society that had never attributed much importance to women's work, inasmuch as it was always considered an accessory to the real "official" work of men. From this point of view, it is quite meaningful, even strikingly so, to list the orders inspired by Maddalena of Canossa: the Institute of the Sons of Charity of Rosmini; the Daughters of the Heart of Jesus of Anna Brunetti; the Sisters of the Holy Family of Leopoldine Naudet; the Little Sisters of Charity of Maria Addolorata of Teodora Compostrini; the Servants of Mary of Emilia Ottolini; the Canal ai Servi Institute of Anna Maria Marovich; the Maidservants of the Child Jesus of Elena Silvestri; the Daughters of the Sacred Heart of Jesus of Teresa Eustochio Verzeri; the Pious Teachers of Our Lady of the Sorrows of Elisabetta Renzi; the Sisters of the Most Precious Blood of Maria Bucchi; and the Daughters of the Church of Oliva Bonaldo.

Later on, schools were opened in missionary regions as well; the first six religious women left for China in 1860. Little by little, others then departed for Hong Kong, Macao, Singapore, Malaysia, Argentina, Africa, Australia, Brazil, Japan, and the United States. They founded institutes specialized in educating the physically and mentally handicapped, as well as hospitals, leprosariums, and clinics. It was an immense work that cannot help but amaze us, considering that at the beginning of the 20th century these adventurous women numbered only 500 and that, despite the growth that has raised their membership to more than 4,000 today, their number is still tiny compared to their presence and activity in the world.

It would be fitting to trace a true, concrete history of this enormous contribution to the life of the neediest human groups, not simply a story summed up in the biographies of the founders. It is a story of daily effort and relationships with the countless persons who have been helped in every way by women truly acting according to their definition of themselves: "servants of the poor." The story of religious women is instead still at its beginning. The silence regarding them is part of that terrifying silence that has accompanied the female presence until today, both inside and outside the Church.

What the Church (and historians with it) has never chosen to accentuate is the greatness of the women who have thought and worked in the true sense of thinking and working, in the male sense of *acting*. Even regarding women who have left both family and country, going off to work and die in faraway countries in the same poverty and suffering as those they have sought to help, Pope John Paul II puts the accent on "martyrs," that is, those who have been killed "for the faith." Silence is kept concerning those who have spent their lives caring for the needy the world over, often dying their same deaths of typhus and cholera, living in mud huts and famine, in what once drove Daniele Comboni to cry out, when establishing a group of religious women missionaries in Africa: "Here there is a need for flesh to slaughter!"[134]

It has been religious women who have taken care of all those who, in the eyes of society, were only rejects: deaf mutes, the newborn, the blind, orphans, the elderly, prostitutes, slaves of poverty and victims of the African slave trade. They have done so with all the limitations and shortcomings, even of an intellectual nature, that their condition as women and as religious implies, seeing that they were often self-taught and pioneers in what they did. But they did it.

History has always left their work in the shadows, even that written by the men of the Church. This derogatory attitude emerges in the fact that it is much easier to find bibliographic material on women "mystics," "visionaries" and cloistered nuns who were "sacrificial victims," than on the actions of women who, though subjugated to the obedience of male authorities, have tried to affirm their interpretation of the Gospel by working for the poor throughout the world, armed only with a "habit" as testimony of their belonging to Christ. Their presence has "preached" the Gospel more than any potent word, because it indicated true liberty simply through their work of love and care for the "smallest." Jesus' affirmation: "By this you will recognize them," has been women's only faith. Their silence concerning theological theories, their humility in believing that as women they could do nothing except "serve" has enabled the Church to make itself known throughout the world; while those in power in the Church, the confessors and bishops, have done everything possible to hide the work of the religious women. Many men have contributed to this effort at concealment: historians and politicians, believers and non-believers. Since the sector eluded their absolute authority, it was not functional to the obedience required of women. Above all, it contrasted with the sacrificial passivity assigned to the female sex. As further proof of this, we find an undeniable piece of evidence: The Church has declared as "Doctors" Catherine of Siena, Teresa of Avila, and Thérèse of Lisieux, that is, three women "mystics" who endorsed with their very lives as mystics the heavenly messages they bore, the "truth" underlying the power of the church. It was Pope John Paul II who recently declared Thérèse of Lisieux a "Doctor"; although not really a mystic, she was considered one because she had offered herself up as a victim. She was thus functional to the only commandment useful to the powerful: sacrifice, the voluntary death of the woman-victim.

At the same time, not even the religious women who (beginning with Angela Merici) first threw into a crisis the model of the "dead women," the concrete victims of the cloistered tomb, were able to reject or uproot it once they became culturally and intellectually aware of it. This incapacity sprang (and still springs) from that other, vaster, more "global" model assigned to women: marriage, either to a man or to God.

The women-brides of God have become freer; they can come out into the open more than the women-brides of men because, paradoxically, they are more potent, belonging as they do to the most potent man. Marriage and the kinship structure, which obliges religious women to call each other sisters or mothers, liberates and, at the same time, imprisons them. If Paul of Tarsus is the person who most gravely betrayed the thought of Jesus, he did so because he was incapable of imagining a society, and even God, without kinship structures. That is why religious women, who nonetheless have substituted society for such a long time now, having perceived more or less consciously the duties and responsibilities of society itself, have never allowed their own intelligence to exercise itself by studying the causes of the problems they have faced. Rather, they have limited themselves to studying the means for overcoming the consequences of those problems. This has been the most serious limitation in their actions; a limitation that has also prevented them from contributing to scientific knowledge in the fields where they have been active, even in the medical-nursing one, in which for many centuries they were they only people to operate.

Humanity had to await the appearance of a woman who, though fervently Christian, never thought of becoming a bride of God, a laywoman who was intelligent and, as an Englishwoman, relatively extraneous to the model of obedience, silence and humility that had been imposed on the women of central and southern Europe: Florence Nightingale.

Statistics are my Gospel

Through an extraordinary web of historical and social coincidences, that laywoman, Florence Nightingale, assumed many behavioral patterns from the religious women, and adopted them when she organized her nursing schools. But, at the same time, she brought to such schools a professional awareness and a desire for "technical" knowledge in caring for the ill that had been lacking among the religious women. Florence Nightingale is more famous than any female religious founder, because she is a laywoman, and because she used the normal channels of communication in society without having to hide behind silence and humility. First of all, her secularity led the civil world to accept the need for moral correctness which came to her from Christianity, and which was lacking in most of the lay nurses of her time. In fact, the latter came from the lowliest, most degraded environments of society since — except in the case of religious women — any service dedicated to the "body" was considered "low," and even obscene when carried out by women for people outside their own families. Thus, such women were often ignorant and, for various reasons, already outside the circle of "honest" women. Until Florence Nightingale transformed the work of nurses into a profession, they were considered house-servants who just happened to be hired to work in hospitals.

Furthermore, hospitals were places of extreme poverty, and physical and moral disorder. They were gathering places for alcoholics and the mentally handicapped, for the rejects and the alienated, because of illnesses defined as obscene, such as syphilis, and because of illegitimate births by prostitutes with open wounds and sexual infections. Virtually until our century, the hospital was for the desperate, a gathering place for the dregs of society. Yet religious women, those ministers to the sick, could pass safely through the wards, because they were protected by their consecration to God, armed by their vows of chastity and their religious habits, which imposed universal respect for their persons. Their figures were perceived as being outside the norm and extraneous to any earthly or worldly lowliness, but this same respect kept their work from being evaluated on a professional scale. Wherever knowledge was lacking, their dedication was called on in substitution, along with their voluntary sacrifice, without recompense, and their customary orderliness, discipline, obedience, and silence: supremely useful gifts, in an environment of ill people. Moreover, from the physician's point of view, no nurse was better than a sister of charity: She did not steal, she never talked back, and she criticized nothing of what was done. She respected male authority as being representative of God's.

We find so many surprising traits in Florence Nightingale, and although she is seemingly very well known, in reality much of her life is still to be studied and understood. She was born and lived in the century of Romanticism, fatherlands, and Restorations — not only political and religious ones, but, above all, in an intimate closure against any breath of freedom of thought and action for women. Nonetheless, Florence Nightingale was receptive to social aspects that even today seem less attractive to women. In her scientific attitude toward reality, she favored the statistical measurement of any phenomenon, because she was convinced that like all other phenomena, the social ones also possess a predictable, observable, and controllable order. She was thus attracted by the "external" action of the individual: by one's relations with the collectivity and groups, and by human interaction with the rest of nature. She saw illness in its own context: in the union between the human body and all things surrounding it and interacting with it. In short, and this is one of the most striking elements in Nightingale's thought, God is present even in the order of chaos, and therefore this order has laws that can be studied. They exist just as surely as God does.

Where women have almost exclusively seen the psychological aspect — intimacy, sensitivity, the individuality of life — Florence Nightingale instead sees not only the human body immersed in all the other phenomena of nature, but, indeed, the mathematical necessity of this immersion, since the order of natural phenomena is the expression of God's absolute rationality. In Florence, as in all the women we have met in our story, we find a woman inspired by an absolute religious faith. But unlike what women usually think and do when they are deeply religious, entrusting themselves to divine will in the implicit pretense of knowing it through their own, Florence loves the rational research concerning the existence of this will in everything that is manifest in nature, even that particular nature which pertains to the ill. In other words, we discern a scientific attitude toward the world in Florence Nightingale that is typically male.

This cannot help but surprise us in a young woman of the 19th century who was perhaps a bit better educated than others of her time, but in areas separate from the scientific. Hers was a well-to-do family of great landowners, and therefore it was quite distant from the winds of change and freedom: winds that blew in the industrial society of the 19th century, rather than in the one living off the land. Furthermore, Victorian England foresaw no destiny for women apart from marriage and motherhood, so that, although rich and well-educated, Florence surely represented an exception in her will to work in society and her desire to be free from matrimonial prospects that seemed "similar to suicide" to her. Florence Nightingale's life then reflects the long journey made by women in history, but it also differs from it. Religion sustains women in their efforts at liberation because it encourages them to free themselves from what Balzac (in perfect agreement with our severe English girl) defines as a "matrimonial tomb" that buries women; it is religion that convinces them that their fate is "different" inasmuch as it is chosen by God. In fact, Florence wrote in her diary that God had established something unique for her.

After spending a period training as a nurse in a hospital and in an orphanage run by Protestant deaconesses in Dusseldorf, Germany, and then at a hospital in the St. Germain quarter in Paris, Florence returned to London in 1853, and began to work in a sanatorium for women. In reality, however, Florence never performed real nursing work, since she had always been chosen to direct and supervise not only the work of other nurses, but the "system" of assistance in particular: the functioning of equipment, the purity of medicines, and the cleanliness of the surroundings, reflecting on the results obtained and the need of professional training for nurses.

Her chance came in 1854 when British and French troops invaded the Crimea to support the Turkish forces that had been attacked by Russia. Together with the euphoria over the victorious siege against the naval base of Sebastopol, the journalists' reports reached Great Britain with descriptions of the British sick and wounded who had died without receiving any treatment. There was not one single qualified nurse in the British military hospital at Scutari, nor was there any equipment; whereas the French had sent 50 Sisters of Mercy to the Crimea. They belonged to a congregation of Irish origin, from which Nightingale herself had recruited some of her nurses.[135]

Florence obtained permission from the War Minister to set out with a group of 38 nurses for Turkey. Arriving at Scutari on the day of the terrible battle of Inkerman, she was overwhelmed at the catastrophic conditions in which the wounded had to be treated. Filth reigned supreme, beginning with the open-air latrines that ran through the halls and wards where the sick lay on straw mats infested with every imaginable insect. It immediately struck Florence that those who were dying of cholera and typhus greatly outnumbered the ones who died of wounds. In February 1855, the mortality rate at the British military hospital was 42.7%. Despite Florence's great gifts for organization, the military authorities were hostile to her, both because she was female and because she was not bound to the army by any ties of subordination. Moreover, Florence invested the money offered by generous philanthropists and by the *Times*, which had placed great trust in her, for the needs of the hospital; but she also invested her own property, which gave her complete autonomy in deciding what needs had to be provided for financially.

Using this money freehandedly, Florence began by setting up an efficient center of activity: a laundry room where water was boiled in great cauldrons. The hospital was furnished with a variety of useful equipment from this center, from tin bathtubs (which the military doctors would never have dreamed of for their patients), to disinfectants, to soft, clean sheets and pillows, for Florence had seen that the wounded preferred doing without bed linens rather than lie on those provided by the military. Extremely busy during the day with organizational problems, Florence dedicated her night hours to visiting the wards, determined to keep women away from night duty, because of certain improper episodes that had reached her ears. Hence the legend of the guardian angel of the Crimea, based on a *Times* report describing her as she walked alone, a small lamp in hand, through kilometers and kilometers of suffering men.

The poet Henry Wadsworth Longfellow was so deeply struck by this image that he placed it in his fine lines: "Lo! In that house of misery / a Lady with a lamp I see."

Six months after Florence's arrival, the mortality rate at the hospital had fallen from 42.7 percent to 2.2 percent. These figures were eloquent enough in themselves. In any case, once Florence had returned to England, she decided to conquer the last remaining resistance of the political and military authorities by writing down systematically all the data she had gathered, which might prove useful in organizing medical care in the way she desired.

In 1850, statistical research was still in a pioneering stage. The Belgian sociologist Lambert Quètelet was its major advocate, but it was not until 1841 that he managed to set up a central bureau of statistics in his country. At any rate, the enemies of the methods of social statistics were many, especially since the very concept of the "average man," based on probability, seemed to imply a limitation of one's freedom as an individual. It was precisely this aspect, instead, that fascinated the religious spirit of Florence, who admired order in all things. Even in her earlier days at Scutari, she had introduced the practice of recording events taking place in the hospital. The need for such records emerged all the more urgently, since prior to her arrival no one had even known the exact number of the dead. The great quantity of data that she had taken back to England thus became her strong point. Armed with charts which she herself had ideated, she demonstrated that the mortality rate of soldiers in Great Britain during peacetime was almost double that of male civilians of the same age. Florence finally attracted the attention of Queen Victoria, Prince Albert, and the Prime Minister, Lord Palmerston.

On the basis of her information, a task force was commissioned to study health care in the army. This Royal Commission obviously aroused the ire and opposition of the military authorities. Contrary to what had been done by all the religious women committed to social care before her, Nightingale wrote an 800-page book on health organization, publishing it at her own expense in order to distribute it among politicians. It was the famous *Notes on Matters Affecting the Health, Efficiency and Hospital*

Administration of the British Army, and included a section made up of statistics and diagrams. The outcome was that the army surrendered. Codes of behavior were established for military health personnel, and even a military medical school was established. Immediately after this victory, Florence went on to study the health conditions of the British soldiers stationed in India (then a British protectorate), and to introduce there as well the necessary reforms with which she had experimented at length in the Crimea and at home.

Finally, Florence dedicated herself to her old dream: professional training for nurses. With the 50,000 pounds from a public donation in honor of the "Popular Heroine," she founded the Nightingale Training School for Nurses. Here, for the first time, those principles were to be put into practice that she had reflected on during her long years of study and hospital experience: the need for specialized nursing care, the need for technical training for nurses in hospitals specifically organized for that purpose, and finally the need for nursing students to live in a house suitable to their professional formation and moral discipline. Clearly, this last point was inspired by the admiration Florence had always felt for the nursing nuns and their type of life.[136]

One of the repercussions that Florence Nightingale's work provoked worldwide was the idea of special care for those wounded in war: In 1863, this took shape as the International Red Cross. The humanitarian motive that had led the Maidens of Charity onto the battlefield had taken two centuries to reach secular society, and to become a common value. In any event, with the departure of Florence and her nurses for the Crimea, this motive had appeared to all as a need and duty, just as there was a growing awareness for the need for nurses' training. In the wake of the "Lady with a lamp," Red Cross volunteers were included in armies, and ever since then, nurses have always accompanied and assisted in relieving the immense suffering of wars on endless battlefields from the late 19th century to the present day. However, like the religious women, the members of the Red Cross have never raised their voices against the male delirium.

Today as yesterday, history asks women this question: "Why don't you speak out?"

12

New Martyrs

An Exception: Joan of Arc Saves Man for Earthly Life

Throughout the history of Christian Europe, religious women have always perceived martyrdom as a supreme opportunity for self-achievement. The reason, of which they are quite unaware, is that martyrdom corresponds to their role as "victims." This brings us to the most complex point, and the hardest to explain, in the interchange between individual and culture. The attribution of this "role" by society, in its primary, remote, wholly unconscious state, is transmitted by the group to the single individual through a myriad of messages that are almost impossible to analyze, since they form all the symbolic and concrete strata of life. Yet they are messages that reach individuals in such an obvious form and, at the same time, such a "fitting" one, that they can hardly be perceived with true awareness. The imitative learning of language and its implicit social and cultural meanings suffices to explain the formation of an individual responsibility that conforms to the "unexpressed" symbolic values (that is, those which are never discussed) underlying society. However, if we add to this imitative learning (one therefore exclusively external) the fact that in most cases, women have been excluded from any possibility of "reflection" concerning learning, and kept distant not so much from "knowledge," as from that level of psychological, social, and cultural awareness that only the exercise of knowledge allows, then perhaps we can understand why women have embraced their fate as victims with a will that is seemingly *absolute*, but in reality totally *dominated*. In so doing, they have constituted themselves as *heroes*. This, in fact, is the function of the hero: to impersonate the irremovable ideals codified by the group to the maximum degree, reinforcing them through their absolute achievement and exalting with one's life and death the positive nature of such ideals, which thus cannot and must not change.

Despite their apparent continuity with traditional cultural models, the new martyrs thus deny that function of total rebellion, and subversive victory, over established society that was proper to the martyrs of the early centuries. On the contrary, these women, the modern martyrs (whom we can only mention briefly here), have bowed down completely to the role dictated by the ecclesiastic authorities and secular society, making no critical reconsideration nor the slightest rebellion; indeed, they re-codify the values imposed by the dominant structures through their "heroism."

The most illuminating example in this perspective is that of Joan of Arc, despite all appearances to the contrary. The clearest proof of her adherence to the established order can be seen by the fact that, after killing her as a "heretic," the Church almost immediately rehabilitated her, canonizing her with the "usual" formula of "virgin." What are the most difficult aspects to understand, if we place Joan in the religious, political, cultural, and historical context in which she found herself living "as a woman"? Herein, indeed, lies the uniqueness of her action: a woman, a girl from a small French province of the 15th century, confronts a political and military situation, though the actors of political and military situations have always been exclusively male. Had a man done what Joan did, there would have been no scandal, no surprise and, probably, no accusation of heresy or burning at the stake. Joan turns the ideal woman's traditional task upside down: By saving the man for an otherworldly life, she embraces a task analogous to the one of the male-as-Prince Charming who saves the woman for earthly life. Not only is Joan a woman, she does not even belong to those noble families that guided the destinies of European states throughout the Middle Ages and modern history. In such families, women were informed of events and could influence them, albeit from backstage: those complicated events of religious or political power that so often resulted in major or minor wars. She was neither an empress nor an abbess of a great convent (roles that in certain cases allowed a woman to perform an important role, albeit an informal one).

How can we explain, then, the "patriotic" fervor of a young country girl, and her conviction that she had to take up arms personally in order to "combat" the enemy of the legitimate king? Joan's motivation is similar to that given by so many other religious women. Such women have taken their lives in their hands in order to elude the destiny of obedience and absolute passivity assigned them, by throwing themselves wholeheartedly into works of reform and change, even though they always moved within the framework of official religion. In doing so, they have always claimed: "It is God who has revealed this to me, God who wants this." Here is a psychological mechanism for defense and attack that is common to those who, like women, possess no power, be it personal or group-oriented, except, naturally, an illusion of reality, or a deliberate invention of this supposed will of God. We always find ourselves facing this problem when trying to reconstruct the history of women.

Nor was there any other way out. In a world allowing no creative activity outside that of the relationship with God, women have necessarily "created" only in that area. Hildegard of Bingen preaches to the world, claiming that she draws knowledge from the visions granted her by God; Catherine of Siena takes up the pen in order to exhort the pope to leave the seat of Avignon and return to Rome, she too claiming to be inspired by God; Teresa of Avila and many other women mystics reform the monastic rule, found new institutes, impose new devotions, exhort bishops and popes to perform important politico-religious actions, while hiding behind the will of God who illumines them through extraordinary revelations. Joan too claims that it is God who urges her on, through the "voices" that repeatedly exhort: "*Va, fille Dieu, va!*" As she would painstakingly explain during the trial, they are not only "voices," but also bright flashes of light, visions of winged angels, the faces of St. Catherine and St. Margaret: all hallucinations present in the lives of many other women mystics.

But what she says she must do is wholly anomalous; she must combat personally, instead of exhorting the "right" people to do so. And for a cause whose religious element has only the consistency of a light veil: to drive the English out of the French land and crown the legitimate king, the heir of the French dynasty, and so prevent the passage of the throne to the enemy. It is this, however, although justified by the usual revelation from God, which remains completely unexplainable. Neither Jules Michelet, who wrote an impassioned essay about Joan of Arc in 1853, nor George Bernard Shaw, who, conversely, attempted with his *Saint Joan* to draw Joan back into the tragicomic fate of any religious hero, succeeded in presenting an explanation that was the slightest bit convincing. It is too easy and wrong, at any rate, to transform Joan into a romantic *ante litteram*, a 19th-century heroine who just happened to live in the 15th century, as Michelet thinks; or else, as George Bernard Shaw would have it, to see her as the first Protestant, a kind of skirt-wearing Luther. Joan is a woman, as values go, and thus cannot identify herself either as a patriot or as a theologian. True, she has courage, intelligence, good sense, and self-confidence, but the framework in which she moves, both personally and in her political vision, is entirely pervaded by the premises of the Catholic Church. To consecrate King Charles VII at Reims at any cost, in order to testify to his divine right to reign, is the most Catholic thing possible at the historical moment in which she found herself living. The "voices" too, like all her other visions, achieve sense and legitimacy only in a context of great devotion and faithfulness to the Church, whereas they would become one of the points of major conflict and negation on the part of Protestants.

Joan is judged as a "heretic" because this was the only way to convict her in an ecclesiastic tribunal and trial. But her judges knew that they *had* to convict her exclusively for political reasons, so that the entire trial was carried out under the false pretence, the only "valid" one, of questioning Joan's orthodoxy. Thus she was accused of being an instrument of the devil; she was accused of presumption in that she considered herself the privileged receiver of revelations and commandments that came directly from God. It is therefore as a "woman" that she was condemned, because all these motivations were socially valid only in relation to the female image codified during her time. Her canonization by Pope Benedict XV in 1920 explicitly recognized the primacy of the individual Christian conscience in relation to ecclesiastic and hierarchical power. Shortly before, in 1918, the new code of canonical law had declared that all punishments not named therein were to be considered abrogated: therefore, torture and capital punishment for *heresy*. (This type of abrogation represents an extreme precaution on the part of the Church, since it never wants to openly revoke its practices.) Four centuries had passed, at any rate, since the trial rehabilitating Joan, and the Church, while declaring her a "saint," still did not have the courage to recognize her as a "martyr," which Joan *is*. She accepted death in order to testify to her faith, a much more difficult testimony than one validated by the faith recognized by the authorities, and by the group that usually surrounds and sustains a martyr, albeit silently. Joan is alone; perhaps she is the loneliest martyr in history because, even though so many others have been condemned for refusing to bend their conscience to that of the established power, they were men, and thus accustomed to considering it their right to think and to judge the world around them. Joan, instead, was a woman, and by definition incapable of thinking or theorizing anything at all.

The actions she performs are thus totally autonomous, indeed, discouraged and derided by everyone, starting with her father (including everything that a father then represented). The certainty with which she opposes the authority of bishops, inquisitors, theologians, and university professors, in affirming that she must obey God rather than them, is so incompatible with the formation of the female consciousness that it leaves us flabbergasted. True, Joan was sustained by "voices," by faith, and by the certainty that faith granted her in believing that the "voices" expressed

God's will concerned her. But a reading of the trial records shows how far the intelligence and freedom inspiring her go beyond this type of faith. Probably, in order to try to understand Joan, we must follow a very different path from the seemingly most obvious, religious one.

Hers is an explosive personality, perhaps influenced by the ideals of chivalry and courtly love that lead her to see the figure of the king as a divine Prince Charming. With ingenuous, crystal-clear romanticism, she sees him as needful of her help, and needful of the unwavering certainty of an earthly Beatrice in order to reach his throne. What an extraordinary inversion of roles in her creative fantasy! But although Joan is a wholly unique figure in the history of women, we also find in her the same old desperate will to live out an absolute love relationship and create a lover for herself who is so potent and so impotent as to need her in order to exist: Joan evokes for us the road of dreams followed by all women. It is men/males who have theorized, sung, dreamed of romantic love, but it is women who experience it, and believe in it so much as to create it, make it "come true," and of course lose themselves in it.

Indeed, men accept and recognize the contradiction between thinking and acting, between reality and the ideal. Women, instead, cannot resign themselves to the fact that there is an immeasurable leap between what is hoped, desired, loved, and dreamed of, and "life." Perhaps this is why they have still not succeeded in producing art, true art, or true philosophy. Above all, they have never succeeded in producing music. Art, philosophy, and music are possible if one accepts the detachment from reality, or rather, accepts the existence of a "non-real," non-livable reality, for nothing is more real and unreal than music. This process is clearly discernible in women "mystics": they set off down the road to madness and hallucination, because they want to experience the transcendent at any cost and achieve what by definition is unachievable: physical union with God.

Even among women, however, Joan remains an inexplicable figure (or only partially so), because she makes two passages from the symbolic to the concrete. First, with the "voice" that tells her: "Go!" and then, with the real "going." Masculinity and femininity combine in Joan; they fuse into a single personality, and that is why no artist could ever have invented or created her. As a man/male, the artist knows how to invent a double personality, maintaining it in its synchronic, parallel duplicity and never unifying it. Here are the Doctor Jekylls, the Dorian Grays, the true "male": one who accepts the contradiction in oneself by creating it and achieving it. Have women been dominated by the absolute that men have invented and imposed on them? If so, to what extent? This is what history must still reveal.

The Great Danger of Christian Infiltration: Women Missionaries' Hands

While the case of Joan of Arc is wholly exceptional, there are many others that, conversely, conform to a kind of "norm" of female heroism. This norm leads us to understand the extent to which women have been subjugated by the habit of obedience, humility, and self-expropriation in never judging anything with their own intelligence, with a minimum of detachment from what Christian theology, impersonated in the authorities, obviously presented as right. This phenomenon has clearly emerged, for example, when women have set out as missionaries. Ready for martyrdom, they embrace the task perennially advocated by the Church, that of carrying the knowledge of the Gospel and love of Christ everywhere in the world, without ever doubting their right or duty to extirpate other religions and customs. In reality, women have never directly clashed with the religions of other peoples, for no other religion or faith has ever organized the care of the sick, children, and the poor as Christianity has done from the very beginning. Jesus exhorted his followers to do so, but his work has been put into action to such an overwhelming extent because it is addressed to women. No other religion, in fact, beginning with Judaism, has ever failed to exhort its faithful to help the weak, but no other religion has ever relied on women. Therefore, charitable care has always stopped at the theoretical enunciation of good sentiments and intentions. The sign indicated by Jesus: "By this you will recognize them," has become the unit of measurement for Christians because, above and beyond all the frightful abuses, deceits, betrayals, violence, and massacres that the male followers of Christ have shown themselves capable of committing, the "works" of women have never stopped "bearing witness" to him. Many Christian women have been killed because theirs was the strongest testimony. But even when the ecclesiastic organization, monastic vows, and the power of the church provoked the strongest rebellion — that is, in revolutionary France — religious women were eventually allowed to continue working in hospitals and aiding those in need. The secular state could not do without them. And so, even while a great number of them were sent innocently to the guillotine, women started out again to help the poor in France, Italy, and all other countries shaken by revolutions. Like the Ursulines, they changed from teachers into nurses, working in silence, so strong was their belief that caring for the sick and bearing witness to Christ were one and the same. And yet that is exactly why the Maidens of Charity and the Ursulines had been condemned to death: They testified to something with their lives that contradicted the accusations made against the Church, the religious orders, and the overwhelming power of the ecclesiastic authorities, their wealth, and the lies they all preached. Women were the true "soldiers" of Christ, and so they had to be eliminated with even greater rage and decision, so that no doubt infiltrated into the revolutionaries' certainty and the irrationality of power.

Seven Franciscan nuns, whose institute, the Missionaries of Mary, had formed a small bridgehead in China in 1886, were killed during the persecution of 1900. As has generally occurred with all "new martyrs," they were considered guilty of representing the danger of Christian penetration better than anyone else. This is more evidence of the religious women's influence in the spread of Christianity; it was their actions that "spoke" louder than any theoretical sermon. The language of concrete, immediate care for the fundamental needs of any human being and group needs no translation to be understood and accepted. It cannot be contradicted or denied by any religious or political premise.

The Franciscan Missionaries of Mary were founded in 1877 by Gélène de Chappotine de Neuville, a woman moved by a profound desire to "act." After living as a religious in the Société de Marie Reparatrice, she left it to dedicate herself fully to missionary work. Her ideal, one that only a woman could have dreamed up, was to combine the contemplative life with the concrete care of the poor, especially the "poorest" poor, those of the female sex, throughout the world. The list of the places where her order has been present is amazing. In dizzying succession, houses opened in Carthage in North Africa, Chefoo in China, Moratuwa in Ceylon, Freiburg in Switzerland, Antwerp in Belgium, Clevedon in England, Quebec in Canada, Lisbon in Portugal, New Antwerp in continental Africa, Beira in Mozambique, Biwasaki in Japan, Eichgraben in Austria, Ambohidratrimo in Madagascar, Worcester in the United States, and Curimon in Chile. Their desire to assist the local populations led women to occupy themselves with everything needed by the poorest and the weakest. Little girls, first of all, since at that time — with the first feminist movement — they became much more aware than the religious women had been in the 17th and 18th centuries of the fact that females were deprived of their most elementary rights. Nursery schools were opened for girls, and training schools in home economics and farming; and then, as with missionary women everywhere: hospitals, clinics, nursing schools, schools for midwives, leper colonies, homes for the aged. It is impossible to give even an approximate idea of the work of the Franciscan Missionaries of Mary. Their number has stabilized at around ten thousand, but their hours of work cannot be counted. Their Christian testimony is frightening for this precise reason. Words, theories, and faiths can all be contradicted and denied by other words, theories, and faiths; but the concrete help that is offered together with the only word, one that missionary women utter in silence, their habit marking them as belonging to Christ, cannot be invalidated in any way. This work is the care they give with their own bodies and their own hands, which touch, wash, medicate, dress, and feed the weakest, most derelict bodies, those of the newborn, the ill, the aged, and the dying. Only death can stop such hands.

Finally, Cloistered Nuns Are Really Killed

At the time of the Revolution, monks and nuns had already left their monasteries in great numbers in France and returned to the secular life, according to the decisions of the Commission des Régulières (1766–68). This commission was the result of the pressures that the Enlightenment and philosophers had exercised over Louis XV concerning the uselessness and harmfulness of monastic vows. Moreover, in the case of women especially, the great majority of their "vocations" had been forced upon them. Thus women who had been imprisoned in the cloistered life returned to liberty after having been shut up in monasteries by their fathers' or male guardians' decisions. Other cases regarded orphans or poor girls who had been taken off the streets by the nuns of various charitable congregations, and who remained in "conservatoires" or shelters for the rest of their lives, becoming nuns in turn, since the ancient régime offered them no prospects for work or marriage.

But some decided to bear witness to their religious faith by refusing to sign the act required by the Republic, thus facing the guillotine with courage and determination. This was the case of the Daughters of Charity who were killed at Dax and Arras; of the 32 religious women of various congregations, but prevalently Ursulines, guillotined at Orange and Valenciennes; of the 16 Carmelite sisters of Compiègne, whose memory still vibrates in the famous *Die Letzte am Schafott* by Gertrud von Le Fort, presented in theatrical form by Georges Bernanos. These were true heroes, in the ancient, perennial, masculine meaning of the term. They were simple soldiers sent to die by the constituted authority, as has always occurred in wars and revolutions, even though everyone knows that it is not soldiers who are responsible for the events against which they must combat. Obedience, the greatest virtue of religious women, is the very same virtue that led the revolutionaries to see the monastic vows as the greatest obstacle for becoming a loyal "citizen" of the Republic. Obedience took these women by the hand and accompanied them to the guillotine, the extreme, deriding culmination of what has always imprisoned women everywhere, the duty to obey. While monasticism had originally presented itself as a form of liberation from obedience to the father, brother, and son, it had nevertheless placed women in total subjugation. Seemingly, it was subjugation to God, the heavenly husband, but in reality it was to the abbess, abbot, confessor, bishop, and pope.

Woman actually carries out her true function only if she becomes a victim, dying for the sake of the group. Woman carries out this function biologically through procreating and maternity; the high mortality rate for women giving birth seemed "natural" to everyone until a century ago, and virtually nothing was done to eliminate the risk. The alternative to this type of "sacrifice" is the symbolic-concrete one. The cloistered nun is a real victim with her vows and seclusion sealing her into the real fullness of a dead life. It is hard to determine to what extent the symbolism of the woman-as-victim has been conscious both in the group and the individual. But in this perspective it is emblematic that many women martyrs of the French Revolution were cloistered nuns, and perceived by themselves, the men of the Revolution, and by the Church as inevitable victims who could only ratify their place and function in the world by voluntarily accepting death. Furthermore, the pope, on whose authority their solemn vows rested, could have ordered the cloistered nuns to sign the Republican Act with the force of imposed obedience, but he did not do so.

The 16 Carmelites guillotined at Compiègne on July 17, 1794 had so clearly and strongly perceived the identity between their consecration-sacrifice as victims and their death sentence that, as the *Acta Sanctorum* relates, they had taken a vow to offer up their lives as soon as the possibility arose of their being condemned to die, and they had renewed this vow daily during their two years of imprisonment preceding the trial, two long years in which they never questioned the reasons behind the events occurring in the society around them, about the actual contents of the oath of liberty and equality that was required of them in order to be saved. If any doubt did emerge, it had to do with whether it was licit to avoid death, and not whether the dictates of the Church were in error. In an attitude of absolute adhesion to the implicit sacrificial values of female monasticism and to the explicit ones of obedience to Pope Pius VI, who had condemned the signing of the constitutional oath as apostasy, the 16 Carmelites of Compiègne went off to the guillotine singing their most meaningful hymns—the *Magnificat, Veni Creator, Salve Regina*—before the amazed, speechless witnesses. The youngest one, Marie Geneviève Meunier, still a novice and so not bound by vows, could have saved herself, but she did not.

The story of the Carmelites of Compiègne became famous, above all, through the *Dialogues des Carmelites* by Georges Bernanos. But this is not surprising when we consider the deep collective significance assumed by the real killing of symbolic victims, such as cloistered nuns. Such killing is the "fortunate" fulfillment, culturally fortunate as well as psychologically, of a destiny that seems empty and sterile, unless it can end in the drama of a non-banal death, that of the suicide-homicide. Nor can we be surprised, in this perspective, that (as he himself revealed) Bernanos, in writing his *Carmelites*, was inspired by the *Story of a Soul* by the little Thérèse of Lisieux. For, in reality, Thérèse is also a victim, a hero, who offered up her life by taking an additional (and actually redundant) vow, the vow of the victim, and who died at a very young age in "holocaust" for many. The sensitivity of the poet perceived the deep structural connection between acceptance of the guillotine and that of tuberculosis, once the cloistered nun has been assigned the role of voluntary victim. Everyone has recognized the presence of beauty in what is sublimely "right" in the martyrdom of the Carmelites, as in Thérèse's, because drama has thus found its true and only conclusion: The group sacrifices the chosen victim, the one who has willfully agreed to be killed.

Indeed, this is what distinguishes homicide from sacrifice: the insistent consent of the victim, the desire to be sacrificed. The need dates back to remote times; it is the need that absolves the group at the very moment it kills. In Isaac we can already see a childlike collaboration in the preparation of the sacrificial rite. For the Romans, even animals were expected to show that they were willing to approach the place where the priest-sacrificer awaited them; they were not to make the assistants guiding them pull them along with ropes, but were to hasten their pace to the killing place.

This desire for suicide has become increasingly clear in our time because the Church is beginning to notice that sacrifice, the killing of a victim, is repugnant to modern sensitivity. The Church is therefore obliged to emphasize its value, by forcefully calling on the group to exalt that ideal once again. Pope John Paul II, whose personality is most strongly structured to the need for a victim, the man who most absolutely identifies himself in the sacrificer-executioner of the Old Testament,[137] almost exclusively canonizes martyrs, both male and female, who have died expressly for the faith. But, above all, he canonizes women who are victims of themselves, who have consecrated themselves as priest-sacrificers. In them, the desire to fulfill their fate of dying for the sake of the group, their suicidal will as "women," is more evident. Wives who sacrifice themselves to husbands in faithfulness to marriage, girls who let themselves be killed in resisting rape, nuns killed by tuberculosis after offering themselves up to the Church, and finally, Pope John Paul II's supreme triumph, a woman, Gianna Beretta Molla, who died in childbirth rather than have an abortion. This is perhaps the most indicative case in the strategy of canonization adopted by this pope. Today, in fact, women can avoid dying in childbirth, at least in the West. And this is why Gianna Beretta Molla has been canonized. Every day in the world, seven hundred women die in childbirth, but from the Christian point of view of martyrdom, they are obviously not of interest. What counts is the victim's suicidal will, and the homicidal one of the group, which does not oppose the suicide; indeed, it rejoices over it. In reality, the biography of Gianna Beretta Molla shows to what extremes the desire to be a victim can drive a person. Gianna, in fact, who died in 1962, was well aware of the risks she was running with another pregnancy at a late age (39 years), having given birth to three children in rapid succession after difficult pregnancies. Furthermore, she was a doctor by profession, so she could evaluate the dangers better than any other woman, dangers not only for herself, but for the child as well, according to the statistics relative to Down syndrome children born to older mothers. Why, then, did she not hesitate? Assuming that as Catholics, neither she nor her husband wanted to adopt any contraceptive precautions, why did she not abstain from sex? Obviously, as always in cases of canonization, her biographies do not confront the problem at all in its human reality, and so do not allow us to respond to the question of Gianna's sacrificial desire.[138]

In any event, as we have seen in the history of religious women, it is impossible to answer this question, for to do so would require an examination of the interchange between the individual and culture, and therefore, of the responsibility of the group that spurs women on to concretize their destiny as victims by themselves. It is this responsibility that the group rejects. The Church rejoices over the death of Gianna, and the pope now points it out to all women as an example to follow, after thousands of years in which an infinite number of women have died in childbirth without a single voice being raised to proclaim their glory as heroes. But no illusion is possible in this sense. The Church has hastened to canonize Gianna only because it has become aware that the time is coming in which women may avoid their destiny as victims.

Illusions of a Feminist Theology: Who Will Take the Place of the Victim?

This is the conclusion, then. No feminist theology is possible, because the sacrificial structure laid down as the foundation of Christianity by St.

Paul, and continually recalled during the two thousand years of Christian history, creates an unsolvable problem for women. A sacrificial religion, first of all, obliges the believer to agree to possess a victim, and immediately afterward, to establish who must be the sacrificer and who the victim. Until today, the victim has been the woman (women). Of course, this also means that the person who has designated the victim, the sacrificer, is also the one who holds power. Clearly, it is according to these brief premises that the structure of a society is delineated; however, in the modern world, people continue to pretend that there is such a thing as a "secular" society that is separate from the religious reality. Protestantism has been an implicit attempt to unhinge the system of power tied to the sacrifice of the victim. But with Luther it was still not clear that the discussion about how real Christ's presence was in the "sacrifice of the Mass" (we tend to forget that the Mass is a "sacrifice") was not merely a dispute among theologians or different interpretations of the Scriptures, but one implying quite a different question instead: Can a society subsist without sacrifice? This and related questions remain unanswered, despite the different versions of Christianity that have emerged throughout the centuries, because, in reality, in the name of theology, one was (and is) discussing the basic roots of group life.

Theoretically, the need for a victim is less strong in Protestantism than in Catholicism, since one continues to hold on to the belief that the true sacrifice, that of the Savior, has been made once and for all, and consequently, the church service is interpreted as a "memorial," a simple memory of Christ's sacrifice. In Catholicism, instead, with the reaffirmed "transubstantiation" of bread and wine into the body and blood of Christ, the sacrifice is real; it is performed again, as on the cross. In reality, both positions avoid the unsolvable problem of whether or not a victim is necessary. In this respect, Catholicism is tragically realistic. Catholic churches are full of crucifixes, martyrs' bodies and bloody scenes, and they declare out loud: "victims, victims, victims."

But the contradictions and ambiguities of Protestantism are perhaps even more significant. First of all, the continuity it claims with the Old Testament, that is, with sacrificial culture par excellence. Early Christianity, and later Catholicism, at least until very recently, instead accentuated the rupture with Judaism, and although the violent dispute over the Jews' failure to acknowledge the advent of the Savior and their killing of the son of God was carried on in theological (and thoroughly anti-Semitic) terms, it was actually dictated by the ineradicable trauma of the absolutely new reality introduced by the Gospel. However, both Churches are in fact based on St. Paul, and not on Jesus, which leads the problem back to its roots:

Paul's declaration that every Christian is and must be *alter Christus*, and that "if there is no shedding of blood, there is no remission" (*Hebrews*, 9:22). Therefore, the victim is necessary.

If that is the way things are, nothing in feminist discussions of theology makes much sense. The request of priesthood for women, for example, finds no justification outside of the superficial one of parity with men, unless we establish first of all what we want to do with a sacrificial religion, and whether or not we want to preserve a group organization based on the system of the power of the sacrificer. To ask for priesthood, in fact, means to become sacrificers. In Protestantism, the priesthood is less "potent" than in Catholicism because of the lack of a real sacrifice of the victim, and that is why it has been easier to create equality for women in the office of pastor in reformed churches. But the problem remains essentially the same. In reality (as abundantly proven in the history of Calvinism, Jansenism, Puritanism, etc.), the reformed confessions are more rigid and coercive than Catholicism because they lack a strong power that can assume "representation" of the group before God; they lack the safety valve of a "sacrificial lamb," that is, a victim delegated to stand for everyone. Therefore, the anxiety of the single believer, who relies only on himself in the presence of divine justice, increases immeasurably.

Women thus find themselves facing an unsolvable problem as they continue to move within the area of codified religions in hopes that great or small adjustments are possible, and to be made in analogy with existing male structures. Is God also a Mother, besides being a Father? Should the masculine grammar of the Scriptures and liturgy be substituted for with a corresponding feminine grammar? Or else, should we invent a "neutral" grammar? Is the Son also a Daughter? Was Jesus sexless? Should we celebrate Mass with Honey instead of wine? All these hypotheses have been advanced, with the enthusiasm and bold certainty typical of feminism, by women theologians, particularly in the United States. But they are clearly illogical, little girls' games. True, stimulated by the cultural and social changes occurring in history, theologians have continually re-elaborated interpretations of the Scriptures with stupefying freehandedness. But today we find ourselves facing a cultural transformation that cannot be compared to any previous transformation, great as it may have been, in Western history. No transformation — not the abolition of slavery, not the invention of the scientific method, technological acceleration, not the establishment of democracy — has brought to light and crushed the underlying roots of culture and the social establishment. This, instead, is what is happening as the stable points of women's place in society are slowly cancelled out. If the earliest organization of human groups in all times and places occurred through matrimonial exchange (and scholars have no doubts about this, be they biologists, anthropologists, archaeologists, ethnologists, or historians); if, as Lévi-Strauss claims, society came to be with the "circulation" of women, then this root, at least in the West (and also on the basis of the first seed sown by Jesus in this direction), is about to be torn out. Women refuse to "circulate." The crisis of the matrimonial exchange is much more than that it appears: It is much more a crisis (as the history we have briefly traced should demonstrate) of the role assigned to "femininity" than the one assigned to women. And it is upon "femininity" that the concept of victim is played out.

We thus come back to the initial problem: Is a victim necessary for the group's survival? And if one is necessary, is there anyone who wants to take the place of the victim now that women are about to abandon it?

Notes

1. Lévi-Strauss, Claude, *Elementary Structures of Kinship*. Boston: Beacon Press, 1969.
2. All Bible quotations in English are from the *New Jerusalem Bible*. New York: Doubleday, 1990.
3. Poirier, Jean, *Ethnologie générale*. Brussels: Gallimard, 1968.
4. Magli, I., *Gesù di Nazaret*. Milan: Rizzoli, 1982.
5. Mansi, G.D., *Sacrorum Conciliorum nova et amplissima collectio*. Florence, 1759, II, c. 1038.
6. Migne, J.-P., *Patrologia Latina*, 77, cc. 1193–1196.
7. Thomas Aquinas, *Summa theologica*, III, q. 80, a. 7, Italian ed., *La Somma Teologica*. Florence: Salani, 1949.
8. Berselli, C., and Gharib, G. (eds.), *Lodi alla Madonna*. Rome: Paoline, 1979.
9. Daniélou, Jean, *The Ministry of Women in the Early Church*. London: Faith Press, 1961; Gribomont, J., "Diaconesse," *Dizionario degli Istituti di Perfezione*, III, cc. 472–473.
10. Clement of Alexandria, *Stromati*, IV, XV, 3–4, in *The Ante-Nicene Fathers*, A.C. Cox et al. (eds.). Grand Rapids, Mich.: Eerdmans, 1977.
11. Rizzelli, G., *Lex Julia de adulteries*. Lecce: Ed. del Grifo, 1997.
12. Jerome, *Contro Gioviniano*, I, 3; *Lettera ad Eustochio*, 22, 15.
13. Migne, J.-P., *Patrologia Graeca*, 47, 513–32.
14. *Conciliorum Oecumenicorum Decreta*. Bologna: Dehoniane, 1991; canon 26.
15. The author is alluding to the fact that in the beginning, the canonesses participated in the liturgy in a particular church, which allowed them to leave the monastery and thus enjoy some small measure of social life.
16. The old study by Schäfer still remains valid: Schäfer, K.H., *Die kanonissenstifter im Deutschen mittelalter*. Stuttgart: Enke, 1907.
17. Molinari, P., and Spinsanti, S., *Nuovo dizionario di spiritualità*. Rome: Paoline, 1985.
18. Magli, I., *Gesù di Nazaret*, op. cit.
19. Lévi-Strauss, Claude, *La vie familiale et sociale des Indiens Nambikwara*. Paris, Plon, 1948.

20. Morris, D., *L'uomo e i suoi gesti*. Milan: Mondadori, 1978.
21. Magli, I., *La sessualità maschile*. Milan: Mondadori, 1989.
22. Moëller, C., *Sagèsse Grecque et paradoxe Chrétien*. Tournai and Paris: Casterman, 1948.
23. Delehaye, H., *Les Passions des Martyres et les genres littéraires*. Brussels: Société des Bollandistes, 1921.
24. Magli, I., *Sulla dignità della Donna*. Parma: Guanda, 1993.
25. Rizzelli, G., *Lex Julia de adulteriis*, op. cit.
26. Edelman, G. M., *Bright Air, Brilliant Fire*. New York: Basic Books, 1992.
27. Thérèse de Lisieux, *Story of a Soul*. Trans. John Clarke. Washington, D.C.: ICS, 1996.
28. Bloch, Marc, *Feudal Society*. Chicago: University of Chicago Press, 1982, 2 vols.
29. Pourrat, P., *La Spiritualité Chrétienne*. Paris: Gabalda, 1931.
30. Lévi-Strauss, Claude, *Le cru et le cuit*. Paris: Plon, 1964.
31. Strathern, M., *Women in Between*. London and New York: Seminar Press, 1972.
32. Palazzoli-Selvini, M., *L'anoressia mentale*. Milan: Feltrinelli, 1963.
33. Cf. Bell, R.M., *Holy Anorexia*. Chicago: University of Chicago Press, 1987.
34. Lévi-Strauss, Claude, *Du miel aux cendres*. Paris: Plon, 1966.
35. De Martino, Ernesto, *Morte e pianto rituale nel mondo antico*. Turin: Boringhieri, 1977.
36. Lunardi, G., and Müller, J.-P., "Reclutamento," in *Dizionario degli Istituti di Perfezione*, VII, c. 1253.
37. Favaro, A., *Galileo Galilei e Suor Maria Celeste*. Florence: Barbera, 1891.
38. Cit. in Desiato, L., *Galileo, mio padre*. Milan: Mondadori, 1983.
39. "Religiosa Historia," XXIX, in Migne, J.-P., *Patrologia Graeca*, LXXXII, cc. 1489–92.
40. Moscati, Sabatino, "Il sacrificio dei fanciulli — Nuove scoperte su un celebre rito cartaginese," in *Rendiconti Pontificia Accademia di Archeologia*, XXXVIII, 1965–66, pp. 61–68.
41. Irblich, E., *Die "Vitae sanctae Wiborade." Ein Heiligen-Leben des 10. Jahrhunderts als Zeitbild*. Friedrichshafen, 1970.
42. AA.VV., "Costume dei monaci e dei religiosi," *Dizionario degli Istituti di Perfezione*, III, cc. 204–49; Augè, M., "L'abito religioso. Studio storico e psico-sociologico dell'abbigliamento religioso," *Il celibato per il Regno*. Milan: Ancora, 1977.
43. Abelard, Peter. *Storia delle mie disgrazie: Lettere d'amore di Abelardo e Eloisa*. Milan: Garzanti, 1974.
44. Malmberg, Denise, *Skammens röda blomma* [*The Red Flower of Shame*], Uppsala: Etnologiska, 1991.
45. Cf. Gougaugh, L., "Chevelure," *Dictionnaire de Spiritualité*, II, 1963, cc. 832–34.
46. Barone-Adesi, G., *Monachesimo ortodosso d'oriente e diritto romano nel tardo antico*. Milan: Giuffrè, 1990.
47. Cf. Le Guern, M., *L'image dans l'oeuvre de Pascal*. Paris: Colin, 1969; Durand, G., *L'imagination symbolique*. Paris: PUF, 1968.
48. See his *Le prediche volgari*. P. Bargellini, ed.; sermon XXX, Milan, 1936.
49. For this historical development, see the still fundamental Grundmann, H., *Movimenti religiosi nel Medioevo*. Bologna: Il Mulino, 1980.

50. For the biopsychic formation of a value, see Edelman, G.M., *Bright Air* ..., op. cit.
51. Magli, I., *La sessualità maschile*, op. cit.
52. Zanette, E., *Suor Arcangela*. Venice: San Giorgio Maggiore, 1960.
53. In addition to *L'inferno monacale*, which was probably written in 1644 and not published for obvious reasons, Arcangela wrote, ironically, *Il Paradiso monacale*, Venice: G. Oddoni, 1643; *La semplicità ingannata*, Leiden: Gio. Sambix, 1654.
54. Brémond, Henri, *Histoire littéraire du sentiment religieux en France*. Paris: Bloud et Gay, 1916.
55. Brémond, H., op. cit.
56. Kroeber, Alfred, *The Nature of Culture*. Chicago: University of Chicago Press, 1952.
57. Magli, I., *Gli Uomini della Penitenza*. Padua: Muzzio, 1995 (1967 1st ed.).
58. Boas, Franz, "The Limitations of the Comparative Method of Anthropology," *Race, Language and Culture*. New York: Macmillan, 1948.
59. *Liber Scivias*, quoted in Fumagalli Beonio Brocchieri, M.T., *In una aria diversa*. Milan: Mondadori, 1992.
60. See Weitlauff, M., "Margherita Ebner ed Enrico di Wordlingen," *Movimento religioso e mistica femminile nel medioevo*. Milan: Paoline, 1993.
61. Teresa of Avila, *Opere*. Rome: Postulazione Generale O.C.D., 1981.
62. Lazzarini, A., "Il miracolo di Bolsena," *Testimonianze e documenti dei secoli XII e XIV.* Rome: Edizioni di Storia e Letteratura, 1952.
63. Folgheraiter, A., *La Meneghina: una donna già chiamata "Beata."* Trent: Grafiche Artigianelli, 1991.
64. Schmitz, Ph., "Visions inédites de S. Elisabeth de Schönau," in *Révue Bénédectine*, 47 (1935), pp. 181–3.
65. Brother Ephraim, *Marta Robin*. Rome: Dehoniane, 1994.
66. Bernardine of Siena, *Prediche volgari*. Siena: 1884.
67. Frugoni, Chiara, *Francesco e l'invenzione delle stimmate*. Turin: Einaudi, 1993.
68. Magli, I., *Gli Uomini della Penitenza*, op. cit.
69. Frugoni, op. cit.
70. See Vauchez, A., "Les stigmates de saint François et leur détracteurs dans les derniers siècles du moyen age," *Mélanges d'archéologie et d'histoire*, LCCC, 1968, pp. 595–625.
71. Frugoni, op. cit.
72. See Delaruelle, E., *L'Eglise au temps du Grand Schisme*. Paris: Bloud-Gay, 1964.
73. Bevignati, G., *Legenda*, Crivelli, E., ed., Siena, 1897.
74. Gertrude of Helfta, *Il messaggio della divina pietà*. Trans. Medici. Florence: Edizioni dei Monaci Benedettini di Praglia, 1923.
75. Angela of Foligno, *Il libro della beata Angela da Foligno*, Milan: Paoline, 1990.
76. Prayer of February 23, 1379, quoted in *Scrittrici mistiche Italiane*. Turin: Marietti, 1988.
77. Catherine of Siena, *Le lettere*, U. Meattini, ed. Turin: Paoline, 1987.
78. *Scrittrici mistiche Italiane*, op. cit.
79. All the citations are from Bridget's *Scelte antologiche da le Rivelazioni*. Trans. R. Cuomo. Rome: Tipografia Poliglotta Vaticana, 1982; based on the Latin

edition of the *Liber celestis* ed. by Bishop Alfonso Pecha de Vadaterra, who had been the Saint's confessor.

80. St. Bridget's *Visioni e Divine Consolazioni* can be read in the Italian translation by Modesto Scarpini, Olivetan priest (the church of Santa Maria Nova that Frances often visited belonged to the Olivetan Order). It was first published in 1923, in a series of texts "for the Faith," edited by Giovanni Papini.

81. Caterina da Genova, *Dialoghi*, in *Opere*, G. de Libero (ed.), Milan: 1963.

82. Teresa of Avila, *Opere*. Rome: Postulazione Generale O.C.D., 1981.

83. Edelman, G.M., *Bright Air* ..., op. cit.

84. Edelman, G.M., *Bright Air*..., op. cit.

85. Rossi, R., *Biografia di una scrittrice*. Rome: Editori Riuniti, 1993.

86. Cf. *Scritti vari* in Teresa of Avila, *Opere*, op. cit., pp. 1478–82.

87. Landini, Carlo A., *Fenomenologia dell'estasi*. Milan: Angeli, 1983.

88. Magli, I., *Gli Uomini della Penitenza*, op. cit.

89. Thérèse of Lisieux, *Story of a Soul*, op. cit.

90. Collin de Plancy, J.A.S., *Dizionario critico delle reliquie*. Rome: Newton Compton, 1982.

91. Thérèse of Lisieux, *Story of a Soul*, op. cit.

92. Magli, I., *La Madonna: Dalla donna alla statua*. Milan: Baldini-Castoldi, 1997.

93. G. Folgarait has counted the epithet "Virgin" addressed to the Madonna 864 times, in Bernardine's Latin sermons alone; cf. *La Vergine bella in S. Bernardino da Siena*. Milan: Ancora, 1939.

94. Grignion de Montfort, Louis-Marie, *Trattato della vera devozione alla S. Vergine*. Rome: Paoline, 1980.

95. *Lettere di Gemma Galgani al Padre Germano*, no. 42, quoted in Zoffoli, E., *La povera Gemma*. Rome: Il Crocifisso, 1957.

96. Cf. Edelman, G.M., *The Remembered Present*. New York: Basic Books, 1989.

97. Edelman, G.M., *The Remembered Present*.

98. Cremisi, T., *Rouen 1431: Il processo di condanna di Giovanna d'Arco*. Parma: Guanda, 1977.

99. Zoffoli, E., *La povera Gemma*, op. cit.

100. Pribram, K.M., *The Languages of the Brain*. Englewood Cliffs, N.J.: Prentice Hall, 1971.

101. Magli, I., *La Femmina dell'uomo*. Bari: Laterza, 1982.

102. Devereux, G., *Essais d'ethnopsychiatrie générale*. Paris: Gallimard, 1973.

103. Brown, P., *The Body and Society*. New York: Columbia University Press, 1988.

104. Brown, Judith C., *Immodest Acts*. New York: Oxford University Press, 1986.

105. Dubois, Jacque, "Oblato," in *Dizionario degli Istituti di Perfezione*, VI vol., cc. 654–676.

106. Vercelloni, V., *Atlante storico dell'idea del giardino europeo*. Milan: Jaca Book, 1990.

107. Martini, G., *Il "vitio nefando" nella Venezia del Seicento*. Rome: Jouvence, 1988.

108. Coleman, P., *Christian Attitudes toward Homosexuality*. London, 1980.

109. St. Bridget, *Le Rivelazioni*, op. cit.

Notes

110. Louise du Néant, *Il Trionfo delle Umiliazioni*, Bergamo, M., ed. Venice: Marsilio, 1990.
111. Lévi-Strauss, *Du miel aux cendres*, op. cit.
112. Pourrat, P. *La Spiritualité Chrétienne*, op cit.
113. Bernardine of Siena, *Prediche volgari*, op. cit.
114. Gauthey, L. *Vie et oeuvres de la Bienheureuse Marguerite Marie Alacoque*, Paris: Gigord, 1915.
115. Mauriac, F,. *S. Margherita da Cortona*, Milan: Mondadori, 1952.
116. Fauchery, P., *La destinée feminine dans le roman européen du dixhuitième siècle*. Paris: Colin, 1972.
117. Laing, R.D., and A. Esterson, *Sanity, Madness and the Family: Families of Schizophrenics*. Turin: Einaudi, 1970.
118. See Papàsogli, B., *Il "fondo" del cuore: Figure dello spazio interiore nel Seicento francese*. Pisa: Goliardica, 1991.
119. Le Brun, J., "Marguerite-Marie Alacoque," *Dictionnaire de Spiritualité*, X, cc. 349–55.
120. Rahner, H., *Ignazio di Loyola e le donne del suo tempo*. Rome: Paoline, 1968.
121. Praz, M., *La Carne, la Morte e il Diavolo nella letteratura romantica*. Florence: Sansoni, 1976.
122. Hamon, A., *Histoire de la dévotion au Sacré Coeur*. Paris: Beauchesne, 1923–1940.
123. Firpo, M., *Riforma protestante ed eresie nell'Italia del Cinquecento*. Bari: Laterza, 1993.
124. Magli, I., *Gli Uomini della Penitenza*, op. cit.
125. Merici, Angela, *Regole, Ricordi, Legati*. Brescia: Queriniana, 1976.
126. Magli, I., *Gli Uomini della Penitenza*, op. cit.
127. Gueudré, M. de Chantal, *Histoire de l'Ordre des Ursulines en France*. Paris: Saint-Paul ed., 1957–60, 2 vols.
128. Lallémand, L., *Histoire de la charité*. Paris: Picard, 3 vols., 1906.
129. de Lellis, Camillo, "Le Regole per ben servire gl'Infermi," in Vanti, M., *S. Giacomo degl'Incurabili di Roma nel Cinquecento*. Rome: Puste, 1938.
130. Dissin, J., *Mrs. Seton, fondatrice delle suore Americane della carità*. Turin, 1963.
131. Celier, L., *Les Filles de la Charité*. Paris, 1928; and Baetman, J., *Les Filles de la Charité*. Evreux, 1936.
132. Jéglot, C., *Les soeurs de la Charité Dominicaines de la Présentation de Tours. Trois Siècles d'histoire*. Paris, 1951.
133. Rosmini, A., "Introduzione," in Bresciani, C., ed., *Elogio della marchesa Maddalena di Canossa*. Verona, 1835.
134. D. Comboni to Mother Bollezzoli, quoted in Mariani, U., *Lucerna Ardens*. Verona: Istituto Missioni Africane, 1946.
135. Concannon, H., *The Irish Sisters of Mercy in the Crimean War*. Dublin: Irish Messenger Office, 1950.
136. Nightingale, F., *Notes on Nursing: What It Is, and What It Is Not*. Philadelphia: Lippincott, 1992.
137. Magli, I., *Sulla dignità della Donna*, op. cit.
138. Pelucchi, G., *Una vita per la vita — Gianna Beretta Molla*. Milan: Paoline, 1989.

Bibliography

AA.VV., *La Ca' Granda – Cinque secoli di storia e d'arte dell'Ospedale Maggiore di Milano*, Milan: Electa, 1981.

____. "Costume dei monaci e dei religiosi," in *Dizionario degli Istituti di Perfezione*, vol. III, cols. 204-249.

Abelard, Peter, *Storia delle mie disgrazie. Lettere d'amore di Abelardo e Eloisa*, trans. Federico Roncoroni, Milan: Garzanti, 1974.

Abrahamsson, Hans, *The Origin of Death*, Uppsala: Almquist and Wiksells, 1951.

Acts of the Christian Martyrs (H. Musurillo, ed.), Oxford: Clarendon Press, 1972.

Adkins, Arthur W. H., *Merit and Responsibility: A Study in Greek Values*, Oxford, 1960.

Angela of Foligno, *Il Libro della beata Angela da Foligno* (S. Andreoli, ed.), Milan: Paoline, 1990.

Anson, John, "Female Monks: The Transvestite Motif in Early Christian Literature," in *Viator*, 5, 1974, pp. 1-32.

Arnheim, Rudolph, *Art and Visual Perception: A Psychology of the Creative Eye*, Berkeley: University of California Press, 1954.

Augè, Matias, "L'abito religioso. Studio storico e psico-sociologico dell'abbigliamento religioso," in *Il celibato per il Regno*, Milan: Ancora, 1977.

Baetman, J., *Les Filles de la Charité*, Evreux, 1936.

Barone-Adesi, Giorgio, *Monachesimo ortodosso d'oriente e diritto romano nel tardo antico*, Milan: Giuffrè, 1990.

Bell, Rudolph M., *Holy Anorexia*, Chicago: University of Chicago Press, 1987.

Bellère du Tronchay (de), Louise, *see* Louise du Néant.

Benedict, Ruth, *Patterns of Culture*, Boston and New York: Houghton Mifflin, 1934.

Bernardine of Siena, *Prediche Volgari* (L. Banchi, ed.), Siena, 1884.

____. *Prediche Volgari* (P. Bargellini, ed.), Milan 1936.

Berselli, Costante, and Gharib, Georges (eds.), *Lodi alla Madonna*, Rome: Paoline, 1979.

Bevignati, Giunta, *Legenda* (Crivelli, ed.), Siena, 1897.

Bihlmeyer, Karl, and Tuechle, Hermann, *Storia della Chiesa*, ed. It., Brescia: Morcelliana, 1956, 3 vols.

Bloch, Marc, *Feudal Society*, Chicago: University of Chicago Press, 1982, 2 vols.

Boas, Franz, "The Limitations of the Comparative Method of Anthropology," in *Race, Language and Culture*, New York: Macmillan, 1948.
Boswell, John, *The Kindness of Strangers: The Abandonment of Children in Western Europe from Late Antiquity to the Renaissance*, New York: Pantheon, 1988.
Bougaud, Emilio, *Histoire de Sainte Chantal*, Paris: Lecoffre, 1861, 2 vols.
_____. *Storia di S. Vincenzo de Paoli*, Turin: Marietti, 1919, 2 vols.
Bréhier, Louis, *Les Origines du Crucifix dans l'art religieux*, Paris, 1904.
Brémond, Henri, *Histoire littéraire du sentiment religieux en France*, Paris: Bloud et Gay, 1916.
Bridget of Sweden, *Le Rivelazioni* (R. Cuomo, ed.), Rome: Tipografia Poliglotta Vaticana, 1982.
_____. *Visioni e divine consolazioni*. Florence: Libreria Editrice, 1923.
Brown, Judith C., *Immodest Acts*, New York: Oxford University Press, 1986.
Brown, Norman O., *Life against Death*, Middletown, Conn.: Wesleyan University, 1959.
Brown, P., *Florence Nightingale: The Tough British Campaigner Who Was the Founder of Modern Nursing*, Exley Publ., 1988.
Brown, Peter, *The Body and Society*, New York: Columbia University Press, 1988.
Cameron, Averil, and Kurt, Amélie (eds.), *Images of Woman in Late Antiquity*, Detroit: Wayne State University Press, 1983.
Cantarella, Eva, *I Supplizi Capitali in Grecia e a Roma*, Milan: Rizzoli, 1996.
Caterina da Genova, *Opere* (G. de Libero, ed.), Milan: 1963.
Catherine of Siena, *Le Lettere* (U. Meattini, ed.), Turin: Paoline, 1987.
Celier, L., *Les Filles de la Charité*, Paris, 1928.
Clement of Alexandria, *Stromati*, IV, XV, 3-4, in *The Ante-Nicene Fathers*, A.C. Cox et al. (eds.), Grand Rapids, Mich.: Eerdmans, 1977.
Coleman, P., *Christian Attitudes toward Homosexuality*, London, 1980.
Collin de Plancy, Jacques-Albin-Simon, *Dizionario critico delle reliquie*, Rome: Newton Compton, 1982.
Concannon, H., *The Irish Sisters of Mercy in the Crimean War*, Dublin: Irish Messenger Office, 1950.
Conciliorum Oecumenicorum Decreta, Bologna: Dehoniane, 1991.
Cremisi, Teresa (ed.), *Rouen 1431: Il processo di condanna di Giovanna d'Arco*, Parma: Guanda, 1977.
Daniélou, Jean, *The Ministry of Women in the Early Church*, London: Faith Press, 1961.
Debongerie, P., "Essai critique sur l'histoire des stigmatisations au Moyen Age," in *Études Carmelitaines*, XX, 1936.
Delaruelle, Étienne, *L'Eglise au temps du Grand Schisme*, Paris: Bloud-Gay, 1964.
Delattre, Pierre, *Les établissements de Jesuites en France depuis quatre siécles*, Enghien: Wettern, 1955.
Delehaye, Hippolyte, *Les Passions des Martyres e les genres littéraires*, Brussels: Société des Bollandistes, 1921.
De Lellis, Camillo, "Le Regole per ben servire gl'Infermi," in M. Vanti, *S. Giacomo degl'Incurabili di Roma nel Cinquecento*, Rome: Puste, 1938.
De Martino, Ernesto, *Morte e pianto rituale nel mondo antico*, Turin: Boringhieri, 1977.
Denzinger, Henrici, *Enchiridion Symbolorum*, Frigurgi Brisg.-Barcinone: Herder, 1955.

Deonna, Woldemar, *Le Symbolisme de l'oeil*, Paris: De Boccard, 1965.
De Sales, François, *Introduzione alla vita devota*, Turin: UTET, 1969.
Desiato, Luca, *Galileo, mio padre*, Milan: Mondadori, 1983.
Devereux, Georges, *Essais d'ethnopsychiatrie générale*, Paris: Gallimard, 1973.
Dienzelbacher, Peter, and Bauer, Dieter R. (eds.), *Movimento religioso femminile nel medioevo*, Milan: Paoline, 1993.
Dieterlen, Germaine, *Essai sur la religion Bambara*, Paris: Presses Universitaire de France, 1951.
Dissin, J., *Mrs. Seton, fondatrice delle suore americane della carità*, Turin, 1963.
Dodds, Eric R., *Pagan and Christian in an Age of Anxiety*, Cambridge: Cambridge University Press, 1965.
Dronke, Peter, *Women Writers of the Middle Ages*, Cambridge: Cambridge University Press, 1983.
Dubois, Jacques, "Oblato," in *Dizionario degli Istituti di Perfezione*, 6, cols. 654-666.
Duby, George, and Duby, A., *Le procès de Jeanne d'Arc*, Paris: Archives Gallimard-Juillard, 1973.
Durand, Gilbert, *L'imagination symbolique*, Paris: Presses Universitaire de France, 1968.
East, E. C., *Géographie historique de l'Europe*, Paris, 1939.
Edelman, Gerald M., *Bright Air, Brilliant Fire*, New York: Basic Books, 1992.
____. *The Remembered Present*, New York: Basic Books, 1989.
Eliade, Mircea, *Myth and Reality*, New York and Evanston: Harper and Row, 1963.
Ephraim, Brother, *Marta, Robin*, Rome: Dehoniane, 1994.
Esterson, Aaron: *see* Laing, Ronald D.
Fauchery, Pierre, *La destinée feminine dans le roman européen du dixhuitième siècle*, Paris: Colin, 1972.
Favaro, Antonio, *Galileo Galilei e Suor Maria Celeste*, Florence: Barbera, 1891.
Firpo, Massimo, *Riforma Protestante ed eresie nell'Italia del cinquecento*, Bari: Laterza, 1993.
Fletcher, Richard, *La conversione dell'Europa*, trans. Stefano di Marino, Milan: Corbaccio, 2000.
Flügel, J. C., *Psychology of Clothes*, London: Hogarth, 1930.
Folgarait, Giulio, *La Vergine bella in S. Bernardino da Siena*, Milan: Ancora, 1939.
Folgheraiter, Alberto, *La Meneghina: una donna già chiamata "Beata,"* Trent: Grafiche Artigianelli, 1991.
Frances of Rome (St.), *Visioni e Divine Consolazioni*, vulgate trans. Modesto Scarpini, Florence: Libreria Editrice Fiorentina, 1923.
Fromm, Erich, *Escape from Freedom*, New York: Holt, Rhinehart and Winston, 1941.
Frugoni, Chiara, *Francesco e l'invenzione delle stimmate*, Turin: Einaudi, 1993.
Fumagalli Beonio Brocchieri, Maria Teresa, *Eloisa e Abelardo*, Milan: Mondadori, 1984.
____. *In una aria diversa*, Milan: Mondadori, 1992.
Gauthey, Léon, *Vie et oeuvres de la Bienheureuse Marguerite Marie Alacoque*, Paris: Gigord, 1915.
Gertrude of Helfta, *Il messaggio della divina pietà*, trans. Medici, Florence: Ed. dei Monaci Benedettini di Praglia, 1923.
Gougaugh, L., "Chevelure," in *Dictionnaire de Spiritualité*, II, 1963, cols. 832-34.

Gribomont, Jean, "Diaconessa," in *Dizionario degli Istituti di Perfezione*, III, cols. 472-473.
Grignion de Montfort, Louis-Marie, *Trattato della vera devozione alla S. Vergine*, Rome: Paoline, 1980.
Grundmann, Herbert, *Movimenti religiosi nel Medioevo*, Bologna: Il Mulino, 1980.
Guerri, Giordano Bruno, *Povera Santa, Povero Assassino*, Milan: Mondadori, 1985.
Halbwacs, Maurice, *Les cadres sociaux de la mémoire*, Paris: Alcan, 1925.
Hamon, Auguste, *Histoire de la dévotion au Sacré Coeur*, Paris: Beauchesne, 1923-1940.
Hancelet-Hustache, J., *Sainte Elisabeth de Hongrie*, Paris, 1947.
Hertz, Robert, *Death and the Right Hand*, New York: Free Press, 1960 (orig. 1909).
Irblich, E., *Die "Vitae sanctae Wiborade." Ein Heiligen-Leben des 10. Jahrhunderts als Zeitbild*, Friedrichshafen, 1970.
Jéglot, C., *Les Soeurs de la Charité Dominicaines de la Présentation de Tours. Trois Siècles d'Histoire*, Paris, 1951.
Jerome, *Adversus Jovinianum*, in *Patrologia Latina*, vol. XXIII, cols. 221-352.
____. *Ad Eustochium*, in *Patrologia Latina*, vol. XXII, cols. 325-327.
Kertzer, David, and Saller, Richard P. (eds.), *The Family in Italy from Antiquity to the Present*, New Haven and London: Yale University Press, 1991.
Kroeber, Alfred L., *The Nature of Culture*, Chicago: University of Chicago Press, 1952.
____, and Kluckhohn, Clyde, *Culture: A Critical Review of Concepts and Definitions*, New York: Vintage Books, 1963.
Kroeber, Alfred L., and Richardson, Jane, "Three Centuries of Women's Dress Fashions: A Quantitative Analysis," in *University of California Anthropological Records*, V (1940), pp. 111-154.
Kurt, Amélie: *see* Cameron, Averil.
Laing, Ronald D., and Esterson, Aaron, *Sanity, Madness and the Family: Families of Schizophrenics*, London: Tavistock Institute, 1964.
Lallémand, Léon, *Histoire de la charité*, Paris, Picard, 1906, 3 vols.
Landini, Carlo Alessandro, *Fenomenologia dell'estasi*, Milan: Angeli, 1983.
Lazzarini, A., "Il miracolo di Bolsena," in *Testimonianze e documenti dei secoli XII–XIV*, Rome, Edizioni di Storia e Letteratura, 1952.
Le Brun, Jacques, "Marguerite-Marie Alacoque," in *Dictionnaire de Spiritualité*, vol. X, cols. 349-55.
Ledóchowska, Teresa, *Angèle Merici et la Compagnie de Sainte Ursule*, Rome and Milan, 1968.
Le Guern, Michel, *L'image dans l'oeuvre de Pascal*, Paris: Colin, 1969.
Léroi-Gouzhan, Andrée, *Il Gesto e la Parola*, Turin: Einaudi, 1977, 2 vols.
Lévi-Strauss, Claude, *Le cru et le cuit*, Paris: Plon, 1964.
____. *Elementary Structures of Kinship*, Boston: Beacon Press, 1969.
____. *Du miel aux cendres*, Paris: Plon, 1957.
____. *La pensée sauvage*, Paris: Plon, 1962.
____. *Les structures élementaires de la parenté*, Paris: Plon, 1969.
____. *La vie familiale et sociale des Indiens Nambikwara*, Paris: Plon, 1948.
Lévy-Bruhl, Lucien, *Le surnaturel et la nature dans la mentalité primitive*, Paris: Presses Universitaire de France, 1963.
Loreaux, Nichole, *Come uccidere tragicamente una donna*, Bari: Laterza, 1988.
Lorenz, Konrad, *Die Rückseite des Spiegels*, Munich: Piper-Co. Verlag, 1973.

Lortz, Joseph, *Storia della Chiesa considerata in prospettiva di storia delle idee*, trans. Lydia Marinconz, Alba: Ed. Paoline, 1972, 2 vols.
Louise du Néant, *Il trionfo delle Umiliazioni* (Mino Bergamo, ed.), Venice: Marsilio, 1990.
Lunardi, Giovanni, and Müller, Jean-Pierre, "Reclutamento," in *Dizionario degli Istituti di Perfezione*, VII, col. 1253.
Magli, Ida, *Cultural Anthropology*, trans. Janet Sethre, Jefferson, N.C., and London: McFarland, 2000.
———. *La femmina dell'uomo*, Bazi: Laterza, 1982.
———. *Gesù di Nazaret*, Milan: Rizzoli, 1982.
———. *La Madonna: Dalla donna alla statua*, Milan, Rizzoli, 1986; new ed. Baldini-Castoldi, 1997.
———. *La sessualità maschile*, Milan: Mondadori, 1989.
———. *Sulla dignità della donna*, Parma: Guanda, 1993.
———. *Teresa di Lisieux*, Milan, Rizzoli, 1984.
———. *Gli Uomini della Penitenza*, Milan: Garzanti, 1978; new ed. Padua: Muzzio, 1995.
Mâle, Émile, *L'art religieux de la fin du Moyen Age en France*, Paris: Colin, 1925.
Malmberg, Denise, *Skammens röda blomma* [*The Red Flower of Shame*], Uppsala: Etnologiska, 1991.
Mansi, Gian Domenico, *Sacrorum Conciliorum nova et amplissima collectio*, Florence, 1759.
Maria Celeste (Galilei), *Lettere al padre* (Giuliana Morandini ed.), Turin: La Rosa, 1983.
Maria Maddalena de' Pazzi, *Lettere scrritte in estasi*, (M. Vaussard ed.), Florence: Libr. Editr. Fiorentina, 1927.
———. *I quaranta giorni*, Palermo: Sellerio, 1996.
Mariani, Umberto, *Lucerna Ardens*, Verona: Istituto Missioni Africane, 1946.
Martini, Gabriele, *Il "vitio nefando" nella Venezia del Seicento*, Rome: Jouvence, 1988.
Mauriac, François, *S. Margherita da Cortona*, Milan: Mondadori, 1952.
Mercier, R., *Pacifique Conquêtes*, Paris, 1949.
Merici, Angela, *Regole, Ricordi, Legati*, Brescia: Queriniana, 1976.
Metz, Réné, *La consécration des vièrges dans l'Église Romaine*, Paris: Presses Universitaires de France, 1954.
Mezard, D., *Doctrine spirituelle de sainte Jeanne-François de Chantal*, Paris: Lethielleux, 1928.
Migne, Jacques Paul, *Patrologia Graeca*, Paris, 1857-66.
———. *Patrologia Latina*, Paris, 1844-64.
Moëller, Charles, *Sagèsse Grecque et paradoxe Chrétien*, Tournai and Paris: Casterman, 1948.
Molinari, Paolo, and Spinsanti, Sandro, *Nuovo Dizionario di Spiritualità*, Rome: Ed. Paoline, 1985.
Morris, D., *L'uomo ei suoi gesti*, Milan, 1978.
Moscati, Sabatino, "Il sacrificio dei fanciulli—Nuove scoperte su un celebre rito cartaginese," in *Rendiconti Pontificia Accademia di Archeologia*, XXXVIII, 1965-66, pp. 61-68.
Müller, Jean Pierre: *see* Lunardi, Giovanni.
New Jerusalem Bible, New York: Doubleday, 1990.
Nietzsche, Friedrich, *L'Anticristo-Maledizione del Cristianesimo*, trans. Ferruccio Masini, Milan: Adelphi, 1982.

Nightingale, Florence, *Notes on Nursing: What It Is, and What It Is Not*, Philadelphia: Lippincott, 1992.
Palazzoli-Selvini, Mara, *L'anoressia mentale*, Milan: Feltrinelli, 1963.
Papàsogli, Benedetta, *Il "fondo" del cuore: Figure dello spazio interiore nel Seicento francese*, Pisa: Goliardica, 1991.
Pelucchi, Giuliana, *Una vita per la vita — Gianna Beretta Molla*, Milan: Ed. Paoline, 1989.
Poirier, Jean, *Ethnologie Générale*, Brussels: Gallimard, 1968.
Pourrat, Paul, *La spiritualité Chrétienne*, Paris: Gabalda, 1931, 4 vols.
Pozzi, Giovanni, and Claudio Leonardi (eds.), *Scrittrici mistiche italiane*, Turin: Marietti, 1988.
Praz, Mario, *La Carne, la Morte e il Diavolo nella letteratura romantica*, Florence: Sansoni Editore, 1976.
Pribram, Karl H., *The Languages of the Brain*, Englewood Cliffs, N.J.: Prentice Hall, 1971.
Rahner, Hugo, *Ignatius von Loyola, Briefwechsel mit Frauen*, Freiburg: Herder, 1956.
Réau, Louis, *Iconographie de l'art Chrétien*, Paris: Press Univ. de France, 1955-59, 6 vols.
Richardson, Jane: *see* Kroeber, Alfred. L.
Ridgely Seymer, Lucy, *A General History of Nursing*, London: Faber and Faber, 1932.
Rizzelli, Giunio, *Lex Julia de adulteriis*, Lecce: Ed. Del Grifo, 1997.
Rocca, Giancarlo, "Figlie della Carità di S. Vincenzo de Paoli," in *Dizionario degli Istituti di Perfezione*, Rome: Ed. Paoline, 1976, vol. III, cols. 1539-1548.
Rosmini, Antonio, "Introduzione" in Bresciani, C., ed., *Elogio della marchesa Maddalena di Canossa*, Verona, 1835.
Rossi, Rosa, *Biografia di una scrittrice*, Rome: Editori Riuniti, 1993.
Russell, Bertrand, *An Inquiry into Meaning and Truth*, London: Allen and Unwin, 1940.
Saller, Richard P.: *see* Kertzer, David.
Schäfer, Karl Heinrich, *Die Kanonissenstifter in Deutschen Mittelalter*, Stuttgart: Enke, 1907.
Shorter, Edward, *A History of Women's Bodies*, New York: Basic Books, 1982.
Sissa, Giulia, *Le corps virginal*, Paris: Vrin, 1987.
Spinsanti, Sandro: *see* Molinari, Paolo.
Stephens, William N., "A Cross-Cultural Study of Menstrual Taboos," in *Genetic Psychology Monographs*, 64 (1961) pp. 3385-416.
Stone, Lawrence, *The Family, Sex and Marriage in England 1500-1800*, London: Weidenfeld and Nicolson, 1977.
Strathern, Marilyn, *Women in Between*, London and New York: Seminar Press, 1972.
Tarabotti, Arcangela, "L'Inferno Monacale," in *Donna e società nel Seicento* (Ginevra Conti Odorisio ed.), Rome: Bulzoni, 1979.
_____. *Il paradiso monacale*, Venice, 1643.
_____. *La semplicita ingannata*, Leiden, 1654.
Teresa of Avila, *Opere*, Rome: Postulazione Generale OCD, 1981.
Thérèse of Lisieux, *Acts du Procès du Beatification*, Rome: Istituto Teologico Theresianum ed., 1973, 2 vols.

_____. *Story of a Soul*, trans. John Clarke, Washington, D.C.: ICS, 1996.
Thomas Aquinas, *Summa Theologica*, Italian ed., *La Somma Teologica*, Florence: Salani, 1949.
Van Gennep, Arnold, *The Rites of Passage*, London: Routledge, 1960.
Vanzan Marchini, Nelli-Elena (ed.), *La Memoria della Salute — Venezia e il suo ospedale dal XVI al XX secolo*, Venice: Arsenale Editrice, 1985.
Vauchez, André, *Les laïcs au Moyen Age*, Paris: Editions du Cerf, 1987.
_____. "Les stigmates de saint François et leur détracteurs dans les derniers siècles du Moyen Age," in *Melanges d'archéologie e d'histoire*, LCCC (1968), pp. 595-625.
Vercelloni, Virgilio, *Atlante storico dell'idea del giardino Europeo*, Milan: Jaca Book, 1990.
Verga, Giovanni, *Storia di una capinera*, Milan: Mondadori, 1980.
von Franz, Marie-Louise, *Passio Perpetuae*, Zurich: Daimon Verlag, 1951.
Watson, Paul F., *The Garden of Love in Tuscan Art of the Early Renaissance*, Philadelphia: Art Alliance Press, 1979.
Weitlauff, Manfred, "Margherita Ebner ed Enrico di Wordlingen," in P. Dinzelbacher and D. R. Bauer (eds.), *Movimento religioso e mistica femminile nel medioevo*, Milan: Ed. Paoline, 1993.
Zahan, Dominique, *Societé d'initiation Bambara*, Paris: La Haye, 1960.
Zanette, Emilio, *Suor Arcangela*, Venice: San Giorgio Maggiore, 1960.
Zoffoli, Enrico, *La povera Gemma*, Rome: Il Crocifisso, 1957.

Index

abbess 2, 34, 48, 68, 78, 79, 80, 81, 82, 108, 117, 125, 188, 191, 194, 195, 258, 265
abbot 2, 34, 53, 70, 78, 88, 90, 125, 126, 185, 265
Abelard, Peter 90, 91, 272, 277
abjection 201, 202, 203, 204, 207, 209; *see also* annihilation
abnormality 140, 162, 175, 182, 213
Abraham 143, 210
Abrahamsson, Hans 277
acculturation 173, 174, 182, 213
Acta 54, 63
Acta Sanctorum 48, 57, 64, 127, 129, 135, 171, 265
acting 9, 11, 19, 45, 83, 92, 101, 126, 157, 168, 189, 234, 249, 261
Acts 15
Acts of the Apostles 22, 163
Acts of the Christian Martyrs 44, 277
Adam 18, 94
Adkins, Arthur W. H. 277
adventure 58, 67, 118, 171, 173, 177, 211
Aeschylus 39
Africa 25, 26, 45, 54, 127, 180, 249, 250, 263
Agatha 62
Agnes 49, 62, 63, 94, 120, 139
Agnes of Bavaria 127
Agnes of Montepulciano 139, 172
Alacoque, Marguerite-Marie 137, 166, 171, 172, 203, 205, 208, 209, 217, 218, 275
Albert 255
Albigensians 106, 118, 121
Aleppo 87
Alexandria 20, 26, 271
Alexis 143
Algiers 244

Alsatia 34
Ambohidratrimo 263
Ambrose of Milan 27, 28, 62, 63
America 3, 45, 91, 95, 187, 244
American school of Anthropology 1
Amnesty International 50
analogy 2, 30, 40, 60, 78, 94, 193, 269
Ancelle della Carità 243
Andalu, convent of 34
Andenne, convent of 34
Andreoli, Sergio 273, 277
Angela of Foligno 138, 166, 170, 273, 277
angels 61, 72, 109, 110, 112, 120, 125, 128, 142, 143, 144, 145, 146, 147, 182, 189, 192, 193, 255, 259
Annales (French school of history) 11
Annales (of C. Baronius) 48
Anne of Austria 243
annihilation 88, 109, 112, 114, 119, 160, 202, 203, 204, 209, 211, 212, 216; self- 81, 201, 202, 204, 209
anorexia 74, 75, 208, 272; mental 74
Anson, John 277
anthropologists 10, 16, 77, 79, 160, 180, 270
Anthropology 1, 8, 10, 12, 67, 162
Antigone 57
anti-pope 143
antiquity 25, 29, 49, 62, 72, 73, 99, 128
Antonello of Monte Savello 143
Antwerp 263
Apennines 187
Apostolic Constitutions 22
Apostolic Letters 22
Appian Way 57
Arcetri 85, 86
archaeologists 270
Argentina 249

285

Arianism 163
arms 14, 59, 63, 116, 127, 137, 139, 140, 146, 168, 210, 247, 258; *see also* body
Arnaldo 138, 139
Arnheim, Rudolph 277
Arras 264
art 66, 67, 116, 122, 152, 216, 261, 277; history 66
artists 62, 65, 99, 122, 165
Ascent of Mount Carmel 160-1
Asia 127, 180
Assisi 92, 138, 164, 168
Athanasius 27
Athens 46
attraction, sexual 64, 95, 97, 185
Augè, Matias 272, 277
Augustine (Bishop of Canterbury) 20
Augustine (of Ippona, Saint) 32, 33, 71, 102, 156, 157, 208, 216; rule of 32
Australia 249
authority 19, 32, 34, 40, 42, 50, 63, 68, 71, 73, 79, 82, 106, 116, 117, 125, 126, 153, 154, 155, 158, 175, 178, 190, 201, 204, 209, 232, 234, 235, 242, 250, 252, 260, 264, 265
Avignon 259
avoidance 1, 22; *see also* taboo
Aztecs 43

Bacon, Francis 77
Baetman, J. 275, 277
Balzac, Honoré (de) 253
Banchi, L. 273, 275, 277
baptism 15, 16, 17, 18, 19, 20, 22, 23, 25, 31, 37, 41, 44, 59, 72, 97, 132, 229
Barat, Sophie 220
Bargellini, Piero 272, 277
Barone-Adesi, Giorgio 272, 277
Baronius, Caesar 48
baroque mysticism 123, 139, 245
Basil 23, 30; rule of 32
Basilides 20
battlefields 241, 244, 256; *see also* Maidens of Charity; Red Cross
Bauer, Dieter R. 279, 283
Bavaria 34
Beatrice 261
Beatrix I 129; *see also* body
Beatrix II of Este 129; *see also* body
beauty 11, 92, 94, 99, 100, 122, 139, 147, 151, 154, 189, 211, 221, 266; female 97; of youth 97
The Beauty and the Beast 60
Bavaria 34

Beguines 99, 106, 130, 131
Beira 263
Belgium 130, 255
Bell, Rudolph M. 272, 277
Bellère du Tronchay, Louise (de) *see* Louise du Néant
belt 81, 92, 100, 185, 186, 230; *see also* hair
Benedict, Ruth 277
Benedict of Norcia 32, 72, 89, 89, 91, 144, 156; *see also* Benedectines: rule of
Benedict XV 260
Benedictines 91, 124, 125, 137, 225, 238; monasticism of 70; rule of 32, 33, 89, 90, 137
Beretta Molla, Gianna 267, 275
Bergamo 248
Bergamo, Mino 209, 274
Bernadette (Soubirous) 129, 177
Bernanos, Georges 216, 264, 266
Bernard of Clairvaux 110, 111, 168, 169, 175
Bernardine of Siena 107, 128, 168, 208, 274, 275, 277
Berselli, Costante 271, 277
Bevignati, Giunta 273, 277
Bible 29, 76, 271, 281
Bihlmeyer, Karl 277
biography 23, 47, 49, 57, 58, 60, 121, 122, 125, 126, 128, 131, 133, 136, 137, 171, 182, 189, 201, 203, 227, 247, 248, 249, 267
biological-cultural clock 75
biology 8, 173; epigenetic 8
Bishops 12, 34, 53, 68, 99, 126, 154, 226, 232, 235, 247, 250, 259, 260
Biwasaki 263
Blair, Lucie 213, 214
Blair family 213
Bloch, Marc 272, 277
blood 40, 42, 43, 45, 49, 50, 82, 90, 91, 92, 120, 135, 137, 139, 171, 178, 181, 203, 208, 229, 268, 269; baptism by 44, 131, 132; bond 40; of Christ 20, 68, 122, 136, 140, 164, 170; continuity by 38; Jesus denied importance of 39; liqueur- (*see also* menstruation; potency) 130; martyrdom 26; women's 51; word and 41
Boas, Franz 121, 273, 278
body 3, 10, 12, 23, 26, 44, 46, 47, 49, 56, 57, 58, 59, 64, 68, 73, 75, 77, 87, 89, 92, 96, 109, 110, 113, 118, 122, 126, 128, 129, 130, 131, 132, 134, 135, 136, 137, 139, 148, 149, 151, 154, 159, 160, 162, 164, 165, 168, 169, 175, 176, 179, 181, 184, 185, 186, 191, 193, 194, 195, 204, 206, 207, 208, 211, 231, 252, 253, 264, 268; of

Index

Christ 20, 68; as container 207; female/women's (*see also* female; virginity) 55, 63, 90, 92, 180, 193, 207, 208; male 253; as object of initiation 16; possessed 68; uncorrupted (*see also* fashion; nudity; oppositions; potency) 128, 148
Bolsena 122, 136, 273
Bona of Pisa 171
Bonaldo, Oliva 249
Bonaventure of Bagnoregio 133
bonds 1, 39, 40; blood 40
Book of Joshua 26
Borromeo, Carlo 231, 232
Bosch, Hieronymus 152
Boswell, John 278
Bougaud, Emilio 278
Bourges 136
Bouxières, convent of 34
brain 7, 174, 274
Brazil 235, 249
breasts 64, 74, 136, 141, 146, 168, 208; cut-off 61, 64, 66
Bréhier, Louis 278
Brémond, Henri 115, 116, 117, 154, 273, 278
Brescia 226, 227, 232
Bresciani, Carlo 248, 275
bride 46, 80, 81, 98, 106, 109, 100, 110, 111, 112, 140, 142, 154, 155, 158, 166, 167, 170, 171, 177, 178, 179, 191, 193, 194, 195, 204, 212, 217, 221, 230, 251; of God 25, 34, 52, 60, 68, 80, 81, 97, 100, 112, 113, 115, 118, 119, 120, 124, 127, 137, 140, 143, 148, 251, 154, 163, 167, 171, 185, 215, 228, 230, 233, 234, 244; *see also* matrimony
bridegroom 68, 80, 81, 98, 100, 109, 112, 142, 162, 165, 169, 182, 191, 204; divine 80, 112, 113, 119, 141, 181, 195; *see also* matrimony
Bridget of Sweden 102, 140, 166, 170, 172, 199, 273, 274, 278; non-revelations of 140
Bridgetines 102
British 254, 256
Brother Elia 131, 132, 211
Brother Ephraim 273, 279
brothers 39, 40, 44, 50, 52, 105, 133, 134, 185, 196, 201
Brothers of Divine Love 228
Brown, Judith C. 187, 274, 278
Brown, Norman O. 278
Brown, P. 278
Brown, Peter 274, 278
Brunetti, Anna 249

Bucchi, Maria 249
Burgundy 34
Byzantium 23

cadavers: contamination of 77; uncorrupted 128
Caesar, Julius 101
Cairo 246
Calvinism 115, 269
Calvino, Giovanni (Jean Calvin) 230
Cameron, Averil 278
Campostrini, Teodora 249
Canaan 9
Canada 235, 263
Canadian Union (of Ursulines) 235
Canal ai Servi Institute 249
canoness 29–35
canonization 123, 129, 185, 260, 267
Canons 29, 30, 31, 32
Canossa 248
Cantarella, Eva 278
capital condemnation 196
carceri 87
carcerate 87
Cardinal of Florence 86
Carlini, Benedetta 187, 188, 189, 192, 195
Carmel, convent of 71, 161
Carmelites 93, 115, 151, 265, 266; of Compiègne 265
Carmine 99
Carolingian Era 31
Carthage 263
Cassian 93; rule of 93
Catherine (martyr) 137, 259
Catherine (Saint, daughter of St. Bridget) 141
Catherine de' Ricci 129, 192
Catherine of Bologna 129
Catherine of Genoa 129, 147, 274
Catherine of Siena 116, 135, 136, 139, 140, 152, 166, 170, 188, 191, 192, 250, 259, 273, 278
Cecilia 49, 55, 56, 57, 58, 60, 120
Celestial Revelations 142
Celier, L. 275, 278
Cella meretricia 63
Cenchreae (church of) 22
cerebral state 180
Chalcis, desert of 74
Chantal, Jeanne (de) 241
Chantal, Gueudré, M (de) 275
Chappotine de Neuville, Gélène (de) 263
Charités, Institutes of 240
Charles VII 259

Charles X Gustav of Sweden 244
Charolles 172
Chartres 246
chastity 70; vow of 25, 44, 52, 55, 59, 70, 73, 78, 172, 187, 235, 242, 252
Chefoo 263
Chester, Leofrie 94
Chiara of Montefalco 134, 135, 170
child 7, 8, 39, 47, 71, 79, 116, 128, 141, 142, 168, 187, 189, 210, 229, 247, 267
childhood 47, 79, 124, 137, 141, 143, 171, 173, 174, 189, 227, 240, 245, 247
China 94, 244, 249, 263
Christ 22, 36, 43, 59, 68, 97, 109, 110, 122, 131, 132, 133, 134, 135, 136, 138, 139, 140, 141, 146, 147, 151, 163, 164, 169, 171, 187, 221, 229, 230, 242, 250, 262, 263, 264, 268; crucified 113, 130, 131, 133, 134, 136, 137, 139, 146, 164, 170, 171, 178, 179, 191, 217; man of sorrows (*see also* passion: of Christ) 163; second *see* Francis of Assisi; *see also* Jesus
Christina 61, 62
Christus vincit, Christus regnat, Christus imperat 221
Chrysostom, John 23, 30
Church: authorities 84, 190, 192, 195, 243; Catholic 3, 33, 149, 151, 154, 155; of the circumcised 17; early 226, 228, 234; Eastern 24; female 63, 68; of the Gentiles 17; history 54, 84, 108, 156, 240; men of 28, 53, 59, 60, 73, 100, 152, 190, 234, 248, 250; "prostitute" 227; reform 154, 169; of Rome 231; Western 24, 31
Cicero 155
circulation: of reformers' texts 227; of women 2, 270
circumcision 15, 16, 17, 18, 164; *see also* initiation rite
Cistercians 135, 137
civil war, Spanish 244
Claire of Assisi 99, 165
Clarke, John 272
Clement of Alexandria 26, 271
Clement II 88
Clement IV 220
Clement XIII 218
Clevedon 263
clitoridectomy 180; *see also* closure
clitoris 180
cloister 1, 24, 60, 68, 81, 83, 84, 85, 91, 100, 106, 107, 108, 114, 119, 123, 154, 174, 184, 186, 215, 221, 225, 226, 227, 229, 230, 233, 235, 238, 241, 244, 250, 251, 264, 265, 266; *see also* imprisonment; prison
Closed Garden 180
closure 2, 91, 107, 180, 181, 234, 252; *see also* oppositions; seal
clothing 12, 13, 14, 33, 49, 56, 59, 92, 96, 99, 186; renunciation of 63, 210
Clytemnestra 39
coitus 111, 112, 118, 208
Colbert, Jean-Baptiste 245
Coldingham, convent of 48
Coleman, P. 274, 278
Colette of Corbie 171
Collegio Romano 219
Collin de Plancy, Jacques-Albin-Simon 274, 278
Cologne 34
Colombanus 72
Colonna 143
Columella, Lucius Junius 98
Comboni, Daniele 250, 275
Commentary on the Letter to the Romans 25, 26
Commission des Régulières 264
Commodus 54, 55
Common Rules 241
Company 150, 218, 219, 220, 244; of Jesus 218; of Saint Ursula 228; of the Servants of the Poor 241
Compiègne, martyrs of 264
Concannon, H. 275, 278
concentration camps 114, 186, 197
Conciliorum Oecumenicorum Decreta 271, 278
concrete-symbolic realism 119, 152
concretization of the symbolic 137
concreteness 67, 114, 119, 123, 139, 158, 159, 179, 204
confessor 14, 20, 53, 82, 90, 116, 124, 125, 130, 138, 139, 141, 143-145, 148, 153, 168, 169, 178, 179, 184, 185, 190, 192, 194, 198, 201, 202, 203, 204, 205, 209-11, 212, 240, 247, 250, 265, 273
Conen de St-Luc, Victoire 222
confraternity 241
congregation 241
Congregation of the Ursulines 225, 228
consciousness 67, 110, 126, 150, 156, 162, 163, 166, 174, 183, 216, 260
consecration of virgins 24, 28, 31, 52, 68, 99, 100, 101, 185, 226
Conservatoires 264
Constitutions 153

contemplation 83, 110, 125, 134, 227; life of 123
contexts 58, 124
Conti Odorisio, Ginevra 282
continence 25, 26
Contrada delle Incarcerate 88
contradictions 1, 19, 20, 38, 39, 40, 41, 59, 71, 94, 205, 230, 261, 268
convent 32–35, 48, 68, 69, 71, 75–80, 82, 83, 84, 85, 88, 90, 105-107, 114, 115, 116, 124, 125, 126, 127, 128, 138, 139, 144, 153, 154, 157, 164, 165, 170-173, 181, 182, 184, 186-189, 192, 195, 196, 197, 198, 199, 207, 212, 225, 226, 230, 231–235, 238, 240, 241, 244, 248, 258; double 108
Convent of the Paraclete 90
cooking 13, 74, 75, 77
Cortona 129, 137, 138, 205, 210, 211, 275
Council of Epaona 23
Council of Ephesus 168
Council of Gangra 99
Council of Laodicea 22
Council of Nicea 20
Council of Nimes 23
Council of Orange 23, 234, 264
Council of Orléans 23
Council of Reims 33
Council of Trent 115, 152, 227
creation 90, 130, 132
Cremisi, Teresa 278
Crescentia 49
Crimean War 254, 255, 256
Crivelli, Bartolomea 191, 273
Crivelli, E. 273
Croce, Giovanni 114
cross 118, 122, 129, 130, 134, 135, 137, 162, 163, 164, 181, 191, 212, 235, 268
crown 62, 101, 137, 141, 170, 176, 193, 259
crucifix 135, 140, 187
Crusades 128, 163
cult 135
Cultural Anthropology 1, 281
culture 1, 2, 7–9, 11, 16, 19–22, 26, 29, 37, 38, 45, 51, 59, 67, 70, 72, 73, 74, 76, 75, 77, 87, 97, 105, 107, 113, 117, 119, 121, 122, 125, 133, 139, 142, 154, 155, 158, 160, 163, 172-174, 176, 182, 183, 190, 193, 206, 207, 213, 214, 228, 257, 267–269
Cuomo, R. 273, 278
Curia 218
Curimon 263
Cyclical laws 51
Cyra 87

Dames de la Charité, Company of 240
Danes 48
Dante Alighieri 142, 144, 145
Daniélou, Jean 271, 278
daughter 34, 46, 61, 79, 85, 86, 88, 127, 212, 213, 214
Daughters of Charity: Company of 240, 241, 242, 244, 264; Canossians 248
Daughters of the Church 249
Daughters of the Sacred Heart of Jesus 249
Dax 264
De Agricultura 99
De centesima, sexagesima, tricesima 25
De Mystica Theologia 110
De resurrectione Beatae Virginis Mariae 126
De Virginibus 62
deaconate 22
deaconess 22, 23, 31, 39, 254
dead-life 265
dead woman 230
death 3, 11, 14, 17-19, 21, 24, 26, 27, 36, 37, 39, 41, 42, 44, 45, 46, 47, 50-52, 54, 55, 57, 59, 61, 62, 64, 65, 68, 70, 77, 81, 84, 87, 88, 95, 96, 99, 100, 101, 109, 114, 115, 128-131, 134-137, 139-141, 163-165, 168, 170, 178, 181, 183, 188, 191, 194, 196, 198, 199, 202, 205–208, 211, 212, 226, 230, 231, 239, 248, 251, 258, 260, 262, 264, 266, 267; beauty of (*see also* beauty 221; life as 162; love until 110, 111, 162; to oneself 43; power of (*see also* power; sacrifice) 132, 265; transcendence of 56; to the world 60
deaf mutes 243, 250
Debougerie, P. 278
decapitation 55, 60, 199; *see also* capital condemnation
Decius Mure, Publius 101
deification 157
Delaruelle, Etiénne 273, 278
Delattre, Pierre 278
Delehaye, Hippolyte 272, 278
De Lellis, Camillus 231, 239, 275, 278
delirium 122, 139, 174, 178, 183, 192, 206; group 178, 179, 181, 182; religious 179
De Martino, Ernesto 272, 278
Democritus 99
Denis the Areopagate 110
Denzinger, Henrici 278
Deonna, Waldemar 278
De Sales, Francis *see* Francis
Descartes, Réné 216
Descalced Carmelites 93; *see also* Carmelites

Desiato, Luca 272, 278
destiny 43, 48, 73, 92, 114, 119, 156, 177, 179, 189, 195, 214, 221, 226, 234, 238, 253, 258, 266, 267
destruction 69, 95, 109, 131, 207, 210; self- 109
Devereux, Georges 274, 278
devil 116, 117, 142, 145, 147, 151, 152, 156, 175, 176, 177, 178, 181, 182, 183, 190, 195, 204, 260
devotion 20, 44, 48, 57, 58, 102, 128, 129, 134, 135, 136, 138, 150, 153, 164, 170, 188, 217, 218, 219, 220, 221, 222, 229, 260
devotions 130, 164, 169, 217, 218, 219, 239, 248, 259
Dialogue on the Two Principal Systems of the World 85
Dialogues 147
Dialogues des Carmelites 266
Didaché 22
Diderot, Denis 195-198
Die Letzte am Schafott 264
Dienzelbacher, Peter 279, 283
Dieterlen, Germaine 279
difference 24, 38, 40, 54, 61, 72, 75, 89, 90, 91, 94, 95, 111, 126, 128, 144, 172, 178, 180, 182, 188, 206, 207, 232, 238; *see also* diversity
Diocletian 60
di Marino, Stefano 279
Diodati, Elia 86
Di Rosa, Pauline 243
disease 52, 143, 178, 221, 226; *see also* sickness
Dissin, J. 275, 279
diversity 44, 45, 91, 101, 109, 165, 182, 205; *see also* difference
Dizionario degli Istituti di Perfezione 3, 271, 272, 274
Doctor Jekyll 261
doctor of the Church 152, 156, 196, 251
Dodds, Eric R. 279
Dolce stil novo 111
Dominic of Guzmàn 100, 149
Dominicans 136, 139, 140, 149, 172, 192, 240, 246; Third Order of 246
Domodossola 248
Donata 54
Dorian Gray 261
Douran 245
drama 80, 83, 184, 213, 266
Dramatic Dialogues 88
dress 89, 90, 95, 101, 176, 242, 264; secular 240; *see also* body; potency

Dronke, Peter 279
Dubois, Jacques 279
Duby, A. 279
Duby, George 279
Dunes, battle of 245
Durand, Gilbert 272, 279
Dusseldorf 254

ears 69, 185, 255
East, Christian world of 24, 26, 30, 31, 100, 101
East, E. C. 279
Ebba the Young 48
Ebner, Marguerite 121, 273
ecclesiastics 33, 34, 123, 127, 154, 186, 227, 240
Ecclesiasticus 14
ecstasies 2, 66, 68, 69, 109, 110, 119, 120, 123, 124, 128, 137, 138, 139, 140, 141, 143, 144, 145, 148, 150, 154, 155, 156, 159, 160, 169, 172, 173, 174, 175, 178-182, 190, 191, 193, 199, 211, 212; hallucinatory (*see also* hallucinations) 121, 150
Edelman, Gerald M. 150, 174, 272, 274, 279
Egbert 125
Egypt 28, 47, 180
Eichgraben 263
Eliade, Mircea 263, 279
Elisabeth of Schönau 273
Elisabeth of Spalbaeck 135
Elizabeth of Hungary 170
Elizabeth of Portugal 129
Emmerick, Catherine 170
emperor of Rome 37, 54, 60
empire 43, 45, 54, 59, 235, 247
encyclopedists 198
England 131, 245, 253, 255, 259, 263, 271; Victorian 253; woman of 251
enlightenment 39, 167, 197, 264
environment 7, 20, 47, 49, 75, 106, 148, 150, 171-174, 177, 182, 197-199, 213, 229, 252
Epaona 23 (*see also* Council of Epaona)
Ephraim, Brother 273, 279
Epinal, convent of 34
Epistula XXII ad Eustochium 74
erection 96, 97, 199, 200
erotic 63, 94, 95, 111, 155, 169, 171, 184-186, 199; object 94
Erstein, convent of 34
Essen, convent of 34
Esterson, Aaron 213, 275, 279, 280
ethnologist 10, 16, 77, 180, 270
ethno-psychiatry 174

Eucharist 23, 43, 72, 100, 122, 127, 139
eunuchs 28, 29, 167
Euphemia of Chalcedon 62
Euripides 39
Europe 3, 32, 38, 39, 52, 71, 75, 76, 84, 91, 99, 105, 107, 111, 125, 127, 143, 148, 160, 167, 170, 171, 174, 186, 189, 190, 215, 227, 229, 239, 245, 257, 258; Central 163; Christian 51, 52, 257; Eastern 235; Southern 251
Eusebius of Caesarea 61
Eve 117, 149, 186
exchange 24, 45, 46, 62, 79, 85, 99, 111, 113, 130, 145, 167, 207, 229, 270; of hearts 118, 119, 130, 136, 191, 192; matrimonial 24, 28
exorcisms 117, 156
experience 2, 27, 42, 69, 72, 73, 75–78, 89, 90, 92, 102, 108-110, 115, 118, 12-125, 139, 145, 148, 158, 159, 160, 162, 163, 164, 165, 166, 171, 179, 189, 190, 193, 206, 211, 216, 217, 225, 226, 227, 245, 256, 261
Expositio 94, 96
eyes 3, 10, 12, 13, 15, 19, 25, 32, 44, 46, 48, 55, 65, 69, 71, 81, 88, 92, 126, 135, 137, 139, 147, 151, 177, 194, 196, 205, 207, 210, 232, 241, 242, 244, 247, 250; torn out 65, 66

face 14, 56, 91, 98, 136, 165; uncovered 101
fairy tales 60, 61, 82; prince of 60
faith 12, 26, 36, 37, 42, 49, 57, 59, 62, 63, 65, 123, 124, 132, 154, 155, 164, 176, 197, 198, 212, 218, 228, 232, 250, 253, 260, 261, 262, 264, 266
falsity 153, 214, 215; see also pretending; representation
fantasy 95, 123
fashion 89, 92, 127, 242; religious system of 92; unisex 94
fate 56, 107, 114, 125, 204, 208, 212, 219, 253, 257, 259, 266
Father, the 40, 111, 151, 163
Fatherlands 251, 252
Fatima 218
Fauchery, Pierre 212, 275, 279
Favaro, Antonio 272, 279
feet 92, 93; female 92, 94, 95; male 96; naked 94, 95; sandaled 94; see also footwear; oppositions
Felicita 41
female 2, 3, 12, 19, 22–24, 30–32, 40, 46, 48, 49–52, 53, 56, 60–65, 75, 77, 78, 80, 89, 91, 92, 94, 95, 98, 107-112, 115, 119, 120, 123, 124, 127-130, 133, 136, 137, 139, 142, 143, 152, 164, 167, 169, 171, 172, 175, 178-180, 185, 187, 189, 191, 196, 198, 199, 201, 203, 204, 207, 208, 210, 212–214, 216, 217, 219–221, 225–227, 232, 235, 241, 249, 252, 254, 260, 262, 263, 266; apparel 97; body 20, 64, 89, 90, 92, 160, 180, 193, 207, 208; institutes 248; monasticism 68, 71, 72, 76, 79, 184, 186, 197, 228, 230, 265; nudity 63, 92, 94, 95, 97; sex (see also sexuality) 38, 69, 70, 74, 86, 90, 97, 100, 116, 143, 166, 177, 209, 246, 250, 263; see also sacrifice
femininity: -annihilation-death 109; of males 109, 167
feminism 2, 40, 40, 84, 97, 160, 200, 263, 267, 269
feminist theology 267
Filles de la Charité 240, 275
fire 13, 71, 74, 77
Firpo, Massimo 275, 279
flagellation 132, 135, 229; as Baptismus (see also blood) 138
Flemish figures 131, 135, 136
Fletcher, Richard 279
Florentine Friar 232; see also Savonarola, Girolamo
Florence 86, 88, 187, 271, 272, 273, 275
Flügel, J.C. 279
Folgarait, Giulio 274, 279
Folgheraiter, Alberto 273, 279
Fonkulgar 141
Fontevrault, convent of 107
food 12, 29, 49, 55, 71, 73–75, 87, 122, 140, 159, 169, 192, 196, 206, 208–210, 231; cooked 51, 71, 74; raw 51, 210, 211
footwear 93, 95
foundation 1, 15, 42, 79, 83, 115, 154, 160, 206, 220, 230, 232, 237, 239, 243, 246, 267
Fourth World Conference on the Rights of Women 33
France 34, 115, 198, 221, 233, 234, 235, 241, 243, 245, 246, 264, 273, 275; revolutionary 262
Frances of Rome 125, 130, 143, 144, 147, 274, 279
Francesco e l'invenzione delle stimmate 273
Francesco Sforza II 230
Francis de Sales 164, 226, 243, 278
Francis of Assisi 92, 99, 129, 133-135, 138; as the second Christ 130, 131, 191
Franciscans 136, 138, 140, 210, 263

Franciscan Missionaries of Mary 263
Franconia 34
freedom 3, 11, 19, 29, 33, 52, 69, 76, 78, 91, 100, 106, 115, 230, 242, 252, 253, 255, 261; *see also* liberty
Freiburg 263
French Revolution 40, 43, 167, 197, 198, 220, 234, 237, 244, 264, 265; Men of 265
Freud, Sigmund 61, 64, 181, 216
Fromm, Erich 279
Frugoni, Chiara 130, 133, 134, 273, 279
Fumagalli Beonio Brocchieri, Maria Teresa 273, 279
function, sexual 62, 63

Galgani, Gemma *see* Gemma Galgani
Galilei, Galileo 77, 85, 86, 154, 174
Galilei, Virginia *see* Sister Maria Celeste 85, 281
Gamba, Marina 85
game 43, 84, 103, 112, 125, 165, 206, 214, 235, 269
Gandersheim, convent of 34, 88
Gangra, council of 99
garden: of the Holy Church 139; place of supreme beauty 189
Gauthey, Léon 275, 279
Gemma 129
Gemma Galgani 162, 170, 177-179, 274
Generosa 54
Genesis 94
genius 8, 15, 118, 123
Gennara 54
Germany 2, 88, 235, 254; empire of 33, 34
Germano (Father Vincenzo Ruoppolo) 274
Gernrode, convent of 34
Gertrude of Helfta 125, 137, 138, 273, 279
Gesù di Nazaret 2, 271, 281
Gharib, Georges 271, 277
Giovanni 57
Giselle 95
Goretti, Maria 50, 59
Gospel According to Matthew (film) 168
Gospels 8, 9, 11, 19, 28, 106, 117, 118, 122, 131, 132, 163, 167, 168, 209, 228, 230, 232, 248, 250, 262, 268
Gougaugh, L. 272, 279
grates 2, 115
Gratian, Jerome 155, 157
Great Britain 254, 255; *see also* England
Greco-Roman culture 17, 19, 26, 36, 42, 47
Greece 36, 39, 44–46, 45, 46, 55, 58, 62, 73, 83, 98, 101

Gregory I, the Great 20, 57
Gregory of Nyssa 23
Gribomont, Jean 271, 279
Grignion de Montfort, Louise-Marie 274, 279
group 79, 179, 250; *see also* power
Grundmann, Herbert 272, 280
Gudmarsson, Ulf 141
Guerri, Giordano Bruno 280
guillotine 222, 234, 244, 262, 264, 265
Guyart, Marie 235
Guyon, Jean-Marie Bouvier de la Motte (Madame de) 205, 208, 209

habit 67, 90, 92, 171, 185, 188, 216, 230, 241, 242, 249, 250, 262, 264; religious 89, 95, 97, 230, 252; secular 230
hagiographers 63, 203
hair 49, 92, 93; cutting of 98, 100; long 57, 63, 93, 94, 97, 99; women's 63, 93, 94, 97, 98, 99, 100
Halbwacs, Maurice 280
hallucinations 121, 122, 126, 145, 156, 158, 162, 169, 173, 174, 176, 179, 182, 183, 189, 190, 216, 259, 261; auditory 183, 189
Hamon, Auguste 275, 280
Hancelet-Hustache, J. 280
hand 41, 55, 92
hating-and-loving 2
head 59; covered or uncovered 97; detached 55, 57, 58; female 100; -hair complex 92,100
health 241, 245, 246; care 255
heart 29, 59, 113, 133, 135, 138, 239; exchange of 110, 128, 136, 191, 192; wounded 123
Hebrew 96, 116, 269
Helfta, Saxon monastery of 137
Hell 114, 117, 142, 147, 152
Heloise 90, 91
heresy 175, 258, 260
heretic 105, 106, 112, 129, 163, 175, 226, 258, 260
Herford, convent of 34
Herkenrode, Cistercian abbey of 135
hermitage 165
hermits 70
hero 42, 44, 45, 46, 50, 58, 119, 146, 257, 259, 164, 266, 267
heroine 221
heroism 44, 45, 50, 62, 217, 221, 258, 262
Hertz, Robert 280
Hildegard of Bingen 120, 121, 124, 170, 188, 259

Histoire littéraire du sentiment réligieux en France 115
Historia Religiosa 87
historians 15, 26, 30, 33, 34, 45, 47, 49, 54, 55, 64, 72, 77, 101, 108, 111, 122, 125, 215, 236, 239, 249, 250, 270
holiness 44
Holy Land 163, 164
Holy Scriptures *see* Scriptures
Homer 71, 46
homicide 266
homosexuality 71, 90, 167, 168, 185, 186, 199; female 186, 187, 197, 199; mental 70, 111, 168
Hong Kong 249
Horace 155
hospital 144, 226, 231, 232, 238, 239, 241, 243, 245, 246, 247, 249, 252, 256, 262, 263; military 186, 254; orders 220
host 26, 59, 136
humility 43, 44, 53, 78, 93, 110, 132, 140, 144, 157, 166, 192, 194, 209, 243, 250-252, 262; *see also* head; oppositions
humiliation 42, 95, 96, 147, 148, 204, 205, 206
Hungarians 88
Hungary 233
Huns 229
hunting 72, 74, 181; *see also* fire; meat
Hymn to the Creatures 165
hysteria 117, 179, 193

iconography 58, 62, 63, 97, 121, 130, 146, 150, 152, 170, 190
Ida of Nivelles 137
ideal 111, 113, 119, 154, 166, 167, 168, 173, 193, 201, 214, 221, 257, 258, 261, 263, 266; love 111; woman 111, 113, 258
identification 47, 58, 59, 63, 65, 91, 109, 111, 132, 133, 163, 169, 188, 213, 239, 242
identity, sexual 112, 166
Ignatius of Loyola 97, 219, 220, 282
images 11, 12, 14, 110, 112, 123, 124, 137, 142, 144, 147, 152, 159, 165, 169, 178, 189, 192, 203, 234; symbolic 102, 134
imagination 48, 55, 57, 94, 109, 119, 132, 142, 144, 170, 189, 198, 272, 279
impotence 93, 173
imprinting of Bride of God 137
imprisonment 49, 83, 85, 87, 88, 91, 114, 115, 126, 127, 186, 187, 194, 199, 203, 215, 234, 241, 264, 265
Impure Acts 187

impurity 9, 10, 17, 18, 20, 29, 58, 73, 187, 195
India 256
individual 7, 8, 22, 27, 32, 37-41, 44, 51, 65, 81, 83, 115, 118, 129, 133, 148, 164, 171, 173, 174, 177, 179, 182, 183, 188-190, 192, 206, 211, 214, 253, 255, 257, 260, 265, 267, 284
inequality 40; *see also* diversity
L'Inferno Monacale 114, 282
infibulation 180; *see also* closure
initiation rite 14, 15, 18; *see also* baptism
Inkerman, battle of 254
Inquisition 85, 86, 149, 152, 153, 229
inquisitors 85, 176, 194, 260
instinct, sexual 7
Institute of Charity (at Domodossola) 248
institutions 2, 15, 16, 22, 23, 28, 29, 30, 31, 32, 33, 34, 35, 43, 44, 68, 79, 84, 85, 88, 89, 100, 108, 114, 115, 117, 119, 132, 144, 152, 154, 178, 179, 180, 185, 187, 196, 197, 214, 219, 220, 225, 234, 239, 241, 244
intelligence 10, 77, 83, 85, 86, 146, 157, 158, 159, 193, 194, 201, 212, 213, 214, 245, 247, 251, 259, 261, 262
International Red Cross 256
Introduction to the Devout Life 164
inventor 132, 133, 203, 218
Irblich, E. 272, 280
Ireland 254, 275, 278
Isaac 210, 266
Islam 3, 97, 180, 227, 246
Istanbul 244
Italy 2, 7, 34, 45, 86, 87, 91, 106, 122, 138, 143, 187, 220, 221, 225-227, 233-235, 239, 241, 248, 262, 274, 280

Jacques de Vitry 121, 130
James of Edessa 23
James of Nisiba 74
Janet, Pierre 179
Jansenism 218, 269
Japan 7, 249, 263
Jéglot, C. 275, 280
Jerome 28, 74, 155, 157, 271
Jerusalem 44, 163, 271, 281
Jesuits 150, 219, 220
Jesus 1-3, 7-15, 17-19, 21, 23, 24, 28-31, 37, 38, 39-41, 43, 44, 47, 82, 84, 99, 102, 106, 108, 109, 111, 115, 118-120, 122, 128-130, 132-134, 136-138, 140-144, 146, 147, 150, 162-164, 167, 168, 170, 172, 176-178, 188, 191-194, 196, 202, 206, 209, 211, 212, 217-221, 242, 244, 249-251, 262, 268-270; *see also* Christ

Jews 9, 11, 12, 14, 15, 16, 17, 18, 19, 20, 21, 28, 29, 37, 40, 41, 96, 98, 101, 121, 166, 268
Joan of Arc 143, 175, 257, 258, 259, 262
John Chrysostom 23, 30
John of Capestrano 175
John of Tella 23
John of the Cross 111, 155, 157, 160, 161, 169
John Paul II 51, 59, 217, 250, 266, 267
Joseph II 234
Judaism 1, 8, 9, 12, 15, 16, 17, 18, 20, 21, 28, 29, 36, 37, 38, 43, 47, 58, 68, 97, 101, 107, 109, 111, 141, 190, 199, 205, 227, 262, 268
Julienne of Cornillon 137
jurists 79, 126, 199
justice 39, 142, 145, 147, 196, 203, 205, 207, 220, 269
Juvinianus 28

Kafka, Franz 112
Kaufungen, convent of 34
Kertzer, David 280
King Kong 61
kinship structure 251
Kluckhohn, Clyde 280
knowledge 9, 16, 17, 73, 76, 77, 105, 112, 116, 118, 123, 124, 126, 139, 148, 158, 159, 160, 162, 164, 170, 172, 174, 176, 185, 186, 188, 193, 194, 201, 202, 209, 216, 217, 225, 227, 231, 233, 240, 243, 247, 251, 252, 257, 259, 262; divine 123; theoretical 189, 247
Kroeber, Alfred L. 273, 280
Kurt, Amélie 278, 280

Labre, Benedetto 203
labyrinth, logical 178
Ladies of the Christian Union of Saint-Chaumond 243
Ladislas 143
Lady Godiva 94
Laing, Ronald D. 213, 275, 280
Lallémand, Leon 275, 280
Landini, Carlo Alessandro 274, 280
language 7; of the body 113; imitative learning of 257; respect 76; theological 162
Laodicea, council of 22
Latin 25, 54, 227, 274; Christian literature in 54
laymen 34, 123, 126, 227
Lazzarini, Antonio 273, 280
Lazzeri, Maria Domenica 122

learning 77, 78, 85, 121, 172, 174, 179, 225, 227, 240, 257; imitative 257
Lebanon 244
Le Brun, Jacques 275, 280
Ledóchowska, Teresa 280
Le Fort, Gertrud (von) 264
legend 57, 62, 63, 94, 126, 172, 229, 255
Legenda Aurea 229
Legenda maior 133
Le Gras, Antoine 240
Le Guern, Michel 272, 280
Leibniz, Gottfried Wilhelm 216
Leo III 57
Leo IV 58
Leo XII 248
Leona 62
Leonardi, Claudio 282
Leonardo da Vinci 154
Leopardi, Giacomo 10, 11
Léroi-Gourhan, Andrée 280
Letter to the Corinthians, I 100
Letter to the Romans 22
Letter to Virgins 27
Die Letzte am Schafott, Die 264
Levi, Primo 114
Lévi-Strauss, Claude 7, 39, 51, 73, 76, 96, 200, 203, 270, 271, 272, 280
Lévy-Bruhl, Lucien 280
Liber Pontificalis 57
Liber revelationum de sacro exercitu Virginum Cononiensium 126
Liber viarum Dei 126
liberation 15, 27, 43, 45, 52, 72, 73, 75, 76, 97, 106, 109, 112, 185, 253, 265
liberty 6, 32, 39, 47, 69, 73, 83, 94, 107, 114, 122, 221
Libri tres visionum 126
Liduina 147
Lieges, diocese of 135
life 3, 7, 10, 11, 15, 17–22, 24–27, 30, 32, 36, 38, 39, 46–48, 50, 51, 53, 56, 57, 60, 68–72, 75, 77, 78, 80, 81, 83–86, 88–91, 100, 106–108, 112, 114, 115, 123–126, 129, 135, 136, 139, 144, 147, 148, 152, 154, 160, 163, 265, 266, 268; as death 162
light 140, 146
Lioger, Caroline 221
lips 48, 65, 199, 209, 211; *see also* body
Lisbon 263
Little Sisters of Charity of Maria Addolorata 249
liturgy 22, 33, 59, 189, 269, 271
Liutgard 136
logic 1, 2, 16, 18, 59, 127, 156, 167, 171,

172, 173, 176, 181, 182, 183, 205, 230; *see also* thought
Lombardy 234
Lombroso, Cesare 65
Longfellow, Henry Wadsworth 255
Lopez Rivas, Maria de Jesus 129
Lord (God) 20, 22, 141, 146, 147, 148, 150, 151, 175, 246, 255
Loreaux, Nichole 280
Lorenz, Konrad 280
Lorraine 34
Lortz, Joseph 280
Louis XIV 246
Louis XV 264
Louise du Néant 202, 274, 280
Lourdes 177, 218
love 106; courtly 261; as death 139; with the heart 136; songs 134
lover 261; divine 82
Low Countries 235
Luc de Tuy 129
Lucca 177
Lucretia 62
Lucy 62, 65
Ludwig IV 127
Lumague, Marie 243
Lunardi, Giovanni 272, 280
Luther, Martin 230
Lutherans 115, 149, 232
Lyon 107

Macao 249
madness 190
Maddalena Gabriella of Canossa 247–249
Madeleine 179
Maderno, Stefano 58
Madonna 2, 20, 111, 117, 120, 146, 150, 167, 168, 188, 193, 218, 219, 239, 271, 274; *see also* Our Lady; Mary (Mother of Jesus); Virgin Mary
La Madonna 274
mad-woman 201
Marian devotion 150, 169, 239
Magnificat 265
Maidens of Charity 256, 262
Maidservants of the Child Jesus 249
Magli, Ida 271-275, 281
Millard, Jean 203
Malaysia 249
male 2, 7, 9, 10, 12, 16, 22, 25, 28, 31, 36, 39, 41, 45, 47, 48, 50–52, 62, 64, 65, 68, 69, 71, 72, 76, 90, 95, 97, 98, 108, 110, 111-116, 127, 155-157, 165-169, 185, 188, 197, 199, 201-203, 206–209, 235, 261;

effeminate 155; institutes 221, 249; physicality 68, 69; *see also* bridegroom; maleness; masculine; penis
maleness 69
Mâle, Émile 281
Malmberg, Denise 92, 272, 281
man: as "most precious merchandise" 200; *see also* male
Mansi, Gian Domenico 271, 281
mantle 150
Manzoni, Alessandro 197
Marana 87
Marcus Aurelius 56
Mare of God 182
Margaret of Cortona 129, 137, 138, 205, 210
Maria Celeste (Galilei) *see* Sister Maria Celeste
Maria de' Medici 240
Maria Maddalena de' Pazzi 281
Mariani, Umberto 275, 281
Marie de Oignies 121, 130, 131
Marillac, Louise (de) 239, 240, 242, 247
Marinconz, Lydia 280
Mark, Gospel of 39
Marovich, Anna Maria 249
Martha 9
Martini, Gabriele 274, 281
martyrdom 25–28, 36, 41-45, 47–49, 51, 52, 54, 55, 59, 60–63, 65, 91, 99, 110, 112, 120, 152, 163, 164, 185, 217, 229, 257, 262, 266, 267; female 45, 51, 55, 57, 59, 60, 62, 63, 65; *see also* martyrs
martyrs 3, 25, 26, 42–44, 48–51, 53–63, 65, 96, 120, 163, 164, 198, 229, 250, 257, 258, 263, 266, 268; new 44, 258, 263; virgin-martyrs 55, 57, 58, 59, 60, 61; women as 49, 50, 51, 59, 60, 64, 94, 99, 120, 265; *see also* martyrdom
Marx, Carl 13
Marxism 77
Mary (Mother of Jesus) 14, 142, 162, 168, 239
Mary (sister of Lazarus) 9, 162
Mary Magdalen 9, 63, 94, 144, 210
Mary of Egypt 63, 93
Masaccio, Tommaso 99
masculine 9, 16, 20, 30, 31, 50, 54, 102, 109, 111, 124, 160, 167, 176, 248, 264, 269; *see also* male; sex
Masini, Ferruccio 281
Mass 125, 132, 149, 152, 187, 268, 269; Requiem 88
Matilda of Hacheborn 171

Matilde of Canossa 247
matriarchy 2, 79; *see also* abbess; mother; power
matrimony 24, 27, 28, 31, 33, 34, 124, 193, 226, 229, 253, 270
Matthew, Gospel of 26, 168
Mattiotti, Giovanni 144
Mauriac, François 210, 275, 281
Maximilian 61
Mayas 43
meat 72, 74, 131, 145
Meattini, Umberto 273
mediators 23, 76
Medici, Rodolfo 273, 279
Melchites 100
mendicant orders 227
menstruation 18, 20, 22, 23, 24, 74, 75, 90–93, 98, 168, 181, 203, 208
Mercier, R. 281
Merici, Angela 106, 225–228, 232, 234, 235, 237, 238, 240, 241, 245–247, 251, 275, 280, 281
method 1, 160, 216, 269; non-masculine 10
Metz, Réné 281
Meunier, Marie Geneviève 265
Mexico 244
Mezard, D. 281
Michelangelo 154
Michelet, Jules 259
Middle Ages 23, 33, 72, 73, 75, 92, 94, 109, 117, 127, 141, 149, 170, 171, 174, 189, 258
Mignani, Laura 129
Migne, Jacques Paul 271, 281
Milan 96, 230–234, 247, 248
military 42, 50, 176, 186, 254, 256, 258
mind 11, 86, 95, 162, 180, 204, 216
Ministers to the Sick 231
miracles 44, 59, 122, 128, 131, 133, 134, 136, 139, 155, 187, 190, 191, 194
Miserentissimus Redemptor 218
Missionaries of Mary 263
model 47, 71, 79, 90, 106, 107, 127, 133, 148, 154, 155, 162, 173, 221, 251, 258; *see also* patterns
Moëller, Charles 272, 281
Molinari, Paolo 271, 281
Mons, convent of 34
Montefalco 134
Morandini, Giuliana 281
Moratuwa 263
Morris, Desmond 271
Morte e pianto rituale nel mondo antico 77
Moscati, Sabatino 272, 281

Moses 20, 116, 147
mother 32, 51, 65, 165, 187, 204, 214, 225, 238, 241, 251, 267; power of 79
motherhood 52, 138, 198, 229, 233, 240, 253
motivation, sexual 89
Mount La Verna 133
Moustier, convent of 34
Müller, Jean Pierre 272, 280, 281
music 216, 221, 231, 233, 240, 261, 271
Mussolini, Benito 96
Musurillo, H. 277
mutilation 17, 29; *see also* circumcision; clitoridectomy; eunuchs
mystery 17, 23, 78, 96, 100, 101, 159

nakedness 63, 90, 92, 93, 94, 96, 168, 211; *see also* dress; head; feet; nudity; oppositions
Nambikwara 38, 271
Napoleon 220, 244, 247, 248
nation 3, 221
Natural History 94
nature 1, 11, 12, 15, 22, 47, 50, 51, 57, 61, 65, 69, 75, 89, 96, 97, 117, 131-133, 139, 145, 149, 155, 165, 195, 203, 205, 233, 235, 250, 253, 258, 273; beyond 61, 203; super- 61
The Nature of Culture 119, 273
Naudet, Leopoldine 249
Nazis 96, 114
Neri, Philip 111, 135, 168, 228, 231, 239
neuronal groups 173
neuronic path 172
neuropathology 183
Nevers 177
New Antwerp 263
New Jerusalem Bible 271
New World 235
New York 244
Newton, Isaac 77
Nicodemism 230
Nicodemus 230
Nietzsche, Friedrich 52, 281
Nightingale, Florence 251-254, 256, 275, 281
Nightingale Training School for Nurses 256
Nimes, Council of 23
Nivelles, convent of 34, 137
non-being 114, 159, 175, 178, 190, 212
non-knowing 123
non-thinking 123; *see also* thought
Norbert of Xanten 108

Nordhausen, convent of 34
normality 130, 158, 174, 175
Normality and Madness in the Family 213
nose 48, 65, 97, 199, 211
Notes on Matters Affecting the Health, Efficiency and Hospital 255, 256
nothingness 123, 178, 194
nudity 63, 92, 94, 95, 96, 97; *see also* body; dress; nakedness
Nun of Monza 197
nuns 23, 32, 33, 48, 53, 59, 60, 68, 71, 73, 78–82, 83, 84, 90, 91, 92, 97, 99, 101, 106, 107, 108, 114, 124, 125, 134, 135, 137, 148, 153, 154, 165, 184–186, 187, 189, 191, 193, 194–197, 199, 202, 209, 212, 220, 226, 230, 232, 235, 238, 244, 248, 250, 256, 263–266
Nuns of the Retreat, Institute of 222
nurses 53, 239, 252, 253, 254, 256, 262; *see also* nursing
nursing 73, 74, 105, 208, 231, 237, 243, 247, 251, 254, 256, 263, 275; *see also* nurses
nymphs 94; *see also* feet

obedience 26, 44, 47, 53, 78, 81, 111, 141, 143, 147, 149, 151, 153, 156, 176, 190, 197, 201, 212, 217, 221, 227, 228, 233, 235, 241–243, 250–252, 258, 262, 265
object 2, 10, 49, 57, 59, 64, 77, 81, 87, 94, 110, 111, 113, 118, 136, 167, 168, 184, 197, 229; sexual 64
objectification 3, 77, 188, 215
oblation 84, 187
office, divine 34, 47, 54, 81, 225, 269
Old Testament 3, 189, 190, 266, 268
Olivetan Order 274
Olympia 23
omnipotence 157, 173, 183
On Virgins 27
On Widows 28
oppositions 160 *and infra*; of emptiness-fullness 159; of head-feet 96; of high-short 95, 97, 155; of male-female 40, 65, 166, 186, 208; of nature-cuture 72, 75, 93, 96, 97; of open-closed 47, 140, 168, 180; of raw-cooked 51, 210, 211; of right-left 41, 129, 130, 136
opposing categories 59, 155; *see also* oppositions
opposites *see* oppositions
Orange 23, 234, 264
oratoire 115
Order of St. Dominic 149

Order of the Carmelites 151, 154
Order of the Dominicans 149
orders 23, 54, 69, 80, 90, 152, 157, 165, 182, 192, 220, 239, 240, 241, 244, 253, 255, 258, 263; as deaconate (*see also* deaconess) 22, 23; male 108; mendicant 108; monastic 32, 84, 88, 90, 93, 149; natural 51; Ursuline 235
Orestes 39
Origen 25, 26, 27
original sin 1, 17, 18, 94, 97, 166, 186, 208
Orléans, Council of 23
orphanages 241, 254
Orsini 143
Ospedale Grande 247
Ottolini, Emilia 249
Ottonian Era 34
Our Lady 128, 141, 142, 144, 150, 168, 177, 180, 237, 249; *see also* Madonna; Mary (Mother of Jesus); Virgin Mary
Our Lady Help of Christians 243

Pacomian monasteries 185
Pacomian Palestine 17, 21, 60, 72, 99
Pacomius 72, 78
Palazzoli-Selvini, Mara 75, 272, 281
Palmerston, Henry John Temple 255
Papacy 247
Papàsogli, Benedetta 275, 281
Paphnunzius 88
Papini, Giovanni 274
Paraclete, convent of 90
Paris 179, 219, 222, 235, 240, 242, 254; University of 175
parish priests 247
Pascal, Blaise 102, 216
Pascal I 58
Pascoli, Giovanni 10
Pasolini, Pier Paolo 168
passion 55, 56, 60–62, 102, 106, 113, 120, 128, 130–139, 141, 146, 147, 163, 164, 170, 171, 176, 178, 188, 196, 212; of Christ 102, 132, 134, 138, 141, 171
passivity 44, 92, 98, 110, 111, 250, 258
pathology 53, 119, 139, 183, 208; of consciousness 183; physical 135; spiritual 135
patriotism 258, 259
patterns 21, 37, 39, 44, 75, 119, 220, 251, 284; sacral 227
Paul of Tarsus 8, 11, 16–19, 22, 24, 36, 39, 41, 43, 52, 59, 96, 100, 109, 110, 133, 144, 163, 167, 169, 206, 251, 206, 251, 268, 269
Pecha de Vadaterra, Alfonso 273

Pelucchi, Giuliana 275, 281
penance 70, 74, 75, 80, 86, 88, 147, 181, 185, 196, 207
penates 58
penis 29, 41, 64, 65, 96, 97, 155, 166, 168, 181, 193, 199, 200
penitence 25, 43, 63, 72, 86, 93, 117, 122, 138, 147, 154, 165, 169, 171, 195, 202, 203, 208, 209, 210, 211; culture of 125, 133, 139
Penitential Psalms 86
perception 44, 158, 159, 183, 207, 214; altered 179
perfection 25, 26, 27, 44, 57, 65, 81, 82, 83, 88, 110, 113, 127, 128, 133, 148, 149, 153, 156, 158, 165, 178, 212, 226, 227, 228, 235, 239, 253
Perpetua 41, 56, 120
Pescia 189
Peter (Saint) 16, 17
Peter Damiani 175
Peter Leopold I 234
Pharaoh 95
pharisees 12
Philip, Abbot of Clairvaux 135
Philomena 60
Phoebe 22, 39
Pious Teachers of Our Lady of the Sorrows 249
Pious Union 241
Pisa 99, 171, 187, 275
Pisano, Giunta 135
Pius VI 265
Pius XI 218
Pliny 94
poet 7
poetry 76, 116, 118, 216, 221
Poirier, Jean 16, 271, 282
Poissy 240
Poland 244
politicians 10, 250, 255
politics 3, 10, 14, 29, 34, 45, 46, 48, 67, 71, 76, 140, 154, 167, 169, 170, 183, 196, 219, 233, 243, 252, 255, 258, 259, 260, 263
Ponte delle Grazie 88
Ponzani, Lorenzo 143
poor 3, 31, 38, 53, 60, 71, 72, 78, 93–95, 106, 107, 118, 123, 131, 143, 144, 148, 151, 155, 177–179, 185, 211, 216, 228, 231-233, 237, 238, 240–250, 262–264
Pope 55, 58–60, 68, 85, 88, 95, 140, 143, 217, 218, 248, 250, 259, 260, 265–267; anti- 143
possession 18, 62, 64, 68, 69, 95, 97, 98, 99, 109, 110, 111, 112, 154, 155, 156, 164, 166, 167, 170, 171, 174, 175, 177, 193, 210, 217, 240; diabolic 175, 176; sexual 64, 109, 111, 178
potency 16, 29, 37, 41, 42, 44, 50, 56, 57, 59, 60, 61, 68, 72, 75, 76, 93, 94, 95, 96, 97, 98, 99, 101, 109, 112, 113, 136, 155, 164, 166, 175, 192, 208, 209, 230, 250, 251, 261, 269; of blood 136; of death 37, 41; erective 41; female 97, 175; of man 60, 251; of objects 44; of the word 37, 41, 50, 67, 76;
Pott's disease 178
Pourrat, Paul 73, 272, 275, 282
Poussay, convent of 34
Poussepin, Marie 245, 246, 247
poverty 3, 44, 78, 83, 93, 95, 106, 107, 108, 117, 131, 138, 142, 188, 211, 228, 242, 246, 250, 252
power 2, 3, 8, 10, 12, 15, 17, 23, 29, 34, 42, 43, 46, 47, 51-53, 56, 60, 64, 67–69, 71, 73, 79–83, 93, 95, 105-108, 112, 116, 117, 123, 125, 132, 152-154, 156, 160, 175, 178, 182, 183, 188, 190, 201-204, 206, 212, 217–219, 227–229, 242–244, 250, 258–260, 262, 263, 268, 269; male 40, 47, 76, 108, 119, 154; maternal 2
Pozzi, Giovanni 282
Praz, Mario 275, 282
preachers: Dominican 117; itinerant 106
preaching 19, 76, 107, 108, 145, 149, 227; popular 227
prepuce 16, 164
pretending 34, 138, 153, 155, 179, 186, 192, 193, 268; *see also* representation
Pretestatus, cemetery of 58
prey, sexual 64
Pribram, Karl H. 180, 274, 282
priest 23, 67, 68, 97, 99, 101, 111, 117, 132, 144, 145, 151, 191, 210, 266, 274; as bride of God 97; -sacrificer 266
priesthood 107, 132, 167, 185, 269
Priests Victims of the Sacred Heart of Jesus 221
Prince Charming 60, 229, 261, 113, 258
prioress 153
Priscilla, cemetery of 60
prison 33, 40, 59, 122, 160, 194, 195, 196, 212, 238, 243; monastic 153
prisoners 45, 46, 50, 113, 115, 119, 123, 143, 156, 233, 234
procreation 16, 22, 27, 33, 51, 70, 187, 198, 207, 208, 217, 238
profane 59, 118

Promessi sposi 197
prostitutes 46, 65, 88, 99, 144, 179, 187, 196, 198, 211, 226, 227, 232, 250, 252
prostitute's cell 63, 64
Protestantism 149, 268, 169; *see also* Protestants; Reformation
Protestants 58, 150, 155, 226, 227, 228, 231, 232, 254, 259, 260, 268, 269; *see also* Protestantism
Proto-gospel of James 141
Proust, Marcel 123
Providence des Filles de Dieu 243
Provveditori sopra i Monasteri 199
Pseudo-Cyprianus 25
psychiatry 74, 74, 75, 158, 193, 213, 214
psychoanalysis 73, 159
psychology 28, 30, 32, 37, 46, 48, 50, 63, 68–70, 73–75, 79–81, 86, 90, 102, 108, 111, 112, 114, 116, 124, 128, 132, 138, 148, 153, 154, 163, 166, 167, 170, 171, 185, 188, 189, 195, 197, 200–202, 214–216, 238, 239, 247, 253, 257, 259
psychosis 93, 122, 130, 131, 137, 138, 139, 146, 178, 179, 181, 193, 208, 209, 214, 216
psychosomatic symptoms 132
public exposure 63; *see also* nakedness; nudity
Publius Decius 101
purification 1, 16, 18, 29, 75
Puritanism 269
purity 18, 20, 26, 29, 58, 63, 94, 108, 109, 129, 147, 150, 152, 168, 178, 205, 217, 232, 254

Quattro Coronati 58
Quebec 263
Quendlinburg, convent of 34
Quételet, Lambert 255
Quimper 222

Rahner, Hugo 275, 282
Raimondo of Capua 139
Rampolla del Tindaro, Mariano 57
Rancé, Armand Jeanhe le Boutheillier (de) 74
rape 48, 59, 65, 98, 232, 266; of nuns 232
rapture 119, 123, 149, 173, 179, 190
Ratio studiorum 219
rationality 56, 205, 253
Ravenna, mosaics of 58, 60
rays 112, 130, 135, 140, 146, 149, 191; *see also* light
reality 11, 14, 18, 38, 40, 41, 46, 48, 54, 67, 79, 82–84, 91, 102, 118, 119, 122, 124, 138, 140, 144, 153, 163, 164, 166, 173–175, 178, 179, 181-183, 185, 190-193, 202, 205, 206, 214, 215, 218, 225, 238, 259, 261, 268; earthly 23, 114; of life 47; principle 118, 157, 158, 178, 191, 206; social 114
realism 152
Réau, Louis 282
rebellion 11, 40, 75, 107, 114, 124, 194, 216, 258, 262; social 198
recluses 60, 86, 87, 88, 129, 135
red carpet 95
Red Cross 256
The Red Shoes 94
Redi, Anna Maria 129
reflection 54, 71, 76, 80, 100, 102, 110, 122, 137, 143, 157, 160, 188, 196, 216, 217, 248, 257; *see also* thought
reform 105, 112, 115, 117, 154, 169, 226, 227, 228, 258, 259; counter- 105
Reformation 58, 101, 155, 228
regality 221
Règles 246
Regula 72, 131
Regula non bullata 131
Reims 33, 259
relics 57, 58; cult of 56, 135, 164, 170
religions 15, 43, 44, 77, 262, 269
Remiremont, convent of 34
Renaissance 94, 106, 148
Reni, Guido 168
Renzi, Elisabetta 249
repetition 23, 37, 43, 48, 134, 158, 189, 214
representation 68, 82, 83, 117, 176, 190, 192, 195, 212, 269; self- 154; *see also* pretending
Republican Act 265
Requiem Mass 88
Restoration 220
revelation 2, 16, 101, 102, 110, 117, 125, 128, 137, 138, 140, 141, 142, 151, 152, 156, 171, 175, 189, 194, 199, 217, 218, 259, 260; *see also* veil
Revelations 199
revolution 7, 8, 10, 12, 15, 30, 40, 45, 50, 63, 107; French 167, 197, 198, 220, 234, 237, 244, 264, 265; Reform 115
Richardson, Jane 280, 282
Richer, Julie 243
Ridgely Seymer, Lucy 282
ring 192, 195; wedding 110, 119, 123, 128, 173, 191
Risorgimento 220

Rita of Cascia 129
Rizzelli, Giunio 271, 277, 282
Robert of Arbrissel 107, 108
robes 11, 12, 32; golden 58
Robin, Marthe (*called also* Marta) 126, 273
Rocca, Giancarlo 282
Rodersdorf, convent of 171
role 2, 9, 22, 23, 32, 34, 36, 50, 51, 74–76, 78, 80, 83, 85, 88, 105, 115-117, 119, 156, 160, 167, 173, 174, 176, 198, 204, 214, 217, 239, 257, 258, 266, 270
Romania 233
Romans 17, 19, 22, 24, 25, 26, 36, 37, 39, 42, 43, 44–47, 49, 54, 55, 56, 58, 59, 62, 74, 76, 85, 94, 96, 98, 100, 168, 178, 218, 266; *see also* Rome
romantic love 110, 165, 239, 261; and God 165
Romanticism 252, 261
Rome 3, 17, 49, 54, 57, 60, 62, 72, 86, 88, 98, 99, 125, 130, 141, 143, 144, 147, 219, 227, 231, 248, 259; Sack of 230, 232
Roncoroni, Federico 277
Rosmini, Antonio 275, 282
Rossi, Rosa 274, 282
Rosvita of Gandersheim 88
rules 2, 8, 30, 34, 53, 70, 72, 74, 75, 81, 78, 89–91, 93, 125, 137, 152, 153, 154, 156, 187, 196, 201, 241, 242, 249
Rule of St. Augustine 32
Rule of Teresa of Avila 154
Russell, Bertrand 282
Russia 45, 254

Il Sabato del villaggio 11
Sacco, convent of 139
sacred 15, 18, 21, 24, 44, 83, 84, 98, 118, 154, 172, 189
Sacred Heart 129, 170, 218; *see also* Alacoque, Marguerite-Marie; Jesuits
sacrifice 2, 16, 24, 25, 29, 36, 37, 42–44, 51-53, 59, 61, 73, 79, 80, 81, 83, 87, 88, 132, 143, 190, 191, 205, 210, 214, 215, 217, 221, 233, 235, 242, 251, 252, 265, 266, 268, 269
sacrificer 132, 163, 191, 202, 203, 206, 266, 268, 269; -executioner (*see also* confessor; spiritual director) 266
sacrificial religion 43
Sadducees 12
Sade, Donatien-Alphonse-Francois (Marquis de) 202
safety 3, 246, 269

St. Catherine at Saint-Trond, monastery of 137
St. Damian, hermitage of 165
St. Germain 254
St. Magnus 88
St. Jacques 235
Saint Joan 259
St. Ursula 126, 229, 232
saints 12, 20, 44, 47, 53, 56–59, 75, 97, 112, 119–124, 128, 130, 132-136, 138, 140, 141, 147, 149, 152, 155, 163, 170, 175, 176, 178, 182, 185, 188, 191, 192, 193, 195, 204, 217, 225, 232, 244, 260, 273
Sainte-Odile, convent of 34
Salamanca, University of 219
Saller, Richard P. 280, 282
Salomon 88
Salpêtrière 179, 202
salvation 21, 37, 38, 41, 44, 59, 70, 83, 109, 125, 135, 141, 163, 187, 218, 229, 232; *see also* safety
Salve Regina 265
Samaritan woman 9, 10
San Sepolcro 171; convent of 199
sanatorium 243, 254
sanctity 75, 88, 113, 124, 129, 133, 164, 175
sandals 93, 94; *see also* feet
Santa Croce 88
Santa Lucia charity 248
Santa Maria in Vallicella 168
Santa Maria Nova 274
Santa Prassede 17
Santa Sabina 17
Santa Teresa di Lisieux 2
Sant'Apollinare 60, 62
Savior 38, 163, 170, 218, 268; Jesus as 17
Savonarola, Girolamo 227, 232
Saxony 34
Scarpini, Modesto 274
Schäfer, Karl Heinrich 271, 282
Schmitz, Philip 273
science 10, 160, 174, 216
Scillitans 54
Scillium 54
Scotland 48
Scriptures 8, 19, 78, 91, 268, 269
Scutari, hospital of 254, 255
seal 16, 17, 133, 180, 234, 243
sealed fountain 20, 180; *see also* closure
Sebastian 111
Sebastopol 254
Second Lateran Council 32
Second Vatican Council 242
Seconda 54

Sedan, battle of 244
self-hypnosis 158
self-identification 91, 242
Servants of Mary 239, 249
Sethre, Janet 281
Seton, Elizabeth Anne 244, 275
sex: female 38, 69, 70, 74, 86, 90, 97, 100, 116, 143, 166, 177, 209, 246, 250, 263; organs 93; *see also* sexuality
sexes 94, 111, 126, 127, 207, 245
sexuality 22, 24, 25, 26, 27, 28, 29, 41, 42, 51, 52, 59, 64, 70, 71, 89, 90, 92, 97, 98, 100, 101, 111, 118, 124, 138, 158, 166, 167, 184, 185, 186, 187, 198, 200, 208, 210, 238; female 184, 186, 208; male 41, 52, 64; *see also* homosexuality; virginity
Sfondrati, Francesco 58
Shamanic flight 182
shaving 97, 98, 99, 234; *see also* hair
Shaw, George Bernard 259
shoes 93, 94, 95, 96, 97; *see also* feet
Shorter, Edward 282
Shroud of Turin 136
sickness 135; *see also* disease
Signorelli, Luca 62
signs 92, 192-194; sexual 92
silence 17, 19, 53, 75, 76, 78, 82, 87, 90, 100, 142, 158, 180, 185, 186, 191, 197, 210, 215, 238, 239, 249, 250, 251, 252, 262, 264
Silvestri, Elena 249
sin 18, 25, 36, 68, 70, 72, 109, 140, 142, 144, 145, 148, 150, 151, 168, 186, 187, 196, 197, 198, 199, 205, 210, 211, 220; original 17, 18, 94, 97, 166, 186, 208; sexual 185, 187, 197, 199, 200, 210
sinner 148, 151, 205, 210
Sinforosa 65
Singapore 249
Sissa, Giulia 282
Sister Maria Celeste 85, 86, 281
Sister Suzanne 197
Sister Teresa 198
Sisters 100, 127, 172, 249, 251
Sisters of Mercy 254, 275
Sisters of St. Clare 100, 172
Sisters of the Holy Family 249
Sisters of the Most Precious Blood 249
Société de Marie Reparatrice 263
sodomy 50, 168, 195, 199; *see also* homosexuality
soldiers 98, 129, 255, 256, 263, 264
Solomon 12
son 7, 37, 38, 39, 46, 47, 85, 90, 140, 143, 167, 210, 240, 265, 268

Song of Songs 169, 180
Songs of the Bride 169
Sons of Charity 248, 249
Sophocles 39
Soubiran La Louvière, Sophie-Augustine (de) 243
Soubirous, Bernadette *see* Bernadette
soul 26, 39, 47, 77, 83, 109, 112, 129, 136, 138, 140, 142, 145, 146, 147, 149-151, 159, 169, 204; femininity of 169
space 14, 68, 69, 83, 87, 154, 159; male 47; sacred 44, 59
Spain 233, 244
spear 129, 134, 136, 176
Spinsanti, Sandro 271, 282
Spiritual Canons 20
spiritual director 14, 20, 82, 90, 116, 117, 121, 124, 130, 139, 143, 144, 169, 179, 210, 219
Splenditello 192
state 18, 20, 22, 27, 28, 42, 47, 84, 88, 105, 109, 110, 127, 128, 138, 149, 158, 176, 180, 193, 214, 225, 227, 231, 234, 237, 244–248, 257; secular
statistics 34, 48, 53, 84, 120, 127, 252, 255, 256, 267; social 255
Stephens, William N. 282
stigmata 110, 113, 119, 120, 127, 129-131, 133-138, 140, 155, 170, 173, 174, 177-179, 187, 188, 191, 194, 195; invisible 140, 147, 192
stigmatization 132, 133, 191
Stone, Lawrence 282
Storia di una capinera 114
story 3, 9, 12, 48, 53, 55, 56, 61, 83, 88, 105, 114, 124, 126, 133, 135, 136, 140, 147, 187, 196, 202, 229, 234, 239, 247, 249, 253, 265
Story of a Soul 83, 266, 272, 274
Strathern, Marilyn 272, 282
structures 1, 14, 15, 18, 21, 24, 25, 31, 32, 33, 38, 40, 48, 68, 69, 71, 72, 73, 88, 105, 106, 117, 126, 127, 132, 154, 160, 180, 218, 226, 227, 233, 242, 243, 251, 258, 267, 268; male 269
suicide 132, 266, 267
Summa Theologica 20
superculture 72
Sweden 2, 92
sylphs 94; *see also* feet
symbolism 28, 61, 67, 68, 106, 169, 179, 265; *see also* symbolism
symbols 18, 28, 43, 57, 62, 63, 67, 83, 92, 95, 102, 130, 163, 215, 220, 221; con-

cretization of 137; of power 67; power of 67; *see also* symbols
Syria 23, 87
system 1, 18, 20, 56, 63, 70, 72, 89, 92, 96, 150, 153, 164, 190, 192, 201, 206, 218, 254, 268, 269; of taboos 18

taboo 1, 18, 20, 29, 63, 65, 68, 91, 125, 154, 184, 185, 187
Tarabotti, Arcangela 6, 114, 273, 282
Tarragona 21
Tarzan 61
teaching 91, 245, 246, 247
Telemachus 46
Teresa of Avila 125, 129, 138, 148, 166, 184, 188, 196, 250, 259, 273, 274, 282
testicles 29
Thais 88
Theatine (convent) 189
themes 10, 43, 60, 65, 123, 124, 149, 152, 170, 171, 172, 174, 175, 221, 227; cultural 42
Theodora 30
Theodoretus of Cyrus 87
Theodosia of Caesarea 60
theologians 12, 23, 53, 82, 116, 136, 147, 175, 199, 208, 232, 235, 260, 268, 269
theology 2, 15, 18, 24, 27, 43, 71, 84, 102, 107, 115, 116, 122, 125, 126, 144, 148, 149, 154, 155, 156, 158, 160, 162, 166, 170, 172, 174, 193, 195, 205, 217, 218, 227, 229, 230, 231, 232, 244, 250, 262, 267, 268, 269
Thérèse of Lisieux 83, 84, 152, 163, 165, 177, 205, 215, 250, 266, 272, 274, 282
Thomas Aquinas 136, 271
Thomas of Cantimpré 136
thought 1, 8, 10, 12-14, 18, 20–22, 24, 29, 33, 36, 37, 40, 42, 64, 77, 78, 85, 86, 95, 105, 106, 114, 123, 125, 129, 136, 138, 142, 143, 145, 150, 152, 155, 157, 159, 160, 165, 169, 172, 174, 180, 188, 195, 198, 199, 202, 205, 209, 211, 217, 227, 229, 244, 245, 249, 251-253; critical 134; imaginary 174; mystic 159; objectifying projection of 188; perceptive 174; symbolic (*see also* logic) 188
Tiber River 88, 101
time 2, 9, 10, 12, 15, 17, 18, 20–22, 24–27, 32, 34, 50-53, 55–57, 63, 64, 69, 73, 75, 76, 81, 83, 85, 95, 97, 98, 101, 105, 108, 110, 113, 114, 121, 124-126, 128, 131, 136, 137, 139, 140, 141, 149, 151, 153, 160, 163, 167-169, 173, 175, 180-182, 184, 185, 187, 188-190, 195, 197, 198, 201, 204, 210, 212, 213, 217, 219, 220, 225, 228, 230, 233, 234, 238–243, 245, 246, 249, 251-253, 256, 257, 260, 263, 264, 266, 267; conception of 38; liturgical 39, 71; monastic 71
Times 254, 255
tomb 59, 139, 251, 253; cell- 60; matrimonial 253; *see also* closure
Tommaso da Celano 130, 133
transcendence 24, 28, 37, 51, 56, 68, 94, 95, 96, 97, 99, 101, 111, 113, 117, 118, 136, 139, 143, 146, 155, 158, 159, 175, 179, 181, 183, 190, 192, 193, 203
Trappists 74
Trastevere 58, 144
Trent 115, 152, 227, 248, 273
Trotti Durini, Carolina 247
tuberculosis 177, 178, 221, 243, 245, 266
Turkey 254

union, sexual 158
United Nations 246
United States 3, 244, 249, 263, 269; *see also* America
unreality 68, 173, 175, 176, 212, 216; *see also* reality
untouchability 63
Urban I 56
Urban VIII 140
Ursula 126, 228, 229, 232
Ursulines 115, 225, 228, 230, 232, 233, 234, 235, 236, 237, 238, 241, 243, 262, 264, 275

Valenciennes 234, 264
Valerianus 55
value 10, 26, 27, 36, 37, 39, 40, 41, 42, 43, 49, 50, 51, 52, 56, 59, 60, 62, 75, 76, 80, 81, 83, 106, 111, 117, 126, 160, 198, 215, 217, 228, 229, 242, 256, 266, 273; biopsychic formation of 273
values 7, 8, 25, 26, 27, 35, 72, 73, 75, 76, 83, 84, 91, 119, 125, 128, 129, 155, 170, 187, 214, 215, 257, 258, 259, 265
Van Gennep, Arnold 282
Vanti, Mario. 275
Vanzan Marchini, Nelli-Elena 282
Vatican 33, 187
Vatican II 101, 242
Vauchez, André 273, 282
Vaussard, Maurice 281
veil 14, 30, 91, 92, 99-102, 164, 186, 212, 234, 241, 259; of the Temple 101; and veiling 102; of Veronica 164

velatio 100, 101
Vellano 187
Veni Creator 265
Venice 94, 114, 199, 248, 273, 274
Venus of Brassempouy 98
Vercelloni, Virgilio 274, 282
Verga, Giovanni 114, 283
Verona 247, 248, 275
Veronica 164
Verzeri, Teresa Eustochio 249
Vestal 47, 55, 56
Vestia (martyr) 54
Via Nomentana, martyrs of 62
victims 26, 36, 43, 44, 49, 51–53, 64–66, 79, 83, 84, 86–88, 107, 111, 112, 115, 132, 163, 177-179, 191, 202–205, 211, 215, 216, 218, 220, 221, 244, 250, 251, 257, 265–270; sacrifical 2, 3, 36, 101, 212, 250
Victoria 255
Vigilius 57
Vincent de Paul 240, 247; order of 202
violence 8, 11, 12, 55, 61, 64, 65, 66, 72, 98, 99, 105, 106, 111, 131, 163, 164, 165, 169, 198, 210, 211, 262; sexual 50
vir 28, 49
virgins 22, 24–31, 47, 49, 51, 52, 53, 55, 56, 57, 58, 59, 60, 61–64, 63, 68, 74, 88, 97, 98-101, 126, 129, 141, 143, 168, 175, 176, 185, 226, 229, 232–235, 242, 258; and martyrs 58, 59, 61
Virgin Mary 142; *see also* Madonna; Mary (Mother of Jesus); Our Lady
virginity 20, 21, 23–28, 30, 46, 47–51, 55–57, 59–61, 63, 64, 68, 97–99, 129, 141, 147, 167, 168, 175, 176, 180, 181, 185, 198, 208, 217, 226, 228, 229, 234, 235; defense of 55, 57, 59, 60, 229
virility 16, 50, 72, 76, 97, 178
virtue 28, 29, 47, 49, 50, 52, 60, 62, 75, 124, 140, 151, 152, 165, 166, 187, 194, 201, 202, 207, 228, 264
vis 41, 97, 155; *see also* potency
vision 2, 10, 14, 24, 43, 47, 68, 102, 110, 114, 117, 120–126, 128, 130, 131, 133, 135-137, 141-143, 144-147, 149-151, 152, 154, 155, 156, 158-160, 168, 169, 170, 172, 173, 174, 175, 177, 181-183, 187, 189, 190, 192, 193, 194, 195, 206, 211, 212, 214, 217, 226, 227, 259, 260; *see also* hallucinations
Visitandines 226, 241, 243
Vita prima 130
vocation 31, 52, 143, 197, 198

voice 62, 68, 76, 81, 110, 114, 116, 123, 126, 141, 155, 157, 170, 173, 175, 176, 181, 189, 193, 195, 196, 256, 259, 260, 261, 267
void 15, 119, 123, 139, 192, 204, 208
von Franz, Marie-Louise 283
vows 31, 32, 44, 60, 70, 78, 82, 86, 101, 106, 115, 124, 141, 147, 153, 172, 187, 209, 212, 220, 221, 226, 240, 242, 244, 252, 265, 266

Waldensians 93, 99, 106, 118
war 10, 42, 46, 48, 98, 128, 143, 155, 175, 176, 221, 245, 256, 258, 264
Warsaw, siege of 244
water 10, 13, 16, 17, 18, 55, 71, 77, 121, 132, 146, 165, 189, 254
wedding 47, 55, 56, 98, 100, 110, 112, 119, 123, 128, 140, 173, 181, 191, 192, 238; night 47, 55, 56, 98, 100, 181; ring 112, 140, 192
Watson, Paul F. 283
Weitlauff, Manfred 273, 283
West 3, 19, 20, 23, 24, 26, 31, 74, 94, 97, 101, 102, 111, 120, 182, 214, 267, 270
Western history 1, 64, 269
Wiborade 88
widowhood 22, 27, 127, 128, 240
widows 21, 22, 26, 28, 46, 59, 88, 107, 127, 128, 235
wine 68, 72, 122, 187, 268, 269
wives 46, 127, 153, 154, 204, 238
woman-victim 209, 251
women 3, 9, 10, 12–20, 22–24, 26–32, 39–41, 45–51, 53–56, 59–62, 64, 65, 68–80, 82–91, 94–96, 102, 105-108, 111, 113, 114, 116-119, 121-130, 132, 134-147, 150, 152-162, 164-166, 168-177, 179, 181, 182, 184, 186-192, 194, 196-206, 210–220, 225–227, 229, 231, 232, 235, 237–243, 245–249, 250, 252, 253, 255–259, 261-269; -brides of God 25, 34, 52, 112, 115, 120, 163, 167, 185, 228, 230, 233, 234, 244, 251; -brides of men 251; and death 57
women's history 1
women's studies 1
Woolf, Virginia 78
Worcester 263
word 7, 8, 9, 16, 23, 29, 36, 37, 39, 41, 50, 54, 62, 67, 69, 75, 76, 78, 79, 82, 83, 87, 89, 91, 113, 114, 116, 118, 122, 123, 131, 134, 138, 140, 151, 153, 155, 156, 161, 165, 166, 182, 190, 196, 209, 210–212, 227, 228, 231, 244, 248, 253, 263, 264; false 53; potent 155, 175, 250

work 1, 2, 3, 10, 12-15, 24, 32, 33, 57, 59, 66, 68, 71, 78, 84, 85, 92, 106, 108, 115, 122, 144, 149, 164, 167, 179, 198, 207, 210, 213, 227, 231-235, 237–239, 241, 243–250, 252–254, 256, 262–264
World War II 91, 98
wound 3, 61, 77, 112, 122, 128, 129, 130–138, 146–148, 170, 172, 176, 178, 191, 193, 203, 208, 209, 212, 252, 254; rib 129, 137, 170

writers 8, 11, 124, 128, 138, 163, 219
writing 78, 90, 144, 154, 186, 188, 197, 205, 237, 246, 255, 266
writings 19, 20, 30, 89, 124, 126, 153, 156

Zahan, Dominique 283
Zanette, Emilio 114, 273, 283
Zoffoli, Enrico 274, 283

www.ingramcontent.com/pod-product-compliance
Ingram Content Group UK Ltd.
Pitfield, Milton Keynes, MK11 3LW, UK
UKHW041925140426
5217IPUK00014B/321